SAFE FOR DEMOCRACY

Safe for Democracy

The Anglo-American Response
to Revolution, 1913–1923

LLOYD C. GARDNER

New York   Oxford
OXFORD UNIVERSITY PRESS
1984

Copyright © 1984 by Oxford University Press, Inc.

Library of Congress Cataloging in Publication Data

Gardner, Lloyd C., 1934–
Safe for democracy.

Includes bibliographical references and index.
1. United States—Foreign relations—Great Britain.
2. Great Britain—Foreign relations—United States.
3. United States—Foreign relations—1913–1921.
4. United States—Foreign relations—1921–1923.
5. Great Britain—Foreign relations—1910–1936.
6. Wilson, Woodrow, 1856–1924.   7. Lloyd George, David,
1863–1945. 8. World War, 1914–1918—Diplomatic history.
I. Title.
E183.8.G7G23   1984   327'.09'041   83-26790
ISBN 0-19-503429-5

Printing (last digit): 9 8 7 6 5 4 3 2 1

Printed in the United States of America

To my children,

Rebecca, Erin, and Timothy.

They know how much this book has meant;
I hope they know how much more they mean.

Introduction

When Woodrow Wilson arrived at the Capitol on the evening of April 2, 1917, it was not to ask Congress to intervene in a European war. His quest was for a new world. Only that outcome of the Great War could ensure the conversion of the "irrational" revolutionary impulses that surged up in the late imperial era from Mexico to China into steady forces supporting world equilibrium. "When you have the foundations of established order," Wilson told Mexican newspaper editors in 1918, "and the world has come to its senses again, we shall, I hope, have the very best connections that will assure us all a permanent cordiality and friendship."*

Long before he had accepted American participation in the war as both inevitable and necessary, Wilson had called the Mexican Revolution a "wedge" in American politics. By that he meant that the industrial era had produced a genuine world politics. Wars could never be localized "private quarrels" any more; revolutions could no longer be considered mere "native uprisings." What was happening in Mexico would shape the future of the world in the same way the French Revolution had earlier altered European society and politics. Wilson believed this before he made his decision to ask for war; but if there had been any question, events in Russia settled the issue. "It is no doubt true as Mr. House told me in so many words," British foreign secretary Arthur Balfour reported to London on April 27, 1917, "that but for Russian Revolution and famous German telegram to Mexico, President would have found it very difficult to take decisive step. . . ."**

*"An Address to a Party of Mexican Editors," June 7, 1918, in Ray Stannard Baker and William E. Dodd, eds., *The Public Papers of Woodrow Wilson*, 6 vols. (New York, 1925–27), 5:223–28.
**Balfour to Lloyd George, April 27, 1917, FO 371 3119/86512, Public Record Office, London.

British prime minister David Lloyd George did not get involved in Mexican or Chinese questions as Wilson did. But from the time of the overthrow of the tsar in Russia in March 1917, he was as absorbed as the president was in devising a strategy to meet the revolutionary challenge. In British politics, revolution was more than a "wedge"; it was a likely cause of military defeat in the war and a real threat to postwar security.

Some of the materials for this book were researched in 1965–66, when I held a Social Science Research Council Fellowship. A John Simon Guggenheim Fellowship in 1973–74 and a Fulbright Professorship at the University of Birmingham in 1975–76 gave me the opportunity to complete the bulk of the work in the Public Record Office and in various private collections. I should like to thank all those connected with these organizations for making the book possible. I would also like to thank the archivists in the many libraries and research centers who have helped me with access to documents. Extracts from Crown-copyright material in the Public Record Office, London, appear by permission of the Controller of H.M. Stationery Office.

Inevitably, such lists leave out other persons who have contributed greatly to my research and writing. But I must give special thanks to Arthur S. Link for allowing me to consult the vast collection of Wilson materials he has assembled at Princeton University for the publication of the Wilson Papers. I am also indebted to him for many conversations on Wilson's role in attempting to construct a liberal alternative to revolution. Over the years, as well, I have learned so much from Arno Mayer, also of Princeton, both from his books and conversation, that it is a pleasure to acknowledge my debt here. In the course of doing the research for this, and a subsequent volume on the Roosevelt-Churchill era, I met Professor Christopher Thorne of the University of Sussex. He is a model scholar and a great companion on what he once called "the journey of enquiry."

At Rutgers, Professor Michael Adas read the manuscript when it was nearly twice the size it finally turned out to be. No greater burden can be put on a friendship between historians than to read a rough draft. Warren F. Kimball lets me try out all my ideas on him, and helps me to sort out the occasional insight from the truly insignificant. Samuel Baily never lets me forget that American diplomatic historians are all too narrow in their outlooks. He is as well a great good friend for all seasons.

I can never finish a book without expressing my gratitude to the oldest of these friends, Walter LaFeber of Cornell University, Thomas McCormick of Wisconsin, and William Appleman Williams of Oregon State University. Like Michael Adas, Walter LaFeber did double duty by reading the "whole thing." Thanks again. At Oxford, Sheldon Meyer may have thought he would never see the end of this project. I hope other authors are fortunate enough to work with an editor of Sheldon's skill and patience. I should also like to thank his colleagues Leona Capeless and copy editor Tessa DeCarlo, who have provided expert help and advice in adding much more than the final touches to this project. Thanks, finally, to my literary agent and friend Gerald MacCauley, who successfully keeps abreast of developments both in the historical world and Little League coaching.

East Brunswick, New Jersey L. G.
July 4, 1983

Contents

SAFE FOR DEMOCRACY

PROLOGUE

Wilson in London

What a place the President held in the hearts and hopes of the world when he sailed to us in the George Washington! *What a great man came to Europe in those early days of our victory.*

John Maynard Keynes, 1919

On board the *George Washington* as it neared Europe, Wilson spoke confidently of America's ability to fulfill the world's hopes. They had not come this far, he reminded members of the peace mission, simply to restore the old order. The conference that was about to open in Paris must not become another Congress of Vienna, another tragic victory for the enemies of progress. It was their business to fight for a new order, "agreeably if we can, disagreeably if necessary." Because Europe's existing leaders were "too weatherwise to see the weather," it was up to them to get in touch with the "real masses." A peace treaty without justice as its foundation would produce not another war, but a world cataclysm.

"The conservatives do not realize," he went on, "what forces are loose in the world at the present time. Liberalism is the only thing that can save civilization from chaos—from a flood of ultra-radicalism that will swamp the world. . . . Liberalism must be more liberal than ever before, it must even be radical, if civilization is to escape the typhoon."[1]

Once arrived in Paris, Wilson told a welcoming socialist delegation, "This has indeed been a people's war. It has been waged against absolutism and militarism, and these enemies of liberty must from this time forth be shut out from the possibility of working their cruel will upon mankind."[2] Everything about the president's demeanor proved that here

[1]

was a man inspired by a vision, but more than that, possessed by a prophecy.

On December 26, 1918, Wilson crossed the channel to Dover, where a huge crowd awaited him. Schoolchildren strewed flowers along his path. "I have conversed with the soldiers," the American leader declared in London. Not all of them had understood at first what they had fought for—and at last had won. But they would not mistake the meaning of their victory. "They fought to do away with an old order and to establish a new one, and the center and characteristic of the old order was that unstable thing which we used to call the 'balance of power'—a thing in which the balance was determined by the sword. . . . [T]hat sort of thing should end now and forever. . . . [I]t was my paramount duty to turn away even from the imperative tasks at home to lend such counsel and aid as I could to this great, may I not say, final enterprise of humanity."[3]

American intervention had decided the outcome of the war, Wilson seemed to be saying, but also of all the past errors made by humankind. The royal banquet planned in Wilson's honor was one of unsurpassed splendor, David Lloyd George would recall many years later; but from a joyous occasion the scene at Buckingham Palace was suddenly transformed into an allegorical representation of the second coming of Oliver Cromwell when the president entered "clad in an ordinary black dress suit without a medal to adorn his breast." Who could miss the striking contrast he made to the "resplendent uniforms of every cut and color" and the "dream of magnificence" that greeted him? Who could fail to watch his progress across the hall without wondering what this new Cromwell demanded of the war-weary "old world," hiding its fears about the future behind the gala dress and ceremonial trumpets?

George V welcomed Wilson with a speech of cordial friendship. "Wilson replied," continues Lloyd George's account, "with the perfect enunciation, measured emphasis and cold tones with which I was to become so familiar in the coming months. There was no glow of friendship or of gladness at meeting men who had been partners in a common enterprise and had so narrowly escaped a common danger."[4]

> *You must not speak of us who come over here as cousins, still less as brothers; we are neither. Neither must you think of us as Anglo-Saxons, for that term can no longer be rightly applied to the people of the United States. Nor must too much importance in this connection be attached to the fact that English is our common language. . . . No, there are only two things which can establish and maintain closer*

relations between your country and mine: they are community of ideals and of interests.

Woodrow Wilson,
private conversation at Buckingham Palace,
December 1918

What Wilson would have written of David Lloyd George had he left an account of their meeting cannot be known. He did tell an adviser that he thought he might get on fairly well with the prime minister, if he could trust "the Little Man."[5] By temperament, however, Wilson was less curious than other politicians about what shaped his contemporaries' outlook. And in this case it seemed unnecessary anyway. "Never," said John Maynard Keynes, "had a philosopher held such weapons wherewith to bind the Princes of the world." British policymakers knew that Wilson possessed almost unlimited physical power to enforce his will on the peace conference. The Allies were dependent upon America for food and finances, no less in peace than they had been in war.[6]

In practically every way, Lloyd George was Wilson's opposite. He led an empire in decline. That was the most obvious difference, perhaps, and it dictated a different political strategy for coping with the "ultra-radicalism" that threatened to swamp the world. Unlike Wilson, Lloyd George appeared to have no central core, no permanent attachment to a "liberal" ideology, only a conviction that a politician must play many roles in a lifetime. Lloyd George enjoyed them all. "To Lloyd George no policy was permanent, no pledge final. He became like a trick rider at the circus, as he was compelled to leap from one back to another in his party-colored team."[7]

Lloyd George's private conversations with Wilson during this visit to London before the peace conference were interrupted by two events. The first was news that British election returns had given the prime minister a huge majority, a vote of confidence for handling British interests at the peace conference. He had made that leap safely. Congratulations were offered by those around the table. But Wilson sat silent, holding aloof. Later he explained privately to the prime minister that he had not wished to appear to be interferring in British politics. Perhaps that was so. Lloyd George assured Wilson that he was not offended. But both men knew the president had suffered an important electoral defeat at home, had failed to persuade voters to return a Democratic majority to Congress. Pique may have kept Wilson silent. More probably the incident reflected deeper uncertainties undermining the president's self-confidence as the peace conference began. Where Wilson delivered election sermons (a very old American tradition), Lloyd George led rallies (a more ancient political tradition).

Both men had gone into the elections proposing a liberal program. Wilson had promised a peace based upon the Fourteen Points and the proposed League of Nations, and had been disappointed. Lloyd George had, perhaps reluctantly, joined in the chorus demanding a victors' peace, punishment of Germany tenfold, and had been rewarded. The prime minister took his cue from the audience always, snapping up its phrases, arriving with it at the obvious conclusion. "It must," he had proclaimed at Newcastle-on-Tyne, "be a just peace, a sternly just peace (loud cheers), a relentlessly just peace (renewed cheers). Justice must not be merely vindicated in the victory, it must be vindicated in the settlement as well." Interrupted during another speech, Lloyd George agreed with the voice demanding that Germany pay to the "uttermost farthing." And for good measure he added, "[W]e will search their pockets for it."[8]

Wilson's failure to congratulate Lloyd George thus had in it something more, probably, than either the desire not to interfere or simple pique. There was almost certainly a fear about the future. Wilson had taken his nation into war convinced that, so long as the war raged, the struggle on the battlefield would usurp the fight for liberalism at home. His was the enormous task of preventing the war from aiding the forces of reaction, of justifying all the terrible suffering with a peace that would permit the fight for liberal aims to be carried on no longer simply on a national basis, but as part of a worldwide endeavor. He did not lack an appreciation of the art of politics. But he feared that false promises to the masses that Germany could be made to pay for the war would wreck a liberal peace program. At the very least it would divide the liberal alliance that supported a League of Nations. One part of the alliance had already fallen away, a result of Bolshevik appeals for working-class support of the Russian Revolution.

The second interruption of the Wilson–Lloyd George talks was the arrival of an open letter from the Bolshevik representative, Maxim Litvinov, offering to negotiate a "peaceful settlement" of all outstanding questions. Citing the Wilsonian principle of self-determination, Litvinov asked that consideration be given to helping the Soviets restore Russia, not to destroying the experiment. One might believe in the ideals of the revolution or not, said Litvinov, but surely there was no justification for sending foreign troops to fight against it, or for arming and supporting classes "interested in the restoration of the old system of exploitation of man by man. . . ." In a second, private message, the Bolshevik representative held out the prospect of "concessions" to secure peace, and reviewed how the reintegration of Russia into the world economy would accrue to "the benefit of all countries badly in need of foodstuffs and raw materials."[9]

Once again, it appeared, Wilson was to be faced with a sudden reversal by Lloyd George. In the immediate aftermath of the Bolshevik Revolution the Allies had begun importuning the president, asking that he join them in an effort to restore the eastern front, which meant intervention against the Bolsheviks. Wilson had held out, finally agreeing in the summer of 1918 to send troops—but only, he insisted, to aid Czechoslovakian prisoners of War recently released by the Bolsheviks to make their way to Far Eastern embarkation points. Nothing must be done, he thought, that would either stimulate Russian nationalism on behalf of the Bolsheviks, or create a situation which would lead to the breakup and partition of Russia.

Lloyd George, however, was already scouting the political terrain for a new Russian policy. Labour party leaders, and laborers, were making a fuss about Russia. But the "Hands Off Russia" rallies were only part of the reason Lloyd George sought to redefine the Russian problem. During the election he had denounced Labour leaders as men who really believed in Bolshevism for England: "Supposing the Labour Party won. The moment they got in these are the men who would run the Government. That is exactly what happened in Russia."[10] When he met with French Prime Minister Georges Clemenceau in early December 1918, however, Lloyd George proposed that, since the Bolsheviks had the support of the majority of the Russian people, they should be represented at the peace conference. Other members of the British cabinet, including Foreign Secretary Arthur Balfour, agreed with Clemenceau that such a radical shift on Russia was out of the question. Very well, said the prime minister, they would wait until Wilson came.[11]

Litvinov's letters had had an impact on Lloyd George. German reparations might win an election, but over the long run these blood payments offered no more substance as a solution to the "social problem" than did his denunciations of Labour politicians as Bolshevists. His conversations with Wilson on this point proved disappointing. The president did make it plain that he thought military intervention useless, and that American troops would soon be withdrawn from Archangel and Murmansk. But the Siberian situation, said Wilson, presented a somewhat more difficult issue. The Japanese were behaving as if they owned Siberia, and clearly something would have to be done to disabuse them. And on the key question of representation at the peace conference, the president did not display "any keenness" to sit across from a Bolshevik delegate.[12]

*My mind is not clear as to what is the proper immedi-
ate course in Russia. There are many more elements*

at work there than I conjecture you are aware of, and
it is harder to get out than it was to go in.

Woodrow Wilson, private letter,
November 1918

By his own account, Wilson had "sweat blood" over the Russian question. And the end was not in sight. "Their invasion," he said of the Bolsheviks, "was mainly an invasion of ideas and you could not defeat ideas by armies." His policy, he then explained to the editor of the *Manchester Guardian,* "all through had been not to attack Russia, but to help her."[13] Yet he was determined to repel the Bolshevik invasion. Whatever Lloyd George was up to, however he intended to juggle Germany and Russia, buy off opponents with visions of reparations or, it now appeared, the fabulous Russian market hinted at by Litvinov, Wilson would not allow America to become party to a despoliation of the liberal conscience.

Though he led a government that had much more reason to fear revolutionary agitation (or perhaps because he did), Lloyd George had a far more relaxed attitude than those who suffered such pangs of conscience over Russia. Once, when an anguished associate brought him a firsthand witness to the Red terror, the prime minister put off talking about the subject while he continued to entertain a band of Welsh singers. "For several hours they sang Welsh hymns in the most beautiful manner," recalled Winston Churchill. When Lloyd George did at last permit an interruption, he dismissed his visitor's warnings with an almost flippant comment that revolutions, like diseases, ran a regular course.[14]

Wilson was not so austere, however, nor Lloyd George so relaxed as to ignore their common interest in minimizing Anglo-American differences. The American president's position as putative leader of a world movement—which to some Allied politicians was more frightening than Lenin's militant Bolshevism, because more appealing to "reasonable" men—gave him, temporarily, a political authority that rose above the leverage America enjoyed as the world's newest "superpower." How he used that authority was a matter of great concern, not least to himself. He might indeed take command of the constituencies Allied leaders needed to continue ruling at home—but would he only succeed in isolating himself "as spokesman for a cause without power"?[15]

There were indications that Wilson sensed the danger. His talks with Lloyd George in London had given the prime minister no sure guide to what Wilson would do at the peace conference. But a day or so before he crossed the Channel, the president had dined at the British embassy in Paris. After dinner the ambassador, Lord Derby, had sought to draw him out on "Freedom of the Seas," colonies, and the League of Nations.

Everything must stand or fall on the success of the League, the president replied. But he had not meant to imply that England and America were to relinquish their navies. "That we should between us do the whole of the marine policing of the world and that the size of our navies should be determined by agreement between ourselves," he went on, would not be affected by the principles he had put forward under the rubric "Freedom of the Seas." "[T]ogether we should have vastly preponderating navies over any forces that could be possibly brought against us."[16]

Lord Derby listened carefully to all this, perplexed about the real Wilson. Was it this man who sat here sounding not unlike a European statesman, talking about power and navies? Or was it the man who had stayed out of the war for so long, talking about a "peace without victory"? The president's close adviser Colonel Edward M. House might provide the answer. "I spoke to him," Derby then reported to London, "about the various weird creatures that the President was supposed to want to see, and he told me the whole of that was dropped. . . ." Derby had assumed that Wilson wanted to be put in touch with "radicals," so he was relieved to learn that the president had no intention of leading the European left or of seeking the aid of socialists of the ilk of "Ramsay MacDonald & Co."[17]

Yet the real Wilson was not to be fathomed in one conversation, or many. More doctrinaire than Lloyd George, he was equally elusive. "You know," Wilson said in his final address in Great Britain before the peace conference, to an audience at the Free Trade Hall, Manchester, "you know that the United States has always felt from the very beginning of her history that she must keep herself separate from any kind of connection with European politics, and I want to say frankly to you that she is not now interested in European politics. But she is interested in the partnership of right between American and Europe. . . . Never before in the history of the world, I believe, has there been such a keen international consciousness as there is now."[18]

Wilson was undoubtedly right: never before had there been such a keen international consciousness. A partnership of right, but backed by vastly preponderating navies—if that was what Wilson meant, Lloyd George could understand "Wilsonism," even if the president had proved reluctant to discuss specifics while he was in London. More to the point, however, did Wilson really believe that the League of Nations would supersede centuries of European politics, or, for that matter, decades of American politics? Did he imagine it would make up for the failures of imperialism? Lloyd George could not think so. Wilson had envisioned the dawn of a new day, an age of enlightenment symbolized by the creation of the League of Nations. Lloyd George must have wondered, as the president left to return to Paris, what the new day would look like at the end of the peace conference.

I

The
Failure of Imperialism

Wise old England! How she fortifies her island Realm, and yet all the while develops and improves the energies of her people, while she does not hesitate to undertake the police regulation of the world! She knows, moreover, when and where and how to establish the necessary police stations.

William H. Seward,
Travels Around the World, 1873.

Where fifty years ago we had every liberty of movement to go where we chose, we have had within the last twenty years scarcely walking-room; where we had walking room, now we have scarcely elbow-room; and now, where England has hardly elbow-room, she will very soon have hardly room to move.

Lord Curzon, 1895

CHAPTER ONE

What Comes of Empire

This growing stake of our wealthy classes in countries over which they have no political control is a revolutionary force in modern politics; it means a constantly growing tendency to use their political power as citizens of this State to interfere with the political condition of those States where they have an industrial stake.

John A. Hobson,
Imperialism, 1902

David Lloyd George had pushed his way to the front of the national political scene during the Boer War. The young Liberal from Wales had brazenly attacked the colonial secretary, Joseph Chamberlain, in the latter's home city, Birmingham. He had asserted that Chamberlain was a war profiteer, exploiting the situation in South Africa to swell the profits of his family's armaments firms.[1]

Conservatives struck back with accusations that votes given to the "radicals" meant "smacks in the face for our country." "Every seat lost to the government," declared Chamberlain, "was a seat gained by the Boers." The "Khaki" election of 1900 returned a strong majority for the government, but the popular vote was more equal: 2.4 million for the government against 2 million for the Liberals.[2] The issues raised during the Boer War, which lasted from October 1899 until the summer of 1902, would set the political agenda down to the eve of the Great War in 1914. It was a humiliating experience. Arrayed against the power of the British empire was a batch of irregulars, Dutch-ancestored farmers, who managed to hold off the best the British could put up against them for nearly three years.

But that was not the worst. From the outset, when Germany's Kaiser Wilhelm II sent a telegram congratulating Boer leader Paul Kruger on his escape from the British, the war had great-power ramifications. "I have great sympathy for the Boers and great respect and liking for them," Theodore Roosevelt wrote a German friend in 1899, "but I think they are battling on the wrong side in the fight for civilization and will have to go under." TR's ambiguity was typical. Many American leaders felt British motives were sordid—"What a corrupting thing the lust for gold is!" former President Benjamin Harrison wrote privately—but they balanced criticism with a concern for the fate of the empire, having themselves undertaken to do the "world's work" in the Philippines and Cuba.[3]

The tactics used by the British in fighting the Boers, moreover, were reminiscent of Spanish efforts to prevent Cuban rebels from winning their fight for freedom, and thus deepened American ambiguity. The only way to defeat the Boers, British military leaders decided, was to separate them from their sources of supply. And the only way to do that was to put Boer women and children in concentration camps. Thousands died of disease. Reports of conditions in the camps sent a shock wave through Parliament, and reverberations around the world.

Now Lloyd George and the other "pro-Boer" Liberals had something to sink their teeth into—something much more politically satisfying than personal scandal. By stressing the horrible consequences of imperialism abroad, the Liberals could get a handle on the much trickier problem of its impact at home. Outside the immediate arena of parliamentary maneuvering, British intellectuals were also seeking to come to terms not only with the Boer War, but with all the implications of the phenomenon called the "New Imperialism."

In the thirty years before 1900, Great Britain had added territories to the empire totaling 4,754,000 square miles, an area considerably larger than the United States, with an estimated population of 88,000,000. France brought under the tricolor over 3,500,000 square miles, with 37,000,000 inhabitants. Germany ranked third, with 1,027,120 square miles and 14,687,000 colonial dependents. What had set off the race? Who had fired the starting gun? "When I left office in 1880," said Lord Salisbury, the Conservative leader, "nobody thought about Africa. When I returned to it in 1885, the nations of Europe were almost quarreling with each other as to the various portions of Africa which they could obtain. I do not exactly know the cause of the sudden revolution. But there it is. It is a great force—a great force—a great civilizing, Christianizing force."

In private, he was more candid. If free trade had remained the rule, Africa would have remained unpartitioned. But "inasmuch as protection-ist Powers may, and do, possess themselves of new tracts of Africa and then proceed to stifle or cramp our trade with differential duties and irritating restrictions . . . then it becomes a necessity for us to protect ourselves. . . ." All Great Britain ever wanted was a fair field and no favor—the Open Door. "[I]t is to secure this for our commerce and our civilization that we are forced to extend our direct political influence over a large part of Africa."[5]

The Boer War was a bad ending. Whether it had been undertaken at the behest of one or two capitalist speculators, or with some larger purpose in mind, the war in South Africa could not be justified, economically or morally. Analysis of the "New Imperialism," wrote one critic, demonstrated that despite Salisbury's acceptance of the claim, trade did not follow the flag, and that imperialism itself, "with its natural supports, militarism, oligarchy, bureaucracy, protection, concentration of capital and violent trade fluctuations," was the supreme danger to modern national states.[6]

If Britain's declining economic fortunes were the problem, imperialism was the wrong remedy. Indeed, in the very era that all this territory, and all those people, were being added to Her Majesty's realm, Britain's share of the world's trade continued to slip. In the 1880s Britain was overtaken in steel production by the United States, and in the next decade by Germany. By 1900 Britain was still the greatest manufacturing and trading power in the world, but the gap was narrowing. All the while, however, income from foreign investments continued to grow. The result was a deceptive balance sheet that masked the true situation. It showed Britain in the black when in fact a rising excess of imports over exports revealed that British manufacturers were less and less competitive.[7]

From these statistics critics drew several interconnected conclusions. Based firmly on free trade premises, some indicted the "New Imperialism" as a distortion of capitalism, a victory for a privileged class of investors and financiers (the decendants, spiritually at least, of Richard Cobden's old enemies, the landed aristocracy), and an obstacle to British industry. Brushing aside Salisbury's explanation that imperialism was a defensive maneuver, a reaction to the initiatives of "protectionist Powers," writers like John A. Hobson contended that the imperialists deliberately ignored statistics that showed trade did not follow the flag because their policies were dictated by the "special interests."

It was true that Britain's rivals had annexed territories and then closed them off, but the glut of capital and manufacturing power which was now endemic in the industrial world could not be relieved by such methods. Instead of using the power of government to support the parasitic classes who, it was commonly assumed by critics, were behind the Boer War, the government should be instrumental in raising consuming power. Thus

Hobson wrote in his 1902 treatise, *Imperialism,* the following Lincolnesque peroration:

> The power of the imperialist forces within the nation to use the national resources for their private gain, by operating the instrument of the State, can only be overthrown by the establishment of a genuine democracy, the direction of public policy by the people for the people through representatives over whom they exercise a real control.[8]

A proper government policy would release consumer demand at home, reducing reliance upon foreign trade and making unnecessary the solution to the "social problem" being advocated by Joseph Chamberlain, an empire *Zollverein.* The emotions stirred by the Boer War are evident throughout Hobson's work, and help to explain the emphasis he placed upon the "special interests" and his contention that imperialism was a "depraved choice of national life." He never really came to grips, perhaps, with the practical choices confronting policymakers, nor did his analysis of the economic taproot of imperialism—the special interests—provide an adequate basis for political action outside those choices. Like Woodrow Wilson after him, Hobson imagined it was really not a difficult matter to recognize the deficiencies of imperialism—and to correct national life accordingly.

He argued, for example, that the problems confronting Britain could be reduced to the question of intensive versus extensive cultivation:

> A rude or ignorant farmer, where land is plentiful, is apt to spread his capital and labor over a large area, taking in new tracts and cultivating them poorly. A skilled, scientific farmer will study a smaller patch of land, cultivate it thoroughly, and utilize its diverse properties, adapting it to the special needs of his most remunerative markets.[9]

> *Never was there such an absurd waste of power, such ridiculous inconsequences of policy—not for want of men, but for want of any effective central authority, or dominant idea, to make them work together. Joe is a strong man. Under other stars he might be as big as Cavour or Bismarck.*
>
> Sir Alfred Milner, 1902

Where Hobson and other critics of the New Imperialism imagined that the authors of the Boer War were determined to force foreign trade into narrower (and unnatural) outlets in order to maximize profits for a privileged group—bringing on the inevitable twin disasters of international rivalry and class war at home—Joseph Chamberlain used the same analogy of careful husbandry to describe a Conservative way out of the dark forest of industrial unrest and the thickening gloom on the international horizon. "I regard many of our Colonies as being in the condition of undeveloped estates, and estates which can never be developed without Imperial assistance. . . ." Only by such a policy, he went on, could he see "any solution of those great social problems by which we are surrounded. Plenty of employment and a contented people go together. . . ."[10]

As colonial secretary inside Lord Salisbury's cabinet, Chamberlain played a key role in the events that led to the Boer War. But he was not motivated by hopes of personal gain. He had viewed Kruger's Transvaal Republic as bad for the British in south Africa, and bad for imperial unity in general, since the mid-1880s. And as imperial rivalries grew intense near the close of the century, Chamberlain saw successful resolution of African questions as the basis for a general settlement with Germany. The settlement he imagined with Germany would allow Great Britain a breathing space in which to deal successfully with its major internal problems.

Such hopes were far too optimistic. Germany was not to be bought off with a general partition, especially not now, when questions of pride were at stake. Yet when the colonial secretary dispatched Sir Alfred Milner to South Africa to deal with Kruger, peacefully if possible, but by whatever means necessary, he had not been afraid of the consequences of imposing "reform" with arms. Kruger denounced Milner's offers as amounting to a demand that the Boers yield to British suzerainty, and a war followed. Chamberlain was still not discouraged when the war went badly and internal unrest rapidly and radically changed British politics. He used the situation as an urgent argument inside the cabinet for opening negotiations for an Anglo-German alliance.

Chamberlain was nothing if not innovative. Too much so for old Lord Salisbury, who could not imagine abandoning splendid isolation. Perhaps the colonial secretary would have gotten further with his arguments if the Foreign Office had not weighed in on Salisbury's side. "If we had a formal alliance with Germany," contended the respected Sir Francis Bertie, "we should either have to shape our conduct over a large extent of the globe in accordance with her views and subordinate our policy to hers . . . , or, if we acted independently, whenever we took measures necessary for the protection of our interests in some distant part of the world we might be told by Germany that we were bringing about a situation which might lead to an attack on us by France and Russia obliging Germany without sufficient cause to take up arms in our defence, or Germany might find some moment opportune for herself, but inconvenient for us, for bringing on a war on a question in which we might not have a great interest."[11]

Bertie also agreed with Salisbury that the supposed dangers of isolation had been overdrawn. The proof was what had *not* happened because of the Boer War. With a quarter of a million men tied up in South Africa, with sentiment in most countries running strongly against the British, and with more than one power only too happy to inflict a further humiliation on Britain, it had still not been possible for other nations to form a coalition to call upon London to stop warring against the Boers and accept arbitration.

What Chamberlain had had in mind was more than an alliance of the sort familiar to Foreign Office officials. He imagined a pact of conservative powers that could stand together ideologically as well as politically. Yet Bertie's argument was a telling one, for if Germany faced the same internal threat as Great Britain, it could not behave as a status quo power internationally. As closely watched in European capitals as trade statistics in this era were the figures revealing the rapid spread of a new force: trade unionism. In 1890, Britain, with 8 percent of its industrial workers in unions, already had the most organized labor force in the world. Union membership doubled from two million in 1906 to over four million by the beginning of the Great War in 1914.

Taking note of the emergence of labor as a separate political force in British politics, Lord Randolph Churchill had predicted in 1892 that if the "Constitutional Party," the Conservatives, shut their ears to labor demands, "the Labour interest may identify what it will take to be defects in the Constitutional Party with the Constitution itself, and in a moment of indiscriminating impulse may use its power to sweep both away."[12] A decade later Joseph Chamberlain offered Conservatives a solution: expand the Constitution by taking in the colonies—if not politically, then economically. For Germany, however, such an option did not exist. Its empire in Africa was not useful in the same ways. Neither did it provide the starting point for an understanding between conservative powers to resolve internal difficulties.

Even more than his German "departure," moreover, Chamberlain's new tariff reform proposals caused consternation in Conservative circles. Lord Randolph's son, Winston, who would break with the party over the issue, caught the mood of the times. Chamberlain felt, Churchill wrote in the first volume of *The World Crisis,* the ever-growing tide rising "against the ruling combination." Impelled by the ardor of his nature, he launched a desperate remedy onto the troubled political seas:

The Opposition was advancing hopefully towards power, heralded by a storm of angry outcry. He would show them, and show doubting or weary friends as well, how it was possible to quell indignation by violence and from the very heart of reaction to draw the means of popular victory. He unfurled the flag of Protection.[13]

In 1903 Chamberlain resigned as minster of colonies to lead the fight for tariff reform. "I represent Labour," he declared. "I represent Labour . . . which thinks not of itself as a class, opposed to any other class in the community, but as responsible for the obligations of the country and the Empire to which it belongs. . . ."[14] The problem was that Labour, like the Conservatives, was still free-trade-minded. So Chamberlain was highly vulnerable to an attack that stressed higher costs to the working-man. Anticipating the attack, the advocate of "imperial preference" had offered workers a pension plan to compensate for the "higher loaf." "We come to this—if you are to give a preference to the colonies . . . you must put a tax on food," Chamberlain admitted. To his Liberal opponents he added, "I make the hon. gentlemen opposite a present of that."[15]

A silent groan went through Tory ranks at that remark. Salisbury's successor as prime minister, Arthur Balfour, had tried to put the best face on Chamberlain's campaign. The government's view, he explained in the House of Commons, was to consider the world as it was, not as it had been in Cobden's day. It was time to look into the possibility of retaliatory tariffs. Was it not also possible to gather evidence to see if fiscal arrangements could be devised to bind the empire closer together? Then, if public opinion moved in this direction, "we ought to do something to put the British Empire in an economic position which would make it an equal to the magnificent position obtained by the United States."[16]

Germany under Kaiser Wilhelm became a disturber of the peace, and, increasingly, a likely military foe, but Balfour's reference to the United States, another high-tariff protectionist power, dramatized the universal nature of the problem that had to be addressed. The kaiser complained of encirclement, but it was Britain whose internal politics had been put askew by nations that encircled their own domestic markets. A disunited Conservative party was swept aside by the Liberals in January 1906. Chamberlain had not won over the working class or, at the other end of the economic spectrum, the City bankers, who feared any policy that might endanger investment opportunities. Improving trade figures suggested, moreover, that Chamberlain's concern for the manufacturer was unnecessary—or at least premature.[17]

Chamberlain had expected defeat, had regarded it as a stage on the way to ultimate vindication. He also consoled himself with the thought that now Balfour would see there was no alternative to breaking the

deadlock within the party in favor of protection. Within six months, however, Chamberlain had suffered a stroke that removed him from the
political scene. With his retirement all the urgence went out of the tariff
reform campaign. Balfour took the defeat in stride, as befitted one of his
background; he was a nephew of Lord Salisbury. In fact, he confessed, he
was filled with a "kind of illegitimate exhilaration at the catastrophe which
has occurred." He found he was more interested in politics than he had
been for some time. In various letters—to the king's secretary, to Lady
Salisbury—Balfour sketched out an analysis of the defeat that implied a
deeper concern for the future than his urbane exterior revealed. "We
have here to do with something much more important than the swing of
the pendulum or all the squabbles about Free Trade and Fiscal Reform,"
he wrote. "We are face to face (no doubt in a milder form) with the
Socialistic difficulties which loom so large on the Continent." And again,
"If I read the signs aright, what has occurred has nothing whatever to do
with any of the things we have been squabbling about over the last few
years . . . what is going on here is the faint echo of the same movement
which has produced massacres in St. Petersburg, riots in Vienna, and
Socialist processions in Berlin."[18]

> *I don't know exactly what I am, but I am sure I am
> not a Liberal. They have no sympathy with the people.*
>
> David Lloyd George, 1913

A total of 53 Labourite members sat in the new Parliament, along with 83
Irish nationalists and 377 Liberals. Little wonder Balfour felt himself and
his party face to face with "Socialistic difficulties." The dominant figure
across the floor was not the prime minister, Sir Henry Campbell-Banner-
man, but David Lloyd George. Named chancellor of the exchequer in
1908, Lloyd George would introduce the "Socialist Budget" of 1909, a
benchmark in British politics that divided the Liberal party in much the
same manner as his old rival, Chamberlain, had rent the Conservatives
asunder with tariff reform.

   Lloyd George, who had barely escaped physical harm during the Boer
War when he attacked Chamberlain from a speaker's platform in Birmingham, had continued his assault on the floor of Commons, deriding
the latter's pension scheme as a swindle to win votes for greedy capitalists.
He soon emerged as the most effective voice for the "radical" case against
the "Imperialists." After the war, Lloyd George likened "Africa Joe" to
German statesmen:

Mr. Chamberlain fancies himself as a sort of little Bismarck. The notion has turned his head. He is the man who will consolidate the Empire, the man of blood and iron—rather the man of screws [a reference to the Chamberlain family business]; that is all the iron in Mr. Chamberlain's Imperialism. After the pattern of Bismarck, he has his social program and his *Zollverein* . . . but we want no Empire made in Germany."[19]

"We have a great Labour Party sprung up," Lloyd George warned a Liberal rally. "Unless we can prove, as I think we can, that there is no necessity for a separate party to press forward the legitimate claims of Labour, you will find that . . . the Liberal Party will be practically wiped out and that, in its place, you will get a more extreme and revolutionary party. . . ."[20] It looked very much as if that was the way things were heading. Beginning in 1908 British industry was swept by a tidal wave of labor militancy. Ten million work days were lost to strikes in 1908, and again in 1910 and 1911. The next year the figure rose to forty million. In 1911 Home Secretary Winston Churchill took precautionary steps: fifty thousand troops were supplied with twenty rounds of ammunition each to take up strategic positions in the event of a general rail strike.[21]

Throughout these years, nevertheless, both Churchill and Lloyd George suspected that the Conservatives were out to regain office by focusing public attention on German arms spending. The way to defuse both threats, Lloyd George told an Austrian newspaper, was to take a leaf from Chamberlain's book. He wished to see an "entente" develop between Germany and England, Lloyd George explained, so that the two nations could devote themselves "wholly to the tasks of peace, of progress and of social reform."[22]

Neither Conservative nor Liberal efforts to enlist Germany's aid for their own purposes had much chance. But in those prewar days, that did not matter so much. In 1909 Lloyd George introduced the Liberal party's famous budget; it was more than a budget, of course, it was a political program of new tax proposals and principles. Conservatives cried socialism. Determined not to provide Lloyd George with more kindling to pile on the funeral pyre of traditional Conservatism, Arthur Balfour looked for some way to buy time. It was no good simply shouting defiance. In a letter that, in the end, never left his desk, Balfour tried to spell out his thoughts on possible foreign policy remedies. Addressed to Theodore Roosevelt, who was soon to leave the presidency but presumably would retain his great influence within the Republican elite, Balfour's plea was for greater Anglo-American understanding. A principal object of Germany's decision to build a great fleet, it went on, was to be able—at some future moment—to dictate British policy, even within the confines of the empire itself. "No, I will not allow Imperial Preference," Balfour could imagine the kaiser declaring. "I will fight if I don't get most favored nation treatment myself and I will arouse the world against you."

Such were the stakes of international politics at the conclusion of the New Imperialism; and here, also, was the nexus of foreign and domestic policy. If the German menace was as real, and as sophisticated, as the former prime minister seemed to think, then of course Lloyd George's proposed social program was too costly. Taxes at levels high enough to pay for both the defense of the empire and social reform could not be sustained without depriving the upper classes of needed incentive. Even if it were possible to overcome this obstacle, the social program would still cost too much psychologically, for it would weaken the nation's will to survive by exacerbating class divisions, casting doubt on patriotic concerns, and generally undermining faith in national leaders and institutions.

Probably the salvation of British politics rested in finding a moderate radicalism, but what Lloyd George and his Liberal colleagues had started, under prevailing conditions, could not easily be contained within traditional borders. Working together, America and Great Britain could survive the coming years of crisis and, hopefully, perfect long-range solutions to both national and international problems. Roosevelt's new role as world statesman, Balfour thought, would put him in a strong position to advocate a close Anglo-American understanding. Besides, powerful as it was rapidly becoming, the United States needed aid as well. America was consolidating its empire. "She is already beginning to feel the need of territorial expansion. She has large sums of money invested abroad, millions of pounds worth at sea. She cannot afford not to be a world power."

The only matter to be decided, he thought, was whether foresighted leaders in both nations would recognize their mutual interest, and act accordingly. An Anglo-American combination would dominate the world. "The balance of power, which is the subject matter of foreign politics today, would be permanently upset." Balfour's words had an explicit double meaning. America could not afford not to be a world power for the same reason that Britain could not; world power status was now a requirement for national cohesion. And the balance of power Balfour referred to was internal as well as external.[23]

Roosevelt actually replied, after a fashion, to this unsent communication. On May 31, 1910, Roosevelt accepted an invitation to address a prominent audience in the London Guildhall. He said he had two purposes in mind in speaking out. He wished to enter a plea for good will and understanding among *all* civilized nations engaged in "bringing abreast of our civilization those lands where there is an older civilization which has somehow gone crooked. . . . It is of interest to all civilized men that a similar success shall attend alike the Englishman and the German as they work in East Africa; exactly as it has been a benefit to every one that America took possession of the Philippines." Clearly, Roosevelt could see no special relationship, or at least none binding the Anglo-American powers to common political action to forestall Germany.

His second purpose was to issue a call to imperial duty, a reiteration of two-fisted Progressivism, later known as Social Imperialism in Europe, as against the sort of reform by craven pacificists who turned their backs on the "White Man's Burden." Sentimental concerns must not replace righteousness, he insisted, in dealing with the "so-called Egyptian Nationalist Party." Referring to the assassination of pro-British Boutros Pasha, Roosevelt delivered a stern warning on the evils of mollycoddling that implied much about dealing with domestic violence. "When a people treats assassination as the cornerstone of self-government," he declared, "it forfeits all right to be treated as worthy of self-government."[24]

So while Roosevelt's Guildhall speech probably disappointed those who yearned for a closer understanding with the United States, it encouraged resistance to socialism, if not specifically to Lloyd George's new agenda. The chancellor had his hands full anyway, as the general election of January 1910—called by the new prime minister, Herbert Asquith, to break the impasse over the budget caused by the House of Lords—resolved nothing. The Liberal majority in the House was in fact destroyed, forcing them to rely upon Labour and Irish Nationalists.

The continuing deadlock prompted Lloyd George to pursue a "national settlement" on his own initiative. The scheme that the chancellor advanced in August 1910 had its origins in a plan for securing bipartisan approval for various pending welfare measures. But it quickly grew into something quite different. Having received an enthusiastic response from Churchill, Lloyd George explained his coalition idea to other Liberal chiefs and then to Balfour and Conservative leaders. Such a national government could bring the resources of talent from both parties "into joint stock in order to liquidate arrears which, if much longer neglected, may end in national impoverishment, if not insolvency."[25]

Apparently Lloyd George promised a great many things to a great many people in the course of canvassing support for a coalition government, including empire tariff preferences should an impartial commission of experts so recommend. The covering memorandum he drafted stressed declining exports, coupled with foreign "dumping," as major factors in growing unemployment and a discontented working class, leading possibly to class war and revolution. This theme figured prominently also in his *War Memoirs,* written twenty years after: "The shadow of unemployment was rising ominously above the horizon. Our international rivals were forging ahead at a great rate and jeopardizing our hold on the markets of the world. There was an arrest in that expansion of our foreign trade which had contributed to the phenomenal prosperity of the previous half-century, and of which we had made such a muddled and selfish use."[26]

This first attempt to avoid a division of British politics between labor and capital failed. During the war Lloyd George would get his chance to play the mediator's role, ably seconded this time by Balfour. Already in July 1911, however, Lloyd George had shifted his attention and efforts from the domestic agenda to foreign affairs. How much the failure of his national coalition plan weighed in this decision is impossible to say, but when the latest German provocation, the Agadir crisis, produced a genuine war scare, he and his associates knew that a consensus on domestic issues was out of the question until the external menace had been faced.

Whether or not the kaiser intended war, and that was still unclear, he had become the overriding political issue in Britain, if only because the Conservatives made him so. Under these circumstances, the only thing a Liberal could do, it appeared, was to sound more patriotic than the opposition. Troubled by the impact of the kaiser's challenge, Lloyd George argued with a friend, C. P. Scott, editor of the *Manchester Guardian*, that the latter should not publish a lead article undermining the government's position against allowing Berlin to seize the Moroccan port city. There was a real danger, he told the disbelieving editor, that Germany sought to fulfill Napoleon's old ambition.

In fact, Liberals found themselves in a political no-man's-land, stranded between the external challenge and the mounting pressure behind them at home. Bankers and merchants at the Lord Mayor's dinner at Mansion House on July 21, 1911, had steeled themselves for the chancellor of the exchequer's speech, expecting an attack like those he once reserved for the hated landlords of Wales. Instead, he attacked Germany. If peace could be preserved only by allowing British views to be ignored at Agadir, said Lloyd George, "then I say emphatically that peace at that price would be a humiliation intolerable for a great country like ours to endure."[27]

Several explanations for the Mansion House speech have been offered by historians removed from the events that prompted it by more than half a century. At the outset it should be obvious that Lloyd George's radicalism did not make him a pacificist, either temperamentally or politically. Second, German naval building had become something more than a nuisance that allowed Conservatives to divert attention from the real threat to British security, the accumulated grievances of the working class. Increasingly frustrated by naval difficulties, those who had stood out against Germanophobia, especially Lloyd George and Churchill, risked compromising their future political careers. They could resign in protest at the stand taken by the government, writes Richard Shannon, "or they could stay on and vent their exasperation against the Germans." The shift in Liberal thought was marked, in this analysis, by Churchill's move from the Home Office (where he had come under considerable criticism for involving the army in an industrial dispute) to the Admiralty, where his bellicosity found more useful occupation.[28]

Lloyd George's reputation as a mediator in industrial disputes, on the other hand, and his cleverness in always achieving a settlement, suggested to historian A. J. P. Taylor another interpretation of the Mansion House speech:

> He was out to conciliate the men, and he extracted concessions from the employers by any means that occurred to him. It is tempting to surmise that he made his Mansion House speech of 21 July 1911, stirring up the Agadir crisis, so as to frighten the railway companies with the spectre of war into settling the great railway strike much in favor of the unions some three weeks later.[29]

Either interpretation highlights the Liberal predicament in the last years before the Great War. Their bid to resolve the nation's pressing problems had met with no greater success than Chamberlain's combined imperial tariff reform and great power alliance program, either in its original form or as amended by Balfour in his unsent letter to Theodore Roosevelt. So while Lloyd George might have no compunction about scaring the railway companies with a German bogeyman, he suffered considerably over the next months trying to decide for himself if the bogeyman was, after all, real. He probably did not decide finally until after the Germans had committed their last act of disregard for the "old" principles: the violation of Belgian neutrality.

It came down to this. The Germans, unwittingly of course, were in league with the Conservatives to destroy Liberalism. No one knew what would emerge to take its place. During the summer of 1914 the British government was deadlocked over Ireland's future, an age-old question that now threatened to overwhelm the nation's capacity to find its way out of political danger. Stretched thin by all the events since the Boer War, British political institutions seemed on the verge of being rent completely.

Settlement of the Irish question, Churchill argued, would immediately have brought back thoughts of unity and cooperation, "which had so intensely appealed to the leading men on both sides, ever since Mr. Lloyd George had mooted them in 1910." Failure to settle, the more likely outcome, would mean "something very like civil war and the plunge into

depths of which no one could make any measure." Ireland was the principal subject of the cabinet meeting on July 24, 1914:

> The discussion had reached its inconclusive end, and the Cabinet
> was about to separate, when the quiet grave tones of Sir Edward
> Grey's voice were heard reading a document which had just been
> brought to him from the Foreign Office. It was the Austrian note
> to Serbia. He had been reading or speaking for several minutes
> before I could disengage my mind from the tedious and bewilder-
> ing debate which had just closed. We were all very tired, but
> gradually as the phrases and sentences followed one another, im-
> pressions of a wholly different character began to form in my
> mind. . . . The parishes of Fermanagh and Tyrone faded back into
> the mists and squalls of Ireland, and a strange light began immedi-
> ately, but by perceptible gradations, to fall and grow upon the map
> of Europe.[30]

Churchill's additional reflections upon charges that were later placed
against Sir Edward Grey for not having made Britain's intentions plain
sooner make the point in a less dramatic—but even more convincing—
manner. Suppose the foreign secretary had proposed a formal alliance
with France and Russia? The consequent military conventions would have
required the raising of an army by compulsion. "The Cabinet of the day
would never have agreed to it." And even if it had, the House of Commons would never have agreed to be guided by its advice.[31]

Liberals were not united behind Grey as late as August 1, 1914. It was
thought that as many as ten ministers might resign if Prime Minister
Asquith sought a war vote that day. Even after the German invasion of
Belgium, two actually did resign rather than follow Grey into war. Lloyd
George was not one of them, but he had been stirring around in recent
weeks, thinking again of the prospects for a Liberal initiative for an alliance, this time with Labour, in the next election.[32]

But then it all became clear. If the Conservatives had got what they
thought they wanted, a nation united once again, why should they be the
only ones to gain politically? Patriotic enthusiasm could be the means for
securing Liberal ends as well. And this could be accomplished without
yielding to Labour's smothering socialist embrace. How different it would
all be from the troubled days of the Boer War—different for those who
answered Lord Kitchener's appeal for recruits, different for the people at
home, different, finally, for Lloyd George, whose Defence of the Realm
Act No. 2 assured the nation that industry would not be permitted to
make the war into a reactionary enterprise. Conservatives had preserved
the House of Lords, but it—and all their old bastions—would shrink into
insignificance as the new England was built throughout the land.[33]

CHAPTER TWO

The American Answer

We have gained an outlook, have seen the bigness of the world and the widening circle of our prosperity and influence and are not afraid of what we will find over the big curve.

Woodrow Wilson, 1900

Unlike David Lloyd George, Woodrow Wilson did not emerge as a sword bearer in the anti-imperialist campaign many liberal reformers carried on as the century began. Wilson held a very different view. He believed that the Spanish-American War would turn out to be almost as important to his countrymen as the American Revolution itself. "Some gentlemen who are violent anti-imperialists," he said in 1902, "whatever that means, tell us we are damaging our own natures by our treatment of the Philippines." They were wrong. "[I]f we do right anywhere we shan't damage our principles."[1]

To liberal imperialists on both sides of the Atlantic, domestic reform and foreign expansion went together. Indeed, the real danger, as they perceived it, was that the "violent anti-imperialists" would block the way of America's fulfilling its true destiny. What the nation proposed to do for those remote islands, Wilson claimed, it would also do for itself, and for the world. The responsibility involved in taking the Philippines was not to the capitalists or the "special interests," but to the people. If right was done, the rest would follow. When the revolutionary war came to an end in North America, Wilson argued, the changes it wrought were felt back in Europe. Great Britain "began to see what light the notable thing done in America shed upon its own affairs. The king was to be grappled with at home, the Parliament was to be freed from his power, and the ministers who ruled England were to be made the real servants of the people. . . . We had begun the work of freeing England when we completed the work of freeing ourselves."[2]

Less well articulated by others, perhaps, Wilson's notion that Americans were now doing the world's work was a popular theme. The recent years of European expansion, in this formulation, were like those of George III's reign, an unhappy time when the liberties of the colonies had been endangered by a grasping tyranny. "No war ever transformed us quite as the war with Spain transformed us. No previous years ever ran with so swift a change as the years since 1898. We have witnessed a new revolution. We have seen the transformation of America completed."[3]

Powerful claims indeed. Surely Wilson was aware that apologists for imperialism, European or American, spoke such words to avoid meeting the arguments of critics. But if Wilson's interpretation of the new vistas opened by national expansion was hardly novel, his emphasis upon America's example to the world was different. Meanwhile, others drew attention to the contrast between the faltering British mission, as evidenced in the prolonged struggle to subdue the Boers and America's swift triumph over Spanish colonists. "England's failure in South Africa," Theodore Roosevelt confided to a friend, "and our own success with Spain and the Philippines have been symptomatic of . . . changed conditions."[4]

"More than ordinary significance attaches to the fact that in the same year, 1898, in which the United States appeared, somewhat against her will, as a great military and colonizing power," observed young journalist Ray Stannard Baker, later Wilson's chosen biographer, "she also attained supremacy among the nations as the greatest of the world's exporters of home products." These were achievements of paramount importance, dwarfing the narrow significance of Manila Bay or San Juan Hill. "[T]he struggle with England for trade supremacy was hardly less stern than the shorter and fiercer war with Spain, and its effects may reach further into history."[5]

Thoughts about the balance of power or America's new commercial ascendancy were never absent from Wilson's analysis, but he was concerned as well with the future security of democracy. America was obliged to seek its expansion abroad, or witness its decline at home. Hence the explicit connection he made between the American Revolution and the Spanish-American War. His views were also consistent with John A. Hobson's interpretation of imperialism: that it was a matter of choice, not circumstance. America's destiny carried it to the Philippines. Its principles would rescue it from the dangers it encountered there, and from the errors Europeans had made. "We need not fear the expanding scene,"

Wilson said in 1902. It was plain destiny "that we should come to this, and if we have kept our ideals clear, unmarred, commanding through the great century and the moving scenes that made us a nation, we may keep them also through the century that shall see us a great power in the world."[6]

It had not always seemed so sure.

> We may hold all the ground we have (or its equivalent) and more than all, and yet America may be the primate nation in trade. That is what I think.
>
> William E. Gladstone, 1878

Observed from the United States, the new imperialism puzzled and disturbed post–Civil War leaders. It was unnatural. The founders of the Republican party had expected, as William H. Seward put it, that the freeing of the South from its bondage to England would produce a chain reaction. Canada would soon be free. Colonialism would gradually fade away. But instead it expanded. How long would it be, Americans wondered, until European industrial expansion demanded the "Africanization" of Latin America?[7]

In 1879 a French company headed by Ferdinand de Lesseps, the builder of Suez, proposed to construct a ship canal through the Isthmus of Panama. Although disassociated from the French government, the project aroused American fears. President Rutherford B. Hayes refused to believe any disclaimers. "The policy of this country is a canal under American control," Hayes said in a special message to Congress. "The United States can not consent to the surrender of this control to any European power or to any combination of European powers."[8]

Hayes issued his warning three years before the British occupied Egypt, but it required no special gift to identify the main themes and trends of the age, or to see that Central America could become as dependent upon a European-built canal as the medieval fiefdom was on the noble lord's castle it surrounded. The economic system had changed, but little else. "The industrial world," wrote the American economic historian Carroll D. Wright, the nation's first commissioner of labor, "has reached a crisis in production, the result of stimulation fostered by various causes." Nations were being forced to find outlets where they could. The United States could not stay out of the race much longer. "With this development there may be something in the Mexican question," Wright mused, "that we do not yet study or comprehend. Politically, the control of Mexico by the United States might bring serious questions; industrially, such control should be seriously considered. Certainly the United States would be false to the interests of their people if they allowed the control of Mexico to go into other hands than their own, or its vast resources to remain but partially developed."[9]

What engaged the attention of Wright and his contemporaries even more than the threat of a Suez-style imperialism was the tariff question, however. From Civil War days, Republicans had argued that a low tariff meant permanent subservience to Great Britain. The South was a prime example of a "colonial" area, and of what would happen again if the Democrats ever regained power. In 1888 Republican Benjamin Harrison anathematized the Democrats as unreformed sycophants of the British throne. "Within the past year I have been reading . . . the story of our diplomatic relations with England during the Civil War," he said. He had discovered that British policymakers sympathized with the southern cause only in the "expectancy of free trade with the Confederacy." Lest Americans feel that they could relax, having ended this dark conspiracy, Harrison reminded audiences that Great Britain was still perfidious Albion, still out "to coin commercial advantage out of the distress of other nations."[10]

British free trade now posed as a liberal cause, Harrison and his secretary of state, James G. Blaine, insisted, but it was nothing of the kind. Blaine had a chance to debate the point, in print, with the Right Honorable William E. Gladstone, the outstanding Liberal leader and former prime minister, in the January 1890 issue of the *North American Review*.[11] Gladstone felt it his duty to enlighten the benighted protectionists who held sway in Washington. Their arguments, he began, came as a "pleasant novelty" to modern Englishmen, "but once upon a time we British folk were surfeited, nay, almost bored to death, with it. It is simply the old song of our squires, which they sang with perfect assurance to defend the Corn Laws. . . ." And to what point had the squires' hoary refrain advanced over the years? "Like a phonograph of Mr. Edison, the American Protectionist simply repeats on his side of the Atlantic what has been first and often, and long ago, said on ours."

Truth was that if America adopted a free trade system, "she will by degrees, perhaps not slow degrees outstrip us in the race," and lay claim to the proud place England had achieved in world commerce. No other nation could do it. Yet it could not be denied that America might achieve the same dominant economic status under protection. The United States might indeed conquer in the marketplace with protectionist devices, but it could become the "teacher to us of the old world" only by "rejecting and denouncing all the miserable degrading sophistries by which the arch-enemy, ever devising more and more subtle schemes against us, seeks at one stroke perhaps to lower us beneath the brutes, assuredly to cut us off from the hope and from the source of the final good."

Whether reforming prostitutes or protectionists, Gladstone never failed to put the issue on top of a church steeple well, above, he had no doubt, the ability of his opponents to reach up and pull it down. Blaine was not inclined to climb to such heights. But neither was he willing to accept the implication that protectionism would reverse civilization's march toward the promised land of world harmony. In his reply in the *North American Review,* the secretary of state reminded Gladstone of something the latter had said on another occasion, that Americans produced "too much cloth and too much iron" and should concentrate instead on "low-priced cereals and low-priced cotton." At bottom, these were the true British sentiments, Blaine charged: "that the mechanic arts and the manufacturing processes should be left to Great Britain and the production of raw material should be left to America." And what was this, he asked, but a return to the rule of the squires, escorted by the naive free traders in all their frightful innocence. The squires' power had been broken in America, not by free trade, but by protection. Modern-day British squires were manufacturers, but they were just as happy as the old landowners to see everyone else live as peasants.

If Americans had not cast off Britain's baneful influence, Blaine continued, the United States would have sunk below Canada and Australia. Mr. Gladstone now admitted that Americans enjoyed a wonderful increase of wealth under protection, but averred that it would have soared higher under free trade. Perhaps that was so. But it was only fair to point out that Gladstone's views did not represent modern Europe's judgment on the subject. "The most eminent statesman on the continent of Europe holds opinions on this subject directly the reverse of those held by the most eminent statesman of Great Britain." America could leave Mr. Gladstone to Prince Bismarck of Germany.

Blaine's theme was British meddling. It provided common ground for Republicans and Democrats, and, as would become clear in Wilson's day, for reformers and liberal imperialists, who could all agree on the need to halt British advances into Latin America. Thus in the mid-1890s it was Grover Cleveland, a low tariff Democrat, who stood up against London over the question of Venezuela's boundaries, backed by the radical reformer Henry Demarest Lloyd. The British had taken the side of their colony British Guiana in a dispute that suggested to Americans nothing less than an effort to grab off yet another piece of valuable territory. The specifics were less important than the impression that fixed itself in

American minds of the British lion, having gorged itself in Africa and Asia, stalking new prey in the Western Hemisphere.

In a special message to Congress on December 17, 1895, Cleveland announced that he would resist as "willful aggression upon . . . [America's] rights and interests" the appropriation of any lands or the exercise of any jurisdiction over lands belonging to Venezuela. He was fully alive, Cleveland warned, to "all the consequences that may follow." On this date, writes Walter LaFeber, "the world heard of the American challenge to the British Empire."[12]

Hardly soon enough, thought Henry Demarest Lloyd, who, along with many others critical of Cleveland's conservatism on financial affairs, associated such a challenge with the fundamentals of change at home. Lloyd was ready for war, if need be, to save the world from colonialism and America "from her apparently impending Midas-like doom. . . . The Great Britain of Lord Salisbury, of India, of Africa, of Ireland, of the House of Lords, and the English landed system, encroaching upon a neighboring Republic, refusing arbitration, represents to me in this day the same forces as those which in the past have stood against Liberty and Progress."[13]

To the extent that Americans stood united against British expansionism, the arguments that Gladstone had put forward to dissuade protectionists never had much chance. Under Gladstone, perhaps, the American fear was of what would later be called "free trade imperialism"; under Salisbury the British threat was much the same, even if different in name. Opposition to London often had the same impact in the United States that Berlin's supposed (and real) designs had in England, though of course the issue was less immediate in a military sense.

However that may be, Cleveland left himself some room to maneuver if things got really bad. As it happened, he did not need an out. Lord Salisbury was duly outraged at this preposterous behavior in Washington, but his advisers kept reminding him that the bumptious Mr. Cleveland was hardly in the same category as the German kaiser, who was building his fleet, jostling the British in Africa, showing an unhealthy interest in the conflict with the Boers, or the Russian tsar, who was creeping along the newly laid tracks of the Trans-Siberian Railroad into the Far Eastern scene. In brief, the lion backed off. The settlement of the Venezuelan dispute through a face-saving arbitrationlike device ushered in an era of Anglo-American good feeling. But men on both sides of the Atlantic knew that it was not any "special relationship" between them, but the changing of world relationships around them that counted. Nothing else really mattered.

> *Snatch of Lord Cromer, Jeff Davis a touch of him.*
> *A little of Lincoln, but not very much of him;*
> *Kitchener, Bismarck, Germany's Will,*
> *Jupiter, Chamberlain, Buffalo Bill.*
>
> Description of Theodore Roosevelt
> quoted by Woodrow Wilson, 1902

Americans mostly agreed with Woodrow Wilson about the Spanish-American War. It was a real turning point. Whether one rejoiced that Europe had been driven out of another part of America, looked upon Cuba and the Phillippines as stepping-stones to hidden treasures in Latin America and Asia, or mused about the impact of such responsibilities upon domestic politics, the keynote was the coming American supremacy. President William McKinley, who had endured the Populist challenge and then the slings and taunts of jingoes who thought him too slow to respond to the sinking of the *Maine,* was positively enthusiastic about embracing the world:

> The period of exclusiveness is past. The expansion of our commerce is the pressing problem. Commercial wars are unprofitable. A policy of good will and friendly trade relations will prevent reprisals. Reciprocity treaties are in harmony with the times, measures of retaliation are not.[14]

In myriad ways, then, America's appearance on the world stage promised change, including, of course, a change in the battle at home between protectionists and free traders. How far down this path McKinley would have traveled cannot be known, as he received a fatal wound from an assassin's bullet the day after he issued this appeal to reconsider traditional party positions on the tariff.

But McKinley's interest was certainly more than rhetorical. He had appointed a special reciprocity commissioner, John A. Kasson, and told him to investigate possible trade treaties with European nations. He hoped as well that better rules for international trade, and greater access to the world market, would help to tame the business cycle and check any resurgence of radical Populism. Kasson was sure treaties could be negotiated. But time was short. Great Britain was now on the defensive, Kasson advised McKinley's successor, Theodore Roosevelt; it was preparing protectionist defenses against the American commercial invasion no less than imperial Germany was. "Both agrarians and manufacturers abroad are appealing to their governments for new measures against the 'American invasion.' . . . We have come to the parting of the ways. We must go to the left on the Spanish road of Exclusiveness and industrial stagnation in our home market, and for our insular possessions; or go to the right on the smooth highway of Reciprocity and industrial expansion."[15]

TR had grave doubts that reciprocity was anything like a "smooth highway," fearing it was only another path paved with good intentions. True, foreign trade was becoming more important. Between 1895 and 1900, manufactured exports had risen by 172 percent, to more than $350 million annually, and total exports by nearly 100 percent, to $1.37 billion annually. Predictions of future trends dwarfed even these sums. But would the European industrial powers really show themselves to be so complaisant as Kasson imagined? Was it to be seriously argued that they would simply allow the United States to take over the world—peacefully? And were vested interests at home so eager for the reciprocity program that they would be willing to make sacrifices for its promise of a better tomorrow, when they had it so good today?

Roosevelt and Salisbury were men of different generations, but the innovations suggested by Kasson and others struck the younger man as fully as dangerous as what Chamberlain proposed to solve England's problems. Roosevelt's informal advisers, men such as Brooks Adams and Alfred Thayer Mahan, strengthened his conviction that the central fact in the world was the struggle for survival, and no reciprocity program he had heard of would alter that reality. Europe's statesmen, his advisers told him, were now all neo-mercantilists, empire builders who cast jealous eyes upon America's vast home market. They were not likely to give away very much without assurances of access to American wealth. Whether America stayed with protectionism or sought some alternative in reciprocity, the dangers of the future could not be avoided. TR agreed: "I think that no greater calamity could happen to this country at present than to stop building up the navy."[16]

A decent military establishment benefited the nation in several ways. It would allow the United States to exercise its proper options in a world filled with rivals, just as TR's "Square Deal" policy at home maintained the internal "balance of power" between competing class interests. Alarmed by the rapid changes brought about by the industrial revolution, spurred by the ubiquitous Social Darwinism of the age, political leaders looked everywhere for signs of vulnerability and unfitness. Above all, they believed, a nation must not succumb to passivism, must not drop out of the race. A strong military establishment was an antidote to socialism at home and its accompanying symptom of softheadedness about foreign affairs.

When Columbia University president Nicholas Murray Butler warned Roosevelt that he risked giving the Democrats the initiative on foreign economic policy questions, TR responded that, while a great many people said they were in favor of a reciprocity program, few ever showed up to do the work. It took two years, for example, to get Congress to accept a less than generous trade treaty with Cuba, whose bargaining power was practically nil. "The western farmer is anxious to have the tariff revised in the direction of lower duties upon the so-called trust products . . . ," TR pointed out, but "he does not like to have even an appearance of a reduction of duty on a farm product as the first step towards reciprocity."[17] Maybe, when the time was really ripe, the public would come together behind a demand for a different trade and tariff policy. Meanwhile, it wanted an army and navy.[18] For practical political reasons, then, as well as because of his more general assumptions about human nature and international relations, Roosevelt had little patience with theories of natural harmony.

In mid-July 1902, Joseph Chamberlain offered Roosevelt congratulations on putting down the Philippine insurrection. "This extension of American influence and dominion will work for the happiness of the native population," predicted the British colonial secretary, and the "experience in the problems of government under such circumstances will help the American people to understand our world-work, and I hope to sympathize with it."[19] TR did sympathize—up to a point. And he did believe that an informal consortium of the great powers was essential to maintaining world peace. If America's voice was to be heard, however, it was all the more necessary to have military credibility. "Speak softly and carry a big stick" was not, therefore, the boast of a jingo—well, not only that—but the voice of Progressivism.* Roosevelt's emerging career as mediator in the affairs of the powers was premised upon a persistent Progressive belief that, while international rivalry was inevitable, there were situations that, precisely because of America's relative isolation, lent themselves to experiments in cooperation. Perhaps it might even be possible to ameliorate the growing trade rivalries and fears by demonstrating possibilities for cooperation in the "outside" world. If so, that would make the tasks of the political leader far less risky, both at home and abroad.

Thus, TR's eagerness to referee the Russo-Japanese peace negotiations in 1905, and his willingness to call the great powers together at Algeciras, Spain, to resolve a potentially dangerous dispute over Morocco, can be viewed as products of the same forces, however different in result, that led Joseph Chamberlain to advocate a combined program of tariff reform

---

*Wilson's conversion to "military preparedness" in 1916 might be cited as a parallel. By the time America entered the war in 1917 he had convinced himself, with a lot of help from close advisers and British prime minister David Lloyd George, that the only way he could claim a seat at the peace table (and thereby advance Progressive goals) would be to pay the admission price in the trenches first. And, again like TR, Wilson imagined that the fate of American politics would be determined as much (or, now, more) by what happened in Paris as by what happened at home. See Lloyd C. Gardner, *A Covenant with Power: America and World Order from Wilson to Reagan* (New York, 1984), chap. 1.

(really empire protectionism) and treaties with Germany and America to delineate "boundaries." Both believed, furthermore, that the future would be determined in large part by the way in which relations were managed between the industrial nations and the "semi-barbarous" peoples of the outside world. Relief from the increasingly vexed social questions at home were to be found there, but not if the powers got mixed up about their respective missions and fell out among themselves. Roosevelt put it this way:

> Over the entire world, of recent years, wars between the great civilized powers have become less and less frequent. Wars with barbarous or semi-barbarous peoples come in an entirely different category, being merely a most regrettable but necessary international police duty which must be performed for the sake of the welfare of mankind.[20]

Roosevelt had once condemned Illinois governor John Peter Altgeld for pardoning the Haymarket rioters, and he had little difficulty drawing an analogy between the danger of insurrection at home and a failure to fulfill police duties abroad. Resistance to American pacification efforts in the Philippines, he asserted, should be equated with support for an "Indian uprising."

> Encouragement, direct or indirect, to these insurrectors stands on the same footing as encouragement to hostile Indians in the days when we still had Indian Wars. Exactly as our aim is to give to the Indian who remains peaceful the fullest and amplest consideration, but to have it understood that we will show no weakness if he goes on the warpath, so we must make it evident . . . that while we will do everything in our power for the Filipino who is peaceful, we will take the sternest measures with the Filipino who follows the path of the insurrector and the ladrone.[21]

That, as Roosevelt saw it, was the meaning of Progressivism. Writing to an English friend in 1906, TR explained that it had been his purpose to supervise and control "the business use of wealth so that it shall not be used in an unethical or anti-social spirit. . . ." Yet he had never hesitated to make it equally plain "that we intend fearlessly to put down anything in the nature of mob violence, and that we set our faces like flint against the preachers who appeal to or excite the dark and evil passions of men."[22]

> *Democracy is not so much a form of government as a set of principles. Other forms of government may be equally effi-*

> *cient; many forms of government are more efficient,—know*
> *better ways of integrating and purifying administration*
> *than we have yet learned, more successful methods of im-*
> *parting drill and order to restless and undeveloped peoples*
> *than we are likely to hit upon of ourselves, a more telling*
> *way of getting and a more effectual way of keeping leader-*
> *ship in a world of competitive policies, doubtful concerts,*
> *and international rivalries.*
>
> Woodrow Wilson, 1900

Wilson shared many things with Theodore Roosevelt. Like TR he had never doubted that America had a world mission to perform in the Philippines, and like him he expanded American power in the Caribbean. And like TR, Wilson had an urgent calling to mediate between the industrial nations. But Wilson came to have grave doubts about the "balance of power" as a guiding principle in either domestic or foreign affairs. Roosevelt's plan for saving democracy by controlling the corporations struck him as equivalent to saying that the best way to punish reckless driving would be to arrest the automobile.

A number of factors prevented Wilson from embracing a full-blown social imperialist outlook. "Democracy is not so much a form of government," he had said, "as a set of principles." TR's New Nationalism would bend those principles out of shape, perhaps to the point where American democracy would no longer be recognizable. In its place would be a strange form of government indeed: something that looked like socialism at home and international capitalism abroad. Hence when he became president in 1913, Wilson resisted plans for continuing the Republican emphasis on cooperation among the powers to formulate a response to the Mexican and Chinese revolutions. That approach, he believed, promoted only an international cartel of "special interests" banded together out of a narrow concern for profit.

His views also resembled those of David Lloyd George before the Great War, therefore, especially when the latter was criticizing "Africa Joe's" schemes for imperial consolidation and an Anglo-German alliance. He was never so radical, of course, as Lloyd George. And at the time he entered the White House, Wilson had little to offer beyond a mild reformist program and traditional southern low tariff postulates better suited to an earlier age. While it was clear that the giant corporations that now dominated economic and, increasingly, political life had been nourished on a steady diet of Republican high tariffs, it was equally obvious that the Republicans had become the corporations' servants in other ways, bringing them what they demanded under the rubric of "Dollar Diplomacy."

As matters stood, the corporations already posed a growing menace to American political traditions and institutions, not least (although this was not so well understood) because they threatened to raise up radical counterparts. The nation had already witnessed a Populist scare in the 1890s, and if some future demagogue managed to combine agrarian and Labor protest, the outlook was grim indeed. TR's New Nationalism was setting a precedent that a successor to William Jennings Bryan could stand on its head. In 1907 Wilson, then president of Princeton University, warned an audience that reformers were talking too "exclusively of the capitalistic class." There was an equally formidable enemy to freedom and equality, "and that is the class formed by the labor organizations," who represented only a minority interest among working people, but who yearned to exert monopolistic controls every bit as much as did the trusts.[23]

Whether they knew it or not, therefore, the Republicans were steering the country straight toward some form of socialism. "There is a great and apparently growing body of opinion in the country," Wilson wrote in the *Atlantic Monthly,*

> which approves of a radical change in the character of our institutions and the objects of our law, which wishes to see government, and the federal government at that, regulate business. Some men who entertain this wish perceive that it is socialistic, some do not. But of course it is socialistic. Government cannot properly or intelligently regulate business without fully comprehending it in its details as well as in its larger aspects; it cannot comprehend it except through the instrumentality of expert commissions; it cannot use expert commissions long for purposes of regulations without itself by degrees undertaking actually to order and conduct what it began by regulating. We are at present on the high road to government ownership of many sorts, or to some other method of control which will in practice be as complete as actual ownership.[24]

It occurred to Wilson that the Republicans were merely repeating the "experiment of paternalism" which had led to the American Revolution and "against which our whole political history has been a brilliant and successful protest." Some day soon it would be realized that the only course for the nation would be to "re-Americanize our government. . . ."[25] Wilson gave much thought to these problems during 1907, a time when he was considering a political career seriously. The statement about re-Americanizing the government came, in fact, from a statement he had titled "A Credo." The basic thrust of the document was an effort to define himself as a strict constitutionalist, who believed with all his heart that the president must not try to intimidate Congress or the courts.

Three years later, in the wake of a struggle over the fate of the new graduate school at Princeton, Wilson thought he saw the looming clouds of revolution gathering over America. In a surprising speech to Princeton alumni, who received his words in stunned silence, Wilson declared that the nation's churches and educational institutions had failed the people. They served only the classes, not the masses. Citing de Toqueville as his authority, the Princeton leader predicted a time of choice. "If she loses her self possession America will stagger like France through fields of blood before she again finds peace and prosperity under the leadership of men who understand her needs."[26]

Wilson was moving closer to the conviction that of those available, he himself best understood the nation's needs. The conservative Wilson of 1907 had appealed to various men interested in placing brakes upon the Progressive movement in New Jersey—and perhaps nationally. These men apparently misread the situation, or failed to keep up with Wilson's rapid transformation. The machine candidate for governor in 1910, Wilson cut loose immediately once in office, and pushed through his own reform program. His was the most spectacular rise to national leadership in the history of American politics, and already by the spring of 1911 he was being thought of as a leading contender for the Democratic presidential nomination.[27]

The election of 1912 shaped up as the most interesting election since 1860. Besides the likely standard-bearers of the two major parties, President William Howard Taft and Woodrow Wilson, there were two challengers from the outside: Bull Moose candidate Theodore Roosevelt and Socialist Eugene Debs. The situation was indeed not unlike the one in Great Britain that had prompted David Lloyd George to produce his memorandum calling for a coalition to handle a political agenda that none of the parties alone, Liberal, Conservative or Labour, could manage in safety. If there was considerably less urgency about the American political scene in 1911 and 1912, and practically no thought given to the other crisis, in foreign policy, there was plenty of excitement.

In prenomination speeches, Wilson tried to set an agenda. The world of the twentieth century, he would begin, had not made the Constitution obsolete. But the new era required national leaders who could recognize that fixed points were harder to find in the modern Darwinian world than they had been in the eighteenth century, the Newtonian era of the Founding Fathers. "We must have some central points of guidance. This is the adjustment to environment; this is the Darwinization of the Government of the United States."[28]

In one sense, Wilson was preaching paradox. According to Darwin, simpler creatures evolved into more complex ones. The candidate's proposed New Freedom appeared to many to be an effort to reverse that process. Yet there was a strong response, not only from voters but also from Progressive intellectuals. Discounting those who turned to Wilson out of despair at William Howard Taft, there was still a sizable number who had glimpsed the same future Wilson had seen: a cartelized America lurching from one political extreme to another, dominated by political parties that had become abject servants of capital and labor.

Wilson had wanted to make the tariff a central issue, but his campaign began to pick up steam only when he focused on the threat to traditional freedom implied by Roosevelt's solution to the problems of modern society. Roosevelt proposed to legalize the monopolies, said Wilson, adding, "I do not look forward with pleasure to the time when the juggernauts are licensed and driven by commissioners of the United States." The line between TR's dangerous paternalism, however, and Wilson's New Freedom was not always so clear. If Wilson continued to object to class legislation on behalf of corporations or workers, he nevertheless insisted that laws to protect the workingmen where they could not protect themselves, as in the case of their workplace environment, would not be anything but "a measure taken in the interest of the whole people. . . ."[29]

Wilson still talked about the tariff. Indeed, while he seldom mentioned foreign affairs as such, his speeches hammered on the theme that the Republicans, by their selfish concern only for the trusts, had neglected the most pressing problem in a capitalistic society: the expansion of the marketplace. "We must . . . fill the seas again with our own fleets," he said in his acceptance speech. "Our domestic markets no longer suffice. We need foreign markets." The Panama Canal was eloquent evidence of an awakening to the need for foreign trade. "We are not building the canal and pouring out million upon million of money upon its construction merely to establish a water connection between the two coasts of the continent, important and desirable as that may be, particularly from the point of view of naval defense. It is meant to be a great international highway." It was meant to be America's Suez.[30]

Speaking to a farmers' group a week after he accepted the nomination, Wilson repeated each of these warnings and arguments. "If prosperity is not to be checked in this country we must broaden our borders and make conquest of the markets of the world. . . . [If] you keep on with this tariff business, we will have to have a special board of guardians to look after the United States." After this reference to TR's New Nationalism, the candidate predicted "a great, handsome, peaceful, hopeful revolution on the fifth day of November 1912. . . ." Afterwards, he went on, people would go about their business wondering what it was they had feared. "We feared chains and we have won liberty. We feared to touch anything for fear we should mar it, and now everything wears the bright face of prosperity. And we know that the right is also the profitable thing, and that nobody can serve a nation without also serving himself."[31]

Lost in all this enthusiasm for a New Freedom was any clear picture of where Wilson actually stood on a whole series of critical issues. He resisted paternalism and state intervention as remedies to the ills of modern capitalist society; he placed great faith in the reassertion of individual responsibility as a primary answer; and he was serenely confident in the operations of a free—and expanded—marketplace. Yet those proposals that he did espouse for correcting abuses in the workplace required an even stronger role for government, not only to enact but to enforce. In sum, the line between the New Freedom and the New Nationalism, even during the 1912 campaign, was less distinct than either candidate cared to admit.

> *As America turns upon herself her seething millions and the cauldron grows hotter and hotter, is it not the great duty of America to see that her men remain free and happy under the conditions that have now sprung up? It is true that we needed a frontier so much that after the Spanish War we annexed a new frontier some seven thousand miles off in the Pacific.*
>
> Woodrow Wilson, February 1902

Wilson's mind constantly turned back to metaphors of freedom and restraint. The promise of America was a promise of freedom, unlimited frontiers, and economic opportunity. Roosevelt's way promised nothing but a "straitjacket," a denial of everything that had made the nation the last, best hope of mankind. In Cleveland, Ohio, as the campaign of 1912 approached its end, Wilson discovered yet another variation on that theme. "I have always thought of Ohio," he said, "as the first territory into which the freeing forces of America seemed to go and encamp. . . ." The other forces, now headed by Roosevelt, aimed at complete control of the nation's economic development. Ohioans, along with the rest of the nation, were to choose which set of principles were to be enthroned in the government.[32]

Both the New Nationalists and the Taft stand-patters had ignored the lesson their Republican forebears had tried to teach. William McKinley had attempted to move the nation toward reciprocity, Wilson said in Canton, McKinley's birthplace. "You will remember how he joined in opinion with what Mr. Blaine had said before him: that we had set up in this country too rigid a system of restriction on the movement of trade and the development of manufacture; that we must look forward to a time, which ought to come very soon, when we should enter into reciprocal relations of trade with the chief countries of the world. . . . McKinley saw what his successors did not see. He saw that we had made for ourselves a straitjacket. . . ."[33]

An unexpected emphasis was given to Wilson's remarks about the dangers represented by Roosevelt's campaign when, three days later, TR was shot in the chest as he left a Milwaukee hotel on the way to a speaking engagement. The wound was not serious, but it left an impression of stirred passions and unknown perils along the path Roosevelt trod. Whatever others thought, it must have reconfirmed for Wilson what he had written to an associate about the precarious state of national health. "In every one of my speeches in which I have put forth what seemed radical doctrine," he had confided to William Gibbs McAdoo in 1911, "I have accompanied the radical exposition with a statement of the absolute necessity that we should be careful; that we should remember the delicate tissue of the economic body politic. . . ."[34]

His heritage as well as his analysis of modern conditions prepared Wilson to believe that an assault on the tariff would work a transformation in world politics as well as strengthen national institutions. It would complete that "peaceful, hopeful revolution" he had foreseen. Wilson got his low tariff, the Underwood Act of 1913. Congratulations poured in. Ambassador Walter Hines Page in London saw the new tariff as a turning point no less significant than Britain's repeal of the Corn Laws. He had been telling British leaders, Page wrote, "that the passing of commercial supremacy to the United States will be dated in the economic histories from the tariff act of 1913. . . ." Wilson replied that he was not constituted to enjoy a sense of triumph, "but I do know in my mind that what we are accomplishing with regard to the tariff is going to be just as epoch-making as you indicate and in just the way you foresee."[35]

Wilson did not exaggerate his feelings. He was as confident as the Civil War generation had been that America would lead the way in breaking down the power of imperialism. Protectionism had been a mistake that had straitjacketed the American market, stifled the growth of liberalism, and created the twin dangers of radicalism and reaction. Tariff reduction was not all there was to the New Freedom, but it was seen as an essential first step. Aside from any immediate economic benefits, moreover, it stamped the Democratic administration as determined to "re-Americanize" the political scene. It was that notion as much as anything else that led Wilson to declare the Underwood Tariff an "epoch-making" event.

What was imperialism, after all, but the banding together of the "special interests" to dominate national governments and turn them into their servants? In an unpublished essay written in 1907, Wilson put the situation this way:

> Since trade ignores national boundaries and the manufacturer insists on having the world as a market, the flag of his nation must follow him, and the doors of the nations which are closed against him must be battered down. Concessions obtained by financiers must be safeguarded by ministers of state, even if the sovereignty of unwilling nations be outraged in the process. Colonies must be obtained or planted, in order that no useful corner of the world may be overlooked or left unused.[36]

Under these conditions, peace was a matter of conference and international combination. He did not advocate that the United States adopt these methods for its own; Wilson constantly talked about the Philippines as a sacred trust. What he did believe was that the United States under a New Nationalist program would, perforce, opt for high tariffs and become just another imperialist power—with devastating results for American politics and world peace.

The president's closest associates across the spectrum shared these beliefs, from the conservative businessman he named commerce secretary, William C. Redfield, to the former Populist, William Jennings Bryan, who became secretary of state. Redfield remains a little-noticed member of the cabinet, but Wilson listened closely to him about concerns of the business community.[37] Shortly before he joined the cabinet, Redfield authored an essay on modern business conditions, entitled *The New Industrial Day*, that sounded remarkably like Wilson's own analysis. Redfield wrote, "We have gone out into the world because we must. The product of our mills, our men and our minds has grown so large that it has burst through territorial and traditional lines. . . . Our foreign trade is . . . a safety valve that relieves the pressure of over-production at home."[38]

William Jennings Bryan was proud of his ability to demonstrate that Taft's "Dollar Diplomacy" had worked against the interests of American commerce. Like the imperialist policies of Europe, "Dollar Diplomacy" had been characterized by the effort to coerce smaller countries into compliance. Once foreign nations realized that the Democratic administration was not going to have anything to do with such unscrupulous behavior, Bryan declared, they would welcome American capital and American capitalists. "Many rich fields are awaiting development—the development of Central and South America is still in its infancy—and our nation is the nation to which our sister republics to the south of the

United States naturally look for such assistance as they need. . . . Why should they not look upon the United States as the great clearing house of their national wealth?"[39]

"The effort to get a few dollars by the employment of unfair and offensive methods has prevented our industries from securing that large and lucrative business which would have come with a more liberal policy—for a just policy is a liberal policy."[40] What is so striking about this formulation—and the others as well—is Bryan's discussion of what could be, not what was. The emphasis is on the future. If the American economy is to develop as in the past, if the dangers of radicalism are to be avoided, then the changes in policy starting with the new tariff and the break with "Dollar Diplomacy" had to be followed with concrete steps toward a more active world role. Otherwise it was all for naught.

Progressive Oswald Garrison Villard was unhappily surprised to learn of Wilson's strong views about expanding the navy and managing the affairs of smaller nations. It might not be Theodore Roosevelt or Taft talking to him, but Villard's interview with the candidate on August 14, 1912, left him troubled. The best face he could put on it was that Wilson was ignorant of foreign affairs:

> To my regret I found that the Governor favors a large navy, and that he has been quite deluded by all that silly jingo talk about Germany making a raid on South America. He also alarmed me by saying that this was a period when the big nations of the earth were not going to put up with misbehavior by the small ones.[41]

Wilson never spoke so many words about specific foreign policy issues during the campaign as in these private remarks to Villard. It was probably not because of ignorance, however.* As in the case of domestic policy, Wilson espoused seemingly contradictory views on foreign affairs. Lowering the tariff would reduce the causes of international friction, but America needed a navy nevertheless. Imperialism was an error, but the big nations "were not going to put up with misbehavior by the small ones."

Prudence and simple recognition of facts about great-power rivalries explain much of the apparent discrepancy. For further clarification it is necessary to introduce Colonel Edward M. House, Wilson's closest adviser and confidant. From before he entered the White House until midway in the Paris Peace Conference, Wilson relied on House for political and diplomatic advice. He entrusted him with the most delicate and far-reaching missions since the assignment Ben Franklin undertook in Paris during

---

*On his way over to the Paris Peace Conference, Wilson told news reporters that he had always believed that Germany had been on the verge of the commercial conquest of the world in 1913, but that the German military party had insisted upon taking a "short cut" and plunging the world into war.[42]

the American Revolution. House's foreign policy views, however, were more closely in line with those of Roosevelt-style Progressives. In an anonymously published novel, *Philip Dru: Administrator,* House presented a hero who, having dispatched the plutocracy at home and replaced it with scientific commissions charged with governing America, turns to the world scene to find that while he had been occupied with clearing out the rubbish of a robber baron regime, Germany and Japan had taken advantage of the situation to form an alliance against the United States. Now, Dru could really go to work.

He was successful immediately in detaching Great Britain from this unholy collaboration, with the result that the would-be usurpers were stopped dead in their tracks. According to Dru's plan, the secret pacts made among America's rivals were then replaced by a network of treaties that reduced armaments and lowered customs barriers. Spheres of influence were clearly defined under these arrangements, "and an era of friendly commercial rivalry established."[43] In *Philip Dru,* and in real life as Wilson's alter ego, House imagined a world directorate, as he suggested to German ambassador Count Johann von Bernstorff in May 1913, that would insure proper development of the "waste places" of the earth, and maintain "an open door and equal opportunity to everyone everywhere."[44]

On the eve of the outbreak of war in Europe, House was busy telling leaders in the rival capitals that America would consider joining a consortium of powers to establish "some plan" for lending money at reasonable rates to occupants of the

> waste places of the earth, and on the other hand, to bring about conditions by which such loans may be reasonably safe. If this can be brought about, it will not only do away with much of the international friction which such things [loans] cause, but it will be a step forward towards bringing about a stable and healthful condition in those unhappy countries which are now misgoverned and exploited both at home and abroad.[45]

When war came such dreams faded, of course. But the war highlighted, in House's and Wilson's minds, the peril to a "stable and healthful condition" in all countries that would exist unless a new international order was erected after the shooting ended. Long before the Bolshevik Revolution, indeed after less than a month of war, House had concluded that if the Allies won, Russia would be dominant on the continent, and if the Central Powers triumphed, "it means the unspeakable tyranny of militarism for generations to come." Either way, America's future would be fundamentally altered. "We will have to abandon the path which you are blazing as a standard for future generations . . . and build up a military machine of vast proportions."[46]

If House was willing to follow a much more Rooseveltian path in international and domestic affairs—indeed, relished the opportunity, so long as Wilson held the reins—nevertheless he also spoke in terms of paradox. The longer the war went on, the more it became certain that American liberalism could not survive in an atmosphere dominated by European militarism. In its place, moreover, TR's New Nationalism was only the most moderate of postwar alternatives available for political leaders to consider. To be sure, neither House nor Wilson ever spelled out the situation in such precise terms. Moreover the latter's grasp of its essentials was reshaped, and headed in a different direction, as the events of the Mexican and Chinese revolutions unfolded. What was essential, it became more and more clear, was to detach England from the "old world" of secret diplomacy, as Philip Dru had undertaken to do, in the name of a genuinely American progressive world order. That would be difficult indeed.

And so was Lloyd George's task. An outsider from Wales who had begun his political career in controversy, he shared Wilson's conviction that imperialism had failed to address intranational as well as international conditions. Where the American leader attempted to ward off cartelization of national and international life by reestablishing a free marketplace, however, Lloyd George sought to meet the socialist threat by beating the Conservatives at their own game.

Eventually Lloyd George would seek to enlist Wilson's aid in his various maneuverings and encourage him to enter the war so as to take his seat at the head of the peace table. But as events in far-off storm centers, Mexico and China, would soon demonstrate, Great Britain and the United States would have a hard time agreeing on ways to make the postwar world safe for democracy.

CHAPTER THREE

Intervention in Mexico

*There can be no certain prospect of peace in America
until Gen. Huerta has surrendered his usurped authority in Mexico; until it is understood on all hands,
indeed, that such pretended governments will not be
contenanced or dealt with by the Government of the
United States.*

Woodrow Wilson,
First Annual Message, December 1913

Woodrow Wilson was perfectly willing for the Mexican Revolution to
become an international issue. Indeed, he welcomed the prospect of confrontation. Encouraged by advisers eager to do the world's work, the
president early decided that Mexico should be the place, and the Mexican
Revolution the proper occasion, for teaching the old order about modern
conditions, and the perils of ignoring their imperatives.

Never mind that Wilson's original view of the Mexican situation was
shallow, both as to the causes of the disturbance there and its likely outcome, or that he never gave up the thought that revolutions in general
would yield to American instruction if handled properly. He saw clearly
enough, if only because of the repercussions in the United States, that
Mexico was likely to be the beginning of an international movement
against the nineteenth-century imperial order. His blind spots are well
known, from his rather uncritical celebration of the American role in the
Philippines to his TR-like actions in the Caribbean. He convinced himself
that America's emerging "duty" toward the submerged masses of Mexico
was in an entirely different category. Acceptable or not to critics, Wilson's
distinction was a meaningful one for the times, for it posited that if there

was to be a chance for liberalism to assert itself in terms less dangerous to its ultimate survival than those of social imperialism, and if it was to avoid being cast aside in favor of frankly radical solutions of the left or right, the way America responded to Mexico mattered a great deal. According to this formulation, failure to appear sympathetic to popular feelings in Mexico for change would likely rebound in America, weakening the liberal alliance and forcing a search for more radical leaders.

From the beginning, however, Great Britain appeared to be the major obstacle in Wilson's way. The leading power in the imperialist league, England had the most to lose in Mexico. The direct investments put at risk by the revolution were, moreover, only a fragment of a much greater danger. Any change in the status quo, whether nearer at hand, say in the Balkans, or as far removed from European politics as Mexico, was very likely to be disadvantageous, and therefore was to be avoided. The Americans, it was said in London, simply did not realize the folly of playing around with revolutionaries. The most incompetent government America had ever had, wrote British ambassador Sir Cecil Spring-Rice in a moment of exasperation, was "embarking light heartedly" on a path it did not realize would eventually lead it to undertake a complete protectorate over the Central American and Caribbean area.[1]

Even so, there arose in certain American minds the unfounded notion that the ruling Liberal party in England would welcome Wilson's intervention. "The whole Liberal fight here," American ambassador Walter Hines Page wrote the president in a moment of naive self-congratulation, "is confessedly to bring this Kingdom, as far as they know how and dare to try, up to the economic level and practice of the United States: that's their standard and aim."[2] Page had not specified Mexico, nor had he, in this sentence, spoken about a desire to emulate American political behavior. The "Liberal fight" was to become more like America on an economic level, but that was just the point. To become more like America economically required abandoning old ways politically, and leaving behind the reactionary impulse that had produced the new imperialism in Asia and Africa, and that had shaped (or rather misshaped) countries like Mexico for too long.

What other result but revolution could one expect? And given the unholy alliance of reactionary imperialist nations, what other outside force was there, except America, to lead the way to safety? Page preached Anglo-Saxon unity. Anglo-American intervention in Mexico could be justified as the sort of "police duty that all great nations have to do. . . . It's merely using the British fleet and ours to make the world understand that the time has come for orderliness and peace and for the honest development of backward, turbulent lands and peoples."[3]

Convinced that he had a special part to play as leader of the liberal forces working to make the world safe for democracy, Wilson posited a different role for America. Mexico's fate was about to be decided, but far more importantly, so was the character of the governments within the industrial nations—including America. The president was under no illusion about the power of the great economic forces and their ability to survive a reformist administration in Washington. Only by making some fundamental change first could one contemplate the sort of benevolent trusteeship Page, Colonel House, and others proposed as a solution to relations between industrial nations and the rest of the world.

So even before he fully understood all the causes of the Mexican Revolution, Wilson sensed that the issues were rooted in questions that went back as far as the French Revolution and that reached ahead into the increasingly uncertain future.

> *It is particularly unfortunate that this should have taken place in a leading country of Latin America, where if we have any moral work to do, it is to discourage violence and uphold law.*
>
> William Bayard Hale,
> Wilson's "special agent," 1913

Even those in America who paid little or no attention to Mexico had been shocked by President Madero's murder in early 1913. Madero had come to power three years earlier, in 1910, the result of a peaceful coup d'etat against aging, in fact ancient, dictator Porfirio Díaz. Madero's attempt to emulate the modern liberal principles of advanced thought in Europe was probably too abstract for the realities of Mexican life at the time, but that did not lessen the shock of his murder at the hands of General Victoriano Huerta, who, in an arrogant display of unconcern for world reaction, set himself up as Mexico's new ruler. Reports coming to Washington via both public and private channels confirmed the rumors of the American ambassador's connivance in Madero's death. If not the actual author of Madero's betrayal, Ambassador Henry Lane Wilson was said to be deeply implicated in the intrigues leading to his overthrow. Progressive commentators agreed: America's reputation had suffered, and would continue to suffer, until this ghastly "error" had been repudiated.[4]

Foreign capitalists, however, had greeted Madero's original "revolution" ambivalently. Some felt it was merely a prelude to worse things. In this bearish view, either Madero would move in more radical directions, or he would soon succumb to the agrarian "wild men," Pancho Villa and Emiliano Zapata. Either way, the effort to liberalize Mexico would produce nothing except Indian rule and anarchy.[5] A consensus was lacking, however, as it would be throughout the years of the revolution. One prominent representative of capitalist interests, Judge Lebbeus R. Wilfley, wrote President William Howard Taft that Díaz's days had been numbered anyway. A little reform would not hurt, especially if it contained a much bigger explosion. Military intervention, on the other hand, would be unpopular in *both* countries, stirring up questions about "Dollar Diplomacy." "Moreover," Wilfley concluded, "Intervention would probably unsettle an order of things in all Latin America which it might be well to conserve at this time."[6]

Taft was in no hurry to precipitate an even worse state of affairs, in either country, and so imposed an arms embargo along with a proclamation warning American citizens not to become involved in Mexico's internal affairs. Secretary of State Philander C. Knox encouraged New York bankers to go ahead with a proposed loan of $10 million to the Mexican government. Even as gloom spread throughout the business community, the bankers persisted in seeing a silver lining. Mexican finances bordered on "hopeless confusion and bankruptcy," reported American diplomats from the capital city, but the bankers were not disheartened. To the contrary, in their eyes the financial situation meant that Madero would have to agree to external supervision, something on the order of Cuba, Santo Domingo, and Nicaragua.[7]

Ambassador Henry Lane Wilson had no faith in any of these schemes. Madero simply would not do; he was not suited for the role imagined for him by the bankers. Thus from the day Madero entered Chapultepec Castle, the American ambassador was his enemy. Wilson made no effort to hide his feelings, nor to disguise his association with the new Mexican president's sworn foes. Madero was no more fortunate, moreover, in dealing with agrarian revolutionaries in the countryside. And when the crisis came, he could not count on anyone's support.

On February 9, 1913, Felix Díaz, nephew of the deposed dictator, rode into Mexico City at the head of an armed force. The final blow, however, was struck by Madero's own military commander, General Huerta, who decided that Mexico had suffered long enough from this experiment in liberal democracy. Ten days later, accordingly, Huerta placed Madero under arrest and assumed the title of provisional president. Ambassador Wilson was quite content with the outcome and, fulfilling his duty as he saw it to protect foreign interests, summoned both Díaz and Huerta to the American embassy. Unless the fighting between them stopped immediately, he told them, the European powers would force the United States to intervene. The implication went the other way as well: if they did come to terms, they could expect protection from the United States. Under what became known as the "Pact of the Embassy," Huerta retained the presidency until elections could be held, with the promise that he would support Díaz's candidacy at that time.

Satisfied he had covered all contingencies, Ambassador Wilson set the diplomatic process to work on Huerta's behalf. On the evening of February 20, 1913, members of the diplomatic corps were called to the embassy to hear what had transpired. Explanations over, Wilson asked them all to attend Huerta's initial diplomatic reception. He reminded his colleagues how essential it was in these cases to demonstrate "immediate support" for a new government. Wilson's hints that a display of support for Huerta would discourage further attempts at revolution did not go unnoticed.[8] Sir Francis Stronge, the British minister, cabled home that in private conversations Henry Lane Wilson had assured him that he accepted the "official" version of Madero's death—shot during an escape attempt—but that there was not much doubt about who had really given the execution order. These were necessary fictions, additional prerequisites for restoring order. Best not to inquire too much under the circumstances. And in any event, Stronge believed, Wilson had acted properly (whatever his involvement) in facilitating a restoration of public health.[9]

Ambassador Wilson, meanwhile, had shifted his attention to more ordinary duties: informing Washington of what had taken place and procuring formal diplomatic recognition of Huerta's regime, so as to insure "the submission and adhesion of all elements in the Republic."[10] That was all that was needed, he urged, to put Mexico back on a secure footing. President Taft and Secretary Knox were not so sure it would be that simple. At hand were reports that Governor Venustiano Carranza of Coahuila had declared he would never accept Huerta's authority. A conservative landowner with well-known political ambitions, Carranza was united, temporarily at least, with Zapata and Villa, and thus lent legitimacy to what was called a Constitutionalist alliance.[11]

Riven by ancient disputes between the rich *haciendas* and the Indian communities, the Mexican countryside had come alive in recent years. If Carranza's Constitutionalist alliance held up, it could still mean a steadily worsening situation for foreign interests, as the thrust of the revolution was sure to be directed against foreign holdings. In any event, Carranza's domination of the Constitutionalist movement would mean that almost the entire thrust would be directed that way while internal conditions became those of civil war and approached anarchy.

Added to traditional disputes were those now developing in commercial agriculture and within the tiny but growing industrial sector. A working-class consciousness was already well rooted in the mines and oil fields. Foreign-owned, these holdings became a focus for the struggle by nationalist Mexicans to claim their own in the world. In the last days of Porfirio Díaz's regime, for example, his inner circle of advisers, an elite group that liked to call itself the *Científicos,* had revealed considerable discontent with the way things were. Although they were hardly as disenchanted as the leaders of the countryside or of the workers, their concerns overlapped, especially those about the foreigner and his privileges. The exact extent of foreign control of the Mexican economy cannot be fully documented, but that matters little. Almost all areas of commerce and industry were under its sway—approximately 97 percent in mining, 98 percent in rubber, and 90 percent in petroleum.[12]

With the stakes so high, it is not surprising that Taft wanted more information about the situation before recognizing Huerta. Besides, if it came to a point where America would have to supervise events in Mexico, it was better that the Democrats take responsibility from the outset, rather than have it become a partisan question. Formal diplomatic recognition, Knox cabled the ambassador without elaborating, "is not to be undertaken just now."[13]

In London, Foreign Office experts were divided about whether His Majesty's Government ought to consult the U.S. Department of State before granting recognition. Everything it learned from Mexico City and Washington only strengthened the view that Sir Francis Stronge had put forward. President Taft was happy, advised Ambassador James Bryce from the American capital, about the way things had turned out, and felt confident that Huerta stood a good chance of restoring order and tranquillity. Since the two generals, Díaz and Huerta, controlled the military, American policymakers believed that the transfer of power agreed upon in the embassy could be realized "under the semblance of a popular election." Bryce added that President-elect Woodrow Wilson was expected to take much the same view.[14]

As it happened, Bryce was misinformed about Taft's confidence in Huerta, let alone about the president-elect's views. To be sure, there was ample room for doubt about both, and Bryce's informants probably thought their conclusions justified. The important thing, however, was that the foreign secretary, Sir Edward Grey, decided that Bryce's reports should not be the determining factor in deciding the recognition question. "Our interests in Mexico are so big," he instructed his colleagues in the Foreign Offfice, "that I think we should take our own line without making it dependent upon that of other Govts."[15]

You will informally and unofficially advise all officials who make inquiry that our Government is deeply interested in the restoration of peace to the end that law may be enforced, that order may be preserved, and that the rights of Americans may be preserved.

William Jennings Bryan to Henry Lane Wilson,
March 8, 1913

Woodrow Wilson came into office with only the barest knowledge of recent events in Mexico. He had been informed of Madero's death, and the rumors surrounding it, but in the weeks before his inauguration, whatever attention he gave to Mexico and Central America concerned fears that "revolutionaries" were plotting to take advantage of the advent of a liberal government in Washington to pursue their own ends. Explaining all this to an early cabinet meeting, the new president vowed to oppose "those who foment troubles for personal aggrandizement in the hope of America winking at revolution and holding hands off." Huerta's coup seemed to fit this definition.[16]

Accordingly, on March 12, 1913, the president issued a statement that, while it did not mention Huerta or specify Mexico, advised the world that the United States would "lend our influence of every kind" against "disorder, personal intrigues, and defiance of constitutional rights." What these statements, private and public, indicated above all else (and certainly beyond any understanding of the specifics of the Mexican situation) was Wilson's eagerness to get off to a fast start in formulating a liberal foreign policy that could be distinguished from Republican "Dollar Diplomacy"— and from European practice.

In mid-April, for example, Wilson and his cabinet talked over reports that all the recent trouble in Mexico originated in a struggle between British and American oil companies, with the former backing General Huerta. And that accounted for the British reaction. If that were so, however, why was it that Ambassador Henry Lane Wilson was so intent upon gaining diplomatic recognition for the general?[17] One upshot of this discussion, and of the rumors of foreign loans destined for Mexico, was an official inquiry put by Secretary of State Bryan as to whether there was any evidence that "Lord Cowdray has been instrumental in any way in this matter." The answer Bryan received from Ambassador Henry Lane Wilson was, yes, the British oil magnate was deeply involved. Why should that be surprising? the ambassador continued. Rival diplomats were openly bragging about "our present unpopularity," and how they were taking advantage of it. "The British minister informed me a few days ago that he thought it entirely fair to make use of the opportunity growing out of the present embarrassed relations . . . to push British enterprises in every direction."[18]

The ambassador had chosen his words maladroitly. To those in power in Washington, however uncertain they were about the facts of the situation since Huerta's takeover, the "present embarrassed relations" did not mean what the ambassador had in mind, delay and indecision, but the blot left on America's reputation by the conspiracy to depose Madero. President Wilson's assault on the fomentors of revolution now seemed to be directed only at Huerta. This was the first example, moreover, of the way the president's public diplomacy would commit him to a course of action beyond recall.

Increasingly desperate, Ambassador Wilson exaggerated the existence of anti-American feeling into a threat that if recognition was not given, the men around Huerta would use Washington's delay to default on Mexico's financial obligations to American bankers.[19] Nothing the ambassador said could carry any weight with Wilson or Bryan, but Wilson did listen to a suggestion from Colonel House. Approached by American citizens with large holdings in Mexico, House agreed to submit their ideas to the White House. In brief, these were that nothing would be lost by giving General Huerta a chance to fulfill his "Pact of the Embassy" promise to hold elections. If Huerta failed to restore peace, the colonel's visitors had warned, 'it meant either intervention or [Mexico's] disintegration into smaller units."[20] (Indeed, when things got worse in Mexico in later years, several American capitalists urged support for separatist movements in the northern states.)[21]

President Wilson actually did draw up instructions to the American embassy in Mexico City combining an offer of American diplomatic recognition with a demand for a cease-fire and early elections. He soon had second thoughts, however, and abandoned the whole scheme. The most significant part of the unused draft, it would soon appear, was the president's warning to Huerta not to seek European "assistance in consideration of special advantages accorded their citizens or subjects."[22]

Unfortunately for Anglo-American relations, the advice Sir Edward Grey was getting from Washington still did not reflect the true situation there. His new envoy, Sir Cecil Spring-Rice, informed London that the only thing that held back the new administration from granting diplomatic recognition was lack of confidence in General Huerta's ability to hold the lid on and restore order. American bankers were pushing hard for recognition, nevertheless, and some plan would be tried.[23] Those were the views of Colonel House's visitors, approximately, but they were not Wilson's, which had already taken a turn toward seeing the pressure for recognition as European-stimulated.

Grey's efforts to appear sympathetic with President Wilson's dilemma as presented by Spring-Rice only added to American suspicions. In a telegram drafted with the State Department in mind, Grey explained that British recognition was provisional only, and that it had been granted after Henry Lane Wilson had led the entire diplomatic community in paying their respects to the general at a Chapultepec reception. America already bore responsibility for the new government in Mexico, in other words, and it was now more dangerous to back out than to go ahead.[24] Wilson agreed that it was wrong to back out. Having ordered Ambassador Henry Lane Wilson home, the president sent in his place a diplomat of the new school, former Minnesota governor John Lind, with a loan offer that promised aid to Mexico if Huerta would step aside. "We offer our good offices, not only because of our genuine desire to play the part of a friend," read Wilson's instructions to Lind, "but also because we are expected by the powers of the world to act as Mexico's nearest friend."[25]

Lind's eagerness to serve the president was never in doubt, but not so his diplomatic abilities. Once in Mexico he confided "very confidentially" to Sir Francis Stronge that since the "Pact of the Embassy" had been signed under American aegis, the United States government had a solemn responsibility to see that it was carried out. Stronge was flabbergasted. Was His Majesty's Government now to understand that President Wilson stood behind the pact—and not just the erring (and recalled) Henry Lane Wilson? If so, then Washington was surely obliged to grant Huerta recognition before it demanded that the general fulfill his side of the bargain. Truth was, he reported to London, Washington wanted to have it both ways: it wished to invoke the pact as convenient justification for claiming a special role, while at the same time seeking to enlist the aid of other nations in ousting Huerta. Whatever else Lind intended, it was clear that his superiors wanted Mexico all to themselves.[26]

Lind's offer of an American loan if Huerta would agree to go peacefully reconfirmed Stronge's first impression, but it got the American nowhere. All it accomplished was to provide an opportunity for General Huerta to mobilize nationalist feelings with his indignant refusal to contenance such bribery, the most heinous since the offer to Judas Iscariot. Informed of this outcome, President Wilson advised Congress on August 27, 1813 that Huerta's rejection of "our friendship" had created new circumstances that "will inevitably bring its own alternative in the whole aspect of affairs." For the second time within six months, Wilson had publicly committed himself to making Mexico a laboratory to test out a new diplomacy. He would adopt a policy of "watchful waiting," he said, and for the time being would content himself with imposing an arms embargo on all "factions" in Mexico.[27]

Lind had withdrawn to an American warship off the coast of Veracruz, where he conducted his own watchful waiting close by the Constitutionalist stronghold there. He was already blaming the British for his
inability to achieve Huerta's removal, and giving consideration to encouraging England's economic rivals in Mexico as a means of bringing His
Majesty's Government around to the American point of view.[28] The news
that London was sending out a new minister to replace Stronge dashed
hopes in Washington that Grey was reconsidering his hasty action in
recognizing Huerta. To send a replacement made the policy more definite; that the replacement was Sir Lionel Carden meant that Wilson
would have his confrontation.

Carden had a reputation for eagle-baiting that went back at least a
decade, when, it was asserted, he had tried his best to disturb the smooth
running of the Cuban-American commercial treaty. Sir Lionel reveled in
the knowledge that Americans hated him, and was dead set upon living
up to every word that had been written about him. "He is the handsome,
perfectly groomed, tall, fresh-complexioned, white-mustached, unmistakable Briton," was the sardonic comment of an American diplomat's wife
stationed in Mexico City.[29]

The guiding principle of Anglo-Mexican relations, Carden had written in a memorandum for Grey, must be to prevent British policy from
drifting into a groove designed by American whims or pretensions. The
recent history of the Monroe Doctrine demonstrated Washington's propensity to meddle in the domestic affairs of its weaker neighbors, he went
on, a propensity that would neither bring about improved political conditions nor remove the causes of unrest. Far from following the economic
liberalism they talked so much about, moreover, the Americans had
sought a virtual monopoly over Latin American finance, commerce, and
public works. Their overbearing attitude was now reaching a climax in
Mexico, unfortunately for everyone with holdings there. But it was not
too late to insist that General Huerta be given a free hand to suppress the
rebellion, and afforded all possible moral and financial support. That was
the only way to protect British interests, Carden concluded, and, he might
as well have added, set limits upon American pretensions.[30]

Carden thus arrived in Veracruz with a well-advertised mission and an
overheated contempt for his untutored and bumptious American adversar-
ies. John Lind invited him to lunch on board the flagship of the American
flotilla, no doubt to impress on Sir Lionel that these were now American waters. As expected, and probably hoped, the conversation went badly. It convinced him, Lind reported, that Lord Cowdray was pulling all the strings,
and controlled Huerta "absolutely." It was just as the Constitutionalists had
been saying: no elections held by Huerta could produce an honest result.[31]

Lind's report of his interview with Carden reached Washington at approximately the same time that word came of the arrest of 110 members of the Mexican Chamber of Deputies. Standing near Huerta as the general met with the diplomatic corps to explain this action was Sir Lionel Carden, who had just arrived to present his credentials. It was quite a "love-feast," quipped the American diplomat's wife Edith O'Shaughnessy. "[A]t the delicate moment of his birth and first struggling cry as a dictator," there was Sir Lionel, to watch over Huerta like a godfather. "Mexico must be compared to a sick man who needed an operation to save his life," claimed Huerta, putting the best face he could on the illegal arrests. What he should have said, grumbled John Lind in Veracruz, was that Sir Lionel Carden had deemed them a necessity. The Britisher had very likely planned the arrests and written Huerta's speech for him.[32]

In Washington, meanwhile, Wilson was less concerned with assessing Carden's personal responsibility, but he was angered by this untoward turn of events. Huerta had been on the verge of collapse, he wrote in a memorandum intended for European capitals, when Carden arrived to take charge of the general's rehabilitation. Without foreign assistance, Huerta's bloody reign would have come to a quick end. "Will the other governments cooperate with the United States, or is their policy and intention to antagonize and thwart us and make our task one of domination and force," was how Wilson posed the question. There followed a recitation of the sinister forces at work in Mexico that conspired to deprive the Mexican people of their political rights and economic well-being.

> If the influences at work in Mexico were entirely domestic, this government would be willing to trust the people to protect themselves against any ambitious leader who might arise, but since such a leader relies for his strength, not upon the sympathy of his own people, but upon the the influence of foreign people, this Government, whether that foreign capital is from the United States or from other countries, would be derelict in its duty if by silence or inaction it seemed to sympathize with such an interference in the rights and welfare of Mexico.[33]

Several Wilsonian themes first emerge in the sentences quoted here from these unsent diplomatic notes. First, it is clear that, while he still did not understand all the forces at work in Mexico, the president saw the situation in a much broader context than merely the duty to redress the consequences of Henry Lane Wilson's shameful behavior. Second, he now believed American foreign capital was at least as responsible as that from other countries. Finally, the connection of the Mexican Revolution with the outcome of the political struggles going on within the industrial nations, the question of whether reform at home could work without breaking the thralldom of the "special interests" abroad, had become a central (if still vague) matter for consideration.

The president also touched upon, more directly than ever before, the "covenant with power" that he would accept to justify intervention in Mexico against "outside" forces, and the decision to go to war in 1917 to make the world safe for democracy. The United States, he said, waited to see if the other industrial nations would cooperate—or would they seek to "thwart us and make our task one of domination and force"? Here was treacherous ground for liberals. No one knew that better than Wilson.

> *Settlement by civil war carried to its bitter conclusion is a*
> *terrible thing, but it must come now, whether we wish it or*
> *not, unless some outside power is to undertake to sweep*
> *Mexico with its armed forces from end to end, which would*
> *be the mere beginning of a still more difficult problem.*
>
> Woodrow Wilson, 1914

America was not motivated by a desire for more territory, Wilson said in his famous Mobile address on October 27, 1913. Having eliminated imperialism as a justification for intervention, the president went on to describe a possible cause for action. "We have seen material interests threaten constitutional freedom in the United States," he said. "Therefore we will now know how to sympathize with those in the rest of America who have to contend with such powers, not only within their borders but from outside their borders also."[34]

A few days later Wilson outlined to Colonel House a possible solution to the impasse. In former years the Monroe Doctrine had been aimed at preventing any political control of Latin America by European nations, the president said, according to House's record of the discussion. Financial control was equally reprehensible, and more likely in the modern world. He was certain that Carden's mission was to make Mexico safe for Lord Cowdray. And since London would not recall its representative, something dramatic would have to be done:

> The President has in mind to declare war against Mexico even though the actual armed entrance into Mexico is not made. His purpose in this is to keep the powers from interfering and entirely out of the situation. He will first blockade the ports, thereby cutting off all revenue from the Mexican Government which will have a tendency to break down Huerta's resistance.[35]

House encouraged the idea. It reminded him of the sort of ploy that Philip Dru had used to break up the anti-American alliance. In House's novel, moreover, Dru had led an army to victory over a Mexican dictator whose behavior toward foreign property and foreign lives had made necessary either American intervention or European invasion. "In another generation," Dru proclaims at the moment of victory, "this beautiful land will be teeming with an educated, prosperous and contented people, who will regard the battlefield as the birthplace of their redemption."[36]

Wilson did not declare war—not yet, anyway—and he received a special emissary from Sir Edward Grey with assurances that his principal objective was to protect property and lives, and to promote harmony among the industrial nations. "With this object in view," Sir William Tyrrell reported to the foreign secretary, "the President has made up his mind to teach these countries a lesson by insisting on the removal of Huerta."[37]

The Wilson-Tyrrell conversations provide a crucial insight into the president's character: Wilson's ability to compartmentalize his mind. He was aware by this time, if only from the protests of the "special interests," that opposing Huerta carried great risks in terms of life and property. And his bland assurances to Sir William hardly squared with his private notes denouncing European intervention. The disparity in these instances was growing, not diminishing. Soon, moreover, Huerta's removal would become incidental to a much more ambitious foreign policy that Wilson could not even begin to glimpse the end of. Sir Edward Grey zeroed in on that danger at once. All well and good, mused the foreign secretary about Wilson's assurances, but what was to come after? How did the president imagine, Grey asked Ambassador Page, "seeing that the greater part of Mexico was being ravaged by bands, elections for a Constitutional Government were to be held when Huerta retired?" Page admitted the difficulty.[38]

Truth was, Wilson was also scared about the Constitutionalists. A few days before Tyrrell's visit in mid-November 1913, the president had sent William Bayard Hale to see Venustiano Carranza. Hale was to tell the "First Chief" that the United States was considering lifting the arms embargo. But the Mexican leader must not assume he was being given carte blanche. The United States wished to avoid intervention. "If the lives and property of Americans and all other foreigners are safeguarded we believe intervention may avoided," Wilson warned. "If not we foresee we shall be forced to do it. We rely upon them to see to it that there is no occasion for it in their territory."[39]

Carranza's response was so negative, so full of unhappy portent, that Wilson actually sought to reopen negotiations with Huerta with an eye toward persuading him to resign in favor of a provisional government of elder statesmen. Sir Edward Grey welcomed this overture. Certainly such a solution was better than allowing the Constitutionalist marauders to come to power, and he so instructed Lionel Carden. Despite this pressure to accede, Huerta struck a defiant pose, saying, "We cannot accept the intervention of any foreign power."[40]

"It looks pretty hopeless to us both," lamented Colonel House after talking with the president. Wilson was still thinking about lifting the arms embargo. Presumably that would insure a Carranza triumph. But what did that mean? "He had been told that Carranza's program was to kill Huerta and his Cabinet. . . . They also purposed doing away with the land monopoly and dispersing it among the proletariat."[41]

Grey received the news that Wilson had lifted the arms embargo with a shrug. "I should have no objection of letting things go on to a fight to the finish," he told Page, "if only the finish were likely to come soon." Sir Edward's composure was soon put to the test, however, by the president's suddent enthusiasm for a possible alternative to Carranza, General Pancho Villa.[42] A sort of Robin Hood, Wilson mused to Ambassador Spring-Rice, a man who had spent "a not uneventful life in robbing the rich in order to give to the poor." His great virtue, though, was that he knew his own limitations. "He knew he could fight," Wilson told Spring-Rice, "but he knew also that he could not govern. Villa was the sword of the revolution, and it was possible that someone would be found who would manage the political affairs of the revolution when accomplished under capable and disinterested advice." And that was not all. "So long as the present system under which whole provinces were owned by one man continued to exist," Wilson went on, "so long there would be perpetual trouble in the political world." The Constitutionalists had many faults, but they did represent the just claims of the agricultural population. "This was especially true of Villa."[43]

The president made the rounds of Europeans diplomats in an effort to persuade them of Villa's qualifications. "Speaking of Villa," a French military attaché reported, Wilson "expressed his admiration that this highwayman has gradually succeeded in instilling sufficient discipline into his troops to convert them into an army. Perhaps, he added, this man today represents the only instrument of civilization in Mexico. His firm authority allows him to create order and to educate the turbulent mass of peons so prone to pillage."[44]

None of this was convincing to Wilson's listeners.[45] For them the question became, Which was the greater danger—Wilson's faith in Villa, or Villa himself? Eventually, of course, it would appear that Carranza was, and the Constitution of 1917 with its antiforeign clauses, but in 1914 it seemed unlikely in the extreme that anything but anarchy would come out of the revolution. The issue between London and Washington came to a head on February 16, 1914, when Villa ordered the execution of William Benton, a British citizen. Spring-Rice warned Secretary of State Bryan that this act would cause an uproar across the ocean. Bryan was not conciliatory, not at all. Why had the "civilized" nations over there acquiesced in Huerta's crimes? he retorted. "We are giving them [the Constitutionalists] arms as you are giving Huerta arms," he continued, "we are friends with them, as you are friends with Huerta. We are no more responsible [for Benton's death] than you are for all the crimes Huerta has committed."[46]

Spring-Rice did not back off. If His Majesty's Government was really as intimate with Huerta as the U.S. secretary of state wished to believe, and if an American subject had been killed, then Washington could be assured that the British would "do something."[47] What concerned American policymakers, however, was that the "something" they themselves were doing was not enough. Lifting the arms embargo was not working to oust Huerta, at least not very quickly. John Lind was frantic. "Our country cannot afford to surrender either to this man or to his European ally," he told Bryan. The time had passed for being overly scrupulous "about the fiction of neutrality." Wilson had announced to the world that Huerta must go. And so he must, for America's sake.[48]

Lind's warlike metaphors recalled Wilson's idea that he would declare war on Mexico so as to defeat European machinations in the hemisphere. Now, however, Wilson was counseling patience. Eventually Huerta would have to retire. "A country the size and power of the United States can afford to wait just as long as it pleases," insisted the president. But outward calm belied the apprehension felt in the White House. There were reports of German plans to intervene, of large arms shipments from Japan as well as other European countries. British diplomats in Mexico City were predicting an early Huerta victory.[49]

It looked very much, in other words, as if the Europeans had decided amongst themselves what they must do to save Huerta. Efforts to secure firm assurances from the Constitutionalists that they would protect foreigners, meanwhile, had still not yielded any positive result that could be presented by Washington to forestall European intervention. On April 8, 1914, Grey cabled Spring-Rice that Lord Cowdray had just warned him that if Huerta were forced to evacuate Tampico, the enormous British oil fields in that area would be endangered. The ambassador then decided that he must personally convince the Americans not to allow their "wards" to cause trouble between London and Washington. Sir Edward Grey was averse to headlong action, Spring-Rice told Bryan, but public opinion "would take a very serious view of [the] menace to such immense British interests within eighteen miles of British ships. . . . [I]t was impossible to predict what action would be taken."[50]

Whatever Bryan thought, Sir Edward Grey was shocked when he learned of Spring-Rice's initiative. He had not meant that the ambassador should even hint at a troop landing, "because such a measure has not even been thought of." The State Department was a busy place in the wake of Spring-Rice's visit. Messages went out to Admiral Frank Fletcher, commander of the flotilla, and to the consul at Tampico, instructing them to impress on all Mexican leaders, Huertista and anti-Huerta alike, that attacks on foreign property would trigger a grave situation. If such attacks took place, the United States would have to consider taking measures to protect those holdings.[51]

As it happened, these cables arrived at their destinations some hours after one of Huerta's local commanders had arrested several American sailors who had come ashore for mail and supplies. The men had been released within hours, but Admiral Henry Mayo decided that the flag had suffered an insult and must be duly honored by a twenty-one gun salute—within twenty-four hours. "Really," as Wilson himself said later, "it was a psychological moment."[52]

Spring-Rice had exceeded his instructions, but American policymakers had heard him go on about the situation in Mexico on several occasions, and there could be little doubt about the momentum building in favor of some decisive action. In any event, Wilson seized the "psychological moment" to land American forces at Tampico and Veracruz. He had declared his war. The ostensible reason for this incursion into Mexican territory was not the confused negotiations over a salute to the flag, moreover, but to prevent a German steamer from landing a cargo of munitions and machine guns. "The Huertistas intend to use these guns on our own boys," the president told the cabinet. That would have been truthful, of course, only if he expected the flag incident to lead to a final showdown.[53]

He was to be disappointed, at least in the short run. The Americans encountered fierce resistance from local Mexican forces. In the fighting 126 Mexicans and 19 Americans died, while another 195 Mexicans and 71 Americans suffered wounds. Tragic as that was, Wilson now faced the prospect of a Huerta-Carranza alliance to repel the Yankee invaders.[54] That catastrophe was avoided by a mediation offer from the "ABC Powers," Argentina, Brazil, and Chile. At first the offer meant only that a cooling-off period was available to all the parties, but the president had in mind something much more permanent. Even after Huerta followed Porfirio Díaz into exile, the American occupation forces remained. Secretary of War Lindley Garrison urged Wilson to finish the job, march to Mexico

City and set up a government that would last. Wilson recoiled: "All the world has been shocked ever since the time of the revolution in France that Europe should have undertaken to nullify what has been done there, no matter what the excesses committed."[55]

Hence Wilson made no move, as Garrison's proposal suggested he ought, to prevent Carranza from taking power in the summer of 1914. Militarily the secretary of war's argument was dubious, but that was not the deciding factor. Mexico was to be Wilson's laboratory, his great experiment. He did make several efforts to secure protection for life and property (sometimes in ultimatum-sounding notes) by pointing out in various ways that, ultimately, the revolution would fail without his sanction. The president also used these occasions, it should be noted, to try to force the Constitutionalists to honor their pledges to the Mexican people. As his response to Garrison further demonstrated, he had already abandoned the notion that Mexico's ills could be cured simply by the holding of elections, and was ready to grant the Constitutionalists time to impose their revolution before they risked asking for a popular mandate. That was an important step for Wilson.

Without using American military or economic coercion, then, he would gradually lead the Constitutionalists to see the light. Wilson genuinely believed that he had saved the Mexican revolution from European intervention at Veracruz, and nothing could ever persuade him otherwise. By the same token, however, nothing could convince him to set up American rule in Mexico City, not Carranza's threats to property nor political warnings at home.

Over the next three years, Carranza made war against his former allies in the struggle against Huerta, announced a number of measures designed to place limits on the power of foreign interests, and in general displayed a bellicosity that kept him at odds with the industrial powers. Even before he ordered the withdrawal of American troops from Mexico, however, Wilson had begun to grasp another point: Carranza could not respond to Wilson's diplomatic notes without compromising his own position as leader of the Mexican Revolution. There was a strange sort of bond between Wilson and Carranza, based on what Mexico was teaching Wilson and their common determination to see the revolution succeed.

The American president was a lifetime student of political institutions and theory. He watched events in Mexico with a keen sense of the imperfections of democracy. He was convinced, as he had said, that European intervention against the French Revolution had been a terrible mistake that had contributed to the less than firm foundation democracy had had in continental Europe ever since, a foundation now under greater stress than ever before. The American Revolution had succeeded, on the other

hand, because it had been isolated from Europe's turmoil by an ocean and
by the wisdom of the Founding Fathers in avoiding connections, political
or ideological, with the old world. What Mexico had to have, therefore,
was an *American* revolution, if it was to break free from foreign economic
dominion, avoid a violent lurching back and forth between reaction and
anarchy, and, most important, not set the wrong precedent as the world
moved out from under the shadow of the dying imperial order. The only
sure way to have that happen was for the United States to seal off Mexico
from European interference until that change had been accomplished.[56]

This did not come to Wilson in a single flash of understanding, nor
did he always honor his own best insights, as later events in Russia would
demonstrate so tragically; yet his was the most thoroughgoing critique of
imperialism made by a leader of a capitalist nation before World War I,
extending as it did beyond the tenets of the social imperialists. Wilson
chose an auspicious occasion for his first elaboration of his Mexican findings—the Fourth of July, 1914. At Independence Hall in Philadelphia,
he delivered a report to the nation on economic imperialism that remains
Progressivism's fullest statement of the problem. Traditionally, he began,
the government was called upon to support its citizens abroad. "But there
ought to be a limit to that. . . . If American enterprise in foreign countries, particularly in those foreign countries that are not strong enough to
resist us, takes the shape of imposing upon and exploiting the mass of the
people . . . , it ought to be checked and not encouraged. I am willing to
get anything for an American that money and enterprise can obtain,
except the suppression of the rights of other men. I will not help any man
buy a power which he ought not to exercise over his fellow beings."

In Mexico, he went on, foreign domination meant that only 15 percent of the population enjoyed rights citizens in the United States took for
granted; only 15 percent participated in government or owned the land
they lived upon. A great deal had been said about the horrors of revolution in Mexico, loss of property, loss of life. "Men's individual rights have
no doubt been invaded, and the invasion of those rights has been attended by many deplorable circumstances which ought sometime, in the
proper way, to be accounted for. But back of it all is the struggle of a
people to come into its own, and, while we look upon the incidents in the
foreground, let us not forget the great tragic reality in the background
which towers above the whole picture."[57]

Encompassed in these few words was a liberal interpretation of the
origins and consequences of imperialism that would make Wilson a hero
to many on the left in Europe as well as America. Unsparing in its criticism of American capitalism, inspiring in its promise for the future of
relations between nations, it had been occasioned, paradoxically, by the

intervention at Veracruz and its aftermath. To critics, of course, it was a curious and ultimately foolhardy exercise in self-justification: what else could Wilson tell the nation after what had happened, and the loss of life?

But however one viewed the speech, Wilson's goal was set. He must now persuade the British, and the other European nations perhaps, to see the situation as he did. In a private communication to Sir Edward Grey, the president drew an analogy between Mexico and Ireland. Could not Ambassador Page "filter" this thought into London society? he asked "A landless people will always furnish the inflammable material for a revolution." Just as the land question underlay the settlement of Irish affairs, so did it determine prospects for a Mexican settlement.[58] Sir Edward thought Wilson's discourses on the land question, while perhaps commendably humanitarian, revealed a poor understanding of the actual situation. "Mexico was really an Indian state," he told Page. Where were the elements that could understand and respond to the U.S. president's policy? No one could maintain control there without using Huerta's methods, Grey insisted.[59]

The outbreak of World War I reduced the possibilities of European intervention in Mexico, though rumor of intrigues and various attempts to shape American policy in response to Constitutionalist misdeeds constantly reminded the president that Mexico's unfinished revolution clouded the future. And this was so in more than one way. Wilson's flirtation with Pancho Villa became a serious affair in 1915 when, despairing of ever convincing Carranza that he needed American guidance, the president authorized his representatives to "subsidize" Villa by permitting him to sell various goods in the United States. As Secretary of State Robert Lansing wrote, "The reason for furnishing Villa with an opportunity to obtain funds is this: We do not wish the Carranza faction to be the only one to deal with in Mexico."[60] To be sure, Wilson still did not envision Villa as Mexico's new ruler. The "sword of the revolution" might have a role to play, however, in making sure that what came out of Mexico was of lasting importance to Wilsonian liberalism.

> *We had to accept in silence the criticism of recognizing Carranza, of not acting vigorously, of withdrawing Pershing without accomplishment, of vacillations, etc., and this had to be done while a presidential campaign was in progress because the national welfare demanded that our lips should be sealed.*
>
> Robert Lansing, 1917

Villa's role thus was to provide the appearance of serious opposition to Carranza, who had reigned in Mexico City for nearly a year—a year filled with civil war and, what was more important, with threats to confiscate foreign property. Wilson's dramatic denunciations of economic imperialism did not mean that he now considered private property "immoral," or that he denied the positive part capitalists had to play in both national and international affairs. Besides, if anything would bring about European intervention, war or no war, it would be an effort by Carranza to make good on his threats.

"Carranza seems so impossible," Lansing explained, "that an appearance, at least, of opposition to him will give us an opportunity to invite a compromise of factions." Villa was the agent of that policy, a designated stand-in until the other preparations were completed for giving Mexico a new government.[61] Wilson thought he was providing an answer to Sir Edward Grey's challenge—where were the elements in Mexico who could respond to Wison's policy—but various other officials hinted to the British that the president had decided to come over to a more pragmatic approach to the Mexican situation.

Chargé Colville Barclay reported from Washington that he had learned "from a good source" that the plan about to be put into operation did not require Carranza's participation. Indeed, it was expected that he would hold aloof from a call for a conference of all the factions. Held under Pan-American auspices, directed behind the scenes by the State Department, the plan, reported Barclay, was for the conference to select one of its number as provisional president of Mexico. Arms and money would then be cut off to all the "recalcitrant factions," i.e., Carranza. "In order to deal with him I understand the United States will hold him personally responsible for the lives and property of foreigners in the districts under his control, they will close his ports, and he will not be able to escape justice, if he murders foreigners or commits other outrages." His source was confident, concluded Barclay, that Carranza had only enough arms and ammunition to hold out for a short time, probably not more than two months.[62]

Perhaps Wilson sensed that something like what Barclay reported was indeed happening, that his policy was fast disappearing into the State Department's institutionalized "Dollar Diplomacy," and was being used as a cover story for a scheme to defraud Mexico—and, worse, the liberal cause worldwide. In any event, he withdrew support for the plan. "It seems to me necessary that a provisional government essentially revolutionary in character should take action to institute reforms by decree before the full forms of the constitution are resumed," he told Lansing. "This was the original program of the revolution and seems to me probably an essential part of it."[63]

As matters stood, the only person in a position to institute those vital reforms was Carranza. A new government of the sort envisioned by the plan would undoubtedly come apart if it sought to get a mandate through elections. Mexico's revolution would be put back to where it was at Madero's death, with the implication that things could turn out much worse that way. If the problem was to get Carranza to leave foreigners and their property alone, the best solution was to get him to concentrate on the land question. Indeed, what had made Villa attractive was precisely his agrarian orientation. Until recently, at least, he had not attempted to tax foreign property in the regions under his control.[64]

Nevertheless, Wilson's decision to set aside the conference solution was a prelude to limited diplomatic recognition of Carranza's government and to a final break with Villa. The term "de facto recognition" was employed, in order to give the impression of a careful, measured step designed to remind Carranza that he was on probation. Wilson saw that he could not really hold the First Chief accountable, however, unless the United States broke with Villa in a way that was clear to Mexico City. Consequently, new orders went out to border patrols instructing them to permit Mexican soldiers to cross United States territory on their way to deliver a devastating surprise attack against Villa's prized Division of the North. Defeated disastrously at Agua Prieta on the Mexican-American border in early November 1915, Villa was reduced permanently to waging a guerrilla war.[65]

But Wilson had not heard the last of Pancho Villa, and his attempt to make a new beginning with Carranza only brought about a new crisis, the worst since Veracruz. On March 9, 1916, a Mexican force of five hundred men attacked the town of Columbus, New Mexico. The raiders were driven back after a six-hour battle, during which one hundred Mexicans and seventeen Americans died. No one had any doubts about who was responsible. Within a week a punitive expedition that eventually reached a total of 10,000 had set out under orders from Washington to destroy Villa's forces. Commanded by General John J. Pershing, the expedition marched deeper and deeper into Mexico—but never even caught sight of its intended foe.[66]

Detachments of Pershing's army did meet up with regular Mexican forces in late June, and were defeated in a small battle that prompted Wilson, before he had full reports of how the fight had started, to draft a message to Congress seeking authority to send troops to occupy all of northern Mexico. That danger passed when he learned that Americans had initiated the exchange. But Wilson was in a bind. Colonel House wondered if the time had not come to settle affairs with Mexico, and if a failure to do so would not damage Wilson's authority in other spheres. If

he withdrew Pershing's expedition without having achieved Villa's capture, the European belligerents would get exactly the wrong impression
of America's sense of purpose and direction.

Wilson saw where this was leading. "Right or wrong," he wrote the
Colonel, "the extremist consequences seem upon us. But INTERVENTION
(that is the rearrangement and control of Mexico's domestic affairs by the
U.S.) there shall not be either now or at any other time if I can prevent
it." In reply, House attempted to console the president, without giving up
the effort to make him see the unwisdom of ruling out recourse to unpleasant alternatives: "I believe . . . that the way the Mexican affair is
handled will have great influence upon the European situation. Heaven
knows, you have done all that a man could to help the people there, and
the fact that they are not able to follow your kindly lead, is no fault of
yours."[67]

British reactions to the Pershing expedition were somewhat along the
lines House anticipated, yet not entirely. Now that Wilson had seen what
trouble his original decision not to get behind Huerta had produced
(though Grey was willing to admit in candid moments that the general
probably could not have survived in any event), the president should be
given a chance to rectify his error. Or so thought British diplomat Thomas
Hohler in Mexico City. Carranza's government was so weak, he insisted,
that "any bluff could easily be run on them." A short campaign, if that were
possible, and if it would bring the right result, appealed to other Foreign
Office officials "as affording the only prospect of speedy return to prosperity of the important British companies in Mexico."

Sir Edward Grey disagreed with this analysis. It was already apparent
that the Pershing expedition's main effect was to unite all factions against
outside force. And while it might be possible to turn out the Carranzistas,
the most likely result would be to increase the lawless areas, politically as
well as territorially. "We cannot promote intervention," concluded the
foreign secretary.[68]

Pursuing a military intervention plan, particularly one led by Woodrow
Wilson, was a risky proposition. If it succeeded it might, for example,
produce an even more radical Mexican government—one that could move
against local commanders, such as Manuel Peláez, who controlled the coast-
al oil fields. A former Villa chieftain, Peláez had informed both American
and British officials that he would like to have an "understanding" with the
oil fields' owners: he would guarantee their properties against Carranza's
edicts, taxes, and military force, while they would assure him of supplies
and ammunition.[69] Learning of these bids, Carranza made known a new
threat. He would burn the wells, he said, if the companies paid Peláez, and
shoot all the managers. Secretary Lansing tried to avoid such a confronta-

tion, pleading in a message to Mexico City that the companies were being forced to pay against their will. Sir Cecil Spring-Rice discovered that the mood in the State Department was much more positive toward Peláez's role. "They consider Peláez is the man most likely and best able to afford protection," he cabled London, and they were going to shut their eyes to the oil companies' supplying him with munitions.[70]

As this message suggested, concern about chaos and anarchy had begun to give way to fears that the Carranza movement, even without the First Chief to guide it, wanted to effect a permanent change in relationships between investors and the Mexican government. Almost from the outset of his reign, indeed even before he entered Mexico City astride a white horse, Carranza had adopted a strident rhetorical style whenever he spoke of foreign interests. A conservative landowner, probably even less inclined to desire fundamental change at home than Madero, Carranza had offered himself as Mexico's savior. No doubt he found it easier to talk about Mexico's "manifest destiny" than to discuss the land question.[71]

Even so, the Constitutionalist alliance shaped Mexican politics, and required much of its leader. The time for rhetoric was fast running out. The raison d'être of the Constitutionalist movement was to produce a constitution. By the late fall of 1916 the work of the drafters was nearly complete. What London and Washington learned of the document did not ease any of the fears about the direction the revolution was going, from uncomplicated apprehension about the future fate of the oil fields to Wilsonian alarm that Carranza would put a dangerous "Mexico for the Mexicans" policy above the goal of eliminating the country's backward-looking, semifeudal—and still dominant—agrarian system.[72]

Finding that the State Department planned to look the other way while the oil companies refurbished Peláez, Sir Edward Grey pondered whether or not there might be common ground in the idea of protecting the oil fields not only by dealing with the local 'military chiefs on the spot," but also more permanently by finding a means of thwarting "expropriation without compensation." In other words, what were the prospects for preventing the Constitution of 1917 from becoming operational—at least until Carranza had been removed or, possibly, brought under financial control?[73]

Foremost among diplomatic concerns about the proposed Constitution was Article 27, which vested all subsoil mineral rights in the nation. In brief, what that meant was that concessions could be awarded only to those foreigners who agreed to become Mexican citizens, abide by the nation's laws, and forsake the old semicolonial right of invoking the aid of their governments in all disputes about taxation and regulation. The desire to rewrite Mexican law in this direction antedated both Carranza and

Madero, back indeed to the last years of Díaz's rule. The diplomats had opposed change then, when they at least could have counted upon a benevolent attitude in Chapultepec Castle. Now they faced not only Carranza but a revolutionary tide.[74]

Robert Lansing had learned of the various antiforeign restrictions in advance of the date for promulgation of the Constitution, and decided to put Carranza on notice. What was proposed, cabled the secretary, was "fraught with possible grave consequences affecting the commercial and political relations of Mexico with other nations." The United States could not acquiesce in any direct or indirect confiscation of foreign-owned properties.[75]

In London, Thomas Hohler, who had replaced Lionel Carden, sought out Walter Hines Page to put to him what must rank as the most amazing suggestion for stopping Carranza and the Constitution of 1917. Being a neutral, Hohler began, the United States stood in a unique position. It could line up all the European powers including (and especially!) Germany. "I could see no ground for objection," Hohler recorded of his conversation with Page, and including Berlin "would bring the further good result of checking the anti-American intrigue by Germany in Mexico which had been causing the U.S. no little uneasiness."[76]

Hohler apparently supposed this ploy would convince Carranza that he had no choice but to cooperate in his country's "reconstruction." Already squeezed for funds, he could not hope to reestablish order without money, and he could not get his hands on any money until order had been reestablished. If the United States agreed to supply him with funds under these conditions, and the other powers all backed the move, the First Chief's arrogant defiance would crumble away, leaving a malleable residue that could be reworked into a much less threatening revolution.[77]

Hohler's proposed alliance was an ingenious but bizarre example of imperialist-era diplomacy. It had no chance of success. But it did suggest that the Great War had evolved in many directions, particularly along ideological lines. Realization of how far that trend had gone awaited events in Russia. But in the meantime the Germans presented British diplomats with a marvelous opportunity to use the Mexican imbroglio to their advantage, and in ways not entirely opposed to Hohler's vision. British intelligence services intercepted a telegram to Mexico City from Berlin that contained an offer of a military alliance should the United States enter the war. The Zimmermann telegram" of January 19, 1917, created a sensation in the American press, and was a factor in Wilson's decision for ask for a declaration of war.[78]

The Zimmermann telegram also provided a reason, however, for not being overly hasty about acknowledging the validity of a constitution written by a government under German "domination." Under Secretary of State Frank Polk and Sir Cecil Spring-Rice talked over this possibility. If Carranza did not take a strong line against German penetration, Polk suggested, that would surely be a reason for withholding de jure diplomatic recognition, and for questioning the Constitution. "At all events," mused the State Department official, "there was always the possibility of having recourse to some of the exiles and other factions whose leaders were comparatively respectable, general discontent with Carranza was so great that these had good chance of easy success."[79]

Polk spoke on no authority but his own. What he said did, however, provide part of a description of Woodrow Wilson's growing entanglement in the Mexican Revolution. Begun as an attack upon the "special interests," especially those based in Europe, personified in the hated presence of Lionel Carden at Huerta's elbow, Wilson's watchful waiting had become sponsorship of a revolution. Unless Mexico moved into the modern age, he had concluded, the imperialist patterns of world order would require, sooner or later, the evolution of "Dollar Diplomacy" into full-scale state capitalism or, contrariwise, state socialism. The Zimmerman telegram was perfectly timed, indeed, but certainly it raised the possibility that the State Department's Mexican policy, as opposed to Wilson's, as hinted by Polk (and earlier by Lansing in 1915, during the Villa episode), would become irresistible. The forces making for the corporatization of the government were well known to Wilson, and deeply feared by him.

Progressivism hung suspended when America entered the war. Yet Wilson feared that Progressivism's failure to come to terms with revolution in Mexico might produce a much greater revulsion against capitalism. He had learned a great deal about the causes of the Mexican Revolution from writers like John Reed and Lincoln Steffens, men whose liberal sympathies developed into attraction for radicalism as the Russian Revolution posed another answer to the problems the president faced.[80]

Steffens and Reed might be accused of simply playing a role, seizing upon journalistic new frontiers in keeping with the time. But beyond that notion was the reality of social upheaval, the first serious challenge to the established world order. Mexico was a part of that. It could not be regarded as, say, Pulitzer and Hearst had looked upon Cuba, a storybook affair peopled with evil Spanish generals and TR's brave Roughriders. The common people in Mexico, Wilson wrote to his future wife, Mrs. Galt, in August 1915, hated the privileged classes. "Therefore," he concluded, "the alliance of the church is necessarily with the 'cientifico' class, who are, as with us, owning and running everything, the reactionary class. Hence the wedge in our own domestic politics."[81]

Hence also the failure of imperialism, at home and abroad.

CHAPTER FOUR

Upheaval in China

China is at the parting of the ways. Whether her destiny is to be one of peaceful and orderly development along the lines of constitutional freedom and self-government, or whether she is torn asunder in civil conflict and international intrigue. . . .

American minister Paul S. Reinsch, 1914

At a moment when things seemed to be going well for Wilson's policy in Mexico, writer John Reed congratulated the president on the far-reaching impact of the reappearance of American idealism on the world scene. What will happen now in China? asked the journalist. "The Chinese Republic has fallen. Yuan Shi Kai is nothing more or less than a dictator of Huerta's stamp." Would the new policy make a difference in China? Wilson doubted that it would: "The power to destroy what any people have consented to is limited. It is limited to organic law, and by the interests of other people and other nations. The relations which we have with other governments whose connection with China is closer than ours, and whose course of action might be diffferent, might prevent us from acting independently of them."[1]

From the first Open Door note in 1899 through the Roosevelt and Taft administrations, American policymakers had sought British cooperation in China. Success never crowned their efforts. Yet expectations had been raised, and Reed's enthusiasm was shared by many who thought the problem had always been that Americans had tried to cooperate on European terms. Wilson's promise in the 1912 campaign to bring a "New Freedom" to American political life implied as well a clean break with

"Dollar Diplomacy" in China, symbolized by the failed Six Power banking consortium. Set up to regulate loans to China, the consortium had never worked well from the start, and when it grew from four powers (France, Germany, Great Britain, and the United States) to six (with Russia and Japan), it became completely unmanageable, and useless to both China and the bankers.

Great Britain wanted out of the consortium, too, but for very different reasons. Sir Edward Grey had imagined that the consortium had been formed for very specific purposes, not as a permanent fixture by which the "China business" would be divided up into six equal parts. Under heavy pressure in Parliament to explain a policy that meant surrendering long-standing British advantages in China, Grey did the best he could to defend the consortium as needed in time of turmoil. But he was as anxious as anyone for it to disappear. "I shall be glad when the time comes when the Six-Powers group can be dissolved," he wrote to Sir John Jordan, British minister in China, on October 31, 1912. "We could arrange this if the Chinese would only make up their minds to negotiate a big reorganization loan with the groups on reasonable terms."[2]

Grey was not pleased, however, by Woodrow Wilson's abrupt and accusatory announcement that the United States government was withdrawing its support from the American banking group in the consortium. America could not shut off China from the outside world, as it would attempt to shut off Mexico, but it could do terrible damage to the British position in China by casting the consortium in the role of an enemy to Chinese nationalism.

> *I believe you have won the lasting gratitude of China. With this nation setting such an example no other nation can force her into unfair terms. They will now become rivals for her friendship.*
>
> William Jennings Bryan to Wilson, March 1913

The origin of the consortium, like everything about it, exhausts the patience of the most dedicated inquirer. It is a study in diplomatic minutiae. Suffice it to say that early in the Taft administration the State Department forced the Chinese to reopen a railway contract that had been all but completed with the participation of British, French, and German bankers. The sorry history of the Hukuang loan is best forgotten, and would be except that the success Washington enjoyed tempted Secretary of State

Philander C. Knox to make a bid to establish a protectorate over *all* China.[3]

On November 6, 1909, Knox proposed that Britain and the United States take the lead in convincing the industrial powers to bring all proposed railways in the Manchurian area of China under an "economic, scientific, and impartial administration." It could be accomplished by an international loan that would guarantee effective supervision of the railroads, and thereby eliminate corruption inside China and curtail industrial rivalry.[4]

Cooperation in this endeavor would set exactly the right example. The "greatest danger" to the China trade, Knox said in a press statement, "arose from disagreements among the western nations." "Nothing would afford so impressive an object lesson to China and the world," it continued, as the sight of the great capitalist nations standing together. The chances for world peace would be greatly improved if the Manchurian area and, implicitly, the rest of China became "an immense commercial neutral zone."[5]

Suggestions like this one, as we have already seen, were common as sparrows in the Progressive Era. They worked best in fiction. Squeezed by diplomatic commitments to Japan, worried about offending Russia, and with Parliament demanding to know what His Majesty's Government was doing to protect British trade interests in China, Sir Edward Grey hoped the Knox scheme would somehow get misplaced. Besides that, he was not altogether happy about America's obsession with its Open Door policy. "I will support the open door in every way that I can," Sir Edward wrote on one occasion to his ambassador in Washington, "having regard to existing engagements. But there are other parts of the world besides Manchuria." And in some of those places, Central and South America for example, British traders had good reason to believe that the United States valued consistency and the Open Door principle hardly at all.[6]

Neither Grey nor Knox was prepared for the sequence of events that followed in China. An imperial decree nationalizing the railroads triggered riots in Szechwan province against the intrusion of central authority and, it was charged, Western capital. Then in October 1911 another local protest at Wuchang set off the explosion that blew away the dessicated remnants of Manchu power, and ended millennia of dynastic rule.[7]

A republic was proclaimed, with the reformer Sun Yat-sen as provisional president. The experiment failed. Out of the confusion arose a very different sort of reformer, Yuan Shih-k'ai, whose reputation stemmed from his role in building a modern army for China in the wake of the humiliating defeat by Japan in 1895. Many nationalists shifted their allegiance to Yuan because he had the army and they lacked mass support—

and financial resources. Sun had no standing with the imperialists, on the other hand, who saw in Yuan the only alternative to chaos.[8]

Yuan kept the title "republic," at least for the present, and awaited the invitations of the consortium. He knew they needed one another. On December 8, 1911, sure enough, Sir Edward Grey himself formally proposed that the French, German, British, and American groups in the consortium grant Yuan a small advance to aid him in "negotiations" with the rebels. A few weeks later J. P. Morgan & Company advised the Department of State that the American members of the consortium had agreed to a suggestion that Russia and Japan become full partners in the enterprise, an enterprise that was beginning to sound very much like the committees established to oversee Egyptian finances, or, more recently, the American protectorates in the Caribbean. When Yuan assumed leadership of the provisional government of China, the bankers announced the opening of negotiations on a huge "reorganization loan" of £ 60 million.[9]

Actual progress, either in convincing Russia and Japan to come aboard or in completing loan negotiations, was slow. The six settled affairs among themselves in late June 1912, but the loan was definitely stalled. Yuan had no intention, it turned out, of offering up China to foreign control. Chinese public opinion, he told American minister William J. Calhoun, would not tolerate such a situation. "We are up against a blank wall," concluded Calhoun. Knox had little faith that it could be scaled. Torn by the desire to save China from without through international cooperation; protests from Americans, who now joined British businessmen in complaining about the consortium "monopoly"; and the suddenly too vivid vision of rampaging "Chinamen," the secretary finally suggested that if the deadlock could not be broken, China should be left free to make other arrangements.[10]

But American leaders were not content to leave it at that. London's refusal to support the neutralization plan when it might have made a difference was rooted in the diplomacy of imperialism, it was charged, specifically in the 1902 Anglo-Japanese alliance and, less directly, in the "balance of power." Taft and Knox thus watched the negotiations for renewal of the Anglo-Japanese pact with growing resentment, a sentiment that would also dominate reactions to British proposals—and particularly, during the war, to British timidity in opposing Japan—throughout the Wilson years. The German ambassador heard Taft bellow out on one occasion, "I wonder what England expects to get from Japan for helping them."[11] These complaints were not meant to go unheard in the right places. From the British embassy in Washington, Mitchell Innes wrote, "I can't help wondering whether the United States would not be glad to drive a wedge between us and Japan."[12]

Although they themselves now felt, however reluctantly, that the consortium had tied things in knots, Taft and his advisers would not concede that the British had anything to complain of about American policy, or even imagine that Sir Edward Grey had any reason to see an "American peril." They were right about the Anglo-Japanese alliance, however, in the sense that the renewal was really a new pact. Originally designed to thwart Russian expansionism and, so far as London was concerned, to protect India, the alliance signed in 1911 was designed, however clumsily, to be an instrument for carving out spheres of influence. Only in this way, it was thought in the Foreign Office, could Japan's desires that the two "should stand together in matters Chinese" be deflected, and only in this way could the Dominions be assured that Japan would not become a threat to their all-white immigration policies. During the negotiations, therefore, Sir Edward had pressed his Japanese counterparts to provide some assurances on their side that they, or rather their government, did not wish to go to "distant places," either as emigrants or as entrepreneurs. He hoped, Grey told Japanese negotiators, that they would confine themselves to Korea, Manchuria, "and other regions in the neighborhood of Japan."[13]

Grey's efforts to limit Japanese claims were all part of a new phase of the Great Game in Asia. The players were not sure of the rules, yet two of them, America and Japan, were aware of their status as would-be successor states to Britain's informal suzerainty in China. Every move required careful thought. But how was one to respond to Woodrow Wilson's seemingly artless public diplomacy? "The conditions of the loan," read his March 18, 1913, newspaper announcement on the stalled consortium loan, "seem to us to touch very nearly the administrative independence of China itself, and this administration does not feel that it ought, even by implication, to be a party to those conditions."[14] The intended slur on certain American bankers (all Republicans?) for having taken part in the negotiations was domestic politics—perhaps—but Wilson's statement also compromised the other consortium members at a time of very delicate relations with China. As with his early pronouncement on Latin America, the president's press-release diplomacy did not go down well in foreign capitals. "The American action is a breach of all diplomatic decency," complained Sir Edward Grey.[15]

Tipping the applecart was all right in domestic politics, but Wilson was getting a quixotic reputation. A few days after the president's scourging of the consortium, moreover, Secretary Bryan called in the representatives of the interested powers to read them a second statement. "The President wishes me to announce to you," he began, "that it is his purpose to recognize the Government of China on the 8th April, upon the meeting of its Constituent Assembly. He wishes me to say that he very earnestly . . . invites the co-operation of your Government and its action to the same effect at the same time."[16]

What was this but a bid to take the lead in China? All the powers wanted Yuan to succeed; they also wanted him to see that it was in China's best interest to cooperate with them. American ability to influence Yuan in any direction was practically nil, yet here was the new president and his lieutenant going off like the Don himself and Sancho Panza. Perhaps Wilson's foolhardy efforts to rout the bankers would not mislead Yuan, but even so there were the Japanese to consider. Sir Edward's Japanese policy was very simple: let them have a share. But if the Americans kept up this Progressive posturing, the ideological anti-Western undercurrent in Japan (and Asia?) would sweep them all out to sea.[17]

> The Chinese Government would be glad if the American Government would give such assurances to American capitalists as would induce the latter to resume the lending of money to China.
>
> Premier Hsung Hsi-ling, 1913

Inside, China, meanwhile, Woodrow Wilson's policy was having an unanticipated boomerang effect. In his March 18 statement the president had sung the praises of American merchants, manufacturers, contractors, and engineers. He enjoined them to provide China with goods and services; he promised that his administration would give them "the banking and other financial facilities which they now lack and without which they are at a serious disadvantage as compared with their industrial and commercial rivals. This is its duty."[18] Gradually, however, it began to be realized in Washington that the *Chinese* thought the Americans had weakened themselves by Wilson's decision to disassociate the government from the consortium bankers. Chinese officials, reported chargé Edward T. Williams, were sorely disappointed that the United States government did not offer better incentives to its capitalists. A change was urgently needed, he added, because of the unsettled state of political affairs, and because of the fact that the Chinese government was generally involved in practically all industrial enterprises. Most important of all, America's economic position in the new China depended upon getting in on the ground floor.[19]

Williams never really got a satisfactory response to this message, and had to content himself with passing on standard disclaimers about the reluctance of American capital to venture abroad, even when it enjoyed perfect security. The dilemma seemed permanent: if the United States took the lead in trying to curb exploitation of China by shackling its capitalists, the only effect was to increase the opportunity for others to step into the breach. Still more frustrating, the effort to encourage cooperation on a "higher plane," only succeeded in stimulating fears of an American moral protectorate.

Wilson's emissary to China, Paul S. Reinsch, thus arrived at a time when it appeared that the bold new initiative had fizzled. Everyone he met, Reinsch recalled later, "talked as if it were all up with American enterprise in China." The American business community regarded the appointment of a "literary and university man" as proof positive that no attention would be paid to economic interests.[20] Desirous of correcting that impression, Reinsch listened closely to Premier Hsung's continuing complaint about American timidity, and how it contrasted with Russian and Japanese moves in Mongolia and Manchuria. Could not the United States enlist both Great Britain and Germany in a combined effort to block the schemes of China's adventurous neighbors?[21]

Reinsch would have liked nothing better, of course. Among the many inducements the premier suggested were promises of a huge naval contract, a monopoly tobacco contract, and an offer to the Standard Oil Company to develop the mineral resources of Shansi and Shensi provinces. "China was offering the United States," said Hsung, "more farreaching opportunities than had been offered to any other nation."[22]

Hsung's missionary work was unnecessary. Reinsch was already a true believer before he left the United States. Picking up on Edward Williams' theme, Reinsch did all he could to convince his superiors that they must rethink their new China policy. Only in that way could the United States thwart the designs of those less interested in China's welfare. Spheres of influence, those ugly testaments to imperialism in China, were being tried again. Open Door architect John Hay's ghost was surely uneasy. Economic investments were the only means at hand to prevent the imperialists from finishing the job they had started earlier. They were, said Reinsch, investments in the "integrity of the Chinese Republic," and this noble task required American businessmen to seek out opportunities in all parts of China.[23]

Reinsch's crusade bore all the markings of an old-time religious revival, with its banners proclaiming American concern for China's "integrity." But it was stopped short by the outbreak of World World I even before it got going. British diplomats had watched the American's progress with much skepticism about the outcome, anyway, and with growing concern that all he would accomplish would be to spur on equally dedicated Japanese missionaries at the head of a rival parade. At the same time that Paul Reinsch had been trying to decide how to develop one or more projects of truly "national" scope, Foreign Office Asian experts were considering among themselves how best to fend off a Japanese economic offensive in Central and South China. On February 23, 1914, Sir Edward Grey had made his final offer. His Majesty's Government, he said, would permit Tokyo to build a single railroad from Fukien to Nanchang, but would not allow a widespread expansion of non-British industrial interests into the heart of its traditional sphere of influence, the Yangtze Valley. His position in Parliament, he had insisted to the Japanese, would be made impossible "if I recognized spheres of influence for other countries without having any British sphere recognized by them." Indeed, the Japanese should see that the best approach to "problems that have arisen since the revolution" in China was to exercise mutual restraint. It was Tokyo's responsibility, he concluded, to join with its British ally to conduct a policy "by which all future friction between the Powers will be avoided."[24]

Grey made a determined effort to line up the French behind this policy, which he differentiated from the forced cooperation of the consortium era. "Nothing could illustrate the failure of the old system more luminously than the Anglo-French disputes that have arisen since individual firms were set at liberty to proceed with industrial enterprises," read a mid-March memorandum to the French embassy, "and the competition for concessions has been re-opened with fresh vigor under the changed conditions of China." Attempts to force joint enterprise schemes or, more ominously, to invade recognized spheres of influence would only produce general disorder. "[T]he intrusion of the nationals of a particular Power into the heart of the acknowledged zone of another, strikes at the very principle which His Majesty's Government are bent on maintaining. . . ."[25]

The French should know that London was always willing to take up their cause with the Chinese in any dispute pertaining to the fair treatment of foreign interests. "His Majesty's Government also desire the French Government to know that they are in no sense discriminating against them, but are asserting their privileged position in the Yang-tze region against all Powers having interests in China, and they will be only too glad to see the French Government doing likewise in the area that tradition earmarks as their exclusive sphere."[26]

British backs were up, and were also against the wall. Sir John Jordan told his Japanese counterpart in Peking, for example, that Japan had already derived great advantages from the annexation of Korea and the forward move into south Manchuria. "For all this," he lectured the Japanese minister, "she was indebted largely to her political alliance with us, and it seemed only fair that she should devote her energies to developing the immense region which lay within her own sphere rather than in blocking our enterprise in the only region that was left to us."[27]

London wanted Jordan's opinion on another matter, however, that bore directly on the bargain Grey wanted to strike with the French and the Japanese. Word had come to London of a monopoly concession awarded to the American Standard Oil Company covering exploration rights in Shensi and Chihli provinces, areas of prime concern to Tokyo in north China. Jordan recommended that Japan protest the award. The dominant view in London was the same. "We have many irons in the fire in China just now," noted one Foreign Office official, "and if we can benefit from protests raised by these Powers, without having to move ourselves, so much the better." Not so, actually, for in that case London could not really continue to argue that the Anglo-Japanese alliance offered Tokyo any special benefits or protections against third powers.[28]

Yet what other option was there? In the spring of 1914 the Foreign Office was not a little disappointed that its China policy—so carefully designed by Sir Edward Grey along Newtonian lines, with each power keeping to its own zone—encountered indifference at home. For whatever reason, those British firms with the most at stake in China were languishing in a state of torpor. "British industrial interests," admonished Sir John Jordan, "should be made to realize that China is, so to speak, being put up to auction, and that [the] best lots will soon be disposed of."[29]

Japan did indeed protest, to no avail.[30] And there matters stood in August 1914, with one English-speaking power extolling the virtues and principles of the classical world of Sir Isaac Newton and its fixed points, while the other called for a Darwinian social contest to discover who among the powers was the fittest to tutor China. With the outbreak of war in August 1914, moreover, it appeared that Europe's days in Asia were about over.

"Asia is growing rapidly in political power," warned President Wilson's old friend, and would-be diplomat, Charles R. Crane. "With that situation facing the Christian world for it to engage in this fearful war, is to run the risk of placing Europe at the mercy of Asia."[31] Crane was a Japanophobe of long standing. He had been named minister to China by William Howard Taft, but his outspoken views had cut short his diplomatic career even before he left the United States. Recalled then, now he could claim ample justification for his gloomy assessments, and have reason to expect Wilson would listen with an attentive ear.

And sure enough, Japan did not hesitate but stepped forward boldly, invoking its obligations under the Anglo-Japanese alliance to justify an attack on the Shantung Peninsula. If Washington was alarmed, however, Sir Edward Grey took this in stride, seeing an opportunity to perfect his earlier scheme. The most likely manifestation of the "Yellow Peril," as imagined in Great Britain as well as in the United States, was of a Japanese-led China. If Tokyo could be awarded the German leasehold over Shan-tung, and perhaps a handful of Germany's Pacific islands, Japan should be content. With that enlarged stake, indeed, it should become a staunch defender of the old system, not a leader of some grotesque pan-Asian movement. After some preliminary sparring, occasioned by Sir Edward's efforts to show the world that Great Britain and Japan had consulted closely together and that the latter had agreed to limit its military activities to "territory in German occupation on the continent of Eastern Asia," serious negotiations began.[32]

German presence in Shantung had not displeased the British, es-pecially since it represented a kind of buffer area between British and Japanese zones of interest. But Japan's succession to the German sphere might have the effect of reinforcing British policy. Perhaps not, of course. Much depended on how it was accomplished. Grey was anxious, for ex-ample, not to have it appear that the white man had been driven from an Asian stronghold. Hence his efforts to make it seem that the British and Japanese were working closely together; hence also the offer he now made to Tokyo urging the Japanese to accept their ally's military aid in carrying out the campaign. British participation in the actual fighting, he suggested, might calm Chinese fears, and actually improve chances that Peking would raise no question about Japan's bid to succeed Germany. If Japan accepted this offer, moreover, it would forestall notions that might otherwise gain currency in both China and Japan that the new occupiers were harbingers of the revolutionary change in relations between Asia and the West.[33]

Not surprisingly, Tokyo declined, contending that this arrangement would only produce postwar complications. Grey then laid his cards on the table:

> I . . . said that I would tell him [the Japanese ambassador] quite frankly, though I could say it privately and unofficially that, after this war, if Germany was beaten, France, Russia and ourselves would naturally get compensation in parts of the world other than China. The only compensation that Japan could get would be in the region of China. It would therefore be unfair for any of us to put forward claims there, depriving Japan of compensation for the blood and treasure that she might have to spend.
>
> The compensation would of course be such as was not inconsis-tent with the integrity and independence of China, and would, I supposed, be the sort of thing about which Baron Kato had spoken to me before he left London.[34]

The reference to discussion of that "sort of thing" in the Grey-Kato conversations earlier, at the time the alliance was renewed, had a special meaning, particularly now that Kato had become the Japanese foreign minister. At that time Grey had guaranteed Japan's right to improve its position in Manchuria and environs, a guarantee that now included Shantung. Kato was no dullard at this game. If Grey wanted the Japanese to accept a role in the old order, indeed now seemed to push rewards upon them for doing so, Kato would accept the British offer. But he would also keep his options open in other directions less pleasing to the British. Japan's public statements indicated that Shantung would eventually be returned to China, however hedged about with conditions the pledge was. This way Kato could trade upon British promises without entirely giving up the notion of leading a general Asian revival. It did appear, as Grey no doubt reflected in moments of wry meditation, that Japan might be safer ensconced in Shantung than left loose to roam over ideological frontiers.

In Washington, as might be expected, all this diplomatic byplay aroused little interest. What concerned American leaders was not what Japan promised to do at some future date, but the fact of the Japanese occupation. Sir Cecil Spring-Rice tried to get State Department officials to see that Britain was the only moderating influence on Japan. It was not an easy assignment. The English-speaking powers had, did they not, a common interest in keeping the Japanese out of white countries. To insist upon such barriers and yet deny Japan an outlet in China as well was impossible. "It is far less dangerous to have them in Shantung than in America and if you dam up the stream in one of its courses you must let it flow freely in the other."[35]

The fall of 1914 was an intensely frustrating season in Washington. Yuan had appealed for American support when the Great War began, urging an increase in American military forces in the international settlements so as to deny to Japan the claim that it had responsibility for "protecting foreign rights." A strong Tokyo protest had led the Chinese leader to retract that bid, but a few day later he called for American mediation to forestall the Japanese campaign against Kiaochow in the Shantung Peninsula. This time Secretary Bryan formally declined the invitation, remarking only that American intervention would exacerbate matters.[36]

Advising Wilson of Japan's assumption of control of the German railroad on the peninsula, Bryan admitted that the Chinese were upset at American inaction. But there did not seem to be anything that "China can do or that we should do."[37] Yuan did not give up easily, however. In a pattern often repeated over the next thirty years, Yuan did his best to precipitate some sort of action. He (and his successors) thought that the best bet was the United States.

Perhaps aware of Japanese plans, Yuan moved to take the initiative first. On January 7, 1915, he informed the Japanese that he was canceling his war zone proclamation concerning Shantung, the legal face-saving device he had used to "allow" Japan to send military forces into the area. If that held up, Tokyo would be obliged to remove its troops at once. Kato promptly denounced Yuan's move as a violation of international law. The troops would stay as long as necessary. Eleven days later Yuan was presented with the infamous Twenty-One Demands by the Japanese minister, who remarked as he did so that the Chinese had an unfortunate penchant for ignoring an old saying, "Befriend the near and antagonize the far."[38]

The first four demands related to Shantung. Of these the most important was a demand that China recognize Tokyo's right to settle with Germany the ultimate disposition of Berlin's treaty rights and concessions. In other words, Peking should not expect to intervene or to invoke the aid of others in an effort to deprive Japan of its spoils of war. The next seven demands were a bid to secure Chinese acquiescence in Japan's hold on Manchuria and eastern Inner Mongolia, while the two articles in the third group of demands pertained primarily to an ironworks complex, the Hanyehping Company, that Japan had financed and wanted to insure its control over. The fourth group required China to deny military bases to any other power, along with harbors or ports.

The fifth group could have meant a Japanese protectorate over China, and certainly took on aspects of such a design in the context of all the previous demands. China was directed, in this group of demands, to hire Japanese advisers in key positions; grant Japanese national rights to establish hospitals, temples, and schools; purchase its arms from Japan; and admit the right of the Japanese claims to supply the capital for future projects in Fukien Province, across from Formosa. The twenty-first demand read, "China to grant Japanese subjects the right of preaching in China."

At the very least, the Twenty-One Demands marked an ambitious imperial program. On the other hand, they also represented, albeit in distorted fashion, what many Asians wished the Chinese Revolution to become—a genuine movement to oust Western influence. Conveyed to Yuan late at night along with an injunction to secrecy, the Japanese program was presented with a curious threat: unless Yuan cooperated, Tokyo would finance the revolutionaries who still sought to overthrow his government. The Chinese official who confided all this to Paul Reinsch added that it was particularly ominous that the paper the Japanese used bore watermarks of dreadnoughts and machine guns.[39]

Reinsch knew what had to be done. He did not expect the United States to go to war over the Twenty-One Demands; what he did expect, however, was that Washington would now use its leverage to force the British to do an about-face. Assured by Sir John Jordan (who had always been skeptical of Grey's approach) that the British would "welcome the support of the United States in opposing Japanese domination in China . . . ," Reinsch recommended a blunt stroke. Since John Hay's time American policy-makers had looked for this opportunity. Now it was here:

> . . . considering not only the value attached to the friendly char-
> acter of American neutrality but also the coercive power which
> rests with our country as an accessible base of supplies, I suggest
> that the British Government would not be disposed to ignore an
> intimation from our government that it could not regard with in-
> difference the usurpation . . . by Japan nor disassociate Great Brit-
> ain from responsibility for such a situation created by its Ally. . . .[40]

Back in Washington Edward T. Williams seconded Reinsch's pro-posal. The real danger, he said, was of Japan achieving control of a powerful Chinese military force. Surely it was not difficult to foresee where these Asian events were leading, Williams insisted. With China's resources at its command, Japan, "which is not restrained by any scruples of the West," becomes "a greater menace than ever to the United States."[41]

Williams also felt that Minister Reinsch was absolutely right about how to proceed. Get the Twenty-One Demands made public. Protest against any that might infringe on specific American rights. "Great Britain proba-bly has her blind eye on the telescope and does not desire to see the danger signal. Nevertheless, if we can get the demands made public she will undoubtedly be glad and aid in bringing about a modification of them."[42]

But the president was uncertain even about how to address the prob-lem. Japanese assurances to Bryan that Tokyo's commitment to the Open Door policy remained intact did not convince, especially since reliable information confirming or denying the Reinsch version of the Twenty-One Demands was slow to emerge. "Just at present," Wilson wrote privately to his minister in the Chinese capital, "it is impossible to see in which direction an open road lies." Direct advice to China might do more harm than good, and was sure to provoke Japan. "I have been trying to play the part of prudent friend by making sure that the repre-sentatives of Great Britain realized the gravity of the situation and just what was being attempted. For the present, I am watching the situation very carefully indeed, ready to step in at any point where it is wise to do so."[43]

> *The American Government has not surrendered any*
> *of its treaty rights in China or abated one iota of its*
> *friendly interest in all that concerns the industrial*
> *and political welfare of China.*
>
> William Jennings Bryan to Paul S. Reinsch,
> April 1915.

As the crisis surrounding the Twenty-One Demands reached a climax in early May 1915, the key element turned out to be neither British complaisance nor American firmness, but Yuan's skill at playing a waiting game. Indeed, the stiffest note that the United States sent was a protest lodged in Peking and Tokyo *after* the Chinese had yielded to a Japanese ultimatum, which, however, only demanded acceptance to points already conceded in lengthy negotiations. None of those given up, moreover, pertained to the notorious fifth group.[44]

But Wilson's instructions to Bryan on May 10, 1915, did reflect the president's sense, growing in the immediate aftermath of the sinking of the *Lusitania*, that the United States had to pursue the same policy in the Pacific and the Atlantic, a policy that would require a complete transformation of the failed rules of the Pax Britannica. It would not do, the president informed his secretary of state, to leave in doubt American acquiescence in any Japanese plan, or any part of any plan, that violated the Open Door policy.[45]

Sending this note to Peking was Wilson's way of putting the other powers on notice as well that China was being asked to reject any advice that they might offer favoring compromise with Japan. Meanwhile, the Twenty-One Demands had caused British policymakers to rethink their Far Eastern strategy. As Reinsch and Williams had argued, London did welcome evidence that Washington was inclined to oppose Japan. Sir Edward Grey's efforts at keeping the Japanese engaged in a diplomatic dialogue and satisfied with an enlarged share had certainly not prevented the unpleasant surprise of Tokyo's demands.[46]

"The present demands . . . if imposed as they stand," minuted Foreign Office China expert Beilby Alston, "subjugate China to Japan's military control forever—for weaker, or for stronger, whichever suits. If for the latter, Japan could, if so minded, with a combination of the two armies, make the Yellow Peril a real danger."[47] Yet when it came right down to it, the governing factor was still British inability to do anything more than keep up the dialogue until the war in Europe ended. Although it grated on British sensibilities and pride, temporary effacement was the best course. Grey agreed: "I think this is the right policy for the moment."[48]

It was hard to say, moreover, what the Americans would actually do about the Japanese challenge. The self-proclaimed champions of China's territorial integrity had yet to prove themselves ready to transform posture into performance. Besides, if it ever came to that, was America's all-or-nothing approach really better than attempting to put limits on Japan's ambitions? To top it off, London had received mixed signals from Washington. Whatever the American notes said, Bryan was thought to be seeking a compromise between Japan and China. In the midst of the Twenty-One Demands crisis, Ambassador Spring-Rice related a conversation with the counselor of the State Department, Robert Lansing, that confirmed the State Department position. Lansing was now Wilson's chief adviser, said Spring-Rice, and his view was that the United States should enter a caveat to the Japanese demands, but make no formal protest. So long as Japanese ambitions were limited to Manchuria and Mongolia, the Wilson administration was inclined "to think this would be useful as [an] outlet to Japanese energies, thus diverting them from this continent."[49]

Diplomats often hear their own words in the voices of others, and Spring-Rice had delivered wrong impressions labeled facts before, as in the Mexican situation. But in this case he was probably right. Lansing was slowly evolving his own solution to the Japanese problem, and superficially at least it looked very much like what Grey was attempting. Spring-Rice would not be around to see how differently it all came out, but in the meantime Lansing was named Secretary of State in the summer of 1915, replacing Bryan, who could no longer accept Wilson's German policy.

Foreign Office caution was well advised under the circumstances. Previous secretaries of state had attempted to persuade London to join in a strong defense of the Open Door policy. Toward this end, Lansing now decided to stand that approach on its head: he sought to enlist Japan in an effort to break down European spheres of influence in China proper. Like Grey he would push the chips toward Japan, offers of economic cooperation as well, and hope Japan would decide instead to play America's game. This was a tricky business, because it meant conceding Manchuria and Mongolia, at least initially, and separating those provinces from the "China question." It also meant convincing Wilson that what looked like a social imperialist solution was compatible with his new diplomacy. Ultimately, if things worked out, everything would be brought back together again, China and the lost provinces and Wilsonian consistency. But Lansing's main objective was the European powers' outdated claims to control spheres of influence. That overcome, he would reorganize the China lineup and bring the Japanese back to a real understanding of their situation, and their dependence upon America. But all this was in the future.

Like his predecessor at the State Department, Lansing was deeply concerned that Paul Reinsch's alarmist outpourings about Japanese expansionism overheated the issue. But he had to agree that the way things were going played into Japanese hands. Wilson's break with the consortium had not released American energies, as anticipated, but had weakened America's presence, as the Chinese had been saying. Independent banking ventures, it turned out, meant private diplomacy, and that meant coming to terms with the Japanese.[50]

Unless the United States were willing to accept what Japan offered, Reinsch cabled Lansing on April 3, 1916, then it would be necessary to establish international control of Chinese finances. It was either that or see Japan call the tune. China faced internal ruin. That situation would last until the outside powers forced an honest, expert administration on whatever regime ruled. The only question that remained was "whether this is to be enforced by Japan alone or by the Powers jointly."[51]

If not a counsel of despair, it seemed pretty close to one to Wilson. "I do not see what is to be done," he confessed to Lansing after reading this message. The president could not find a concrete suggestion to fasten upon anywhere in the recent dispatches out of China. "Have they given you a clue to any definite course of action?"[52] Well, yes, they had, and bit by bit the secretary led Wilson back toward the notion of a bankers' consortium.

It was apparent, to begin with, that the administration's China policy had been based on the premise that, released from the clutches of the bankers' monopoly, Chinese nationalism would prosper. That had not proved to be so. Yuan Shi-k'ai had attempted to ascend the throne of the Manchus. His reign lasted but eighty-two days, from January 1 to March 22, 1916. Over the next twelve years China would have ten heads of state, forty-five cabinets, five legislatures, and seven constitutions, not counting rival governments based in Canton or warlord regimes operating in various places including Manchuria.[53]

Only Japan had a clear-cut China policy, Lansing advised the president. American bankers were fighting among themselves in a most unseemly fashion, while the State Department's information was that the Japanese were deliberately creating disorder in Shantung as part of their overall plan to justify a permanent presence. "The results of Japanese aggression in Manchuria show what we may expect elsewhere," Lansing warned. Skillfully guided by the secretary, Wilson now agreed that the "reasonable course" was first to seek an end to the disagreements in the American financial community that had sprung up around claims, some new, some old, to various pieces of the "China business."[54]

State Department representatives then undertook to convince J. P. Morgan & Company, the leader in the old consortium group, of the president's avid desire for the American members to reconstitute that organization on a broader basis. They might begin, for example, by cooperating with Boston and Chicago firms that had recently gained small contracts in China. Morgan spokesmen were hardly thrilled by the idea, pointing out that the money market was in no shape to absorb much in the way of China loans. Worse, they made it clear that the old consortium firms "disapproved of the policy . . . of irritating Japan by straight loans to China."[55]

Jacob Schiff, another spokesman for the old consortium group, elaborated this point in a letter to Under Secretary Frank L. Polk. The United States should not attempt to prevent Japan from playing the role of big brother in Asia. "The proper remedy to this difficult and complex problem," said Schiff, "appears to me to be that we get alongside Japan in the reorganization of China; that to some extent we join hands with Japan in the labor of modernization. . . ." Schiff's blunt views put off Lansing's advisers. Big brother, indeed, retorted an angry Edward T. Williams. Nothing so noble inspired Japan. "Highwayman of Asia" better described Tokyo's ambition. Japan had no intention of modernizing China, or of allowing anyone else to undertake that assignment. The United States must never hope for such a partnership: "Perhaps it is well for the white race that so much antagonism exists between China and Japan. A union there with universal military service might terrify the world."[56]

Williams's version of the situation, however, was long on indignation and regrettably lacking in recommendation. For the time being the war ruled out confrontation with Tokyo, and over the long run nothing, not even war with Japan, would change the fact that China and Japan had been placed next to one another on this earth. Ambassador George Guthrie in Tokyo reported, moreover, that leading Japanese worried lest the United States employ its war-stimulated financial power to deprive them of a leading role in China: "Forced by the action of America and the British colonies to keep her labor at home, she must find some employment for it and a market for its production. The market must be in China."[57]

Lansing probably understood that kind of argument better than the highly charged pronouncements of Reinsch and Williams. One could do something about such complaints; and if that was what the bankers were saying, the matter became one for the very sort of out-of-court settlement Lansing had been well paid in private life to negotiate. In the back of his mind as well was the thought, shared by Colonel House, that the Asian question must be handled so as not to allow some desperate Chinese leader or faction to draw the United States into an unwanted conflict with Japan.[58]

In a private letter to Lansing, Guthrie had added some information about the visit of Judge Elbert Gary. Japan was short of steel, and would be unable to meet its own needs in the foreseeable future. Therefore a "partnership" with Judge Gary's United States Steel Corporation fired the Japanese imagination. "Businessmen of Japan are coming to feel that the wisest course to pursue is to work, not for political loans in China, but for business co-operation . . . in the development of the transportation facilities and industries of China." Gary's speeches extolling this theme were being quoted with interest and approval, ended Guthrie.[59]

Obviously it was important to Lansing that the head of U.S. Steel had sided with the bankers. China could go the way of harm or the way of peace, Gary was saying in Japan, toward war or internal development. With Japan as the model of Progressivism on the march, China could achieve all it desired through international cooperation.[60] If this were so, then surely Lansing's task was well within the range of the possible. It became a question of how to channel Japanese energies into productive outlets.

Lansing had not forgotten, however, what he had told Wilson: nothing could be accomplished without *everyone*—and that meant the bankers as well—acknowledging that laissez-faire in its international manifestation, private diplomacy, was no longer possible in the century of world capitalism and, it would become clear, of total war. To set his plans in motion, the secretary put Japan and the bankers on notice that the Wilson administration had abandoned its original approach to the Open Door policy and was now determined to defend its economic interests in China. On November 16, 1916, the newspapers carried stories of a $5 million loan agreement signed by Chinese authorities with the Chicago Continental and Commercial Bank. "[A] distinct step . . . to resume business operations on a large scale in China," said the press reports, which also included quotations from a Lansing letter to the banking institution welcoming the loan and giving assurances that "now as in the past," the government intended to provide "all proper diplomatic support and protection to the legitimate enterprises abroad of American citizens." Previous attempts to make such a loan, added the *New York Times*, had foundered "on account of the unwillingness of the United States Government to guarantee to the American financial concerns interested the assistance of the United States in compelling China to live up to its obligations." Now that reluctance had been overcome.[61]

Wilson had not gone that far, but the story suited Lansing's purposes. Readers of the *Times* story in London received the definite impression, for example, that this time America did mean business. "It even seems possible," said one minute in the Foreign Office, "that the USA and not Japan may finance China through the present crisis and, from the point of view of British interests, it is to be hoped that this may be so."[62] Discussion about restarting the consortium, and an exchange with Tokyo in regard to that possibility, had already taken place. Even Sir Edward Grey imagined that the consortium might again have a role to play, given the chaos that followed Yuan's fall, in keeping the peace among the powers. But he did not for a minute intend to fall in behind Lansing's refurbished American extravaganza. He still had good cards to play before that was necessary.

Cautioning Ambassador Page to treat the information confidentially, Grey said he was seeking some way to put the recent dialogue with Japan into a larger framework. His deepest fear, Sir Edward continued, was that a civil war might break out in China. "In that case difficult questions might be raised for all the powers who had interests in China."[63] Rather than subscribe to any foolish American effort to force Japan to stand down, however, Grey and his advisers had in mind harnessing the consortium idea to their prewar strategy in China. If there had been any question about that, Reinsch's renewed drive to interest American financial and industrial interests in old British concessions made it clear that playing up to Washington had its dangers as well. "When the war broke out in 1914," J. D. Gregory reminded his Foreign Office colleagues, "we were engaged in trying to introduce some sort of system into our Chinese railway policy on a basis of spheres of influence—as far as these could be established without prejudice to existing conclaves." All along, Gregory continued, His Majesty's Government had been expecting to proceed more or less on those lines after the war. While it might be pleasant to imagine the Americans giving the Japanese a good lesson in China, reality suggested that more likely Great Britain would be much better off with a "balance of power" in China, and, indeed, that one day the Japanese might even be useful as a check on American ambitions.

Obviously, Lansing's feeling that he had to turn his predecessors' diplomacy upside down to make it work had a sound basis. However that may be, the Foreign Office consensus was that American participation in a revived consortium was "essential." Independent American action, on the other hand, was to be avoided, fully as much as Japan's clumsy bullying of China.[65] On this basis, British policymakers had already begun sounding the Japanese. The advantages of a new consortium, observed yet another official, Thomas Lyons, were self-evident. Germany would be shut out in the immediate postwar period; and China would find itself obliged to take the consortium bid, because, with the United States participating, "all the available cash in the world" would be represented.[66]

When the Japanese were asked about their views, Baron Ishii, the new foreign minister, told the British ambassador that his countrymen had seen Japan's influence in China decline during the years of Yuan's rule. If Japan were now to acquiesce in "this idea of inviting America to partici-pate," the price would be British agreement to a Japanese financial ad-viser in Peking. Grey was not distressed at this request. That would lock Japan in, so to speak, and at least have the virtue of putting an end to independent action from that side.[67]

Lansing's public relations efforts on behalf of the Chicago loan, meanwhile, had had the desired effect from the secretary's point of view of stimulating a Japanese approach to Washington. That was essential for his plan to go into operation. Lansing was perfectly aware of what Tokyo sought: formal recognition of its claim to succeed Germany in Shantung.[68] He enjoyed the thought, moreover, that Japan so clearly saw that even as a neutral the United States was going to have a major voice in determining the post war world order. He was pleased, too, that at last this time Paul Reinsch's blunt talk fit into a larger pattern being designed in Washington.

The prelude to Japanese ambassador Chinda's request for a meeting in mid-January 1917 had been one of Reinsch's sarcastic replies to a Japanese suggestion for economic cooperation. If Japan was serious, he had retorted, then perhaps it would open up Manchuria to American bids for railroad concessions.[69] Chinda opened his remarks to Lansing with a reference to that quip, but before he could finish the secretary expressed great surprise that anyone should imagine America desired to push itself into an area where Tokyo's "special interests" had already been ac-knowledged: "Although no declaration to that effect had been made by the United States yet this Government had repeatedly shown a practical recognition of the fact and did not desire to do anything there to inter-fere with Japan's interests."[70]

Having set his stage, Lansing read the first lines of Act I. In Manchu-ria, Japan's special interests were "conceded," he began, but Shantung was different. No such concession had been made there. Chinda replied by asking, What of Germany's previous rights? These had never been rec-ognized by the United States, said the secretary. Lansing had no intention of trading off Shantung and Manchuria and leaving it at that. By oppos-ing a Japanese succession to German leaseholds he accomplished several things at once. He initiated a diplomatic offensive against other spheres of influence in China, and he sought to establish a distinction between ac-knowledging the existence of certain specific prewar interests, such as the Japanese-owned South Manchurian Railway, and the wholesale transfer of a province from one imperial power to another.

After the Lansing-Chinda conversation, Japan immediately took up Shantung with British policymakers, seeking a formal Allied agreement to its succession.[71] In Washington, Lansing and Spring-Rice debated the merits of an outright concession. The ambassador, playing the advocate, argued that Japanese suspicions could never be alleviated entirely, but that surely it made sense to consult closely with a government "which for geographical reasons, if for no other, must have a peculiar interest in the subject." During their discussion, the secretary noted "with some asperity" that the New York bankers had come to assume that "they alone were the masters of the situation." Well, replied Spring-Rice, it was certainly true that independent action in the past had led to unfortunate results. Hopefully "some means would be found to restore the solidarity of the banking groups of all nations."[72]

Lansing's emphasis on resisting Japan's pretensions in Shantung alerted the Foreign Office that compliance with the latest Japanese requests would not be popular in the United States. Yet against that consideration stood Grey's frequent reassurances to Tokyo and a new development, the Admiralty's desire for Japanese warships in the Mediterranean and the South Atlantic. London's ambassador to Japan, Sir Conyngham Greene, had been told that recognition of Japan's Shantung claims would create a good atmosphere for solving Allied naval problems. Besides, the Japanese foreign minister, Viscount Motono, had said the request was not unprecedented. Had not the Western Allies published their assent to Russian occupation and control of Constantinople? And was it not well known that Italy had entered the war in 1915 by means of a similar special arrangment?[73]

It need not be a public statement, said Viscount Motono. With that caveat, Greene forwarded the request to London with a recommendation that it be approved. The general response was that the Japanese overture offered a chance to make a virtue out of necessity. The war cabinet discussed the issue three times, the last time on February 12, 1917, after the United States had broken off with Germany. The dominant opinion at this session was that His Majesty's Government should act soon, "in order to avoid negotiations on the subject with another Power."

Here was unmistakable evidence: the war cabinet confirmed what the Foreign Office position had been all along. Instead of using the imminent American entrance into the war as a reason for postponing a concession to Japan, it increased the desire policymakers felt to settle. The urgent need to strike a bargain before the United States became involved, with unpredictable diplomatic results, was reflected in Foreign Secretary Arthur Balfour's instructions to Greene:

H.M. Government are quietly resisting attempts to allow the Japanese to get a footing in industrial undertakings in China in provinces bordering India and Thibet, and in the Yangtse Valley. . . . It is doubtful whether, in the present condition of British political and financial helplessness in the Far East, H.M. Government are secure enough to maintain the existing state of things against any pressure that may suddenly arise.[74]

These instructions covered a number of unstated concerns, including the possibility of civil war in China, a Japanese-American conflict, or an American move to oust both British and Japanese interests from leading roles.

> *American intervention in the war may turn out to be*
> *the salvation of our position in the Far East . . . and*
> *so secure our trade interests for the future—besides*
> *other far reaching political considerations.*
>
> Foreign Office minute, 1917

Worried as they might be about the scope of America's war aims, and about Wilson's personal mission to redo the world from the moment of creation down to 1917, the policymakers of Whitehall nevertheless found themselves deeply impressed by the changes wrought by American participation in the war. The question of China's entrance into the war, never seriously considered, now had to be taken into account. Curiously enough, on the other hand, Lansing and Wilson seemed very reluctant to take responsibility for encouraging China to come forward, even under American aegis.

It was Paul Reinsch who seized the moment. The American minister had suspected that some sort of Anglo-Japanese deal was in the works over Shantung. That could be stopped, he thought, and so much more as well, if Washington only understood what power it had over world opinion, what faith was placed in Wilson's leadership by expectant peoples like the Chinese. As early as January 10, 1917, Reinsch had alerted Washington to Chinese fears that their country would be parceled out among the victors. As matters stood, China had no place reserved at the peace table, except as supplicant. Chinese officials told him that they counted on American support to gain a seat on the decision-making side of the table.[75]

As soon as news reached Peking of the American decision to break relations with Germany, Reinsch became active in an effort to persuade Chinese officials to associate themselves with the United States at each step of the way. And to Washington he cabled that a $10 million government-to-government loan would make it possible for China to undertake war preparations. If China broke relations with Germany, Reinsch advised Premier Tuan Ch'i-jui, it could be certain of "an independent position at the peace table. . . ."[76]

Wilson and Lansing understood full well what Reinsch hoped to accomplish. They feared failure. Far from securing China a seat among the powers, wrote the president, "we may be leading China to risk her doom." Lansing liked the idea of creating a Chinese army to defend its territories, but America could not put itself in a position of encouraging China to ignore the risks of incurring Japanese wrath. A telegram went out instructing Reinsch to advise prudence. Peking should consult Allied capitals before acting on this crucial question.[77]

Reinsch simply ignored these instructions. America's decision had already deprived Japan of its strongest weapon, he said, the threat to defect to the Central Powers. "The opportunity is at hand," he wrote privately to Wilson, "for the solving of the Chinese problem for a long time to come in a manner consistent with our national safety and the fundamental rights of China without coming in direct conflict with the position and legitimate interests of other nations."[78]

When his superiors continued to procrastinate, and to seek to dampen his enthusiasm, the minister triumphantly announced that Japan had switched positions. It was now urging China to do more than break relations, indeed to come into the war with Tokyo's blessing and support.[79] The United States was not "bidding against the entente," Lansing rebuked Reinsch. It was still believed in Washington, moreover, that Peking should not give other nations an excuse to take "defensive" measures against an "agressive" China. Nonetheless, the administration was supporting Chinese efforts to obtain American loans, and would seek to assure Peking a seat at the peace conference.[80]

"The entry of America into the war must obviously be a terrible blow to the Japanese," noted Thomas Lyons on April 6, 1917. "Whatever terms we offer, China is bound to follow the lead of the USA, she is sure to be represented at the Peace Conference and is sure to receive the support of an America materially stronger than anything Japan thought she would have to reckon with."[81] Materially stronger also, he might have written, than anything London thought it would have to reckon with.

Though never too sure whether they wanted a rambunctious America demanding a Japanese pullout from Shantung, British policymakers began reconsidering everything Grey had promised Tokyo. At the first Imperial War Conference in March 1917, however, Arthur Balfour had still stressed that Japan could not be denied its opportunity to expand in one area if kept out of the rest of the world, adding only the qualification, "I think Lord Grey carried his doctrine to excess."[82]

When Balfour went to Washington soon after the American decision for war, he had an opportunity to speak with Wilson about the "secret treaties" among the Allies. The president indicated he was aware of the general tenor of the engagements and the likelihood that one or another of the Allies would insist on the strict letter of the treaties. "He evidently thought that in that event [the] US being themselves unfettered might exercise powerful and valuable influence. Were I in his place I should have decided as he has done."[83]

Less enamored of the idea of reconsidering what had been arranged with Japan than some of his advisers, Balfour was happy to wait and see what developed. He was not unreceptive to the argument that American entrance into the war might have the very pleasant side effect of relieving His Majesty's Government of burdens undertaken under extreme circumstances, but he had an uneasy feeling that China's wish for an equal seat at the peace conference would cause trouble.

"We do not want to be outdone by America at this point," minuted J. D. Gregory in an optimistic moment, "and, though it is premature to forecast formal Anglo-American cooperation in China, it is at least politic to assimilate our action to American in the direction of emancipating China (within reasonable limits) from foreign tutelage as a reward for her participation in the war."[84]

China declared war on August 14, 1917. By that time Lansing had decided on his next steps in the campaign against spheres of influence, but things were getting confused. Wilson's world reputation he saw as a hindrance to reassuring Japan, a problem made worse by China's participation in the war for no other reason than to secure equality and increased status. Such fears, whatever Wilson felt, were the real reason Lansing had tried to check Reinsch's enthusiasm. Sympathy for China had become, moreover, one of the left-liberal causes espoused by the president's friends in both America and Europe. Ideological war-making was a perceived danger in many quarters before the Bolshevik Revolution. Its growth after that upheaval touched all issues, from what to do about Germany to reactions to events in Mexico.

II

WAR INTO REVOLUTION

Monarchy and privilege and pride will have it out before they die—at what cost! If they do have a general war they will so set back the march of progress in Europe as to set the day forward for American leadership. Men here see that clearly.

Walter Hines Page to Woodrow Wilson,
July 29, 1914

As someone said to me the other day, the statue of Liberty is an image of gilded bronze hollow inside with its back turned to Europe. The meaning of this is that the liberty the Americans care for is their own liberty and not the world's, their happiness and not ours.

Sir Cecil Spring-Rice to Arthur Balfour,
January 11, 1917

CHAPTER FIVE

Exploding Germany

I want to have the pride of feeling that America, if nobody else, has her self-possession and stands ready to help the rest of the world.

Woodrow Wilson, press conference,
August 3, 1914

The first statement of British war aims in what was to become the Great War had but one essential, the restoration of Belgium. That assumed things could be put back where they were—and should be. Within a few months the restoration of Belgium had become "self-determination" for the small countries surrounding the Central Powers. And there were already hints that a satisfactory peace would require more than a battlefield victory, would demand in fact a change in Germany's internal politics. From the outset Allied statesmen had blamed the "military party" around Kaiser Wilhelm II for the war. If that was indeed the case, and few doubted it, a settlement that did not deprive that caste of any chance to try again was no victory.[1]

Depriving the Prussian Junkers of the privilege of guiding modern Germany was a duty that summoned forth Britain's youth to fight in France, and rallied the political parties behind a wartime truce. At the outset of the crisis that led to war the anti–Boer War Welsh radical David Lloyd George wavered, despite his recent conversion to Germanophobia. He straightened out quickly, however, aided by a vision that put the conflict into a familiar framework. German immorality in attacking Belgium stemmed from the feudal evil genius behind all the kaiser's policies, including the building of a

great fleet. This was truly a just struggle: "It is a great war for the emancipation of Europe from the thraldom of a military caste."[2]

Before it was a Great War in terms of number of men and nations
engaged, or of destruction of life, it was already a great opportunity to
change European politics. Conservatives could embrace that idea as well.
In their view, self-determination had a dual significance. Placing a ring of
new nations around Germany (supported by proper guarantees) would do
away with the immediate danger of a German-led economic union. But to
hold things in place for any great length of time, self-determination had to
take place inside Germany as well. The restoration of the Europe they
knew thus required revolution. The logic seemed paradoxical, but it was
not. A postwar order resurrecting nineteenth-century political standards
and values was illusory, but if Germany could be brought *forward* out of
feudalism, liberal capitalism might again flourish. At least this: a liberal
Germany would reduce the polarization of politics in Central Europe, and
have a healthy influence generally. Put bluntly, it was better to have the
revolution in Germany and have done with it, than to risk allowing the
reactionaries who brought on war, and revolution afterwards, to stay in
power. Finally, once Germany's threat to British economic supremacy had
abated the prewar crisis inside British politics would resolve itself.

Liberals and radicals who supported the war after the fashion of Lloyd
George also saw military victory as essential, and revolution in Germany
as a means to other ends, in fact as the first necessary step in constructing
a new social order on twentieth-century principles. In the politics of peacemaking, their old enemies, the Conservatives, would no doubt make a
strong bid to halt the forces the war had set in motion at a point most
congenial to themselves. Unless the military party was removed from the
German political scene, reactionary forces at home could demand (and no
doubt get) large military budgets and the indefinite postponement of the
prewar social and political agenda.

It is particularly worthy of notice in this regard that where Woodrow
Wilson had made his greatest impact was on foreign affairs, beginning
with his statements on Mexico and China. One speech, his Fourth of July
address in Philadelphia, promised a far more radical change in the order
of things than any legislation enacted under the New Freedom program.
To be sure, it was a promise yet to be fulfilled. But the opposite was true
in British politics. Foreign policy had not been penetrated by the great
hubbub emanating from Parliament when Lloyd George's "People's Budget" was introduced. It remained very securely under the control of Sir
Edward Grey and the professionals, who to all outward appearances had
never even heard about the strikes or the women's demand for the vote
or, above all, the Irish question.

Over the next three years the complications and permutations of these views and political programs transformed diplomacy and international relations into new shapes, shapes beyond anything previously imagined. It was also beyond any European imagination that America would hold the balance in deciding which shapes would dominate, how the world would be made safe for democracy. On August 2, 1914, Ambassador Walter Hines Page wrote from London that the dreadful events of recent days revealed the "deplorable mediaevalism of a large part of Europe." President Wilson must expect an early summons "to point the way back to reason."[3]

> *Was there something very wrong about our civiliza-*
> *tion and the virtues of which we felt so sure? The*
> *Great War has given a terrible answer.*
>
>   Lord Grey, 1925

Sir Edward Grey was in an optimistic mood in the spring of 1914. After several years of rising tensions on the continent, the settlement of the Second Balkan War gave some reason to hope that the alliance system was maturing into a Concert of Europe. He was especially pleased at evidence of Berlin's restraining role upon Austrian ambitions. If a new crisis arose, he thought, this new partnership with Germany would again come to the fore to save the situation.[4]

Four days before the assassination of Archduke Franz Ferdinand by a Serbian patriot, Grey had seen fit to reassure Prince Lichnowsky, the German ambassador, that there was "no alliance or agreement" committing His Majesty's Government beforehand to any course of action. "Grey went on to explain that the British Government does not belong to the Triple Entente group in order to make difficulties greater between the two European groups but on the contrary their wish is to prevent questions throwing the groups into such opposition." If war did occur, Britain would not be on the aggressive side, "for public opinion was against that."[5]

But optimism did not run deep. That spring it was only a patina, beneath which the calm and self-assurance of the Victorian era had eroded. In 1911 Grey had made the same point about public opinion but explained it better. He had said that the "next country, if any, which had a great and successful war, unless it was purely a war of defence against aggression, would be the first to have a social revolution."[6]

As the July crisis deepened across Europe, and Austria's ultimatum to

Serbia hung over all discussions, Grey repeatedly warned both Vienna and Berlin that war between modern nations would lead only to "a state of things worse than that of 1848." Regardless of who won, "many things might be completely swept away."[7] Having failed to prevent war through diplomacy, however, Sir Edward immediately sought to minimize its impact on British thought and politics. At most, he told the House of Commons on August 3, 1914, there would be a commercial recession. "For us with our powerful fleet . . . if we are engaged in war, we shall suffer but little more than we shall suffer even if we stand aside."[8]

This bravado gave way almost immediately to a more realistic view of the war. Its purpose, however, was to set the foundations for an ideological structure of much greater subtlety. Undoubtedly Grey wished to preserve the option of "splendid isolation," if at all possible, for the postwar era, but by presenting the government as unable to keep from being drawn into the war the foreign secretary demonstrated how mindful he remained of his own admonitions that a "great and successful war" would not prevent "a social revolution" unless it was "purely a war of defence."

Grey developed this theme only a few days later in the course of fending off the first American bid to mediate the war. Britain was really a "neutral" participating in the conflict for the benefit of all humankind. Writing to Colville Barclay in the Washington Embassy, he put it this way:

> We had been drawn into the war. We had no objective of our own
> in it, nothing that we particularly sought or had entered the war to
> obtain for ourselves. At the first moment, therefore, that it could
> be stopped honorably on fair terms we should like it to be stopped.

Of course, he continued with practiced urbanity, if the Germans won easily, they would listen to no one. And if the French and Russians won easily, they would insist that Germany "should receive a lesson." Perhaps (it was to be hoped?) neither side would prevail. In that case both sides would become exhausted, and there might arise an opportunity for American mediation. He knew that President Wilson wished for that chance;

> and, whenever there appeared a fair opportunity of stopping the
> war by mediation, we should, I felt sure, throw our influence on
> the side of it, and, having taken part in the war, our influence
> would be stronger than if we had stood outside.[9]

Grey's message can be read several ways: as a coded appeal, for example, to the United States to see that the only way a truly neutral national could behave would be to intervene as soon as possible on the Allied side—as Britain had been *forced* to do—to insure a just end to the conflict. It can also be read more simply as a large dose of soothing syrup to help the scratchy Orders in Council restricting trade with the Central Powers go down American throats as easily as possible.

There is yet a third way. The letter more than implies that after the war British policy would not simply start over along old tracks, but would reach out for some new method of maintaining the peace. In response to a prior German bid to keep Britain from coming into the Continental conflict, Grey had suggested instead "some arrangement" to assure Germany that no hostile policy would be pursued against Berlin's legitimate interests, either by France and Russia or by Great Britain. This idea, he said as Europe mobilized to go to war, had hitherto been "too Utopian to form the subject of definite proposals."[10]

Whether Grey imagined at this time that the United States would at some point really step in with proposals for an expanded Concert of Europe, or something else considered "too Utopian" by Old World leaders, the Liberal foreign secretary had correctly forecast Wilson's intellectual road to April 1917. Wilson would conclude, as had Grey, that a neutral power had a responsibility to insure a just end of the war; and he would decide, after an agonizing three years wandering in the labyrinth of neutrality, that participation in the war itself, and not just in the peace conference, was the only way to fulfill that responsibility. What convinced him, however, was not the logic of Sir Edward Grey, but practical experience, not only with the European situation but with events in Mexico and China. If there was to be serious political change, some way had to be found to accommodate the already powerful challenge those revolutions posed.

When the war began, however, Wilson asked the American people to remain neutral in thought as well as deed. He also appealed for "calmness of thought and steadiness of purpose to help the rest of the world." That was not easy. The economy was in the doldrums. Since April the export surplus—by which Americans settled each year's accounts with their European creditors—had disappeared. Those five months had already seen the greatest surplus of imports over exports since 1895, the nadir of the terrible depression of the 1890s. Wheat and cotton crops in 1914 were the largest in history. What would happen if those crops could not be sold abroad?[11]

Trying to solve that problem, the first he faced as a result of the war, brought the president into conflict with economic leaders who believed that he was deliberately using the war to promote what they regarded as socialism. Wilson, who had campaigned vigorously against Roosevelt's New Nationalism on those very same grounds, thus found himself engaged early on in an internal political dialogue not entirely unlike the one

spreading under the surface of the British war effort. He had called
congressional leaders to the White House on July 31, 1914, to explain
how he planned to head off catastrophe. "Our bountiful crops are ready
to harvest," he told them. "Unless they can be carried to the foreign
markets, they will waste in the warehouses, if they do not rot in the
fields. . . ." Congress then approved a ship transfer bill on August 18,
1914, in an effort to encourage American citizens to reregister vessels
they owned under the American flag. But it refused to allow the administration to purchase fifty-four German ships that had been trapped in
American ports when the war broke out. The British and French had
objected vehemently to Wilson's plan, arguing that placing the ships
under the protection of the American flag would thwart Britain and
France's major sea warfare efforts. Already, then, the impossibility of
traditional neutrality had become evident, as had the probability of being
trapped by Allied policy decisions.[12]

The war would be an external force on American politics, whatever
Wilson did, in this instance by increasing economic pressures and causing
Congress to line up for one side or the other. The war would also become
an immediate internal political force. There were ethnic factors to consider, but in the instance of the ship transfer bill's fate the opening shots
were fired in an ideological battle. Secretary of the Treasury William
Gibbs McAdoo received a telephone call on August 1, 1914, from J. P.
Morgan. The nation's most famous banker told McAdoo that the government's entrance into the shipping field would be considered a "menace"
to private enterprise by the business community. Wilson had made government sponsorship of the merchant marine part of his New Freedom
campaign, along with tariff reduction and banking reform legislation.
These were all part, ironically, of his effort to see that the nation continued to look outward rather than concentrating on government control of
the kind he perceived TR to be thinking about (or, worse, not really
thinking about, only drifting into). Morgan's urgent call put the administration on notice that the economic leaders of American capitalism would
be on the alert to any administration effort to inject "socialism" into the
nation's political veins as a remedy for war sickness.[13]

Morgan's more narrow interest as a private shipbuilder was no doubt a
big factor in his response to the proposed legislation, but he was also
expressing a general conservative concern. Boston banker Henry Lee
Higginson, for example, wrote the president to support legislation similar
to the ship transfer bill, but any other emergency measure he opposed;
any other government initiative in general he opposed. English statesmen
of both parties (he did not mention Labour), he wrote in one letter, had
quite wisely joined hands "in putting off the burning question, and in

looking only to the good of Europe." America was rich, in good condition, and could assume the leading commercial position in the world. Wilson should concentrate on that. He should set as his first task the alleviation of business perplexity and anxiety. "It would do the nation a world of good if every measure under discussion were torpedoed; if all attacks here or there were to cease; and if Congress were to go home at once."[14]

The metaphor was an apt one for wartime. Seth Low, president of the New York Chamber of Commerce, had another in mind. If the administration kept on pushing for the Clayton Anti-Trust Act in the light of the war crisis, it could be the "last straw that breaks the camel's back." Moreover, American business, that heavily burdened camel, stood in the middle of dangerous rapids. The cotton glut threatened the earning capacity of the railroads. And beneath the surface of those roiling waters the financial problems of the country were of the "gravest possible character."[15]

The point, of course, was not that Morgan opposed the ship bill, or that Higginson wanted Congress to pack up and go home, or that Low feared for the camel's safety. It was how the nation would respond, politically, to the shock of war. By placing an "embargo on the commerce of the world," as the president put it on one occasion, the European conflict endangered the stability of domestic political structures in the New World as well, and upped the ante in a game of chance between reform and radicalism. Wilson had repeatedly stressed that his program would give business the one thing it needed most: relief from uncertainty. In his judgment, he told businessmen, "nothing was more dangerous than uncertainty; . . . it had become evident through a long series of years that a policy such as the Democratic party was now pursuing was absolutely necessary to satisfy the conscience of the country and its perceptions of the prevailing conditions of business; . . . it was a great deal better to do the thing moderately and soberly now than to wait until more radical forces had accumulated and it was necessary to go much further."[16]

A decision to button up the domestic reform program had been urged by conservatives as soon as the war began. Wilson was also concerned not to injure the delicate tissue of the body politic at this critical moment. Looking ahead was not easy, but what would a German victory mean to America's future? Which political forces would gain, and which lose? Colonel House wrote Wilson on August 22 that the war was indeed "a most disturbing and uncertain element." If the Germans succeeded, he predicted, that might well force the nation "to abandon the path which you are blazing as a standard for future generations, with permanent peace as its goal and a new international ethical code as its guiding star. . . ." And if Berlin set the terms for international behavior, the

United States would have to "build up a military machine of vast proportions."[17]

House saw himself as a mediator between radicalism and reaction, but Wilson's outlook was determined by a keener political awareness of the pitfalls in whichever path the nation chose. Experiences like those that came out of the ship bill controversy pushed him toward the conclusion that the "special interests" would deny liberals an opportunity to carry through a moderate program, that they would use the war to distract the nation's attention. Yet he feared that they might be right: a reform program could, in the context of dramatic war-inspired change, become radicalism. And this would be especially so if each nation acted in isolation during and after the war. There would be many instances to illustrate the danger.*

> *The world is upon a strain as never before in its history, and something is sure to crack somewhere before a great while. It looks as if our best move just now is to wait until the fissure appears.*
>
> Colonel House to Wilson,
> March 20, 1915

Soon after the war began Colonel House found the president in a somber mood. Wilson was by no means sure that a second term would allow him to pick up the Progressive theme that had dominated in 1912. War had broken that momentum, and deadlock seemed likely:

> [T]he thing that frightened him was that it was impossible to make such an effort in the future as he had made in the past or to accomplish anything like what he had accomplished in a legislative way. He feared the country would expect him to continue as he had up to now, which would be impossible.

House assured his friend that the country would neither expect nor want such things. Other questions would matter more. "I referred pointedly to his foreign policy which if properly followed, would bring him world-wide recognition." By "properly followed" the colonel meant not

---

* Perhaps the most difficult problem Wilson poses for the historian is how to reconcile his openness to seeking change, as in Mexico and China, with his consistent fear of radicalism in domestic politics. Wilson was able to satisfy himself with his plans for a League of Nations; for whatever he told jealous senators, he had no doubt but that the League would have a tremendous impact on the success or failure of domestic political institutions as the contradictions of the industrial age drove nation after nation toward some form of the New Nationalism or socialism. See, for example, Lloyd C. Gardner, *A Covenant with Power: America and World Order from Wilson to Reagan* (New York, 1984), chap. 1.

victory over Germany, but a chance to preside over a peace conference. He expected the battlefield to be indecisive. When the nations fighting on both sides came to that understanding, Wilson would have his chance.[18]

So far the British had refused to meet on any level with German representatives to talk about ending the war, noted House, another indication that they would need outside help. At this stage America's role should be to point out the consequences of seeking victory in the old sense. Aside from mutual exhaustion, the leaders of the two alliances would find themselves eclipsed in the postwar era. "If Germany and Austria are entirely crushed," House noted "neither of us could see any way by which Russia could be restrained. He [Wilson] thought I should bring this strongly to Sir Edward Grey's attention."[19]

This discussion launched Colonel House's famous mediation efforts, which occupied so much of the president's time and attention over the next two years and which, it can be argued, drove him to a decision for war in 1917. Certainly it was the primary ideological consideration. House's missions had no real chance of success, except to lay groundwork. But both sides wanted to appear reasonable to the Americans, and open to serious peace negotiations. Ambassador Spring-Rice appreciated the colonel's efforts to secure talks based on the restoration of Belgium, for example, but pointed out that there were certain complications: France would expect the return of Alsace-Lorraine, and Russia desired Constantinople.[20]

Spring-Rice also warned House that all the European capitals were apparently in a funk, worried about revolution. Far from discouraging House, however, this information only whetted his appetite for finding a way for Wilson to take charge of the forces for change. As it happened, Spring-Rice's cautionary statement was a partial translation of something Sir Edward Grey had said in a letter instructing the ambassador to do what he could to dampen American enthusiasm for attempts at mediation. As an alternative to this sort of intervention, the foreign secretary had mused about the possibility of bringing about the democratization of Germany by the spontaneous action of the German people. This notion and kindred ideas about the politics of war were already engaging considerable attention on both sides of the Atlantic, and across the trenches.[21]

Sir Edward's ruminations reached Wilson directly early in 1915 when Chandler P. Anderson, an expert on the legal aspects of naval warfare, returned from a stint in the American embassy in London. The foreign secretary was anxious, Anderson related, that the president understand the full complexity of the situation, including certain things he could not commit to writing in a formal state paper. At issue was not only what France and Russia might demand, but also Japan's "bill" at the end of the war. Anderson went on:

He had said that up to this time capital had ruled the world; that this war showed that the capitalists had made a mess of it, and that capital itself was being destroyed to such an extent that it had practically disappeared and would have to be recreated before it could play its former part in the economic subdivisions of the state; that being so, he predicted that when the war was over, labor might rule in place of capital, and would take control of the state in order to provide employment for itself.

Wilson interrupted at this point to say that Grey's views were exceedingly interesting. It had not occurred to him before, but they seemed to be "in line with our own form of democratic government where the people were the ruling power." Anderson then continued with Grey's concluding statement expressing a hope that labor would rule in postwar Germany, as that would provide an effective barrier against renewed militarism and aggression.[22]

Grey had not been radicalized. Far from it. In the Foreign Office he was surrounded by advisers pushing for a permanent Anglo-Russian alliance to preserve the peace after victory. This would entail concessions to tsarist expansionism—and certainly more even than would have to be conceded during wartime. Indeed, there might be no end to such a process once started. A similar situation obtained in the Far East, where Japan's "bill" was sure to grow larger. A "great League of Peace" was, as the foreign secretary saw it, the only possible alternative. And only in that way could Britain retain a part of its independence from Europe; otherwise, paradoxically, it would find itself enmeshed in a new alliance system. A democratic, nonmilitaristic Germany was thus essential if future policymakers were to enjoy sufficient leverage against advocates of a dangerously unstable alliance system designed to preserve British power but not likely to succeed doing so.[23]

Thus imagined as an alternative to appeasement, Grey's "great League of Peace" grew out of the original debate in which Chamberlain had argued with Salisbury for an alliance with either Germany or the United States. The old dispute would continue into the 1930s, when the advocates would argue "collective security" versus concessions to the dictators. The role America should play in such schemes was always open to speculation. Thus Grey did not welcome the first House mission. He thought it premature, until the colonel assured him that he had not come to talk peace terms.

There was no chance for peace, House said upon his arrival in London in January 1915, until the Allies had tried out their new armies and, presumably, Germany's position had worsened.[4] He had come instead to talk about a plan to insure permanent peace after victory. With that settled, the two began a discussion of America's role. House had an ingenious solution for the first obstacle to American participation, the various territorial war aims of the belligerents. Wilson could not take part in deciding what happened to Poland, or Alsace-Lorraine, or Constantinople. Instead, the president would take the lead in a "second convention" held simultaneously to define the rules of any future war and to discuss freedom of the seas. Grey warmed to the idea. Britain would be willing, he believed, to agree that merchant shipping in the future, of whatever nature, belligerent or neutral, should be immune to capture. House was of course delighted "to know that Great Britain stood ready to go so far."[25]

Each kept to himself certain caveats. The president's adviser reserved to himself, for example, the thought that if peace had not been restored in a few months, say by August, Wilson should initiate the "second convention." The president would in that case be obliged to minimize the specific war aims that constituted so-called vital issues not only for foreign policy but for domestic peace by inviting both sides to take part without resolution of those issues. If the "far-reaching" questions Americans were concerned about could be settled in this manner, the sticky territorial "controversies" might even disappear.[26]

These musings were interrupted by a message from House's contact in Berlin making it plain that Germany would not take part in any talks that included discussion of an indemnity to Belgium. All the more reason to hope for early German reverses, thought House, but the spadework should go ahead anyway. House waited so long in London, however, that even Wilson become concerned that he might be labeled a British spokesman. As he prepared to cross the Channel to the Continent, the colonel justified the delay by explaining that he had "up my sleeve" a plan for transforming German attitudes. He would say that Wilson had needed the time to convince the British to make concessions at the second convention: "In other words, that, with your initiative and with Germany's cooperation, Great Britain can be induced to make these terms."[27]

The military situation did indeed change, but hardly in the direction House wished. On February 4, 1915, Berlin announced that in two weeks a submarine war zone would go into effect around Great Britain and Ireland. Neutrals were warned against entering these waters, since British vessels sometimes disguised themselves behind foreign flags. In mid-March the colonel found Chancellor Bethmann-Hollweg little inclined to talk about peace. In both England and Germany everything was now geared to achieving military victory—enough victory to pay off an increasingly large debt the governments owed to their people. Thus the left was promised a democratic reorganization of society, and the right its annexationist dreams.[28]

Back in London at the end of April, House found Sir Edward Grey a good deal more cautious. Britain could agree to freedom of the seas only if Germany assented to freedom of the land, which he interpreted to mean secure commitments and disarmament. Grey also suggested that House establish contacts with members of the Conservative party in order to better appreciate the political atmosphere. As House was making these rounds, word came that a German U-boat had sunk the luxury liner *Lusitania*. Nearly 1,200 passengers perished, including 128 Americans.

Wilson sent a sharp note to Berlin, protesting not merely the sinking of the *Lusitania*, but submarine warfare in general. House congratulated him. Grey had said that the United States must either respond thus, he wrote, or lose its influence in the "concert of nations."[29] Indeed, Sir Edward thought that if the president chose to make the incident a *casus belli*, "the influence of the United States in the general aspects of peace will be predominant and perhaps decisive. . . ." In the flush of excitement about the *Lusitania*—and in his desire to put Wilson before the world as liberal leader—House agreed. He had a strategy in mind already. The president could deliver a ringing message to Congress, "placing the blame for this fearful conflict upon the the Kaiser and his military entourage and I would exonerate the great body of German citizenship stating that we were fighting for their deliverance as well as the deliverance of Europe." In other words, House wanted the president to make the fissure in German society appear by outside ideological pressure—not unlike Bolshevik "subversive" methods a few years later as a matter of fact.[30]

Bryan resigned rather than sign a second *Lusitania* note that he feared would result in war, but American public opinion had cooled anyway. The president had inserted into the exchange with Berlin an appeal for "cooperation" to obtain freedom of the seas. In this curious manner, then, the *Lusitania* crisis got turned around into a lead-in for a new dispute with Great Britain. Even before public clamor had subsided after the sinking, Wilson was writing House that "to satisfy our public" it would be necessary to send another note to London about unwarranted interference with American trade. Cotton growers were up in arms about a British plan to declare their product contraband, and the administration had to face the growing fears of senators and representatives (largely of its own party) that the cotton industry was menaced.[31]

Sir Cecil Spring-Rice estimated that Americans would lose the sale of two million bales a year if what had been sold to Germany and Austria could not be disposed of elsewhere. The solution, he thought, was to buy up the American crop and convert potential enemies into staunch supporters of the Allied cause.[32]

Count Bernstorff, the German ambassador, had meanwhile gone out on a limb by promising that U-boat commanders would henceforth abide by the rules of sea warfare as set down in the presubmarine age. Shortly after the British cotton purchase plan was announced, Bernstorff offered to buy several million bales—if delivery was guaranteed. Wilson was not a little discomfited: "That only makes more complexing our questions as to how to deal with England, for apparently we have no choice now but to demand that she respect our rights a good deal better than she has been doing." Germany, Wilson feared, wanted to make the United States play "the role of cat's-paw for her in opening trade to her."[33]

The submarine issue had flared up again with the sinking of the *Arabic* and the *Hesperian* when Wilson wrote House seeking advice. Two things were plain, he said: the country did not want war, and going to war over submarines would be a calamity, because then the United States would be "deprived of all disinterested influence over the settlement." His problems were indeed "complexing," and growing steadily more so. By late summer 1915 the Allies could no longer sustain their purchases from the United States on the basis of short-term private credits. They would have to borrow $500 million on the public loan market, explained Treasury Secretary William Gibbs McAdoo, or halt their purchases. It was illogical to permit munitions sales, he went on, and deny access to the loan market. "To maintain our prosperity, we must finance it. Otherwise it may stop and that would be disastrous." The new secretary of state, Robert Lansing, agreed. Bryan's ramblings about the "true spirit of neutrality" could not be permitted to stand in the way of the national interest. "The result would be restriction of outputs, industrial depression, idle capital and idle labor, numerous failures, suffering among the laboring classes."[34]

Wilson went along with his advisers, but he was uneasy. He had been ever since the question of munitions sales and credits or loans first arose. "There is a moral obligation laid upon us," he said early in 1916, "to keep out of this war if possible. But by the same token there is a moral obligation laid upon us to keep free the courses of our commerce and of our finance."[35] The president did not satisfy his most severe critic, himself, with such statements. War distorted everything. Writing to House on September 7, 1915, Wilson had asked, "Shall we ever get out of the labyrinth made for us all by this German 'frightfulness'?" The labyrinth held many puzzles and dead ends, most still to come, but Wilson knew that it did not start or stop with submarine warfare, and he never thought that his only obligation was to keep free the courses of commerce.[36]

The whole world—including neutrals of the highest purposes and humanitarians with the best of mo-

> *tives—must know that there can be no outside inter-*
> *ference at this stage.*
>
> David Lloyd George, 1916

Colonel House was willing to give it a try; he was willing to try to find a way out of the labyrinth—though it might mean participation in the war. If anything, however, prospects for American mediation were at a lower ebb at the beginning of 1916 than ever before. Discussions of the risks of American mediation had taken place inside the Foreign Office with increasing frequency as the war seemed stalemated. And, increasingly, the talk was about coming to terms with that prospect—but always at some future date.

The most prominent voice in the war cabinet now belonged to David Lloyd George, minister of munitions. He would not become prime minister for several more months, but his reputation was on the rise. He proposed three priorities to guide the government's deliberations. The first was victory without American military intervention, but with continued economic assistance. Next was victory after American military intervention, brought about by German submarine warfare. Last was American mediation to escape the consequences of defeat. Sir Edward Grey, who had already explored up and down each of these avenues, proposed that a special effort be made during the next eight months to mount a final victory campaign. If, after that time, victory still eluded the Allies, then it would be necessary to consider mediation.[37]

House arrived in London again in early January 1916 bringing with him Wilson's new instructions, a very carefully hedged offer to reach agreement with the Allies on peace terms. If the Germans refused to parley, the United States would "probably" enter the war on the side of the Allies.[38] It would be better for the democracies to unite upon some plan, House insisted in his first meeting with Grey, "than for us to drift into the war by breaking diplomatic relations with the Central Powers."[39]

Whatever his true feelings, Sir Edward appeared to concur with what the colonel said. Encouraged, House pressed forward. He would not attempt to argue, he said, that if the Allies turned down Wilson's aid in ending the war the United States would wind up fighting on the side of the Central Powers. But he could suggest that there was a definite possibility of "an isolated life of our own." The United States could, if it chose, build up its army and navy and live perfectly safe in the Western Hemisphere.

Feeling that the atmosphere around him was too full of victory sentiments, House tried to spread a little gloom. He raised the specter of a separate German peace with Russia, and then France. Then who would be isolated? British seapower would not last out three months, "not because it might be defeated at sea, but because all nations would protest against the restrictions of trade."[40] After a flying visit to Paris and Berlin—in the latter capital he declared that "there was not a marketplace or a mosque in the East where the West of to-day was not derided"—the colonel returned to London ready to get down to brass tacks.

This was Wilson's plan: Having ascertained that the terms he offered were satisfactory to the Allies, the president would issue his summons for a peace conference. If Germany refused to heed the summons, the United States would "probably" enter the war. If the conference met, but ended in failure, the United States would leave it a belligerent—provided Berlin had been "unreasonable." The hedges dominated, as Sir Edward might have pointed out. But instead of succumbing to that temptation he signed a memorandum agreeing to these conditions, refusing only to specify a date for setting Wilson's plan in motion. House was mismatched against such a master.

What had been set in motion, really, was the war cabinet's list of priorities. Grey was as honest as the situation permitted, warning House that no one else in the cabinet favored the plan. Actually, House misled himself by failing to question Grey closely enough as to his own views. He erred, perhaps, because he was so busy trying to make British policymakers "feel less hopeful and to show them . . . what a terrible gamble they are taking in not invoking our intervention."[41]

In his communications to Washington, House's optimism ranged from conjecture to outright fantasy. "I am satisfied with the result," the colonel wrote. "They cordially accept the suggestion that you preside over the convention when it is held, provided our general understanding is carried out. No action however is to be taken until they signify their readiness. There is a difference of opinion only as to the time."[42]

A month went by with no signal. Instead, as the war cabinet no doubt hoped would happen, the Germans made a new "mistake": the channel steamer *Sussex* was sunk with the loss of ninety lives, including several Americans. House was for war. But Wilson insisted on playing the hand the colonel had dealt. He would intervene only "upon the hope of ending the war rather than upon a German attack on our rights." House thought the president could finesse this, however, by asking Congress to declare war on the German system, not the people.[43]

House also suggested that Grey be asked whether the United States should break with Germany over submarine warfare. The letter that emerged from this discussion posed a novel argument. American entrance into the war would no doubt prolong the conflict; therefore, if the Allies had any thought of invoking Wilson's aid to end it diplomatically, they should do so immediately, since it seemed probable that the president could not avoid breaking relations with Berlin. Still more curious was another House letter of April 7, 1916, suggesting that "we are not so sure of the support of the American people upon the submarine issue, while we are confident that they would respond to the higher and nobler issue of stopping the war." These letters, sent a day apart, made sense only if the first was read to mean that the Allies were forsaking a chance to end the war by outsmarting Germany, and the second to mean that they were risking military defeat—if Wilson asked for war over submarines and failed, he would be prohibited from responding to a later Allied plea for help.[44]

Whatever the strategy, it produced no change. Grey simply replied that if America felt unable to meet the challenge of submarine warfare, how could the Allies have any faith in its willingness to insist upon the terms required to insure a lasting peace? Given France's greater suffering, moreover, His Majesty's Government was precluded from asking Paris to consider a peace conference at this time.[45]

Grey's cool, almost aloof tone irritated House, so much so, in fact, that he told Count Bernstorff that if his superiors could come to terms with the administration over submarine warfare, that might be a forerunner to peace. Berlin did yield to American wishes, for the time being, but House was off on another tangent. Even before Germany's response to the *Sussex* note was known in Washington, House was urging the president not to "allow" the war to continue beyond autumn. "I am certain he can end it whether the belligerents desire it or not," he confided to his diary. Surely it would not take many more months before both sides would be compelled to recognize the stalemate. "He can so word a demand for a conference that the people of each nation will compel their governments to consent."[46]

"The impression grows," the colonel wrote Sir Edward on May 11, 1916, "that the Allies are more determined upon the punishment of Germany than upon exacting terms that neutral opinion would consider just."[47] It had begun to dawn on Wilson and House, on the other hand, that if the United States did go to war in anger against Germany, there would be no time to prepare a set of war aims. This fear tormented Wilson's adviser. "If we should get into the war," he wrote Grey yet again, "I feel sure it would not be a good thing for England. It would probably lead to the complete crushing of Germany; and Russia, Italy and France would then be more concerned as to the division of spoils than they would for any far-reaching agreement that might be brought about looking to the maintenance of peace in the future and the amelioration of the horrors of war."[48]

For two years, House complained privately, Grey had been telling him that the United States must be willing to do its part in world affairs. "Now that we indicate a willingness to do so, he halts, stammers and questions." Allied cocksureness was becoming as much a threat to America's future well-being as German militarism. "This will grow in the event they have any success themselves, and I can foresee trouble with them." Allied victory now, after passions had been so aroused, Allied victory without America having taken a role in bringing the war to an end, would be as serious a problem as a German triumph. "An international situation can change as quickly as relationships between individuals, that is overnight." After the war the Allies might try to dictate in Europe—"and elsewhere."[49]

A few days later Wilson told House to inform Grey that the submarine issue had been resolved. America was at a turning point. The focus was now on Allied violations of legitimate neutral rights. The United States must either move toward an international peace conference or in the direction of enforcing its rights to trade and the freedom of the seas. "Which does Great Britain prefer? She cannot escape both. To do nothing is now, for us, impossible."[50]

Wilson also wanted his friend to recall exactly what had been agreed to in the memorandum Grey signed in London. He was planning to address the League to Enforce Peace, said the president, and wished to make a concrete proposal based upon their understanding. The Allies had failed to come up to the occasion, he added. "They have been blindly stupid in the policy they have pursued on the seas, and must now take the consequences."[51]

The labyrinth of neutrality now contained two traps: the danger of German militarism triumphant *and* the threat of an "unaided" Allied victory. Grey's reply on May 29, 1916, made the latter appear no less perilous. The "best chance" for the "great scheme" rested in a peace conference obtained by American aid and favorable to the Allies, Grey wrote. "The worst chance would be that it should be proposed in connection with an inconclusive or disastrous peace, accompanied, perhaps promoted, by diplomatic friction by the Allies and the United States over maritime affairs." A premature announcement of nonmilitary intervention would be interpreted to mean that the president desired "a peace favorable to the Central Powers."[52]

Wilson used his speech to the founders of the League to Enforce Peace on May 27, 1916, as an opportunity to begin defining American war aims. Both the substance and tone confirmed British suspicions that American mediation was for them only a last resort. Grey thus wrote to Spring-Rice, "[W]e did not believe anyone could play a great part in securing future peace who was really indifferent to the causes and objects of the war."[53]

The president was not indifferent; his priorities were not compatible, however, with those of the British war cabinet. His speech set these forth as insuring the right of self-determination, securing the rights of small nations, and protecting against future aggression. To achieve them, America would be willing to join a "universal association of nations"—if the peace was a just one.[54]

Wilson's first venture into spelling out war aims was far less radical than what he had said about American capitalism in Mexico two years earlier. Yet in the context of the war it had far more significance, for what he said now was what "advanced" thinkers in Europe were demanding of their governments. The effort to get Wilson committed to the war via the submarine route was, therefore, was at least partly motivated by the need to keep him from intervening through a breach in British politics. It was entirely possible that American entrance into the war could make the divisions inside the Allied nations, as well as inside Germany, intolerable. This concern antedated the revolutionary changes in Russia, though of course it was sharply increased when they occurred. So while Wilson pressed harder for an international solution to American problems, the Allies reacted with greater and greater resistance.

Resentment that Wilson was using American neutrality to place his nation (and himself) in the role of world arbitrator was also a factor in convincing British leaders to respond to French overtures for a postwar economic alliance, directed (Americans were quick to note) not only against the Central Powers, but also against neutrals. Defenders of the plan pointed out that Germany had long dreamed of hegemony in *Mitteleuropa,* and was laying its own plans for an economic war-after-the-war. If, as now seemed likely, a decisive Allied victory on the battlefield could not be obtained, serious thought had to be given to such measures.

The American response was twofold. In the first place, if the Allies formed a bloc, whether or not this was justified as a defensive measure, the only result would be perpetuation of the very conditions that had produced the war—imperialism, secret alliances, and naval buildup—into the indefinite future. Under those conditions American political institutions would have to be dramatically reshaped, and the nation would lose its mission, would no longer be the last, best hope of humankind. Europe's penchant for suicidal behavior would, in this analysis, finally accomplish the destruction of Western civilization.

Even before that happened, however, an Allied economic agreement was sure to injure America's postwar trade position both in Europe and elsewhere. When the Allies nonetheless met in Paris in mid-June 1916 and resolved "to conserve . . . before all others, their natural resources during the whole period of commercial, industrial, agricultural and wartime reconstruction," and produced a list of specific measures to that end, a strong reaction in Washington was inevitable.[55] America was the real target of the Paris Economic Conference (PEC) resolutions, Lansing advised the president. If implemented, they would create a critical situation for American trade. "It must be met in some practical way," Lansing warned, "and the best way to fight combination is by combination."[56]

Clearly the PEC was a product of the old diplomacy, replied the president, and he would not deign to respond by calling a conference of neutrals, as Lansing suggested he should. Restrictive economic alliances bred conflict, both internationally and intranationally. In an interview a few days after his reelection, however, the president struck a different note. Great prosperity would continue, he said, but Congress must enact measures to ensure Americans their postwar markets: "American firms must be given definite authorization to cooperate for foreign selling operations; in plain words to organize for foreign trade just as the 'rings' of England and the cartels of Germany are organized."[57]

He was no happier with this solution, nevertheless, than he had been with his justifications of the munitions trade as part of America's moral responsibility to keep open the courses of commerce. Soon, if these trends were not reversed, America would be compelled not only to "organize" for foreign trade, but (and this no doubt bothered him more than anything else) adopt such policies as natural, even salutary, to the American "way of life." A presidency begun in opposition to the New Nationalism would become its biggest advocate; a search for a way to refresh the spirit of liberalism would end by embracing social imperialism.

As British critics complained, Wilson was no longer much concerned with deciding who had started the war, and for what reasons. The conflict that began in August 1914 was over. The Great War was beginning, a war that would decide the outcome of political struggles in all countries. So, at least, thought Woodrow Wilson.

> *The war is dissolving into a stupendous revolution. A few months ago we still argued about the Bagdad corridor, strategic frontiers, colonies. Those were the stakes of a diplomat's war. The whole perspective is changed today by the revolution in Russia and the intervention of America. The scale of values is transformed for the democracies are unloosed. . . .*
>
> Walter Lippmann, 1917

Of all American policymakers, Robert Lansing was the most consistent advocate of bringing matters to a head with the Central Powers. Yet it was also Lansing who put the Paris Economic Conference into its most sophisticated Wilsonian context. It ranked as one of the Allies' "stupidest blunders," he said. "I was utterly aghast at the utter lack of appreciation of the effect of their action. . . ." Besides arousing American ire, the PEC held back the "revolution" in Germany:

> The announced post-bellum policy of the Allies . . . threw the German capitalists into the arms of the militarists. The reasoning was perfectly plain. Since the military success of the Allies meant the commercial ruin of Germany, the one hope of restoring their industries and trade was by a military victory for Germany. That was the unavoidable logic of the situation.[58]

The Allied blunder did not mean that the United States should keep out of the war. It meant, for Lansing, the opposite. Germany would fight all the harder, making it more, not less, imperative that the United States intervene. Lansing believed, erroneously, that the president was slow to grasp the overriding ideological issue at stake. Determined somehow to "stand forth as the great neutral peacemaker," the president had failed to see "the full significance of this war or the principles at issue. . . . That German imperialistic ambitions threaten free institutions everywhere apparently has not sunk very deeply into his mind. For six months I have talked about the struggle between Autocracy and Democracy, but do not see that I have made any great impression."[59]

Lansing interpreted the House missions as efforts to "compromise" with Germany, when the real object should be to prevent Franco-Russian hegemony in Europe. But the president's behavior during the 1916 election campaign was determined by his conviction that he could not yet determine the peace terms by going to war. As the campaign progressed, moreover, the president often expressed anger (in private, of course) that the Allies were exploiting his vulnerability by ever more obnoxious restrictions on neutral trade, including the notorious "blacklist" of American firms that continued to trade with the Central Powers. "Let us build a navy bigger than hers," he exclaimed to House at one point about British restrictions, "and do what we please."[60]

The very next day, September 25, 1916, Ambassador James Gerard in Berlin reported a dramatic new development. "Germany anxious to make peace," he cabled. If the United States offered its "good offices," Germany would accept in general terms, and declare itself ready to attend a peace conference.[61] Strictest secrecy must be maintained, warned Gerard. It must not get out that the idea originated in Berlin, else it would fail.

What the Germans had in mind was for Wilson to offer his services exactly as Theodore Roosevelt had during the Russo-Japanese War. Chancellor Bethmann-Hollweg was not, however, searching the horizon for a "peacemaker" as Gerard's cable suggested. Rather, he was looking for a means of satisfying world opinion that Germany had exhausted all measures short of ruthless submarine warfare. If Wilson could be persuaded to make an appeal, and if, as expected, the Allies rejected the move, it "would give us a moral justification in the eyes of the world, and in particular of the European neutrals, for withdrawing our promise to America. . . ."[62]

Wilson made no direct response. But on November 17, 1916, the Federal Reserve Board issued a statement warning American banks against "locking up funds in long-term obligations." The statement was as much political as financial: "The United States has now attained a position of wealth and of international financial power, which, in the natural course of events, it could not have reached for a generation. We must be careful not to impair this position of strength and independence."[63] The idea of restricting loans to the Allies "to bring them to their senses" delighted Wilson. "I like it," he wrote. "My only suggestion is that the statement be made a little stronger and more pointed and be made to carry rather explicit advice against these investments. . . ."[64]

In his mind, Wilson was fashioning a method to take advantage of the persistent German hints and the stocktaking advocated by the Federal Reserve Board. Convinced that whatever bid he made for peace negotiations must go beyond what House had offered on his previous missions, the president asked the colonel to write Grey promising "in the strongest terms" to support a league for peace. He was also to say that the American people had about exhausted their patience with "the intolerable conditions of neutrality." Feelings were running as strongly against Great Britain as they had against Germany, "and likely to grow still hotter against an indefinite continuation of the war. . . ." It might be well to close this letter, said Wilson, by intimating to Sir Edward that Ambassador Page's strong pro-Allied views no longer represented the dominant American opinion.[65]

But as Wilson prepared his ground, Bethmann-Hollweg ran out of time. On December 12, 1916, the German chancellor addressed the Allies through various neutrals asking for immediate agreement to a peace conference. His hand forced, Wilson forwarded the offer, along with a statement that he intended to present his own suggestions in the near future. He did so a week later, but instead of suggesting peace parleys, the president's note asked only for the belligerents to state their war aims.[66]

Britain's new prime minister, David Lloyd George, thought it would be unwise to appear recalcitrant, and urged his cabinet colleagues to return a conciliatory answer with concrete suggestions.[67] This cut against the grain. Lloyd George's coalition had been formed precisely to check the drift to "defeatism" by taking the politics out of the war effort. But the Welshman was an agile political leader, perhaps the most agile to occupy Number 10 Downing Street in this century. He could not rule out a drawn war. During the summer of 1916 his predecessor, Prime Minister Herbert Asquith, had called for a debate on war aims and Germany's future. None of the memoranda produced by that debate encouraged the belief that German power could ever be eliminated. Arthur Balfour, for example, thought Europe was likely to remain an armed camp, and that peace would depend "on defensive alliances formed by those who desire to retain their possessions against those who desire to increase them."[68]

If internal change in Germany took place, it could only come as the result of what Lloyd George liked to call a "knock-out blow." Delivering that blow would probably require American participation. Lloyd George, who stood for change at home, never lost sight of the prewar agenda. And he was most like Wilson in seeing that questions of foreign policy whether in regard to Mexico or Germany, had become wedges under domestic policy. The coalition he led had to be able to contain radical demands at home, bring victory in the war, and champion reform of the international system. War aims must include not only territorial issues, but ideological demands as well. At the initial imperial war cabinet meeting in March 1917, the new prime minister told his Dominion counterparts that "if Germany had had a democracy like France, like ourselves, or like Italy, we should not have had this trouble."[69]

He set a goal of a democratic Germany after the war—like Wilson again—as the only way to avoid future trouble, not only on the battlefield, but in politics. Take reparations as an example. If the program he imagined for the postwar era was ever to come to fruition, it would be necessary not only to see that German militarism could not rise again, but also to find revenue sources beyond the tax rolls (if he were to keep the Conservatives in tow) for long-range projects.[70] The radical program he had espoused before the war as chancellor of the exchequer and had fought for against the peers of the realm, the House of Lords, was nothing compared to what would be needed to save British society after the war. "The naked fact is that the country, the mother of free institutions," said a perhaps hyperbolic report of Lloyd George's Ministry for Reconstruction, "was four years ago on the brink of civil war. And if the Germans had not saved us the struggle would have raged not only between Catholic and Protestant Ireland but throughout G.B. between class and class."[71]

After the war the Germans were going to have to save Britain again, by supplying money and, perhaps even more important, by demonstrating that liberalism still had a future. Lloyd George's own charge to his postwar planners advised them to "be fearless."

> No such opportunity had ever been given to any nation before— not even by the French Revolution.
> The nation now was in a moulten condition: it was malleable now, and would continue to be so for a short time after the war, but not for long.[72]

Because he started from many of the same premises as Wilson, his attitude toward the peace initiative has to be looked at in the light of what he hoped to accomplish before the "moulten condition" resolidified. A drawn war—the likely result of any Wilsonian intervention as mediator instead of ally—would have serious repercussions. It would be hard to imagine how the British government could afford to maintain a huge postwar military budget and alliance system and still retain the energy or even the inclination to pursue seriously a "new order" at home. Those were conditions either for national decline or an explosion of radicalism.

The primary task for the Allies, Lloyd George explained, became to make Woodrow Wilson understand that "what could be done after the peace must in no small measure depend on what the peace itself had accomplished."[73] In this analysis, furthermore, "self-determination" took on a special meaning. The phrase was already understood in Allied circles as a code for the breakup of the Austro-Hungarian empire. In Lloyd George's usage it also meant a strategy for placing a check on German expansionist tendencies, both strategically and ideologically. Ideologically, it had been thought from the beginning of the war that Berlin could not be brought to accept internal change until the military party had been completely discredited. That had to be accomplished on the battlefield. Guarantees of the independence of small nations, upheld by some form of international sanction, would thwart German backsliding strategically, while the existence of democratic governments in those nations would provide a constant controlled environment that would exert a healthy influence on Germany's internal politics.[74]

At the end of January 1917, meanwhile, Wilson delivered his "Peace without Victory" speech. He had given up the idea that the Allied or Central governments would respond to his latest appeal. His words were meant, the president wrote privately, for "neither the Senate nor foreign governments . . . [but] directed to the peoples of the countries now at war."[75] Terms imposed on a loser, Wilson had declared, would rest "only as upon quicksand." "I am in effect speaking for liberals and friends of humanity in every nation and of every programme of liberty." Such a statement was nothing if not an affirmation of the need for internal change in *both* alliances.

If America went to war, in other words, it would impose internal change on Germany by military means, and on the Allies by mobilizing a liberal army inside all countries.[76] This final pronouncement of American intentions came none too soon. Since the *Lusitania* crisis in May 1915 Wilson had been haunted by the thought that he might have to go to war "in anger," without stipulating his war aims. Colonel House, who had encouraged the president to think of playing the mediator's role, had, in frustration, twice recommended that Wilson try to put the submarine question into his own framework. Wilson had not been ready.

On January 31, 1917, Berlin ordered a resumption of unrestricted submarine warfare, insisting that Wilson had not been able to gain any concessions in Allied blockade policy and that the "*Sussex* pledge" (by which Germany agreed to conduct submarine warfare according to the old rules of sea warfare) was no longer valid. Even had Wilson been able to obtain the Allied concessions, however, it is clear that the Germans had no intention of losing the war without having exploited the one major advantage they had to the fullest. Ironically, the president's success in extracting the *Sussex* pledge gave German military advisers an argument not to accept peace negotiations until a final underwater offensive had been tried.[77]

Having vowed to hold Germany "strictly accountable" in such an instance, whether it came at a convenient time or not, Wilson ordered diplomatic relations with Berlin broken on February 3, 1917. Ambassador Spring-Rice had anticipated this situation, and predicted the president would soon be face to face with a "most disastrous" condition that would "bring home to the farmers and manufacturers the realities of war."[78] Secretary Lansing was jubilant, assuming an early decision for war. The Allies had to win because democracies were never aggressive or unjust, he told Wilson, and because this was the only way the small countries could be guaranteed their freedom. But Wilson responded to these effusions with a surprisingly cool appraisal, concluding with a comment that he was neither sure that democracies were always unaggressive, nor that it would not be better if the war did end in a draw.[79]

On February 8, 1917, Wilson instructed Ambassador Page to sound out British leaders on the possibility of assuring Vienna that it was not intended that the Austro-Hungarian Empire be dismembered. Austria intensely desired peace, he said, and if the United States did enter the war, it might be useful to avoid a break with Vienna. America could fight and still keep open a diplomatic channel. And if the United States did not go to war, the Allied assurances would permit him "in a very short time" to secure Berlin's acceptance of peace terms in accord with those stated in his recent address to the Senate. Since these instructions went out over Lansing's signature, they were put in the third person:

> The present enthusiastic support which the people of the United States are giving his foreign policy is being given it is very evident because they expect him to use the force and influence of the United States, if he must use force, not to prolong the war, but to insist upon the rights of his own and other peoples which he regards and they regard as the bases and the only bases of peace.[80]

Wilson's "Austrian channel" was nothing less than an attempt to win a decisive political victory over the Entente before he went to war. For this reason he was even willing to set aside his enthusiasm for national self-determination so as to offer Vienna an attractive reason for listening to a new voice that promised redemption.

David Lloyd George was quick to see that the president must not be allowed to have his way, but neither must it appear that to refuse him meant to reject liberal opinion. The prime minister needed the latter force for his own postwar program. He could not openly engage the president in a contest for leadership of the left. Instead, he must bend every effort to convince Wilson that they could work together for the same goals. Hence his reply that Austria did indeed seem to want peace; unfortunately, however, that country was now merely a "convenient fiction," as the Germans even commanded its army. "We have no policy of dismemberment," he continued, but he would have to attend to the opinions of Britain's allies—the Rumanians, the Slavs, the Serbs, and the Italians. "We must look at the war as a whole. . . ."

He had crossed treacherous territory, but now the prime minister was on safe ground. The United States, he hoped, would come into the war. "We want him [Wilson] to come into the war not so much for help with the war as for help with the peace. . . . I mean that he himself must be there in person. If he sits in the conference that makes peace he will exert the greatest influence that any man has ever exerted in expressing the moral value of free government." The belligerents had suffered so badly that their judgment might be impaired. "Those that win will want some concrete gain, old wrongs righted, or boundaries changed." Even Britain will be prevented from returning the German colonies because of South African and Australian security needs. "Nobody therefore can have so commanding a voice as the President. Convey to him this deep conviction of mine."[81]

Colonel House's best efforts paled beside this skillful cajolery. Unlike

House, moreover, or even Sir Edward Grey, the prime minister spoke with the authority of an equal. And another imperative was making itself felt. No more lives had been lost, but German submarine warfare was exacting a toll on the nation's foreign trade. Spring-Rice observed

> congestion in the ports, widespread discomfort and even misery on the coast and inland, even bread riots and a coal famine. The situation is much that of a soda water bottle with the wires cut but the cork unexploded.[82]

His counterpart, Walter Hines Page, reported dark economic news from the other side of the Atlantic. Britain would soon be unable to pay for American goods, because unable to ship gold through the submarine-infested waters. Trade would soon fall to its lowest possible level. "This will, of course, cause a panic in the United States." He elaborated:

> Perhaps our going to war is the only way in which our present prominent trade position can be maintained and a panic averted. The submarine has added the last item to the danger of a financial world crash. During a period of uncertainty about our being drawn into the war, no more considerable credit can be privately placed in the United States, and a collapse may come in the meantime.[83]

At the height of all this uncertainty came the startling news from Petrograd: the tsar had been overthrown! Now it was a "pure" war, democracy against reactionary autocracy.

Lansing hoped the Russian Revolution would pop the cork, but he used a different image. If the president asked Congress for a declaration of war, he wrote House, the United Stated could demonstrate support for Russian liberals—and might even precipitate a revolution in Germany. "If you agree with me that we should act now, will you not please put your shoulder to the wheel?"[84]

Lloyd George, meanwhile, anticipated the impact the revolution would have on Wilson's decision for war. The democratization of Europe was the only sure guarantee of peace, he told the imperial war cabinet. It had come nearer in the last few days. "In fact, if there is wisdom amongst the democratic rulers of Russia, not merely will Russia become a great democratic state but Germany must follow her example inevitably. . . ."[85]

Considered from an ideological perspective, the March Revolution in Russia vindicated Wilson's previous refusals to be drawn into war in simple anger over submarine warfare, and in support of the old order. From that same perspective, how could he now stand by and see the Russian Revolution destroyed by German militarism? Truth was, he might not have a choice anyway. The president had always had difficulty justifying the war trade, even as he celebrated American prosperity. No one was more aware of the economic forces at work than Woodrow Wilson. By April 1917, then, to procrastinate futher was to risk being overwhelmed by circumstances, and would put the future of liberalism at risk. "It is a fearful thing to lead this great peaceful people into war," the president said in his war message on April 2, 1917, "into the most terrible and disastrous of all wars, civilization itself seeming to be in the balance . . ."

And better than most, both Wilson and Lloyd George knew that the balance would not, finally, be decided on the battlefield.

CHAPTER SIX

The Russian Glacier

The last and highest triumph of history would . . . be
the bringing of Russia into the Atlantic combine, and
the just and fair allotment of the whole world among
the regulated activities of the universe.

Henry Adams,
The Education of Henry Adams, 1907

"It is no doubt true as Mr. House told me in so many words that but for
Russian Revolution and famous German telegram to Mexico, President
would have found it very difficult to take decisive step. . . ."[1] Nothing in
the years since Foreign Secretary Arthur Balfour cabled these words back
to London in 1917 has diminished the importance of the Russian Revolution or the Zimmerman telegram as crucial precipitating causes of America's entrance into the Great War, or of ideological perceptions as a long-
term motivating force in Wilson's readiness to take a "decisive step" to set
affairs right in the Old World.

The confluence of dramatic events in the spring of 1917 was noted
and remarked upon everywhere, in the press and in private letters. The
belief that Wilson could seize hold of history as it passed through the
trenches, and redirect its course after the war, was very nearly universal.
Even before the March Revolution, Ambassador David Francis in Petrograd added his voice to those calling for all-out participation to transform
the war into a crusade. War with Germany was unavoidable, he wrote the
president on February 22, 1917. Not only would the Germans threaten
the Monroe Doctrine if they were victorious, but if the Allies won "without the assistance of the United States England would attempt to domi-

nate the commercial world and would come near doing so for a generation or perhaps for a century."[2]

Francis had had his troubles since his appointment in 1916, mostly in
regard to what he believed was a concerted effort by the Allies (especially
England) to secure a privileged place in Russia's postwar economic development. They aimed at nothing less, he thought, than replacing Germany
as Russia's biggest trade partner and mentor.[3] British policymakers, it was
true, did not look upon American commercial advances during the war
with a wholly good-natured smile at Uncle Sam's progress and cleverness.
But worry about the Russian trade was only one of their concerns;
another was trying to figure out what Woodrow Wilson meant to do about
the revolution.

> *Russia was known by those who knew it best to have
> been always in fact democratic at heart. . . .*
>
> Woodrow Wilson, April 2, 1917

The American president's discovery of the democratic spirit in Russia was
a disturbing new element for British policymakers, however much they
too wanted to enlist the new Provisional Government in the war effort.
Sweeping pronouncements about Russia's national character did little to
improve the immediate military situation on the eastern front, and they
stimulated what was developing into a very serious division at home.
Wilson's championing of the revolutionary cause in Russia made life more
difficult for David Lloyd George, until he himself could get a proper grip
on the situation.

It was always best, thought the British, to be wary about saying too
much about Russia. In the four years between 1909 and 1913, Tsar Nicholas II had spent three billion rubles on his army and another billion on
the navy. The army was built up to 114 divisions, as compared to Germany's 96, and it boasted 6,720 mobile guns.[3] Fear of Russia's ambitions
ran deep in England, where memories of the "Eastern question" lingered
even into the final days of the prewar crisis. "We do not aim at Constantinople," Nicholas told the French ambassador early in 1914, "but we need
the guarantee that the Straits will not be closed to us." Then he made a
prediction. "Our commerce will develop with the exploitation—thanks to
railways—of Russia's resources and with the increase of our population
which in thirty years will exceed three hundred millions."[4]

Better not give the tsar too much to count on in the west, thought Sir

Edward Grey, who had refused to give a formal commitment to the Franco-Russian alliance, for which he was later criticized by those who had temporarily forgotten about the Russian danger. As Europe trembled on the edge of war, Grey had scanned the documents for some hint of a way out or, if that failed, of confining the war geographically. Several members of the Asquith cabinet, perhaps as many as three-fourths, were determined not to be drawn into a "European" quarrel, which was a euphemism for a German-Russian showdown. Their last hope was that "if Germany struck at Russia, it ought to be possible for France and Germany to neutralize each other without fighting."[5]

From London's vantage point, much of the secret diplomacy of the Great War was aimed at putting limits on the demands of its allies. It could hardly have been otherwise, since Germany was not the only envious power, nor was the battlefield struggle the only conflict that raged between 1914 and 1918. One strategy was to concede what could not be defended. Hence on November 13, 1914, King George V remarked casually to the Russian ambassador that his cousin Nicholas should have his most sought-after prize. "As to Constantinople," said George, "it is clear it must be yours."[6] But that was all. Negotiations over Constantinople continued for months, with Sir Edward Grey instructing Ambassador Sir George Buchanan not to concede anything that would lessen British opportunities in southeastern Europe or increase the Russian presence in Asia Minor. At the conclusion of these negotiations, Sir George proposed a toast to the "two most powerful Empires in the world," who would surely undertake after the war to assure the world's peace. Nicholas "cordially agreed."[7]

Of all the powers that went to war in August 1914, Russia faced the most severe domestic crisis, and was the least able to cope with the new burden on its economy. Half-developed out of feudalism, plagued by inefficient farming and overcrowded cities at one and the same time, Russia was also the most inclined to resolve its problems by annexationist diversions. "On the very eve of the war," V. I. Lenin, leader of the Bolshevik faction of the Russian socialist movement, would write, "the President of the French Republic, Poincaré, while visiting Nicholas II, was able to see with his own eyes barricades in the streets of St. Petersburg constructed by the hands of the Russian workers."[8]

Before a year was out the Russians had suffered losses of two million, half as casualties, half as prisoners of war. From curbing Russian ambitions, the focus shifted to keeping Russia in the war. On August 19, 1915, Buchanan filed a very gloomy report: "Situation . . . is very serious, and what preoccupies me most is the idea that is gradually permeating [the] populace that Russia is being deserted by the Allies."[9] Lenin's path to power was being made easier, though without his knowledge.

No longer about two great empires dividing the world, Buchanan's audiences with the tsar now took on a very different aspect. On November 5, 1915, the British ambassador said that what he had to impart to Nicholas was of a special nature, so special that no one else should be informed even that the conversation had taken place. Criticisms that had been made of the Russian bureaucracy, began Sir George, were only "too well founded." "Commencing with the munitions question," he went on, "I said that stories brought back by wounded soldiers of disasters and colossal losses caused by lack of munitions that was due to incompetency and corruption of officials had produced widespread discontent." Nicholas admitted there was some truth in the charges, but he remained confident the nation would hold together, and "he had no fear of internal troubles."

Very well, replied Sir George, but "what might happen when the war was over. I had heard very out-spoken language as to the impossibility of allowing a state of things to continue which had brought Russia to the verge of disaster." Did the tsar recognize the peril to the throne? Would he continue to defend a system that had proven its inability to serve Russian needs, no matter the result? Implied rather than stated, such questions hung in the air as Sir George concluded his warning: "If . . . Russia was rent by internal collapse, Germany would seize the opportunity to regain her lost influence in Russia and would endeavor as in the past to sow discord between us by preaching Autocracy at Petrograd and Democracy in London."[10]

British observers thus saw a three-pronged danger developing in Russia. There was still concern about the tsar's long-range ambitions and his use of foreign expansion to divert domestic discontent. There was fear about a continuation of what had proven to be a disastrously ineffective state organization. And there was a premonition of what would happen if that system cracked under the war pressures. But American observers, not yet in the war, were much less cognizant of the complexities of the Russian situation.

Russian-American relations had gone steadily downhill since the turn of the century. St. Petersburg's cool response to John Hay's Open Door note in 1899, its behavior up to the outbreak of the Russo-Japanese War and after in the Far East, and the officially sanctioned anti-Semitism of Nicholas's government all combined to make it difficult for the Wilsonians to give their whole-hearted support to the Allied cause. Colonel House, for example, predicted that an Allied victory meant Russian hegemony on the continent.[11]

American diplomats on the spot in the Russian capital, on the other hand, had tried to spark interest in opening up commercial relations. And as the war went on, they began to notice more response in Washington.[12] Then in early 1916 came the appointment of David R. Francis as ambassador. The former Missouri governor and Democratic stalwart had been renowned in recent years for a strong belief that there was nothing wrong with the American economy that more foreign trade would not cure. "He is a good soul," quipped a sometime diplomat now associated with bankers interested in getting into Russia, "of the stuffed-shirt variety, but he has no more idea of diplomacy than a cow has about running a double six."[13] No doubt Francis was out of his depth in Russia; no doubt, also, over the next several years practically everyone was.

Yet he was no ignoramus. Germany had possessed, and exercised without scruple, he wrote to Colonel House, an overbearing influence in Russia. "The effect of this war upon Russia, while very costly in blood and treasure, will be greatly beneficial in broadening and even liberalizing the views of her people," he went on. Great Britain aspired to succeed Germany and he thought he saw evidence aplenty of these schemes even before he left New York.[14] Upon his arrival in Russia, the ambassador was chagrined to learn just how far advanced the nefarious plans of the Allies really were. It was even worse than he thought. Russian officials warned that they could not sign any commercial treaties until the completion of the work of the Allied Paris Economic Conference. The only way of accounting for this standoffish attitude, Francis believed, "was the influence of England which was desirous that all foreign relations of a commercial or financial character had by Russia should be through London."[15]

Even if Francis's predicted billion-dollar market in postwar Russia never materialized, the ambassador had put his finger on one of Wilson's major concerns: that the postwar era produce something more, much more, than a mere realignment of the old order. Francis was appalled by British success in preventing Russia from obtaining its "independence" economically. Perhaps the only way to break this tightening grip would be to refuse London further loans to carry on the war. "I am almost to the point of advocating such a course. . . ."[16]

While it would be difficult indeed to draw any direct connection between Francis's disgust and the president's actions in late 1916 and on down to the "Peace without Victory" speech in January 1917, the ambassador's analysis closely suited Wilson's own conclusions. On one point, Lloyd George would have agreed with Francis. The Allies had not served Russia as well as they might, and were going to pay a terrible price for their lack of concern. First as minister for munitions, and then as prime minister, David Lloyd George doubted that everything that should have been done had in fact been done to provide Russia with what was needed to sustain the eastern front, or that much effort had gone into coordinating Allied strategy so as to best aid Russia's military efforts. Whatever the future held for Russia, he insisted, more needed to be done now. A conference ought to be held inside Russia as soon as possible. The Americans were watching, said Lloyd George, and if they thought the Allies were a lost cause because of Russia's imminent collapse, that could be disastrous. Some plain words needed to be spoken all around.[17]

A conference was held; words were spoken. And nothing changed. Lloyd George's *War Memoirs* evoke the apprehension many felt, and the growing fatalism about Russia:

> The subterranean fires in Russia had already begun to break through the crust. News came of the assassination of Rasputin— the Czar's protégé and the Czarina's friend—by a cabal of young aristocrats. The anger of the Court found vent in a shifting of Ministers who had failed to protect the favorite. The rumbling underneath became louder, and the seething and spluttering of steam and boiling mud became everywhere more apparent and disquieting.[18]

Aware now of the impending eruption, Allied diplomats seemed linked in a pact to pretend—even to themselves—that it was not so. Buchanan went on pressing Nicholas to start over, to change Russia from above before it was too late. "Your Majesty, if I may be permitted to say so," began Sir George on one occasion in January 1917, "has but one safe course open to you—namely to break down the barrier that separates you from your people and to regain their confidence."

The reply came from a long-dead age, from Louis XVI's Versailles: "Do you mean that I am to regain the confidence of my people or that they are to regain *my* confidence." Buchanan would not be turned aside by a display of ancient hauteur. "You have, sir, come to the parting of the ways," he warned, "and you have now to choose between the two paths. The one will lead you to victory and a glorious peace—the other to revolution and disaster."[19]

Nicholas was right in one regard, however: the feudal chrysalis that had become in his day a sarcophagus could not be shattered, the new Russia not released, by outside diplomatic pressure. In truth, as well, Buchanan was frightened by what he saw. On the very day the March Revolution began, London received this word from its representative: "Excitement will probably quieten down for the present if there is no active provocation to-day."[20] He did not want to see what was so plainly before his eyes. In the aftermath of the successful invasion of the Winter Palace on March 12, 1917, he sent a better piece of political prophecy home: "Parties of the Duma and of Social Revolution though not yet in open opposition are likely to become so very shortly. The former is for war and if it prevails quickly will render Russia stronger than before. The latter is for peace at any price and its advent to power will mean disaster from military point of view." He erred only in thinking that there was a military situation that could be rendered anything but worse.[21]

He also thought that London could make its influence felt in determining the outcome of the struggle for control. It could do so by having labor leaders send expressions of support to the Duma and the war party. The telegram should say that every day's work lost means disaster to their brothers in the trenches, and refer, in closing, to the unity of all classes in England until victory was achieved.[22] The Foreign Office acted quickly, even before signers could be found for "labor's message" to the Duma. The line taken was that Nicholas II had suffered this end because he was unable to overcome the pro-German elements lurking around him. Perhaps that would not go down completely, even in the Duma, but at least it established a connection between reaction and German despotism, and the impossibility of eliminating the former short of military victory. Europe's fate was said to rest with the Russians, for only if the kaiser was also overthrown could the way "be opened for free and peaceful development of European nations." Any slackening of the war effort, any distraction, "means disaster to comrades in trenches and to our common hopes of social regeneration."[23]

So, according to Foreign Office drafters, should British labor speak to revolutionary Russia. At the same time, Buchanan was instructed to consult with his French colleague: "We gather from your telegram that there is no chance of any reversion to the regime which has just fallen, but that the dangers to be faced lie in the direction of socialism and anarchy."[24] An appeal to socialists to keep Russia in the war was a gamble against the odds. Balfour did not want to chance it if there was some other way. Writing to Buchanan privately, the foreign secretary urged him to persuade Nicholas that it would be a "national misfortune" for him to refuse to permit his ill son to succeed him. "I greatly fear that if a Republic be established in the country and the army . . . broken up into Legitimists and Republicans, moderate opinion will be divided and helpless, the Extremists will get hold of the machine, sooner or later there will be a violent reaction in the direction of Autocracy, and in the meanwhile a disgraceful peace will be patched up with Germany."[25]

Provisional Government leaders were also aware of the peril of revolution disintegrating into civil war. Russia was not a republic, Buchanan was told. Its future would be decided by a constituent assembly. "I am most anxious that Government should postpone the holding of elections" for that assembly, Buchanan advised London, "until after the war, not only for military reasons but because I hope by then there will be more chance of return to some form of monarchical Government which is in my opinion the only one possible to hold this vast Empire together. The country is not ripe for a Republic and I doubt very much whether it would be acceptable to the majority of the nation."[26]

"One reason," he continued, "why I advocated in conversation with [Provisional Government foreign secretary Paul] Miliukov for retention of the Grand Duke Nicholas as Commander-in-Chief is that if he wins the confidence of the army and can keep it well in hand there will be a certain chance of the Grand Duke Michael [Nicholas's brother] or some other Grand Duke being eventually declared Emperor with powers clearly defined within the limits of really liberal constitution." Since no other member of the royal family had a son, there was no reason why the succession would not then pass back to the tsarevitch.[27]

The task of welcoming the Russian Revolution and somehow absorbing it into the war effort and war aims of the Allies fell to Andrew Bonar Law, chancellor of the exchequer and Conservative member of the coalition war cabinet. Even when introducing a government resolution of "heartiest congratulations," Bonar Law found himself unable to conceal his fears. Events in Russia should be compared, he said, with the first days of the French Revolution: "We recall with what a glow of hope the fall of the Bastille was received by liberal-minded men throughout the world. . . . We recall, too, how quickly and how sadly that bright dawn was overcast."

This curious advocacy was followed by an even more perplexing statement: "I hope I may be permitted to express a feeling which I believe will be shared by the vast majority of the Members of this House, and which I, at least, hold strongly, a feeling of compassion for the late Czar . . . our loyal Ally, and who had laid upon him by his birth a burden which has proved too heavy for him." When at last Law came to the congratulatory purpose of the resolution, it sounded like an afterthought.[28]

His remarks did not go unchallenged. From the Labour benches came this speech by Arthur Ponsonby:

I trust they [Russia's new leaders] will be allowed to pursue their great and noble work without discord in their own country, and without interference from outside. Let us remember that our Russian Allies have achieved a far greater victory than the conquest of Constantinople [An Hon. Member: "Stop your whining!"]—or any other territory.[29]

Laden with ideological messages, this exchange, which took place well before it was generally feared that Russia would leave the war, puts the Russian Revolution within the realm of political strategy as well as military consideration. It was now important to keep the eastern front active not only to preserve Russian stability, but to maintain Britain's domestic coalition.

How different in tone were Woodrow Wilson's statements about Russia from Bonar Law's cramped efforts! And how impossible to keep them from becoming an issue in British politics. The president spoke from a privileged position: he had never been allied with the tsar, and in fact he would never be truly allied to anyone in the war. By contrast, whichever way Britain's war cabinet responded to events in Russia, its path was fraught with uncertainties about the future, and encumbered with the dead weight of past obligations.

The tenuous negotiations over the possibility of allowing Tsar Nicholas to come to England illustrate the point. On March 19, 1917, two cables were sent from London to Petrograd, one from George V expressing condolences to his cousin and assuring him of his continuing friendship, and the other instructing Buchanan to warn the Provisional Government that any violence done to the tsar or his family would have a "most deplorable" effect on British public opinion.[30]

Foreign Secretary Miliukov declined to transmit the king's message out of fear that it might be "misinterpreted," and used as an excuse by radicals for detaining the former ruler. Miliukov then raised the possibility of Nicholas being allowed to go to England. Miliukov was, in fact, very anxious for an invitation, and wished it to state that the tsar and his family would be expected to stay there for "the remainder of the war."[31] Miliukov, like Buchanan, still hoped for a constitutional monarchy. If the British government took in the tsar, perhaps criticism of the Russian royal family would abate. Perhaps, even, the tsar would be reeducated so that when the Romanovs returned, Nicholas or, more likely, his successor could take up duties similar to those of British monarchs.

The war cabinet showed little inclination to respond positively to these overtures. In fact, Buchanan was now instructed to take care not to "give umbrage to the new Government" by any dealings with the imperial family, "as it is most important that you should retain your authority with all parties especially with the Statesmen whom we desire to keep in power." Instead of England had the tsar thought of either Denmark or Switzerland?[32]

Years later Lloyd George would insist that a favorable response had been sent to Petrograd. In fact, however, it was only after Miliukov pressed the issue a second time that it was decided to send such an invitation. It was better, the war cabinet concluded, to have Nicholas in England than to allow him to become a pawn in the hands of disaffected Russian generals who might try to put him at the head of a counterrevolutionary movement.[33]

Buchanan's conversations in Petrograd convinced him that the Provisional Government was having its own second thoughts and now feared it could not allow Nicholas to leave Russia. Lloyd George also asserted in his *War Memoirs* that despite rising agitation against it in Britain, the invitation was never withdrawn.[34] This was simply not the case. As early as March 30, King George had expressed doubts about permitting his cousin to come to England. Balfour replied to George's secretary that the invitation could hardly be retracted, but the king was truly alarmed. "His Majesty receives letters from people in all classes of life," said the palace, "known or unknown to him, saying how much the matter is being discussed, not only in clubs, but by working men, and the Labour Members in the House of Commons are expressing adverse opinions to the proposal."[35]

The king had his way. On April 13, 1917, the war cabinet instructed Balfour to tell Buchanan that a considerable antimonarchical movement was developing, "including personal attacks upon the King." If Nicholas landed in England, the movement might grow. And with the tsar seated in some royal residence, moreover, it might be difficult to have dealings with the new Russian government. It would be better for Nicholas to find a place in republican France, where the monarchy issue would not arise.[36]

Buchanan was to say nothing, however, unless the Russians again raised the issue. The episode came to an end when, according to Alexander Kerensky's recollections, Sir George came to him with tears in his eyes to deliver a verbal message that Nicholas would not be welcome. Nothing was put in writing. Buchanan thus managed to obey Balfour, yet fulfill an obligation to his hosts. The king become a pawn, that was the meaning of Buchanan's visit to Kerensky, and the Russian Revolution at the center of strategy on political chessboards everywhere.[37]

> *The Socialists would prefer to run a class war rather than the national war. . . .*
>
> Sir George Buchanan, July 1917

What Buchanan asserted applied to Great Britain as much as to Russia, and overcoming the agitation for peace meant getting a handle on political situations in both countries. At least that was the war cabinet view. Meanwhile, Ambassador Francis was ecstatic. "This revolution," he wrote Wilson, "is the practical realization of that principle of government which we have championed and advocated." Formal diplomatic recognition should be extended by America, a welcoming hand to the world's newest liberal revolution from the oldest. If Washington was first, recognition would have a "stupendous moral effect."[38]

Colonel House had no doubts at all. "You will come out of this war as its central figure," he assured the president, "and largely because you stand easily to the fore as the great liberal of modern times. Your first inaugural address, your Mobile speech, and similar utterances have accelerated democracy throughout the world, and I am not too sure that the present outcome [in Russia] is not due largely to your influence."[39]

Russia would need aid—psychological as well as economic—that was simply beyond the capacity of the Allies to give. "Financial aid now from America would be [the] master stroke," concluded Francis.[40] Laden with riches, Russia's fields and forests would permit the rooting of democratic institutions and liberal values, as had once happened in America when the oppressive British colonial regime had come to an end, Francis insisted. The Great War had proved to be Russia's War of Independence.[41]

Recognition was granted soon enough, but the ambassador thought Washington's hesitation to do more inexplicable. A credit was not established until May 1917, and then only for $100 million, barely a fifth of what had been asked. Even this amount was hedged with warnings that no further aid would be forthcoming if Russia should sign a separate peace with Germany.[42]

Washington's priorities had gone awry, Francis thought. "Time is precious," he cabled. The socialistic elements, organized into councils, or soviets, "composed of workingmen and soldiers . . . are advocating abolition of classes and the right of soldiers to disobey their officers."[43] The Petrograd Soviet had done more than that, however. It had passed resolutions of a Wilsonian nature renouncing all annexations and pledging the new Russia to the "establishment of stable peace on the basis of the self-determination of peoples." It had also resolved that the Allies, too, must "renounce their programs of conquest" and, having thus purged themselves, follow Russia's lead in proposing peace to the Central Powers on that basis. These resolutions were intended to bring immediate pressure on the Provisional Government's Duma, but in the confused state of dual authority that prevailed inside Russia over the summer of 1917 they took on at least semiofficial status.[44]

Wilson faced his own image in the Russian mirror, however distorted, and felt as if some alien force had captured his spirit. The president had not the slightest intention of relinquishing control of the peace issue to the Petrograd Soviet, or of risking a German takeover under the guise of a socialist peace. Neither could he turn off the American mobilization effort, short of a decisive German defeat. Wilson had delayed going to war, waiting for the right issue to justify the sacrifice. Now it was unthinkable not to fight, even if the Russian Revolution must be protected against itself.

Echoes from Mexico could be heard here, the same voices that had told Wilson that he must intervene at Veracruz, that he must isolate the Mexican Revolution from European influences. To the degree that the Constitutionalists had succeeded, Wilson thus claimed credit; and to the degree that the Zimmerman telegram evidenced the continuing menace, the president could insist that Russia needed guidance. Whatever validity there was to this Wilsonian syllogism, it perched on the edge of a slippery slope. One slight shove, as Wilson himself knew, and everything would be lost.

Alexander Kerensky, minister of justice in the Provisional Government, thought the radical peace program had much to recommend it. Russia had brought a new force into being, he told Sir George Buchanan on April 8, 1917, which, "by reacting on the internal situation in Germany, might bring about a durable peace." Only the Russian military cared about carrying the flag to Constantinople any more. The rest of the nation desired peace, and welcomed this "new force" as the way to get it.[45]

British and French policymakers were deeply concerned, and with good reason, about the shakiness of moderate opinion in Russia. The Western Allies thought America should send someone who could speak with authority about the president's view that the war must be won on the battlefield if democracy was to be given a chance on a worldwide basis.[46] Ambassador Spring-Rice, meanwhile, told Secretary Lansing that the American Jewish community should be "warned" that if the revolution resulted in a Russian defeat or withdrawal, "Jews will be held mainly responsible."[47]

Lansing took this admonition into account, along with a cable from Ambassador Francis expressing renewed concern about agitation, as he composed a memorandum for Wilson. Something must be done, he wrote, to prevent the Russian "socialist element" from destroying the coherence of the war effort. As the president was already aware, German socialists were all too eager to make contact with their Russian counterparts to lay plans for a separate peace. A commission should be sent at once to counteract these machinations.[48]

The really important thing, Wilson replied, was that those who were sent should be men with the large view, enthusiastic for the success of the revolution, and men who looked the part they were to play.[49] Easier said, it turned out, than done. The president had considerable difficulty in deciding who did and who did not meet the criteria. Samuel Gompers, it appeared, did not. His antisocialist views were well known and "would hardly be influential in the present ruling circles of labor at Petrograd." The problem was to find "a real representative" of American labor who was nevertheless not an antiwar socialist.[50]

The quest for a man to head the commission produced an uproar in liberal circles when it was announced that former secretary of state Elihu Root had been named. Rabbi Stephen Wise, for example, protested that Root stood out in America "as the most eminent and powerful representative of those theories of government and political life to which you [Wilson] as the leader of the American democracy are opposed." Wilson's enigmatic response to such criticism was that he had satisfied himself that Root would be an "admirable choice"—without specifying why.[51]

The reasons for Root's selection may be inferred, at least in part, from Wilson's interest in the views of William English Walling, a prowar socialist who provided him with a rationale for dealing with criticism from the "antiwar left." The Russian working class, said Walling, was in danger of being taken in by the slogan "No annexations, no indemnities." That sincere German socialists had made this Wilsonian prescription their own, or that misguided Americans also supported the idea of immediate peace, made no difference. "Both the German and Russian Socialists mean that not only Germany, but also Austria, Bulgaria and Turkey are to keep absolutely every one of the conquests they had made previously to the present war—leaving the French, Polish, Ruthenian, Rumanian, Italian, Armenian and Syrian populations, now under the Central Empires, in the same position as before," Walling explained.[52]

Walling thus drew a sharp distinction between liberal peace aims, defined primarily by national self-determination, and what he argued were now the aims of socialists on both sides of the war. This made sense to Wilson, and it satisfied his conscience. The socialists wanted an immediate peace so that they could continue the class war; in this way they were no better than the old generation of statesmen who wanted to continue the war-after-the-war according to the schemes of German hegemony or the resolutions of the Paris Economic Conference. When the Bolsheviks came to power, therefore, it was all the more easy for Wilson to conclude that the Russians sought only to make national class wars into a world struggle.

Walling's condemnation of socialist war aims developed by clever men to take advantage of the appalling misery and destruction of the war helps to explain why Wilson was anxious to keep radicals off any mission to Russia, although the choice of Root still seems an odd one even by the president's own criteria. The president also agreed with Walling that Americans should shun, if necessary be prohibited from taking part in, the "so called 'international' Socialist conference at Stockholm now being engineered by Berlin." Secretary Lansing had also alerted the White

House to expect German peace moves, designed, he insisted, only to influence Russian politics. "I am convinced that the sentiment for democracy in Germany is entirely under the control of the Government, which will take every means to give it the appearance of genuineness and the movement an appearance of irresistible popular pressure," he reported.[53]

And from David Francis came confirmation of a sort for both Walling's and Lansing's analyses. The Provisional Government was having a hard time with the Petrograd Soviet, said the ambassador, because the latter placed a "wrong construction" on the president's recent statements about war aims, insisting they meant that Russia's previous arrangements with the Allies were now all invalid. Lansing took the argument a step further: Russia's radical socialists, no doubt under German influence, were using Wilson's words to force the Provisional Government into declarations that would remove the "chief incentive to Russian offensive operations, namely control of the Dardanelles and possession of Constantinople." An adroit scheme it was, concluded Lansing, to take advantage of sentiment for a separate peace.[54]

To remove "any misinterpretations or misunderstandings," Wilson sent a public message to the Provisional Government on May 22, 1917:

> The ruling classes in Germany have begun of late to profess a . . . liberality and justice of purpose, but only to preserve the power they have set up in Germany and the selfish advantages which they have wrongly gained for themselves and their private projects of power all the way from Berlin to Bagdad and beyond. Government after government has by their influence, without open conquest of its territory, been linked together in a net of intrigue directed against nothing less than the peace and liberty of the world. The meshes of that intrigue must be broken, but cannot unless wrongs already done are undone; and adequate measures must be taken to prevent it from ever again being rewoven or repaired.[55]

Wilson's message was admirably designed to take advantage of the liberal and radical interpretations of the war's origins. He hoped to transform that interpretative framework into a compelling reason to seek full military victory. Territorial imperialism had reached around the earth. To undo its "meshes" required more than military victory, but victory was a first prerequisite.

Such reasoning came very close, however (as in Lansing's concern about not depriving the Provisional Government of its "chief incentive" to fight on), to saying that liberal ideology protected military conquest from being a sin. If Wilson felt uneasy with the new turn he had made, he could reread a letter of encouragement he had from Ambassador Walter Hines Page assuring him that nothing could slow the momentum toward a democratic victory. Recently George V had told one of his admirals, reported Page, that he knew he would not die on the throne—"there's too much democracy in the air."[56]

The king's jitters were of little importance compared to the fright his ministers felt about an international socialist conclave scheduled to meet in Stockholm, Sweden. British ambassador Esme Howard had reported that extreme socialists from Germany and Russia were determined to meet in that city to lay plans for forcing an early end to the fighting. A Russian socialist, Lenin, who had been permitted to pass through Germany on his way home from exile in Switzerland, had spent a day in Stockholm en route conferring with radical colleagues from other countries. Afterwards he had vowed to return within a fortnight at the head of a Russian peace delegation. If the Western powers resisted demands for universal peace, this Lenin had said, then Russia would go its way alone.

Lenin's feelings about England, added Howard, were especially bitter, as he felt that His Majesty's Government had done what it could to prevent him from returning to Russia. "I hear . . . that Lenin is a most dangerous man and good organizer and that he is likely to have a considerable backing in Petrograd. He is particularly anti-British and mixed up with Indian revolutionaries. . . . Everything possible should be done to check his activities in Russia."[57]

Lenin would have to be dealt with, when the time came; but that was not now. In the early days of the war, His Majesty's Government had sought to limit Russia's territorial ambitions. Now it was Russia's ideological fantasies that needed checking. "Russian Democracy," Buchanan asserted bluntly, "want to know what they are fighting for and were they to be told that they must go on fighting till objects of our Agreements [the secret treaties] had been realized they would demand separate peace."[58]

A trap for the unwary, thought Foreign Secretary Balfour. How could one stop short of the Allies' territorial war aims now? It was impossible to talk about restoring Germany's African colonies or Turkey's possessions in Mesopotamia. And Great Britain could hardly sacrifice its interests in such areas if the French and Italians insisted, as they surely would, upon all their claims. To go along with the Petrograd Soviet meant undermining political stability within the Allies, opening up a debate that would bring down those governments just as surely as Nicholas II had been deposed.

That might have the Petrograd Soviet cheering, but it meant anarchy and the triumph of German arms, as only the latter would be around to pick up the pieces. Lacking full authority, the Soviet could agitate without being held accountable for what ills befell Russia, what might transpire at Stockholm, or what happened to the Allied governments. Yet the British and French governments both saw the peril of ignoring the peace advocates, and sent special missions to appeal to both the Soviet and the Provisional Government. The British mission, headed by Arthur Henderson, the only Labour party minister in the coalition, had been instructed that Henderson was given authority to replace Buchanan as ambassador to Russia if that became necessary to counter agitation for a separate peace.[59]

British officials had been determined to prevent any socialists from Great Britain from attending the Stockholm conference, and had also instructed Henderson to work instead for a meeting of prowar socialists in London.[60] But then Sir Esme Howard posed an embarrassing question; actually he was passing it on from British labor representatives on their way to Petrograd. What would be the result if no Western spokesmen appeared in Stockholm to refute German charges that it was Britain, and Britain only, that was responsible for prolonging the war by making everyone fight for British war aims and colonial ambitions? If those accusations went unchallenged, Howard answered the question himself, a perilous situation might arise.[61]

David Lloyd George saw the danger if no one went from England: "Any falsehoods that the Germans may choose to propagate . . . will be readily believed."[62] Like Wilson, who wanted to lead the peace forces to military victory, the prime minister wanted to refute the radical socialists by sending to Russia and Stockholm "freely chosen men" who held his views. So while Russia struggled to come to terms with its revolution, the other great powers became more and more mystified by the search for an adequate response to its challenge.

> *In my judgment the demoralized state of affairs will grow worse and worse until some dominant personality arises to end it all.*
>
> Robert Lansing, August 1917

Lloyd George thus faced a complicated task, more so probably than Wilson. The prime minister, while he saw the dangers of allowing "German" arguments to go unanswered at Stockholm, did not want to appear to be yielding to Labour party pressure at home to send a delegate to the conference. He outmaneuvered Ramsay MacDonald, the Independent Labour party leader, only to find that Arthur Henderson had returned from Petrograd a convert to the Stockholm approach for ending the war by international socialist action.[63] Henderson's position was not unreasonable, because it was not based on prattle about the unity of the world's working classes, but on Russian exhaustion. Indeed, he reported to the prime minister, the situation was so grim that Stockholm now looked to be the only way to prevent a separate Russo-German peace. Two opinions contended with one another about how Russia should seek peace, said his memorandum to Lloyd George:

> One is for direct action on Western proletariate [sic] to provoke uprising against capitalism and war together. The other is for Constitutional action by first converting labour and [Social?]ist parties and then trusting to pressure they will exercise on the Government.[64]

The abysmal failure of the Russian summer offensive clinched the matter so far as Henderson was concerned. But inside Britain the steadily declining Russian military position had an entirely opposite political impact. Henderson had brought home with him four members of the Petrograd Soviet, whose mission it was to stimulate broad popular support for a conference to revise Allied war aims. Rumors were circulating, moreover, that Henderson planned to join forces with Ramsay MacDonald to form a great labor-socialist peace movement, and ride to power on the crest of antiwar sentiment. These rumors gained a measure of credibility when the two Englishmen accompanied the Russians to Paris for expanded consultations. It certainly appeared, especially to Conservative members of the coalition government, that the labor left was determined upon some kind of confrontation.[65]

If Henderson and MacDonald had indeed managed to reach common ground (and perhaps even if they had not), the ruling coalition had to react—and soon. On July 30, 1917, the war cabinet resolved that "it was not now desirable for Britain to be represented in Stockholm." Attending the meeting was Sir George Buchanan, whose words about Russia seemed only too appropriate a description of the new development in British politics: "The Socialists would prefer to run a class war rather than the national war. . . ."[66]

However that may be, Lloyd George had about given up on the Russian military situation. His main purpose now was to prevent the success of a Russian ideological offensive, especially since the Americans were finally in the war. It is necessary to keep this priority in mind as one follows the prime minister's zigzagging course over the next several months. And to accomplish his purpose, Lloyd George was perfectly willing to risk the Russian situation, on the battlefield or around Petrograd, getting a whole lot worse.

A reshuffling of the Provisional Government allowed Lloyd George to inquire if Russia still favored participation in Stockholm. The Russian chargé in London, Konstantin Nabokov, took the hint and informed his government that official support for the socialist conference was undermining "the closeness of our union with Great Britain." Could he tell Foreign Secretary Balfour, therefore, that the Provisional Government looked upon Stockholm as merely a party affair, completely separate from Russia's official relations with the Allies?[67]

Before an answer could be received, the war cabinet met and advised Henderson that it would be "more conducive to the maintenance of good relations between the British Government and the Labour Party, that the working men themselves should refuse to attend [the Stockholm conference] rather than that the Government should announce their decision and thereby appear to dictate to the Labour Party."[68] But Henderson no longer felt obliged to carry out the prime minister's orders, and may even have imagined himself, as Lloyd George suspected, the leader of a new political coalition charged with finding a speedy and effective means of ending the war.

Petrograd's reply was not satisfactory from Lloyd George's point of view, but Nabokov managed to give him what he needed anyway in the form of a cover letter that made it seem that the Provisional Government now opposed Stockholm. Nabokov risked little. Kerensky personally opposed Stockholm, often put off and now scheduled for September, and hoped to satisfy the moderates and perhaps the left by securing a formal inter-Allied conference to revise war aims.

Lloyd George would deal with that problem when he had to. Meanwhile, he forwarded copies of Nabokov's cover letter to Henderson, asking that it be read at a labor conference that would meet on August 10, 1917, to discuss sending delegates to Stockholm. Henderson was bamboozled. Fearing that there had actually been a significant change in Petrograd's official attitude, the labor leader brushed aside the Nabokov letter, and used his personal prestige to secure a vote in favor of attending the Stockholm conference.[69] To turn one's back on "poor Russia . . . the infant of Democracies," he asserted, with a "point blank refusal" would have serious implications for Britain's future. "Of this I am convinced, . . . if we today, representing as we do the great British Labour and Socialist movement, determine for the whole period of the war not to use the political weapon to supplement our military victories, not only shall I regret it, but I will venture to predict that you as a Movement will regret it hereafter."[70]

Henderson was not making Russia into another item on Labour's agenda, like wages and hours; he was remaking the agenda! The lines were drawn. The war cabinet demanded Henderson's formal resignation—he had left them in spirit already of his own accord—and refused

passports for British delegates to Stockholm. Henderson took his case to
the House of Commons, where Lloyd George lay in wait for him. It was
really no contest. The prime minister forced an admission that the Nabokov letter had not been communicated to the labor delegates who had
voted to send a mission to Stockholm. Put on the defensive, Henderson
floundered about, unable to properly answer the charge that there had
been "a most drastic change in the whole policy of the Government in
Russia." With a triumphant flourish, the gamekeeper of the House
snapped shut the trap. The change inside Russia, he said, was the reason
why His Majesty's Government had refused passports. Nothing would be
more fatal to Russia's chances "than to hold conferences with the enemy
at the very moment when the first step in the restoration of discipline is to
prevent fraternization with the enemy on the Russian front." Britain's
duty to a loyal ally compelled this action.[71]

Squirm all he wanted, Henderson was caught. No doubt Lloyd George
did want to give Kerensky a fair running. But he had already begun to
write off Russia as a serious military factor in the outcome of the war. No
reason, then, to appease the Soviet.[72] His mind never at rest, Lloyd
George even thought about turning the tables, as it were, and scouting the
possibility of a separate peace in the West. He thought about a deal with
Germany: evacuation of Belgium for a restoration of Berlin's African
colonies. Much depended, of course, on American attitudes, above all on
how fast the United States could actually get into the war.[73]

For the moment, at least, Lloyd George had some breathing space.
Despite Ramsay MacDonald's loud complaints that the prime minister had
misused the Nabokov letter, a second session of the labor conference
voted to support His Majesty's Government. But despite his talk of support for Kerensky, Lloyd George had dealt the beleaguered Russian
leader a sharp blow. In the face of the debate in the House of Commons,
Kerensky felt compelled to deny that any change had taken place in
official Russian attitudes about Stockholm. "The peace program of the
Revolutionary Defensists," wrote one historian, "was a shambles. Thus by
default the Bolsheviks were in a position to attract the support of the
millions of Russians who desired peace above all else."[74]

Thus far Wilson had escaped having to respond to the challenge of
the Russian Revolution. David Francis had complained, to be sure, but the
strongest reaction in Washington, after initial euphoria, had been resentment at the Petrograd Soviet's bid to usurp Wilson's destined role as
arbiter of the peace. Elihu Root's mission posed few questions, and had
simpleminded answers to offer. "Very desirable indeed," Root had cabled,
"to send here immediately as many moving pictures as possible showing
American preparation for war, battleships, troops marching, factories

making munitions, and other things to carry to the mind the idea that America is doing something. These poor fellows have been told that no one is really fighting except Russia and they believe it."[75]

At the beginning of August, however, a new peace appeal emanated from the Holy See in Rome. The pope's manifesto touched on many of the same points Wilson had made before America entered the war. Even so, and even though His Holiness approached the question from a very different standpoint than the Petrograd Soviet, it was unwelcome. Sir Cecil Spring-Rice observed that Washington was put off, since the government was doing its "utmost to kindle a warlike spirit throughout [the] States and to combat pacificists."[76]

The appeal presented other difficulties. Wilson had hoped to avoid an outright refusal of the Petrograd Soviet's demand for an Allied conference on war aims, so sure to be disruptive and so sure to weaken Wilson's own grasp on the knotted threads of peacemaking. For example, he had considered and then rejected a statement that if the Russian government proposed a conference to formulate new war aims, it could not "wisely" be pushed aside. "The democratic feeling of the world is demanding more and more audibly an insistent statement from the nations associated against Germany," he had thought of saying, "which will show that the object of the war is not aggrandizement but the freedom of the peoples to secure independence *within* [?], and free themselves against aggression whether by physical force or successful economic arrangement." This draft of a never-used statement also included a potentially explosive reference to the fact that it would be "exceedingly difficult" to conclude peace on the basis of secret arrangements for dividing Asia Minor.[77]

Both British and Russian diplomats awaited the president's reply to the pope with keen interest. Boris Bakhmeteff, the Provisional Government's new ambassador in Washington, cautioned Colonel House against treating the papal appeal too lightly, lest it worsen the splits among Kerensky's supporters and bring about his downfall. If the pope's overtures were now to be brushed aside, added Bakhmeteff, a schism would open inside Russia into which other countries would also fall.[78]

A way out of this predicament, as House and Wilson saw it, was for the president to say that he was willing to meet with the "German people at any time they are in a position to name their own representatives." To talk about the secret treaties was self-defeating at this point, for Wilson's credibility allowed him to manipulate the Russian situation even more effectively than Lloyd George. Wilson could thus blunt the Petrograd Soviet's peace offensive by reasserting America's single war aim: the creation of a just and humane postwar order.[79]

Robert Lansing offered advice along similar lines. It was very simple, he said. Pope Benedict, fearing socialism, was out to protect the Austrian and German monarchies. "It is not so much democracy as socialism that the Roman Church fears, although both are more or less antagonistic to hierarchical government, and equally so in the denial of temporal power to the church." The pope, "probably unwittingly," was acting at the behest of such reactionary forces. "The intrigues in Russia," argued the secretary, "the Stockholm Conference, the propaganda in this country and in neutral countries, all belong to one general plan of seeking peace while victorious on land and while submarine warfare appears successful."[80]

Without doubt Lansing had learned the knack of appealing to Wilsonian sensibilities. It took a skillful brief to make revolution in Russia appear to be the work of reactionaries. As Wilson went about drafting his reply, he reworked this theme into a picture of the "new-born" Russia at the mercy of German intriguers, burrowing within the revolution to cause its undoing. Later, of course, this notion would provide an ideological foundation for the idea that the Bolsheviks were actual German agents. But in his answer to the pope, the president was concerned with making clear the need for the defeat of the German autocracy. Unless the autocracy was removed, and German connections with foreign intrigue severed, the whole world, including America, would be menaced.[81]

House felt that if Wilson took the offensive and used the opportunity to restate American war aims, he could "almost" bring about a revolution in Germany. "You can make a statement that will not only be the undoing of autocratic Germany, but one that will strengthen the hands of the Russian liberals in their purpose to mould their country into a mighty republic."[82] Yet House had now come to have doubts that military victory was the best answer to the pope. He wanted to explore, at least, arguments for taking command of the peace movement, which meant, he realized, giving first priority to the Russian Revolution. American prestige was at its highest, he reasoned. If the United States insisted on peace before conditions worsened any more on the Russian and French home fronts, and before the war grew unpopular in the United States, the result could be a more satisfactory outcome all around:

> It is more important, I think, that Russia should weld herself into a virile republic than it is that Germany should be beaten to her knees. If internal disorder reaches a point in Russia where Germany can intervene, it is conceivable that in the future she may be able to dominate Russia both politically and economically. Then the clock of progress would indeed be set back.

Besides, he concluded, if Russia did make a go of it, the German autocracy was doomed in a very few years.[83] This intriguing exploration by

Colonel House into the farthest reaches of Wilsonian thought was still based upon a Philip Dru scenario, however sophisticated the balance of power notion had become, or however well disguised. Lansing had a good answer. There was little anyone could do (even the Germans?) to influence events inside Russia, he argued. As in France a century ago, the revolution would pass from moderation to terror, and then back again to reaction. "In my judgment," he advised Wilson, "the demoralized state of affairs will grow worse and worse until some dominant personality arises to end it all."[84]

After all this discussion, Wilson's reply to Pope Benedict avoided specifics. The pope's plan, it said, would permit Germany the opportunity to recuperate and resume unabated its sinister prewar activities. "This power is not the German people," he said. "It is the ruthless master of the German people. It is no business of ours how that great people came under its control or submitted with temporary zest to the domination of its purpose; but it is our business to see to it that the history of the rest of the world is no longer left to its handling."

Wilson's words had an eerie ring. He had said of Mexico once that it was "no business" of anyone's how that people settled their own affairs: if Mexico should be set aflame, then the best thing was to step back from the fire. Now, however, he had penned a rationale for doing the opposite in the case of Germany, and for intervening in Russian affairs as well.

To stop short of military victory, he then concluded, would oblige the world to maintain a constant alert and a permanent combination of nations with but one purpose, to oppose the misled German "people"—the real sufferers, because they were forever to live lives as mere instruments of the autocratic "power." While the statement ignored much of what he had earlier said about the economic roots of the feudal system in regard to Mexico, and was thus much more acceptable to conservatives, Wilson did not fail to bring Russia into the discussion. The way he did so, however, implied that the success of the Russian Revolution now depended on American resistance to a compromise peace. The military alliance that would be needed to hold an undefeated Germany in check, he said, would not protect Russia from "intrigue" and the "manifold subtle interference, and the certain counter-revolution which would be attempted by all the malign influence to which the German Government has of late accustomed the world."[85]

Wilson's reply was masterful. He managed to leave the impression that, now more than ever, only the United States stood above the passions of the moment, as it already stood above the Allies in war aims. The militant antiwar radical Max Eastman sent sincere congratulations: "Now you have declared for substantially the Russian terms—no 'punitive damages,' no 'dismemberment of empires,' 'vindication of sovereignties,' and by making a responsible ministery in Germany the one condition of your entering into negotiations, you have given a concrete meaning to the statement that this is a war for democracy."[86]

Remarkable praise indeed from the American radical left. All the more so because Wilson knew that the world's accolades for his response presumed a sureness on his part that he simply did not feel. Commenting on a report about the French political situation, the president sighed, "They want me to lead them! But where shall I lead them to."[87]

> *What I am opposed to is not the feelings of the pacifists, but their stupidity.*
>
> Woodrow Wilson, November 1917

On August 24, 1917, General Alfred Knox, chief British military adviser in Russia, reported that the newly appointed supreme commander, General Lavr Kornilov, believed that the man who had appointed him, Kerensky, was too weak to restore discipline. Kornilov was contemplating "vigorous political aciton," and wished to know if the Allied governments would support him. The war cabinet demurred—at least for the moment.

Knox was disappointed. The great mass of Russian soliders had never wanted to fight. Workmen were also undisciplined, he said, and were now making "huge economic demands." Employers, including British manufacturers, were responding by closing down factories and moving away. The railroad system was in chaos. The peasants refused to deliver grain to the cities. Yet Kerensky refused to move, still feared to shed blood to restore order. All that was needed was ten thousand loyalists to do the job, enough men to subdue Petrograd—the principal source of disorder throughout Russia. The real danger was that Kornilov would be too late to prevent Kerensky from opening negotiations with Germany for a separtate peace so as to appease the radicals.[88]

Someone in the cabinet suggested that President Wilson be asked to send a note to Kerensky urging him to support Kornilov's plan. Lord Robert Cecil cut that short with the dour observation that it was highly unlikely that the leader of a republican government—especially this leader—would do anything to promote a military dictatorship. When Kornilov moved on Petrograd anyway, the war cabinet offered moral support. "General Korniloff," it went on record as saying, "represented all that was sound and hopeful" inside Russia." Accordingly, Sir George Buchanan was to be instructed to impress upon the Provisional Government the imperative need for coming to terms with him for the sake of the "interests of the Allies and of democracy generally. . . ."[89]

Kornilov's coup failed, but not in time to spare the British and French considerable embarrassment for having intervened in such a clumsy way, nor to save Kerensky from the fallout of a no-confidence vote by the Allies. For Prime Minister Lloyd George there was one consolation. Kornilov's defeat cleared the air. Now it was possible to reevaluate prospects and options without considering Russia's views about anything.

The summer campaign in the west led to the Battle of Passchendaele, which achieved very meager results at a cost of more than three hundred thousand casualties. If the Soviet wanted a conference to revise Allied war aims, Lloyd George again thought of revising them in the east, and approved a harsh note to Kerensky warning that military aid would be cut off unless discipline was restored. Lloyd George was no longer afraid that he might be driving Russia out of the war. So be it. Let Germany lose in the west, and gain in the east.[90]

And once out of the war, Russia could not force its allies to surrender their war aims by insisting upon a conference. The sooner out the better, then, from that perspective. On October 21, 1917, Kerensky, at the end of his tether, announced that Russia would be represented at a forthcoming Allied meeting by a person enjoying the full confidence "of the democratic organizations," someone, moreover, who could present Russia's "terms" for the Allies based on "the principles announced by the Russian revolution." A list of these is enough to explain why Lloyd George was ready to usher Russia out the door. Alsace-Lorraine's future was to be decided by plebiscite. Belgium would be compensated from an international fund. Germany was to retain its colonies. The Suez and Panama canals and the Black Sea straits were all to be neutralized. All nations were to receive equal treatment in postwar economic treaties. Secret diplomacy was to be abolished. And the actual peace negotiations were to be conducted by delegates chosen by legislative assemblies. If the Allies refused to go to Stockholm, in other words, Russia would bring Stockholm to them.[91]

Would a victorious Germany offer much worse terms? Yes, of course, but only a defeated France and Great Britain would accept what Kerensky's representative planned to put on the table. Balfour reacted as one might expect. "To me," he told Nabokov, "it seemed clear that no other nation would, or could, adopt the precedent, and that to allow it [representation by a nongovernment figure] . . . might have most inconvenient consequences." Not only would there be no discussion of war aims at the forthcoming meeting, he concluded, Kerensky's man would not even be given a seat.[92]

Aside from what he was doing internationally, moreover, Kerensky was setting equally bad precedents at home with what London regarded as extreme revolutionary measures. And, as a horrified General Knox reported to London, he was being encouraged by one of Wilson's agents. This man, Raymond Robins, who was attached to the American Red Cross, had even said that the Allies should advise the Provisional Government to distribute land to the peasants immediately. This was the only chance, asserted Robins, to cut the ground from under Lenin and the Bolsheviks, with their slogan "Peace, land, bread," and make possible the regeneration of the Russian army.

"Distribute the land in Russia today," exclaimed Knox, "and in two years we'll be doing it in England!" After a long tirade against both the cowardly Russian soldier and his abject civilian leaders, Knox came straight out with it: "I am not interested in stabilizing Kerensky, I do not believe in Kerensky and his government. It is incompetent and inefficient and worthless." Russia's only hope was a military dictatorship. "These people have to have a whip over them."[93]

Ambassador David Francis had not abandoned the Provisional Government to its fate, but neither did he fear the advent of Soviet power. Should the Petrograd Soviet assume control of the Russian government, it would not survive, in his opinion, and it would be succeeded by those who had a greater resolve and willingness to prosecute the war.[94] Francis was right, up to a point. The men who wrested power from Kerensky came to office with a greater resolve. Only it was to make peace as soon as possible.

The sudden advent of a Bolshevik government in Petrograd under V. I. Lenin and Leon Trotsky was accompanied by less immediate changes inside Russia than had occurred when the tsar was overthrown. Few thought it would last long. Kerensky might not return at the head of an army as he had promised, but somewhere a Bonaparte waited in the wings. It was possible, however, that to save themselves the Bolsheviks might call in the Germans. What they did do was even more infuriating in some ways: they invoked Wilsonian creeds, including self-determination, the American president's main guidepost.

The first "foreign policy" act of the new Bolshevik government in Russia was a peace decree issued on November 8, 1917. The final paragraph was directed not to governments but to the "class-conscious workers" who toiled in all the belligerent countries. "The workers of these countries have been of the greatest service to the cause and progress of socialism." Hence they would understand the new duty history had imposed upon them of "saving mankind from the horrors of war and its consequences. . . ."

In their very first communication with the outside world, then, the

Bolsheviks more than hinted that the working class had a special obligation to the Russian Revolution that took precedence even over the class
war. The two were closely linked at this time, of course, but Lenin himself
was still a bit unsure of his own role; was he history's agent at the van-
guard of the world revolution, or something less important? Either way,
the peace decree was especially worded to catch the eye of Wilsonian
opinion in Europe and America. Lenin believed that the capitalist nations
would not long survive after peace. Their intense fear of Stockholm
offered one proof; their inability to stifle the Russian Revolution in its
early stages was yet another.[95]

Addressed to all the belligerents, the peace decree used Wilsonian
rhetoric in places instead of Marxist phrases, indicating a shrewd calculation that the appeal ought to build on liberal sentiments, and mobilize the
U.S. president's European constituency. It also reflected an appreciation
that, while America's war aims were inevitably capitalist, they differed in
certain respects from those of either European alliance. Even the briefest
glimpse at the tsarist archives would reveal how different, especially in
Ambassador Francis's time, and suggest that America might have a role to
play in the success of the Bolsheviks, even if it was only to delay Allied
intervention.

Indeed, Sir George Buchanan's first thoughts after the Bolshevik sei-
zure of power were precisely along these lines—the very great danger not
of a separate Russo-German peace, but of a separate American policy in
Russia. Only a few days passed before Buchanan wrote a complaining
note about American attitudes. Recalling that Francis had pointedly declined to unite in Allied representations to Kerensky, Sir George now
commented that he saw a pattern developing. "It is pretty clear," he
wrote, "that Americans are apparently with approval of [their] Government playing entirely for [their] own hand and that they are aiming at
making of Russia [an] American preserve from which Britishers shall as
far as possible be excluded."[96]

If America did indeed play a separate role, either because of a clever
Bolshevik seduction or on its own initative, everyone else must accept a
lesser part. Woodrow Wilson would not have denied such ambitions, nor
would he, in later months, deny that he suspected that one reason the
Allies wanted to intervene in Russia was to bolster their own role, quite
apart from the question of reopening the Eastern Front or even annihilat-
ing the Bolsheviks. But he could not see any way American purposes
could be served by direct dealings with the Leninist regime. On November 12, the president addressed members of the American Federation of
Labor. It was his first opportunity to comment on the Russian peace
decree, and he amended his original draft to do so. How could anyone

imagine peace with a still unregenerate Germany? he asked. Referring to the "fatuous . . . dreamers in Russia," Wilson answered his own question. "What I am opposed to is not the feeling of the pacificists, but their stupidity. My heart is with them, but my mind has a contempt for them. I want peace, but I know how to get it, and they do not."[97]

The Russian glacier had broken loose from centuries of feudalism; and nothing in its path seemed safe any longer. The last year of the war would be fought with one eye on Russia, where Lenin sought to consolidate his rule, and one on the places both inside and outside Europe where his example was already becoming a stimulus to radical nationalism.

CHAPTER SEVEN

Ideological Front Lines

An apparition with countenance different from any
yet seen on earth stood in the place of the old Ally. We
saw a state without a nation, an army without a
country, a religion without a God.

Winston Churchill,
The World Crisis, 1929

Churchill's words captured the puzzlement, and the fear. Western states-men had no idea how to blunt revolutionary Russia's call for immediate peace negotiations. Even if one supposed, as most did, that Lenin would fail—fail, that is, not only to force Allied governments to yield to his "diplomacy," but also to sustain a Bolshevik regime inside Russia—might he not succeed in bringing down civilization in his wake?

Afraid of allowing Bolshevism to spread by close contact, policymakers feared still more the consequences of losing touch with its leaders. It was never simply a matter of intervening or not intervening to restore the Eastern Front, nor of attempting to topple the Bolsheviks from power. As Arthur Balfour put it to the British war cabinet, "[I]t is to our advantage to avoid, as long as possible, an open breach with this crazy system. If this be drifting, then I am a drifter by deliberate policy."[1] American observers in Russia similarly warned of the dangers of leaving the Bolsheviks iso-lated, especially now that the tsarist archives had been opened, exposing to the world the Allied secret treaties. Ambassador David Francis, for example, vowed that he would never "talk to a damned Bolshevik," but he sent others to confer with Foreign Affairs Commissar Leon Trotsky while he waited for Kerensky, or some other figure, to return with enough troops to put down the "uprising."[2]

From Moscow, Consul General Maddin Summers also thought it imperative to maintain an American presence. The "immediate problem" was to counteract German propaganda. But there was a long-range consideration as well: "For this purpose as well as to lend moral support to the better elements in Russia, which will regain the upper hand, every effort must be made to maintain every American agency in Russia."[3] The American military attaché, Brigadier General William V. Judson, believed that civilization might not indeed survive the shock of the Russian Revolution. Only Wilson could speak with enough authority and with enough sympathy to the "simple but honest minds" of the Russian masses:

> All order and system are departing. Conditions make possible cataclysm dwarfing great war and tremendous blow to democracy. Resulting world shock apt to lead everywhere to accentuated struggle between extreme socialism and severe reaction, with general setback to democratic systems and civilization.[4]

Judson's words reenforce a point that cannot be made too often: both British and American policymakers, military and political, at a variety of levels and in a number of positions, all perceived the Russian Revolution as a "tremendous blow" to liberal democracy. What they did not yet understand was how to respond, beyond finding some means to deprive the Bolsheviks of their claim to speak for humanity.

> *I have not lost faith in the Russian outcome by any means. Russia, like France in a past century, will no doubt have to go through deep waters but she will come out upon firm land on the other side and her great people, for they are a great people, will in my opinion take their proper place in the world.*
>
> Woodrow Wilson, November 1917

Anti-Bolshevik action, under the guise of restoring the eastern front, was first discussed in the war cabinet as early as November 11, 1917. The issue arose in the form of an inquiry about the Rumanian threat to leave the war. Like Italy, Rumania had negotiated its way into the war, receiving promises from Russia that it would obtain huge chunks of Austro-Hungarian and Serbian territory for participating in the common cause. From one perspective, Russia's demise erased an embarrassing mistake, but a second look revealed other considerations. Anti-Bolshevik forces in southern Russia were said to be rallying around General Alexei Kaledin.

Almost nothing was known about Kaledin or his movement. How many men did he have? Was he the best choice to create a center of resistance?[5]

An overt attempt to send Kaledin military aid might inflame anti-Allied feelings in Russia, "and so defeat the very object we were aiming at." Why not let the Rumanians try to get in touch with the general? It would cost something. Rumania's king had tried to set very advantageous terms. He would try to rally his army, British representatives in Bucharest were told, and "fight his way through to Russia with the object of joining hands with the Cossacks, and perhaps eventually linking up with the British forces in Mesopotamia," but only if the Allies and "if possible" the United States would confirm "their engagements" to his country.[6]

Discussions were adjourned briefly while Balfour and Prime Minister Lloyd George attended an Allied strategy conference at the end of November. It was at this meeting in Paris that Colonel House appeared, for the first time, as a cobelligerent. It was also here that the first doubts were raised about American ability to dominate the policy deliberations and ultimate decisions of its associates.

House had been assured that he would have British backing for a resolution declaring that the Allies were not waging war for any purpose except to banish militarism from the earth and establish the right of all nations to self-determination.[7] No sooner had the talks begun, however, on November 30, 1917, than Balfour preempted the American proposal by asking the conference to consider a suggestion from Sir George Buchanan that the Allies release Russia from its commitment not to make a separate peace. The advantage of this proposal over the American plan was that it would deny the Bolshevik claim that the Allies wanted to prolong the war and bleed Russia to the very end, yet would also take the heat off them to come forward with some self-denying (and divisive) war aims statement.

If Balfour hoped to educate Colonel House about Allied bitterness toward Russia, he succeeded in that as well. The French would have none of Buchanan's argument. Germany would proceed to reduce Russia to a protectorate, they insisted. And instead of the "English proposal," declared Foreign Minister Pichon, the conference should state that "it might be possible" to discuss general peace terms "if Russia could get a decent Government." To give back the Russian promise would be a dreadful mistake that would demoralize large sections of the populace in Allied countries and throw them into the hands of the Bolsheviks.

Italy's Baron Sonnino made the point even more specific. "If we gave Russia back her word," he said, "what would be the effect on Rumania, and on the Serbians, and what . . . would be the effect on Italy?" England had practically "no internal enemy, but it was a very serious matter for

Italy, and might, to-morrow, be serious for France. The moment we gave
the Russians back their word certain parties would get to work to try and
do the same in other countries."

Far from leading the conference toward Wilson's promised land, then,
the colonel found himself shoved off to the side as the other delegates
agreed upon an ambiguous statement that each nation should respond to
the Russian appeal in its own way. "The result has not been satisfactory to
me," House cabled home. Russia was to be told, furthermore, that the
Allies would only talk about war aims with a "stable government" in
power. The decision, in other words, was to meet the Bolsheviks head on
on the question of their legitimacy, hardly a more favorable battleground
than the no-man's-land of war aims. Lenin offered peace to a war-sick
nation. The Allies held out nothing but sermons.[8]

Returning to London, Balfour advised the war Cabinet that Colonel
House had expressed no objections to the plan for sending aid to Kaledin
via the Rumanians. "It . . . would not constitute an intervention in Russian
internal affairs to the same extent as an appeal to General Kaledin from
the Western Allies direct, while it might at the same time afford an opportunity for ascertaining what General Kaledin's real strength and intentions were."[9]

House had been maneuvered, as Wilson would be, by inability to offer
an alternative Russian policy. Both Sir George Buchanan and Sir George
Barclay in Bucharest, meanwhile, had become alarmed at the war cabinet's enthusiasm for Kaledin. Buchanan had met some of Kaledin's associates and found them a bad lot, nothing more than adventurers. The
ambassador's warning against making a misstep that might convert Russia
into a German colony was ignored. In full pursuit of an anti-Bolshevik
savior, the war cabinet instructed Buchanan to send a special agent to
contact Kaledin directly. "In the event of the situation offering reasonable
hopes," read these orders, "Allied assistance will be forthcoming and we
shall be glad to know in what ways this could profitably be given. Your
mission is most urgent and secret but you are not authorized to commit
the Government to any line before reporting."[10]

While Balfour and Lloyd George were casting about in Paris for an
Allied line on Russia, the war cabinet had begun to entertain the most
extravagant hopes for Kaledin, and were considering offering him £10
million. According to the director of military intelligence, a loyalist force
of two million men could be raised with that money. "The proposal is to
support Kaledin, as he is the head of the largest loyal body in Russia.
Either he, or preferably the King of Rumania as the head of a de facto
government with which the President of the U.S.A. could treat, should
ask the U.S. to send a force of say two divisions to Russia nominally to

assist in fighting the Germans, but really to form a rallying point for the loyal element. . . . All reports go to show the cowardice of the mob in Russia, a resolute man backed by a little force could probably do as he liked."[11]

This view, an emotion-laden picture of the Russian Revolution colored by far more than concern over the military front, carried the day. On December 3, 1917, the war cabinet decided to "support any reasonable body in Russia that would actively oppose the Maximalist movement. . . ." All efforts were to be bent to preventing Russia from making a separate peace. Only elements friendly to the Entente were to be supported. That also ruled out a coalition of the left, i.e., of Bolsheviks, Social Revolutionaries, and Mensheviks. "Such a combination would be under Bolshevik influence and would besides consist of talkers and theorists. If on the other hand a southern block could be formed consisting of the Caucasus, the Cossacks, the Ukraine, and the Rumanians it would probably be able to set up a reasonably stable Government and would in any case through its command of oil, coal and corn control the whole of Russia." Buchanan was to implement this policy by whatever means he found expedient. "No regard should be had to expense and you should furnish to Cossacks or Ukrainians any funds necessary by any means you think desirable." Sir George Barclay was similarly instructed: "You are authorized to guarantee Kaledin financial support up to any figure necessary."[12]

These instructions to British diplomats on the ideological front lines can be read as having to do only with military questions, but only if one is also prepared to assert that the secret treaties were void of any purpose save Germany's defeat. This is not to minimize the Allies' outrage at Russia's "betrayal," at being left to face German military might. Wilson, of course, was aggrieved by Russia's theft of his peace program. The president was not terribly upset at House's travail at Paris, or the outcome of the Allied conference. It had not ended with a statement of peace terms at odds with his own pronouncements, and that was enough for the time being.[13]

Neither was the president unhappy with Colonel House for having discussed aid to Kaledin. While it was dangerous to become involved with such a man without even a semblance of a long-range policy in mind, it was still more dangerous to allow the Cossack movement to go to pieces. House had gone so far, however, as to promise that the United States would find money for the anti-Bolshevik leader if he appeared worthy. Any money made available would be given to the Allies for transfer, so that if things went wrong the president could withdraw without embarrassment.[14]

Wilson already had it in mind, moreover, to separate himself from Allied mistakes, past and future. On December 4, 1917, the day after the war cabinet resolved to aid Kaledin, Wilson sent a message to Congress. The Allies had badly mishandled the original Russian request for a re-statement of war aims, he said. Had the Russian people believed in Allied sincerity, "the sad reverses which have recently marked the progress of their affairs toward an ordered and stable government of free men might have been avoided." What was done was done, however. And now the long-suffering Russian people had been led astray by the "masters of German intrigue." No less than the tyrannical tsarist autocracy, the Bol-sheviks were false pretenders. What had taken place in Russia demon-strated yet again that before the peoples of the world could gain control over their destinies, the Berlin conspiracy would have to be taught a "final and convincing lesson."[15]

As in his response earlier to Pope Benedict, Wilson emphasized reac-tionary German forces, as a substitute for the "special interests" he had previously condemned for holding back Mexico and China, almost to the exclusion of all other factors. It was an essentially conservative analysis, not so much in its insistence that the German peril had to be removed before Russia could get on with its revolution, but in its implication that the work of the revolution would be very nearly complete once the Ger-mans were gone. Wilson did not believe that any more than Lenin did, but he had convinced himself that the Bolsheviks, witting or not were working on Germany's behalf.

Actually, he had little choice. The only way to counter Bolshevik insis-tence that there was little to choose between the two sides fighting the war was to insist, in reply, that there was even less to choose between Bolshe-vik peace proposals and German terms. The best that he could do was to continue maintaining that American goals were not determined by Allied ambitions, but by a nobler concern to make the world safe for democracy. Wilson had already ordered George Creel, head of the Committee for Public Information, to spare no effort to get that message to Russia. "Drive ahead full speed regardless expense," Creel in turn ordered his chief agent in Russia. "Coordinate all American Agencies . . . and start aggressive campaign. Use press, billboards, placards and every possible medium to answer lies against America. Make plain our high motives and absolute devotion to democratic ideas. Deny that supplies are going to be stopped and state America' eagerness to help. . . ."[16]

But not help the Bolsheviks. On December 6, 1917, Secretary Lansing cabled David Francis that the "President desires American representatives [to] withhold all direct communication with Bolshevik Government."[17] The reason was simple enough, the secretary wrote in a memorandum to himself, and it was not that the Bolsheviks were German agents. Any sign of diplomatic recognition would only encourage Bolshevik sympathizers in other lands. For a state that believed "in political institutions as they now exist and based on nationality and private property," the only correct approach was "to leave these dangerous idealists alone and have no direct dealings with them." To play up to Lenin would only give him an exalted sense of his power and win his contempt. If the Bolsheviks had their way, he concluded, social distinctions and traditional political and religious institutions would all be swept away, leaving the "ignorant and incapable mass of humanity dominant in the earth."[18]

According to Lansing the president shared these views and had directed him to conduct "our dealings with Russia . . . along those lines."[19] However that may be, talks were soon under way with British officials about possible ways of implementing House's promise to Balfour concerning material aid to General Kaledin.[20] Ambassador Spring-Rice noticed, moreover, that Lansing displayed a surprisingly relaxed attitude about rumors of a Japanese landing at Vladivostok. The secretary had seemed almost nonchalant, remarking that he did not feel it right to deny to the Japanese something that the United States had claimed (and might have to claim again) at Tampico. Japan and the United States had exceptional interests on the continents adjacent to their own possessions, Lansing said: "This geographical situation gave them certain obvious commercial advantages and it also might on occasion impose on them certain political or military duties." Yet there was still a distinction to be made between such duties and European imperialism, he added, for no power had the right to elevate them into claims of a permanent territorial or commercial nature.[21]

In addition to laying groundwork for an interpretation of recent Japanese-American understandings on China, Lansing was here interested in the problem of preventing the Bolsheviks from gaining access to military supplies to use against Kaledin. "[I]f Japan has taken measures to prevent . . . [Vladivostok from] falling into the hands of the Bolsheviki with all the immense accumulation of war material [there]," he told Spring-Rice, he "could not . . . raise objections."[22] Whether or not Lansing merely acted in this manner under Wilson's instructions, the secretary's affirmative use of anti-Bolshevism as a rationale for policy further reduces the plausibility of the idea that German military exploitation was the primary factor in the origins of the American interventionist attitude.

On the main point, aid to Kaledin, there was full agreement. "My dear Mr. Secretary," Wilson said in a brief note, "This has my entire approval. WW."[23] American officials in London were instructed that support was to be given to any movement to keep Russia in the war, "even though its success is only a possibility." The actual aid, however, was to be distributed by the British and French. Whatever was done was to be done without letting the world know that American policy was to show "sympathy for the Kaledine movement, much less of providing financial assistance."[24]

> *Whether their present leaders believe it or not, it is our heartfelt desire and hope that some way may be opened whereby we may be privileged to assist the people of Russia to attain their utmost hope of liberty and ordered peace. . . .*
>
> Woodrow Wilson,
> Fourteen Points speech, January 1918

The first doubts about Kaledin's enterprise arose in London, where both Ambassador Page and Treasury representative Oscar Crosby expressed serious reservations. The latter thought it was unnecessary as well as unwise to share liability for the venture with the Allies, especially as he suspected that the Kaledin movement was motivated by "differences in regard to internal Russian questions" rather than any commitment to continue the war. Dealing with Kaledin also involved getting tied into the "undertakings" to Rumania made before America entered the war.[25]

Second thoughts about the implications of a Japanese landing at Vladivostok, prompted by Allied eagerness to divide responsibility in Russia, raised additional questions about American involvement. Any talk of spheres of influence, or any language that implied America's role would be to assist the Allies, was bound to give Wilson pause.[26] It was one thing to help anti-Bolshevik Russians fight the Germans in the hope that their fellow countrymen would rally to them, quite another to adopt a positive policy favoring the establishment of rival claimants to succeed the Provisional Government, or worse, encouraging the permanent division of the Russian empire as a result of the war. Wilson was determined not to provide the fig leaf of respectability for such a blatant, indeed brazen, reappearance of the old diplomacy.

David Lloyd George, meanwhile, had also reconsidered. Stimulated by the visit of an American, William Boyce Thompson, who had recently arrived in London from Russia, the prime minister began to wonder if a deal could be done with Lenin. "Let's make them our Bolsheviks," said Thompson, who had spent considerable sums from his private fortune in a futile effort to sustain the Provisional Government.[27] Lloyd George always admired the man who challenged orthodoxies. Thompson more than filled that role. Indeed, he told Foreign Office officials, he had spent his own money "disseminating Bolshevik literature by Russian aircraft over the German lines." To continue this work would require continued contacts with Lenin. True, Russia had recently suspended its military efforts, but think of the ideological reinforcements the Bolsheviks offered on the eastern front, reinforcements that made Russia "the gravest conceivable danger to Prussianism." He was on his way home, said Thompson, to enlist President Wilson's support. "And he informed us," minuted one of his listeners, "that the President was already more or less in sympathy with these views."[28]

Many of those who spoke with Thompson came away very impressed, but not the permanent under secretary of the Foreign Office, Lord Charles Hardinage, who saw the danger of regarding the Bolsheviks as would-be rescuers. They came bringing chaos, he argued. Let them alone. And when the inevitable failure came, when famine struck Russia, the forces in south Russia would be able, with British aid, to rally "the more moderate sections of all parties" and would protect "our own interests to the South of the Caucasus."[29]

Inundated by bad news from the military fronts—Italy reeling after defeat at Caporetto, France increasingly unreliable, and Britain itself facing severe manpower shortages—Lloyd George was no longer certain that things would work out the way Hardinage and several of his cabinet colleagues seemed to think. Thompson had convinced him of one thing that would never be absent from his calculations: the Russian Revolution had come to stay. Trotsky and Lenin, whatever else one could say about them, were not in Germany's pay. For the moment, however, all the prime minister could convince the cabinet to do was to establish a special committee to study the financial undertakings the government had assumed in regard to various anti-Bolshevik groups.[30]

Confusion was all the greater because word had now arrived of Wilson's first decision to give all necessary aid to those willing to continue the fight.[31] That was no longer the president's actual position, but it certainly diminished Thompson's claims to special access to the White House. It soon became apparent that the millionaire's plan for coopting the Bolsheviks and aiding their ideological offensive had few supporters in Washington. Only Colonel House seemed at all interested, and he apparently kept his thoughts to his diary. He believed, he wrote there, that the United States should seek a rapprochement with the Bolsheviks and "proffer our financial, industrial and moral support in every way possible."[32]

Lansing's desire to have nothing to do with "these dangerous idealists" remained official policy, but as Ambassador Francis cabled on January 2, 1918, there might be discreet ways of influencing the Bolsheviks not to make a separate peace with Germany. He still had no doubts but that

Lenin and Trotsky aimed at "world-wide social revolution." But that was just the point: a separate peace with Germany might very well allow them to advance that cause.[33] Francis had been alerted by Raymond Robins, who enjoyed access to the revolutionary leaders, that Commissar Trotsky had decided that because of a German "conspiracy" Russia would break off current peace negotiations. Robins was eager to tell Trotsky that if such a rupture actually did take place, Francis would recommend "prompt effective assistance. . . ." "I readily granted" Robins's request, the ambassador cabled Washington. His British and French colleagues had also been advised of Trotsky's intentions, he added, and were also recommending a positive response.[34]

Trotsky's talk of a German conspiracy hardly squared, however, with his message to the peoples and governments of the Allied nations broadcast just a few days before on December 29, 1917. Why had the Entente ruling classes refused the Soviet peace decree? The reason was simple, said the commissar. They did not want to grant self-determination to Ireland, Egypt, India, Madagascar, Indochina, and so on. They would not say so, of course. "For it is clear that to demand self-determination for the peoples that are comprised within the borders of enemy states and to refuse self-determination to the peoples of their own state or of their own colonies would mean the defense of the most naked and the most cynical imperialism." Self-determination for enemy peoples was simply a clever term for military victory. When the Allied governments were forced by their peoples to renounce their claims to rule "the oppressed peoples of their own states," the necessary conditions would exist for revolution inside Germany—and for an end to the war.[35]

Trotsky's words went to the heart of the Wilsonian peace program as it had evolved since American entrance into the war. In both his reply to the pope and in his most recent message to Congress, the president had, in fact, largely sacrificed his earlier commitment to self-determination. What he counted on now was the creation of a liberal postwar order, supported by an association of nations that would be able to check reactionary military tendencies. The Bolshevik Revolution only made it all the more necessary to condemn Germany alone and, he would find, to accept the war guilt clause of the peace treaty. Only in that way would there be enough left of the prewar order on which to build a sound structure.

Suppose, as well, that the Bolsheviks were really only stalling for time, that their purpose was to achieve world revolution immediately. Given the disruptions in society already caused by four years of war, how could it be imagined that the Bolsheviks' professed concern for the welfare of the working classes could be translated by the Soviet program into anything but anarchy and, eventually, a still worse tyranny? Lansing raised several of these points in a memorandum he sent the president about the latest Trotsky pronouncement. "The document is an appeal to the proletariat of all countries," he advised Wilson on January 2, 1918, "to the ignorant and mentally deficient, who by their numbers are urged to become masters. Here seems to me to lie a very real danger in view of the present social unrest throughout the world."[36]

The very next day Wilson voiced his own similar concerns to Ambassador Spring-Rice. At the outset of the war, he began, his principal worry had been with the "imminent danger of civil discord. . . . There was evidence of a long planned agitation which might at any time lead to most serious results."[37] Whatever its origins (Wilson did not name them), this agitation now had the face of Bolshevism. The president then remarked on the Bolshevik appropriation of his own methods. He himself, he said, had appealed to the German people behind the back of their government before the Bolsheviks began issuing manifestos. These declarations had two main points: wars must not be waged for aggressive purposes, and the only proper basis for peace was universal self-determination. But now the Bolsheviks had usurped Wilson's position, and their approach had already had a big impact on Italy, and probably also on England and France. "In the United States active agitation was proceeding."

Here was the genesis of the Fourteen Points speech of January 8, 1918. It provided a response to Trotsky's hints that aid against the Germans would be welcome, and to those of the president's advisers who had been urging him to take up that hint, but it was primarily designed to counter the Soviet ideological assault on the bastions of civilization. Wilson began by lavishing praise upon the Russian representatives at Brest-Litovsk, the scene of the Russo-German peace talks, calling them sincere advocates who could never entertain proposals of conquest and domination. After that, of course, if a separate peace was made, Wilson could picture the Bolsheviks as men false to a sacred trust of the Russian people. He added to this in the speech by stating that the Russians had made their position clear, and had been met by deceit from the other side, as the Germans sought to hide their unswerving aim of keeping every square foot of territory their armed forces had occupied—"every province, every city, every point of vantage."

It was a reasonable conjecture, continued the speech, that the general principles first offered by the Central Powers in response to Russian appeals had originated with the more liberal statesmen of Germany and Austria, men who felt the force "of their own people's thought and purpose." Above this "troubled air" one voice rang clear: the voice of the Russian people. That voice had reached to the far corners of the world. What the president was saying, in such deft fashion, was that the peace program did not belong to the Bolsheviks at all; it had been forced on them in exactly the same way it had been forced on the German and Austrian leaders who had drawn up the liberal response, and now sought to decieve their citizens. How else could the final sentence of this section of the speech be read, except as a hint that the Bolsheviks were already engaged in deceiving the Russian masses: "Whether their present leaders believe it or not, it is our heartfelt desire and hope that some way may be opened whereby we may be privileged to assist the people of Russia to attain their utmost hope of liberty and ordered peace. . . ."

Trotsky had met his match in this initial encounter. If not in disarray, the Bolsheviks were at least put off stride. The Fourteen Points speech demonstrated Wilson's incomparable talents. In Point 6 Wilson promised that all Russian territory would be evacuated, and that the Russian people would be welcomed into international society under institutions of their own choosing. "The treatment accorded Russia by her sister nations in the months to come will be the acid test of their good will, of their comprehension of her needs as distinguished from their own interests, and of their intelligent and unselfish sympathy."

Colonel House thought this section was "the most eloquent part of his message." And so it was. It did not say that the United States would ever recognize a Bolshevik government, and was, in fact, a promise to turn over Russian territory to a government that thought in terms of Russian territory, as opposed to Marxist internationalism. Yet Raymond Robins thought that the speech had converted Lenin, and that now there would be no separate peace. The Soviet leader did welcome the speech, saying that it was a "great step ahead toward the peace of the world," and permitted it to be distributed across Russia.[38]

Edgar Sisson, who handled the negotiations on behalf of the Committee for Public Information for distribution of the speech, was wary of Lenin's seeming eagerness to promote Wilsonian goals. "It will be a mistake for anyone to believe," read his notes of a conversation with Raymond Robins, "that our political democracy can merge with this industrial democracy. The latter will seek revolution against capital until it conquers or is conquered." Sisson knew full well that neither Wilson nor Lenin had been converted. And he was also perceptive enough to take special notice of Lenin's comment about the ambiguity of Wilson's commitment in the speech to an "absolutely impartial adjustment of all colonial claims." It was the only weak clause in the speech, Sisson wrote. "When he went unerringly for it, I knew that he had the gift for finding cracks in any armor." Lenin's final comment also impressed Sisson: "This is all very well as far as it goes, but why not formal recognition, and when."[39]

> *If the present rulers of Russia take action which is independent of their Allies, we have no means of intervening to arrest the catastrophe which is assuredly befalling their country.*
>
> David Lloyd George,
> Trades Union Congress speech,
> January 5, 1918

Lenin had welcomed the Fourteen Points speech because it seemed less menacing than recent Allied moves and statements, not because he wanted aid to fight the Germans. There were rumors of an impending Japanese landing at Vladivostok, and David Lloyd George's recent speech to the Trade Unions Congress had done nothing to dispel the Soviet leader's concern. To the contrary, the prime minister seemed perfectly willing that his words be taken as a wink in Berlin's direction that Germany might be permitted to do as it liked in the east in exchange for granting Allied terms in the west.[40]

"Your Lloyd George," Trotsky said to a British agent in Russia, R. H. Bruce Lockhart, "is like a man playing roulette and scattering chips on every number. . . ." When the British cabinet had originally considered sending aid to Kaledin, the Vladivostok route immediately came to the forefront—and along with it the Japanese problem. If Japan landed forces in Siberia, an intense anti-Allied reaction was likely. To forestall that peril, Lloyd George decided to send Lockhart, in case "anything had to be said to them," i.e., the Bolsheviks.[41]

Lockhart's ostensible mission, then, was to maintain contacts with Lenin and Trotsky in much the same manner as Raymond Robins was serving Wilson. The Japanese were specifically informed of Lockhart's mission because it was imperative, whether anything was to be "said to them" or not, that Tokyo realize Great Britain was not abandoning Russia completely to Germany in the west and Japan in the east. The Japanese foreign minister, Baron Motono, picked up at once on the point. He was surprised, he said, that Mr. Lockhart would be accredited "even unofficially" while plans were going forward for such a different enterprise elsewhere, "say at Vladivostok." Yet he could sympathize with a desire to choose "the safest course," and the wish to support the "better elements in Russia generally." He would like to know more about British methods, for Japan was in a position to act in eastern Siberia "in support of the same good cause."[42]

Sir Conyngham Greene's report of this conversation set off alarm bells in London. The Japanese had been smoked out—but now what? Allied aims in south Russia had no political objectives, Greene was told to say, although of course war exigencies might entail the establishment of an autonomous Georgian state. Protection of Allied supplies at Vladivostok was the paramount issue. If the necessity arose for active measures, Japan would be duly consulted. His Majesty's Government felt sure, this message closed, that it could count on Tokyo's cooperation "in the common interest."[43]

Greene was astounded at these instructions. What century did they think it was in London? One could no longer dismiss Baron Motono with a wave of Victoria's imperial scepter. "We can do nothing to stop them," he cabled back. "We might make a virtue of giving way gracefully, and so have one less military anxiety upon our minds in coming months." Yes, admitted Lord Charles Hardinage, persuading Tokyo to act as mandatory for all the Allies, if not at their behest, required skillful management lest eastern Siberia be reduced to the status of a "Japanese colony at the end of the war."[44]

A debate ensued within the war cabinet, during which ministers contradicted themselves and the prime minister remained indecisive. Everyone agreed that Siberia was too valuable, both for itself and as a link to southern and southeastern Russia, to be allowed to go to Japan. But it was argued at one point that the only way to save Siberia would be to invite the Japanese to send in forces, and in that way topple the Bolshevik regime. This novel argument came from Sir George Buchanan, now returned home permanently, and full of hatred for Lenin and the Bolsheviks.[45]

Buchanan refuted all of Arthur Balfour's arguments that a final break with the Bolsheviks should be avoided. Lenin had made it plain what he intended to do. Look at his contemptuous dismissal of the Constituent Assembly, which had been elected under the Provisional Government to consider Russia's future government. Only Great Britain, Sir George went on, had agreed to receive a representative from the current regime. Inevitably this man must become a propaganda channel, and Sir George would sooner see the rupture than permit such insidious business to go forward. "[S]uch propaganda was dangerous, and attractive to those who had nothing to lose. . . ." Lenin was still on the defensive because of his arrogant behavior in regard to the Constituent Assembly. He needed international sanction. For the moment, the tide had turned, and the opportunity to strike a fatal blow at the Bolsheviks had appeared. With aid from the Japanese or the Americans, or both, military resistance to the Bolsheviks could succeed.[46]

Not once did the German menace or the restoration of the eastern front enter into Buchanan's presentation. The issue was how to crush the Bolshevik movement, outside as well as inside Russia. Those who disagreed did so because they placed a lower priority on immediate action against the new Russian regime. Lord Curzon, former viceroy of India, insisted, for example, that "cooperation" with the Japanese would "enormously enhance the prestige of Asiatics against Europeans, and would consequently react upon the attitude of Indians toward the British." Lloyd George agreed with Buchanan that Bolshevism had become a general menace to civilization, and that its doctrines had attracted adherents even in England. Then he fell to musing about the implications of intervention at Vladivostok, or some other place. "Any attempt of the Germans to interfere in Russia would be like an attempt to burgle a plague-house."[47]

His colleagues decided, nonetheless, to approach the Japanese about occupying the Trans-Siberian Railroad up to the fringes of the Cossack country. Paris and Washington were to be informed of the plan. And so it was left. When one of Balfour's go-betweens, Sir William Wiseman, conveyed the gist of the decision to Colonel House, he chose to emphasize the argument that American interests also lay in seeing Japanese energies taken up with Siberia. That was not a very wise approach, because it only confirmed the president's earlier fears that aid to Kaledin was merely a prelude to the partition of Russia.[48]

There was "nothing wise or practicable in this scheme," the president warned Lansing. Whether Tokyo said yes or no to the proposed invitation, such a request would compromise the Allies by giving the Japanese "a certain moral advantage with respect to any ultimate desires or purposes she may have with regard to the Eastern Provinces of Sibera."[49] On February 4, 1918, Wilson queried the secretary of state twice, with seemingly contradictory implications. In his first note he wrote, "As I understand it, our official representative in Petrograd *is* keeping in touch with the Bolshevik leaders informally. Am I not right?" Later the same day, however, he complained that it was very "annoying" to have "this man [Raymond] Robins, in whom I have no confidence whatever, acting as political adviser in Russia and sending his advice to private individuals." Lansing should see Red Cross officials and have them remind Robins "of his proper functions and their limitations."[50]

Whatever was on Wilson's mind to prompt the notion of a new movement in regard to Russia—and his memos could be read as a hint that he planned to do so—Lansing turned over the first question to his favorite Russian expert, Basil Miles, who produced a somewhat surprising response that criticized the decision not to deal with the Bolsheviks on an official level. Robins had been used as a channel of information, he said, not to communicate anything to Lenin. "All observers returning from Russia seem agreed that the unbending adherence to this policy of holding absolutely aloof has been aggravating; has even tended to throw Bolsheviks into hands of the Germans."[51]

Lansing sent the gist of the Miles memorandum to Wilson on February 9, 1918, along with a covering letter that recommended permitting Robins to act in an informal capacity to establish contacts with the Bolsheviks. Wilson agreed. But neither man dealt directly with the primary issue raised, perhaps because both saw that it would be easier to repudiate Robins than to disavow anything that passed through David Francis.[52]

While British and American policymakers occupied themselves thus, the subjects of their debate were themselves pondering a set of unpleasant options. Lenin's response to the Fourteen Points speech had been one of simple expedience, a question always of gaining time. Trotsky, on the other hand, had come to feel that the revolution in Germany was closer at hand than Comrade Lenin allowed himself, or the party's Central Committee, to believe. Another thought had arisen to trouble Trotsky. What would be the practical consequences of creating the impression that the Russian Bolsheviks had abandoned socialists in other countries? What peril did socialists create for themselves by allowing Wilson's program to hold the field? If for no other reason than to safeguard the future, then, it was imperative to avoid an impression of Bolshevik indifference to what happened outside Russia.[53]

At Brest-Litovsk, accordingly, Trotsky created a sensation by announcing that Russia would not sign a treaty; it would simply stop waging war. This "No war, no peace" formula had several advantages, claimed the commissar when he reported to the Central Committee. They should consider the failed negotiations a triumph over the Germans, who had been outsmarted. "[W]e have made any advance a very embarrassing affair for the German militarists."[54] If the Germans were so foolish as to attack, they would risk a revolution at home and, in consequence, Allied diplomatic recognition of the new regime in Russia.

Recognition, in turn, would provide double protection against a victorious capitalist enemy: Germany held in check by fear of revolution, and Britain, France, and America abandoning intervention schemes to preserve a friendly Russia.[55] As Trotsky rehearsed these presumed benefits of the "No war, no peace" formula, a change was already taking place in London. David Lloyd George had decided to get off the fence.

During a two-day discussion of the Russian problem, prompted by a wire from Petrograd urging that Lockhart be given greater authority to reach a "fuller understanding with the Bolshevik Government," the war cabinet failed to reach an agreement. "My view is that Russia is our most powerful ally now in Germany," insisted Lloyd George. Robert Cecil, who had wavered back and forth, warned that it was a dangerous thing to suppose that revolution was "catching" only in Germany. Did the prime minister really mean to imply aid to the Bolsheviks to bring down the Kaiser? Opening formal relations with the Bolsheviks would have a very serious impact on France and Italy. Not necessarily, answered the prime minister; giving Lockhart greater authority might enable him to reach an understanding on "propaganda."[56]

"The discussion got rather hot at one time," noted cabinet secretary Maurice Hankey, "as they were getting to fundamentals, the rights of property owners etc. . . . A very amusing meeting."[57] Lloyd George emerged from the fray victorious—but only until his instructions were modified in the Foreign Office. On February 9, Lockhart was told that he should assure the Bolshevik leaders that the Allies had no concern to meddle in Russia's internal affairs. Recognition had not been withheld out of fear that such a course "might cause" trouble with the "Bourgeois elements in Russia." For the time being Britain was willing to enter into semiofficial relations, like those that existed with the de facto governments of Finland and the Ukraine. Where the prime minister had suggested that Lockhart be authorized to offer an ideological truce, the Foreign Office stressed instead the "hopeless impasse" that existed on that issue, and warned solemnly that His Majesty's Government would do everything it could to "stop Bolshevik propaganda" in England.

No pretense, then, of liking one another ought to cloud the common interest they shared. "We both desire the overthrow of Militarism in Central Europe." Cooperation toward that end was possible, perhaps invaluable. "I may instance on Trotsky's part," said Balfour's telegram, "the refusal to Germany of supplies which would assist her in prolonging the war and facilitate the efforts of the military party to crush the popular movement in favor of a democratic peace." Meanwhile, he would await Lockhart's specific suggestions as to how he could help either with essential supplies or otherwise.[58]

Sir William Wiseman, who had earlier informed Colonel House of the decision to sound out Tokyo on a Far Eastern intervention, now came back to him with a very different message to deliver, based on Balfour's carefully phrased instructions to Petrograd. Not to be outdone, the colonel declared that the president had decided the time had come to recognize the Bolshevik regime. To do so, said Wilson's special adviser, would encourage "the liberal parties in Germany and Austria," and erase any false impression of Allied support for Russian reactionaries.[59]

Balfour was shocked. His Majesty's Government did not favor recognition, he cabled Washington. The fundamental conflict between the new rulers of Russia and Great Britain had been brought into focus again by Trotsky's desire to send a consul general to India. "That cannot be entertained," the foreign secretary warned Lockhart, even at the cost of reprisals. Avowed Bolshevik policy made it impossible for anyone sent by the Soviets to work in harmony with the existing regime there.[60]

In short, what Balfour and the Foreign Office were offering was their own version of Trotsky's "No war, no peace."

> *Anything may happen, nobody knows, nobody can know, because all the Great Powers are tied up, hard-pressed, compelled to fight on several fronts.*
>
> Lenin on the Treaty of Brest-Litovsk, 1918

From the time of his arrival in Russia, Lockhart had felt that the Foreign Office was making a mistake. Lloyd George was his patron, though he would find the prime minister an elusive supporter. Sometimes he was there, sometimes he was not. Therefore, Lockhart must act on his own. His great ambition was to build something on the Bolsheviks' willingness to cooperate against Germany, something that could prevent postwar ideological conflicts from getting out of hand. He had found Trotsky willing to talk about an agreement, for example, that would provide for a cessation of counterrevolutionary activity in exchange for a halt in Bolshevik agitation.[61]

Trotsky's one aim, Lockhart insisted, was to stimulate the German revolution. London must realize that the opposition parties in Russia, every single one of them, would welcome German intervention. So that meant, Lockhart reasoned, that promoting the German downfall was a defensive measure, not an example of Bolshevik ideological fanaticism. Like it or not, therefore, the most fateful hour had come. The bell was tolling, however, not only on relations with the Bolsheviks, but on Britain's entire future in Russia. "I cannot help feeling that if we let slip this opportunity we are abandoning to Germany the prize that will compensate her for any losses in the West."

Rightly fearing an unsympathetic response from the Foreign Office, Lockhart asked that his message be shown to the prime minister. In the past, of course, it had been Lloyd George who seemed most willing to entertain the idea of a separate peace with Germany, leaving Russia to its fate. "The indictment is unfortunately true," minuted Thomas Lyons of Lockhart's complaint that thus far Britain had supported counterrevolution as its top priority. "[W]e have backed every anti-Bolshevik movement and every one has collapsed." An unrepentant Ronald Graham went further: "The Ukrainian Rada was certainly a bad horse to back and Cossack is almost a non-starter, but Bolshevik would be the worst rogue of the lot on which to lay our money although we may run him as a pacemaker."[62]

A variety of British schemes were underway in Russia as Lyons and

Graham mused over Lockhart's reports, including one that has been described as "nothing less than a blueprint for a British takeover bid for the entire Russian economy—a giant extension of British economic imperialism, whereby a prostrated Russia could be reduced—or elevated—to the status of a British colony." The mechanism for this fantastic scheme was to be put in motion by bids to buy out Russia's major banks and put them under British control. Stranded by Lloyd George's circumspect behavior, isolated from these other doings that put his mission in jeopardy, Lockhart lived constantly on the edge of professional (and even personal) extinction.[63]

To make matters worse, the resumption of the German offensive in the east drove Trotsky into a corner. Lenin had gone along with the "No war, no peace" formula, but now he insisted that if the policy of "revolutionary phrase-making continued," he would resign. Then those who wanted Russia to be the last bastion of a revolution that would not come, who wanted to make themselves martyrs to Western Europe's unenlightened working class, could take over and do as they pleased. Under this pressure, Trotsky dispatched a formal peace offer to the Germans. Unwilling to give it all up, however, Trotsky asked another British diplomat in Petrograd, Frederick Lindley, if Britain and France would give promises of aid if the fighting continued.[64]

Angry perhaps at his own miscalculation, Trotsky blamed Lockhart. "while you are here trying to throw dust in my eyes, your countrymen and the French have been intriguing against us. . . ." The accusation was true and Lockhart knew it. Even Allied diplomats in Petrograd, behind their earnest appeals (the commissar went on, in a crescendo of invective), were plotting to overthrow the Bolsheviks. "Look at this," he declared, shoving at Lockhart a copy of forged documents circulating in Allied circles that purportedly proved that the Bolsheviks were in German pay. "I hope you are proud of your work. Your Foreign Office does not deserve to win a war. Your policy towards Russia right from the beginning has been indecisive and vacillating."[65] However true this last thrust, Trotsky was on the defensive.

A motion to accept the harsh German terms was adopted by the Central Committee on February 24, 1918. Frederick Lindley reflected a moment on the final irony. "Practical result of Russian attempt to secure peace 'without annexations, etc.' has been [the] greatest single annexation which has taken place in Europe since [the] break-up of [the] Roman Empire."[66]

Reluctant to give up *his* version of the Trotsky vision, Lockhart continued to hold out the possibility of Russian resistance to an actual German occupation, and to insist that it was not reasonable to be "unduly pessimistic about our future prospects in Russia."[67] In London, however, the war cabinet quickly decided to renew the Japanese option. The Japanese were about to move anyway, Balfour advised the new British ambassador in Washington, Lord Reading. And given the "bankrupt" Bolshevik surrender policy, he said, it was unlikely that Japanese intervention would stir up pro-Lenin feelings. America's role should now be one of bringing about a coordinated Allied policy in Russia, a policy that would employ Japan to achieve Anglo-American ends.[68]

Never engaged to the extent that the British had been in dealing with Trotsky, policymakers in Washington debated other aspects of the Russian issue. Secretary of State Lansing was interested in finding out more about the so-called Sisson documents, another version of the forgeries that Trotsky had thrust back at Lockhart. Lansing wanted Ambassador Francis to make "every endeavor to obtain further evidence" about German intrigues with the tsarist government as well. To complete "our information in this case," he said, it would be necessary to discover if Lenin had accepted money from Germany, but also if he had agreed not to carry out propaganda against the German and Austrian armies. Otherwise all the documents might prove was that the Bolsheviks had completely outsmarted German intelligence.[69]

Lansing was unhappy at the moment about an Allied resolution at a recent conference condemning Lenin's repudiation of Russia's foreign debt. What bothered him was not that the resolution condemned the action, but that it appeared to "recognize a certain measure of force in acts of the Bolshevik Government."[70] Hence the importance of trying to find more evidence to support the Sisson documents before a pattern settled in that, even in a backhanded way, legitimized the Bolshevik government. For the same reason, the secretary was upset about reports of French willingness to send money and material to the Bolsheviks if the latter agreed to resist the Germans. In response to a French query about possible American cooperation, Lansing had minuted, "This is out of the question. Submitted to the Pres't who says the same thing."[71]

On February 23, 1918, one day before the Central Committee in Petrograd accepted Berlin's terms, Lansing confided to an aide that the U.S. government would refuse aid to Lenin even should the Bolsheviks adopt a policy of resistance. Their regime was a greater danger to America than the Germans, he told Breckinridge Long, because the former denied the principles of nationality and property rights—and had already threatened the United States with revolution. Wartime exigencies shaped Allied tactics, but were not enough reason for the United States to deal with Lenin.[72]

Thus Balfour's suggested role for the United States had been rejected even before it was made. But Lansing's mind was already busy devising an alternative that would enable Washington to exert authority in Russia commensurate with its new military predominance in the west. In mid-February instructions went out to John F. Stevens, head of an old railway mission to the Provisional Government, ordering him to return to Harbin from Japan. Using that Manchurian city as his base of operations, Stevens was to try to make contact with local anti-Bolshevik authorities in an effort to gain control of the Trans-Siberian Railway "both toward Vladivostok and also westwards."[73]

Responses from the field were enthusiastic about the possibility of an American initiative. By making use of Chinese troops and "loyal" Russians, came estimates from Stevens and diplomats in the Far East, control of the Trans-Siberian was possible all the way to Irkutsk in western Siberia. If the United States did not act, on the other hand, Japan would not hesitate to move.[74] Ambassador Francis was more than ready for a change. "In my judgment," he cabled, "terms of peace make Russia German province with good prospects of becoming ally. I renew my recommendation for immediate possession of Vladivostok, Murmansk, and Archangel."[75]

A few days later Francis left Petrograd to reestablish the American embassy at Vologda, some 350 miles to the east. Vologda offered good communications both east and west, and was presumably beyond the range of any German advance. Francis had announced that he was accredited to the Russian people, moreover, and that he had no intention of abandoning them to the Germans or the Bolsheviks. Anticipating the appearance of a new, truly Russian government, the ambassador had set up camp to be close by.[76]

In Moscow, meanwhile, Consul General Maddin Summers and Consul DeWitt C. Poole had worked out the scenario in great detail. The first crucial step was to secure the Siberian Railway, aided by both Chinese and Japanese forces. Stevens would have charge of this operation. A proper line of defense behind the Ural Mountains would thus be erected, and under its protection a "provisional government" established to repulse the expected "German invasion." In no time at all, "representatives of the healthy polictical elements" would rally to this new government, and Russia would be saved.[77]

So far as Colonel House was concerned any plan of this sort, including the one dreamed up so quickly by American second-level officials in reply to Lansing's inquiries, had a fatal flaw: it would have to be worked with Japan. But acquiescence in a Japanese forward move in Siberia would destroy America's special position, the disinterested aloofness that assured Wilson's authority to speak for humankind. "The whole structure which you have built up so carefully may be destroyed over night," he wrote the president, "and our position will be no better than that of the Germans." Filled with hatred toward all Russians, the British and French cared not what happened to those people. House also wrote Balfour directly to ask if the Allies had taken into account the ramifications of using a yellow race to make war against a white one.[78]

The colonel's view prevailed—at least for the moment. On March 5, 1918, the United States informed Japan that even if the firmest self-denying commitments were given, it could not approve of any military action in Russia. The United States entertained the greatest sympathy for that country, continued the message, and for its revolution, "in spite of all the unhappiness and misfortune which has for the time being sprung out of it."[79]

> *This is our last chance.*
> Bruce Lockhart,
> March 5, 1918

Lockhart and Robins, meanwhile, had taken up new positions. Robins's situation was the more precarious, as he enjoyed less access to the corridors of power in Washington. Still, they reinforced one another's belief that by working together they could salvage something out of the wreckage on the eastern front. When Lockhart saw Lenin on March 1, 1918, German armies were still advancing on Petrograd. The Bolshevik leader seemed much less sure of himself in these circumstances than when he had forced through the vote to accept Berlin's terms. "Our ways . . . are not your ways," he told the British agent, but German militarism was for the moment a greater threat. He was ready to risk cooperation, said Lenin, but the British would never see things in that light. Whatever happened, the Germans would have to maintain "larger and not fewer forces in the East." And in the end, Russia would confound the Germans. "Passive resistance—and the expression comes from your own country—is a more potent weapon than any army that cannot fight."[80]

Trotsky could not conceal his excitement at this prospect. Riding a new wave of revolutionary enthusiasm, he told Lockhart that the government would move to Moscow and begin organizing the Ural and Volga districts for massive resistance. But the Allies must not let Japan loose in Siberia, warned the commissar, for that would render all his efforts useless. Coming away from these interviews, Lockhart sent the message the

Bolsheviks no doubt wanted him to send: Hold off on any Japanese scheme until Trotsky had had his chance.[81]

His Majesty's Government would do all it could to aid the Bolsheviks to resist, replied Balfour, but what had they done to help themselves except to issue eloquent proclamations that had neither induced the citizenry to fight nor the Germans to retire? Japan could not be restrained. "She deems her national safety involved in thwarting German penetration to the Pacific coast. We cannot think her wrong. . . ."[82]

Lockhart was making himself something of a nuisance. He doubted, he cabled London, that fear of the Germans had much to do with encouraging the Japanese. The real reason, as the Bolsheviks claimed, was the desire to see the Bolsheviks' destruction. However much Balfour resented such harping on the need for cooperation, he knew that it served one purpose: a record was being made that could square the government with the British people. "I have done this," he explained candidly in a message to Colonel House concerning various proposals to aid Russia, "so that we can put ourselves right with public opinion if and when a statement is made on the whole subject."[83]

President Wilson was similarly occupied. Raymond Robins, like Lockhart, had been hoping that the United States would seize the opportunity presented by the debate over the treaty with Germany in the All-Russian Congress of Soviets to offer aid if the treaty was rejected. He had seen Trotsky on March 5, 1918, and heard a startling proposition. "Do you want to prevent the Brest peace from being ratified?" he recalled Trotsky asking. Robins said that he knew Lenin held strong views on this subject, and asked in reply how the foreign affairs commissar could accomplish what he proposed. Things had changed, said Trotsky, and then he repeated what he had told Lockhart. If Russia could be certain of receiving economic and military aid, the treaty would be rejected and an attempt would be made to reestablish the eastern front in the Urals. Robins wanted this in writing. "You want me to give you my life, don't you," protested Trotsky. No, said Robins, but there must be something specific, something nailed down in Lenin's presence as well.

No doubt Trotsky was making a record to use later just as Balfour and Wilson were, and he most certainly was trying to smoke out Allied intentions. When Robins pressed for details, Trotsky posed a list of hypothetical questions based on the proposition that the treaty had been rejected. What would the United States do if Japan, either in tacit or open alliance with Germany, seized Vladivostok? What would the United States do to prevent a Japanese landing in the Russian Far East? What did Washington think would be available from Great Britain through Murmansk and Archangel? What steps, finally, would the government of Great Britain take to assure this aid, and thus dispel rumors of hostile plans against Russia?[84]

Hedged though it might be, Robins though he was hearing a genuine appeal for American aid. Renewed fighting on the eastern front, he believed, was now only a matter of time. Both Lockhart and Robins were too willing, perhaps, to take these statements for more than they were worth. And they downplayed the obvious motive the Bolshevik leaders had for using any inducements they could to check Japan. Yet Trotsky himself had responded to a request from the Murmansk Soviet for instructions with a blunt statement that to protect the city against the Germans they must accept "any and all assistance" from the Allies.[85]

Trotsky's preoccupation with the Japanese did not trouble Ambassador Francis either. The more the foreign affairs commissar feared Japan, reasoned Francis, the more serious he would have to be about alternative sources of aid. What impressed the ambassador as he read the record of Robins's conversation, however, was the account of the final sentence of Trotsky's statement. "Neither his government," he had said, "nor [the] Russian people would object to America's supervising all shipments from Vladivostok into Russia and virtually controlling operation of Siberian Railway. . . ."[86]

However naive Robins and Lockhart may have been, other evidence existed that pointed to a need to take the appeals seriously—if only to expose the Bolsheviks. And it is clear that one of Washington's concerns was that the appeal *was* serious, and therefore had to be handled with some care. Wilson's efforts to develop a message for the All-Russian Congress of Soviets indicate just how seriously he took the problem. As it happened, Trotsky's inquiries to Robins did not reach Wilson before his message went out from Washington. From what was known already, however, if the president had wished to make a concrete proposal he could have done so. Certainly he had seldom held back from taking the initiative in other instances, especially when the stakes were so high.

The message expressed sympathy for the Russian people, and was taken to mean that the president wished to leave no doubt of his opposition to intervention. Unfortunately, it went on after these assurances, the United States was not in a position to render the direct and effective aid it would wish to give. "I beg to assure the people of Russia through the Congress that it will avail itself of every opportunity to secure for Russia once more complete sovereignty and independence in her own affairs and full restoration to her great role in the life of Europe and the modern world." In his original draft, Wilson had referred in one place to the "Revolution." He readily agreed with State Department views that the wording should be changed to "struggle for freedom."[87]

That alteration is another indication of how carefully Wilson tiptoed around the central issue. He had produced, claimed Colonel House, "one of the most cleverly worded, three sentenced messages extant." It combined several things, including a veiled warning to Japan, into a firm and absolute rejection of Bolshevik overtures. Raymond Robins would later insist that Lenin had held up the proceedings of the Congress of Soviets to allow time for Washington and London to respond to Trotsky's inquiries. Even on the night the Treaty of Brest-Litovsk was ratified, said Robins, Lenin paused a final moment to ask if any word had been received. Robins and Lockhart would always believe that a major opportunity had been allowed to slip away, with tragic consequences.[88]

Nothing in Lenin's attitude toward the West really warrants such a conclusion, but neither is it sufficient to dismiss Robins's account as sheer fantasy. The situation was in a state of flux. Lenin may well have been hoping to hear a negative response to bolster his position or, on the other hand, merely an indication of what American intentions were in regard to a Japanese intervention or British maneuvers now underway near Archangel and Murmansk in the north. Would evidence of American opposition to Allied schemes have changed his mind about the treaty? Unlikely. But Lenin did have to contend with a strong minority opposition, although it was subdued for the moment, and with a changing military situation at his doorstep. If the desire to wage revolutionary war was indefensible, nevertheless protection of the revolution was a duty. Maybe the two could not be separated. In any event, had there been an offer of aid, Lenin could not have concealed it. And even if the absence of an American offer changed nothing that evening—or for the next decade—Soviet relations with the West had been altered, just as Wilson's words had been altered.

Lenin had described the treaty with Germany at a secret party conference as nothing more than "breathing space between wars." It might last only a few days. But whatever time there was could be used to evacuate Petrograd. For that alone he would sign a peace "even a hundred times more humiliating . . . for in doing so I alleviate the sufferings of the workers when the Germans take it; I facilitate the removal from Petersburg of the supplies, ammunition, guns, and other things which I need, because I am a 'defencist,' because I stand for getting the army ready, even if in the farthest rear, where the sick army, which demobilized itself, can be cured." Lenin's adoption of the Menshevik term "defencist" to describe himself was opportunism, but it also suggests that Trotsky's statements to Lockhart and Robins about regrouping in the Urals were not pure fantasy. "[A]n historic crisis is not resolved by one war or by one peace treaty . . . we are not putting an end to our struggle."[89]

That was true, certainly, for Wilson and Lloyd George as well.

CHAPTER EIGHT

Visions in a Clouded Prism

I fear that we are treating the Bolshevik Government as though it were no Government. Under the old regime you would not have gone to Murmansk and Vladivostok without the Tsar's permission. You are out for the same policy as during the French Revolution—seizing Toulon, and one place after another.

David Lloyd George to the war cabinet, April 1918

Not a week had gone by after the Soviet Congress ratified the Treaty of Brest-Litovsk before the Germans launched an all-out offensive to win the war in the west. It would cost them dearly, more than eight hundred thousand casualties, but they inflicted losses of over a million, and drove to within thirty-seven miles of Paris. Thirty-five divisions used in the assault had come from the defunct eastern front. When the attack began, on March 21, 1918, American military forces were still not effectively in operation on the battlefront, although the doughboys would play an important role later in checking the advance on Paris.[1]

Once the German offensive began, the note of desperation in British appeals for Washington's aid in mounting an Allied "counteroffensive" in Russia grew louder and louder. It might be the only way to boost sagging morale, said Sir William Wiseman in conversations with Colonel House. With American troops still not fully engaged, House was willing to credit the argument, and to agree further that "apart from the intrinsic value of the scheme, it may be advisable, and even necessary, to put it into effect for the sake of Allied morale." Perhaps, said Wilson's adviser, Bruce Lockhart could redouble his efforts to secure Russian assent to a Japanese intervention. "This question," Wiseman reported gloomily, "shows disposition always to revert to making assent of Russia indispensable feature of American policy."[2]

> *If . . . we were invited to intervene by any responsible*
> *and representative body, we ought to do so.*
>
> Woodrow Wilson, May 30, 1918

Lockhart's goading cables had won him few friends in London. Considering the way His Majesty's Government had treated the Bolsheviks, read a particularly barbed communication from Petrograd, "they have been wonderfully patient with us. You cannot expect them to say nice things about British capitalists. . . ." No help had been offered from London. Instead Allied agents spent their energy trying to prove Lenin a German hireling. "And our secret service has naturally had no difficulty in buying a wonderful collection of documents. Some of these have been published in *Pravda* as a humorous illustration of what England and France believe."[3]

It was not without a tinge of pleasure, therefore, that the Foreign Office prepared a telegram to Lord Reading in Washington to accompany a memorandum on Lockhart authored by General Alfred Knox. Undermining Lockhart's credibility should be easy, and the sacrifice was apparently necessary to disabuse the Americans about the man's expertise and thereby put an end to House's advocacy of him as a go-between. Balfour left to Reading how and where it should be used.

The gist of Knox's argument was that Lockhart had come under the pernicious influence of Raymond Robins, "a fanatic with the temperament of a hero-worshipping schoolgirl." Former military adviser in Russia, Knox had suggested that the best strategy for dealing with the collapsing Russian army was the knout. Now he made another spectacular recommendation. No matter how stupidly arranged, his memorandum on Lockhart continued, Japanese intervention would do less damage to "our cause" than any more palavering with the Bolsheviks. "The policy of flirtation with the Bolsheviks is both wrong as a policy and immoral." With blithe disregard for the supposed objective of reopening the eastern front, Knox cited Trotsky's announced intention of building a five-hundred-thousand-man Red Army as an illustration of the danger of playing up to such incendiaries.[4]

One could conclude, if so inclined, that Knox was advocating intervention as the best means of preventing Russia from reopening a military front! Whatever use Lord Reading made of this ammunition, Trotsky's supposed military plans posed a predicament for American policymakers as well. Robins, as might be expected, saw another opening in the foreign affairs commissar's invitation to the Allies to send military advisers to help in training the army, while Ambassador Francis's first reaction was akin to that of General Knox. "Prominent government officials," the ambassador cabled from his Vologda outpost in March 22, 1918, the day after the German offensive began, "call our Government imperialistic and even Lenin and Trotsky do not conceal that new army being organized to aid world-wide social revolution and overturn all existing governments."[5]

But he had some second thoughts. Repeating in a later cable his fear that the real objective of the Red Army was world revolution, he said that he had nevertheless instructed his military attaché to open negotiations. A Russian army, he explained, still offered the only possible source of resistance to Germany. But there was another consideration to think about. "My real and strictly confidential reason is that [an] army so organized can by proper methods be taken from Bolshevik control and used against Germans, and even its creators. . . ."[6]

At each turning point, then, the intensifying debate over intervention in the Russian Revolution was shaped by extramilitary questions, from the first proposals to aid Kaledin in December 1917 down to these remarkable comments on the creation of the Red Army. Lansing was perhaps the least circumspect of all in stating his fundamental opposition to dealing with the Bolsheviks, and his determination to see them brought down, but he was also the most persistent in recognizing that the only way to reconcile the Wilsonian and conservative points of view was to prove that the Bolsheviks were indeed German agents.

Trotsky's invitation to participate in building the Red Army was followed by a more subtle inducement to recognition, along economic lines. Lockhart was told that an invitation to the Japanese was not out of the question, under certain conditions. These included something tantamount to official diplomatic recognition, and an arrangement that would force the capitalist West to demonstrate its ever-present cupidity. A fixed price for the Japanese should be agreed upon in advance, explained Trotsky, both economically and territorially. The Soviet government would be a full party to the contract.[7]

Out of the question, responded Balfour. His Majesty's Government would only offer a guarantee that Russian territory would be evacuated at the end of the war, and that while in Russia Allied troops would take no part in political controversies. As for the offer to strike a bargain about territorial and economic concessions, Britain's only desire was "to help Russia not to fleece her." Eventually, of course, Russia would be asked to make good on the Allied loans. But that was a wholly separate question, "not to be raised at the present moment."[8]

At Lloyd George's insistence, however, the question of Trotsky's terms for an invited intervention was referred to Washington.[9] The prime minister apparently hoped he might dissuade his colleagues in the war cabinet from the course chosen when Knox's memorandum was sent to Lord Reading or, alternatively, elicit a definitive statement in favor of counter-revolution and intervention from the United States. If the president agreed to deal with Trotsky, he said, then a firm proposal should be sent to the Soviet government.[10]

Though usually more adept than his war cabinet colleagues in the coalition in running a steeplechase, Lloyd George could never quite get over the Foreign Office barrier. "If recognition . . . is the price to pay," noted J. D. Gregory, a Russian expert, of this latest leap by the prime minister, "it is a great risk—because we shall undoubtedly alienate most of the elements in Russia whose support we require for the restoration of order. It is a vicious circle. Until this point, however, is decided here, it appears impossible to send a formula of invitation to the Powers for joint presentation at Moscow, as Mr. Lockhart suggests."[11]

Gregory knew where the prime minister was heading—back around the course in an opposite direction. Somewhere along his new path he hoped to find Wilson, whose intervention in the British debate over Russia he would welcome. But the president was not to be found, at least not where Lloyd George wanted him. Trotsky's request did throw a new light on the situation, Wilson told Lord Reading, but the Bolsheviks might be setting a trap. He was expecting the arrival daily of Edgar Sisson, the president continued, who was "in charge of documents which were alleged to prove that Trotsky and Lenin were in the pay of [the] German Government." Besides, it was impossible for the United States to send anything more than a regiment to participate in a joint intervention. And finally, it hardly seemed likely that Japan would want American chaperones.[12]

Ambassador Francis had also grown weary of oblique or evasive responses, of halfhearted initiatives, and of Raymond Robins and Bruce Lockhart. Nothing had come of all this talk of an "invited" intervention, and nothing would. It was past time for a decision. "Russia is passing through a dream or orgy from which awakening is possible any day but the longer we wait . . . the stronger foothold Germany will secure." Lenin was hopeless. Only recently the Soviet leader had pronounced the slaughter on the western front morally justified because it weakened all the imperialist governments and brought nearer their day of reckoning and the inevitable "dictatorship of [the] proletariat thoughout the world." The Russo-German treaty was also being justified to Russians because it increased the fury of the war in the west and gave Russia a breathing spell. The issue for Francis was simple: the Bolsheviks were using the war to solidify their power. "I greatly doubt whether Allies can longer afford to overlook principles which Lenin is aggressively championing."[13]

Specific proposals for action came from John F. Stevens and Paul Reinsch in China, both of whom thought the best answer was to get behind Gregorii Semenov, the freewheeling, freebooting local authority in Manchuria. On April 10, 1918, Reinsch reported that the Germans posed no military threat to Siberia. Like Francis, he assumed the threat was otherwise. To save Russia from "German domination," what was needed was economic aid to local authorities, such as the Siberian autonomous government at Tomsk. "Economic support as primary action," he recommended, "military assistance in the background made effective where local anarchy requires, would appear safe policy."[14]

Wilson knew that no policy deserved the title "safe," but a week later he asked Lansing for a memorandum on the emergence of self-governing "nuclei" that seemed to be springing up across Siberia. "It would afford me a great deal of satisfaction to get behind the most nearly representative of them if it can indeed draw leadership and control to itself."[15]

> *My policy regarding Russia is very similar to my Mexican policy. I believe in letting them work out their own salvation, even though they wallow in anarchy a while.*
>
> Woodrow Wilson, October 1918

Wilson was too much a Calvinist to believe that anyone should be allowed to wallow for very long. What he really desired was an interventionist plan that would not permit the "reactionary" tendencies among the Allies (whether Japanese or Anglo-French) to dominate the situation in Russia. The president never believed that talk about restoring the eastern front was anything but a cover story, and anyway Secretary Lansing thought Semenov was a bad vehicle for getting in touch with the self-governing "nuclei" in Siberia. His Russian adviser, Basil Miles, thought better of the idea. It was true that Semenov was backed by the Japanese, and also the British and French, but he had received contributions from the Siberian cooperative societies, presumably the groups Wilson had in mind in his hopeful forecast of things to come. Altogether, he concluded, Semenov was the strongest, most law-abiding, and most popular figure active in Siberia.

Yet any plan to aid him would have to be carefully managed so as to avoid a complete break with the Bolsheviks of the sort that would produce civil war and, quite likely, German domination. Wilson's idea was to allow the Bolsheviks to sustain a semblance of "Russian" control, however perverted their ideology, until the war ended and the true Russian "spirit" could emerge. To accomplish this delicate maneuver would require great skill, but the very instrument to insure its success was at hand. That instrument was the large force of Czechoslovak troops in the east, former prisoners of war who, after the fall of the tsar, had been organized into a Czech Legion. Stranded when Russia left the war, this force tried to regroup so as to join other Czech units now fighting on the western front against the Central Powers. Six thousand had already reached Vladivostok, forty thousand were preparing to try to exodus through Archangel, and an additional fifty thousand were currently being organized into regular military units. They wanted to fight to make Czech nationalism a reality, but their services might well be better employed inside Russia than in the west.[16]

Held in abeyance by Wilson, the Czech Legion would have its part to play. Meanwhile, he mulled over the idea of an economic mission to Siberia. His current plan, Sir William Wiseman reported of a conversation in late May, was to send a civil commission to help with railroads and food supplies and to establish a barter system. Of course, such a scheme would not produce immediate results, but it was the only alternative to allowing a Japanese intervention that would alienate the Russian people, or falling into Trotsky's trap of an invited intervention. What was needed was an invitation from a "responsible and representative" body. And the implication was that this new idea was the only way to see that possibility materialize.[17]

As he would say, Wilson viewed the situation in Russia as presenting issues like those he had encountered in Mexico. If he practiced "watchful waiting" in Siberia, he was ready to act as at Tampico and Veracruz once he concluded that it was essential to hold Archangel and Murmansk. "Every day," began a British appeal, "every day the position of Murmansk is more seriously endangered and, as the United States Government will of course be aware, it is of vital importance to us to retain Murmansk, if we desire to retain any possibility at all of entering Russia." The plea brought swift results. American troops heading for the western front were diverted to join Allied forces preparing for landings in North Russia.[18]

Secretary Lansing, moreover, had come up with an idea about the proposed economic mission to Siberia. It could be patterned after the famous Belgian Relief Commission. Headed by the same man, Herbert

Hoover, who had been so successful with that endeavor, a Russian Relief Commission would be immediately acclaimed as demonstrating American determination to bring about "an orderly government independent of Germany." It would also have the great virtue of disposing of Allied demands for a large-scale military intervention in the Far East.[19]

Colonel House, in a conversation with Wiseman, left the impression that the Russian Relief Commission would provide the wedge needed for America to enter into the whole business in a much bigger way. It would seek an invitation to enter Russia from the Bolshevik authorities, he said, but would go ahead regardless, protected by American troops. The Japanese would also be asked to provide a small guard-duty force. And once Hoover was in Russia, House ended, the president could hardly deny him additional military support—even if it took the form of Japanese troops in large numbers. Wiseman was gratified. At last the Americans were on the right road.[20]

Hoover was willing to serve, but he had difficulty with the logic of the plan. The idea of sending an army to Vladivostok and relief supplies to northern Russia struck him, he wrote the president, as contradictory. "[O]ur ideas of industrial organization," he added, "would scarcely fit into the philosophy of Messrs. Lenin and Trotsky, even if they did not reject the plan utterly as an Allied Trojan horse."[21]

Wilson took the point. No more was heard of a Hoover relief commission for Russia. Instead, the president turned to a cable then on his desk from Paul Reinsch. It would be a great mistake, the minister to China urged, to remove the Czech troops from Siberia when, with only slight support, "they could control all of Siberia against the Germans. . . . If they were not in Siberia it would be worth while to bring them from a distance."[22] With all other alternatives blocked, Wilson could hardly overlook the Czech Legion. "There seems to me," he advised Lansing, "to emerge from this suggestion the shadow of a plan that might be worked out, with Japanese and other assistance. These people are the cousins of the Russians."[23]

Each proposal he considered and rejected narrowed the president's options. He could not expect to control events, and he wished least of all to be forced into accepting a choice between Trotsky and the Allies. Most recently the former had offered yet another invitation to Raymond Robins, a chance to "participate actively in the exploitation of the marine riches of Eastern Siberia, of coal and other mines, as well as in the railroad and marine transportation construction in Siberia and nothern European Russia. . . ." To claim these prizes, all the United States would have to do, of course, was to commit itself to making the Bolshevik government a success.[24]

A historian, Wilson might have reminded himself that Alexander Hamilton had employed a somewhat similar strategy to secure acceptance of the new government in North America in the eighteenth century. His plan for funding the national debt was devised to increase chances that the Europeans would perceive they had an economic stake in the republic's success. Aside from any revulsion the president may have felt about admitting the parallel, and with it Hamilton's estimate of human nature, he did not intend to let himself be outsmarted.

Originally the Czechs had negotiated an agreement with the Bolsheviks that allowed them to travel on the Trans-Siberian Railway to a point of embarkation at Vladivostok. Problems soon arose about restrictions imposed on the arms they were to be allowed to carry. This friction had produced sporadic warfare along the line. The British had taken advantage of the situation to suggest to Dr. Eduard Beneš, a leader of the Czechoslovak National Council, that instead of leaving Russia the troops seek to occupy the Tomsk region, or else proceed to Archangel, where a military base might be established. Eventually it had been put to Beneš that the Czech Legion should join Semenov's campaign.[25]

Bolshevik concern about precisely this sort of maneuvering had been the primary reason for the arms restrictions, and for the outbreaks of fighting. As Wilson pondered his shrinking options, and wondered how long he would have before he actually had to choose an out-and-out anti-Bolshevik plan (a choice that would destroy the liberal alliance he needed for the postwar program put in jeopardy by the now "defective" Russian Revolution), David Lloyd George once more raised the unthinkable. Why not offer the Czechs to Trotsky, he asked his colleagues, along with contingents of British and French forces? If one wanted to block the German advance, here was, indeed, a way to proceed. The prime minister had fewer scruples about dealing with the Bolsheviks on their terms, or on terms that they supposed the capitalists must admit. Why not? was his view always. Balfour admitted that the Czechs were uneasy about being labeled "gendarmes." But rather than adopt the prime minister's suggestion, the war cabinet appointed yet another committee to study the problem.[26]

Its report was predictable. The Czechs should remain in Siberia "to stiffen the Japanese as part of an Allied force of intervention in Russia."[27] Alas for Lloyd George's argument, even Lockhart was now on the side of outright intervention. "It seems clear to me," he cabled on May 9, 1918, "that [the] only aid we shall get from Russia herself will be aid which we are able to organize round our own forces." Negotiations should continue, but only until an ultimatum could be perfected. "For political reasons it is most important that our action should be as swift and as imposing as possible."[28]

The war cabinet also had at hand a cable from Sir Conyngham Greene that supposedly shed new light on the Japanese position. Intervention was much talked about these days, said the ambassador, but only as a means of gaining control of China and establishing a toehold in eastern Siberia. It was now believed in certain quarters that Germany could not be defeated, with the argument being made that Japan must seize the moment to enhance its position. "[I]f we do nothing Japan may herself think her 'opportunity of a 1000 years' has come and, either by supporting Semenov or otherwise, advance to Irkutsk and stay there."[29]

New light or old suspicions, either way Greene's cable dramatized the need for action. Balfour proposed breaking the impasse with Washington by simply announcing that His Majesty's Government was going to act. What would happen then? The Japanese would have to join in, and once they did the Americans could not stand out. The secretary of state for war, Lord Milner, added a clincher. He would rather have, he said, "10,000 Americans in Siberia than in France."[30]

No one disagreed, as Lloyd George was absent that day, and so it was left to Lord Robert Cecil to find out if the Czechs were willing and how the Japanese would react. The former said yes, if the Allies would recognize their "just claims to independence." Japan would also go along, Cecil learned, but the cost would be high—British support for Semenov, politically and otherwise. That was always the problem: how to design an intervention and to control Japanese expansionism at the same time.[31]

But whatever stumbling blocks Cecil encountered with the Japanese, interventionists could now cite Bruce Lockhart's startling conversion to doubters. Bolshevik power was declining, the British agent declared. "Allied intervention will produce a counterrevolution which may easily be successful. . . . Certain . . . parties are ready to support us provided we act quickly. If we do not act immediately they will turn inevitably towards Germany."[32]

Returning from a meeting of the Supreme War Council in Paris, the prime minister tried to slow down this building momentum, headed, he thought, for catastrophe. The American military representative, said Lloyd George, General Tasker Howard Bliss, had stated to the council that his government still opposed military action. Besides, continued the prime minister, he had heard privately that President Wilson was under extreme pressure from West Coast businessmen who feared that if Japan went in, Siberia would be reduced to a province of the Japanese empire. When the prime minister finished, Lord Robert Cecil threatened to resign, but not before he had put Lloyd George on notice that the Germans would soon be at the borders of British India.[33]

Very well, Lloyd George would play on those grounds. Where was he to find someone to organize and inspire the anti-Bolsheviks, "someone like Chinese Gordon, with a streak of genius in him?" Perhaps General Knox might do. Whoever was selected should make his way into Siberia, disguised as a civilian traveler, with plenty of money at his disposal, and then cast off his pretense if developments warranted.[34] Balfour saw where this was going, and rescued the discussion from the brink of absurdity, where the prime minister had skillfully guided it, by asking the secretary of state for war, Lord Milner, to supply him with military proofs that a Siberian means for reopening an effective eastern front actually existed. Whenever President Wilson put him to that challenge he could never retaliate "by quoting detailed arguments by experts."[35]

Lloyd George had not brought the interventionists to a dead halt, but there was no more talk of launching a British initiative and letting Japan do the rest of the convincing. When the requested military paper appeared, Balfour warned Lord Reading that it was "not exactly what the President asks for." Siberia did spell the difference between victory and defeat, asserted the War Office, since if things remained as they were Germany would dominate postwar Russia, along with "most of Asia."

> Even if driven completely out of France, Belgium, and Italy, the Central Powers would still be unbeaten. Unless therefore Russia can reconstitute herself as a military power in the East against the time when the allied armies are withdrawn nothing can prevent the complete absorption of her resources by the Central Powers, which would imply world domination by Germany.[36]

Reading showed it first to Colonel House. It is a panicky document. the latter wrote Wilson. The military argument per se had still not been made. Yet the dangers cited were real. "I believe that something must be done about Russia, otherwise it will become the prey of Germany. It has become now a question of days rather than months." The president should put into operation the plan for a Russian Relief Commission, and announce that since it would need "a safe and orderly field to work in," England, France, Italy, and Japan had been asked to assist. "This program will place the Russian and Eastern situation in your hands and will satisfy the Allies and perhaps reconcile the greater part of Russia towards this kind of intervention."[37]

Whether the president wanted economic intervention brought up again so soon may be doubted. More in tune with Wilson's most recent thinking was Balfour's supplementary cable to Lord Reading. "The Bolsheviks," it said, "who betrayed the Roumanian Army, are apparently now bent on destroying the Czech Army. The Czechs are our Allies, and we must save them if we can. Their position seems to me to render immediate Allied action on their behalf a matter of urgent necessity. Please press this matter at once on the proper authorities."[38]

Balfour had at last hit on the right approach to bring out President Wilson's sense of responsibility, almost as an afterthought, it seemed. In the State Department, a young liberal, William Christian Bullitt, feared that the president was about to abandon his "vision of what is right." "I am so sick at heart," he wrote his patron, Colonel House, "because I feel that we are about to make one of the most tragic blunders in the history of mankind. . . ." The combination pressing for intervention was an unlikely coalition of "gentleman investors" and "well-intentioned" liberals, and all the more powerful for that reason. Ambassador Francis had put the case for both, but the only real beneficiaries would be "landed proprietors, bankers, professional men and commercial men," Bullitt warned.

Wilson was being asked to send an army to Siberia for the welfare "of this crowd," which was as ready to cooperate with the kaiser as with the United States. "How many years and how many American lives will it take to re-establish democracy in Russia?"[39]

> *It goes to pieces like quick-silver under my touch, but I hope I see and can report some progress presently, along the double line of economic assistance and aid to the Czecho-Slovaks.*
>
> Woodrow Wilson, July 8, 1918

On June 28, 1918, the president was reading a cable from Admiral Austin Knight, commander of the Asiatic Fleet. Czech forces occupying large sections of the Trans-Siberian Railway, it said, were under attack from Austro-German prisoners of war, released and armed by the Bolsheviks but commanded by German officers. Where the Czechs had gained control, it went on, the Soviet authorities had been overthrown and replaced by a government "wholly Russian and anti-Bolshevik."[40]

"This is a 'God-send,'" Butler Wright in the State Department had exclaimed to his colleague Basil Miles when Knight's telegram arrived. "It is just the news we want. . . . Let's concentrate on this with all our power at once." Lansing was equally confident of the response in the White House. There was a strong possibility of supplying the Czechs with rifles and ammunition, he told Lord Reading, so that they could protect an American economic mission. Then word came that the Czechs had seized Vladivostok, and were preparing to move west to aid their comrades locked in combat with Bolshevik forces.[41]

Wilson was on the brink. As matters hung in the balance, Robert Lansing sent the president what diplomat-historian George Kennan believes was the "decisive recommendation." It stressed duty. But Lansing also pointed out that it could be made plain that no Allied troops would remain after the Germans had been dispersed "unless Russia wants them." For the secretary, however, the real question was whether the war would last long enough to achieve the full purpose of his proposal. Along with the military contingents sent to aid the Czechs would come a peace commission representing various phases of American society, and equipped to assist in the restoration of "normal conditions of trade, industry and social order." This commission would proceed westward along the Trans-Siberian. "The final destination should depend in large measure upon their reception by the Russians and the resistance made to the military forces."[42]

The governing assumption, in this memorandum as in Admiral Knight's cable, seemed to be that the Bolsheviks had practically lost control of Siberia. Did Wilson share that belief? Did he also believe that a few thousand Czech troops supplemented by Allied forces could actually accomplish an enterprise of such magnitude? Apparently he did. But he also felt that he must now act in order to keep his hands on the reins of Allied policy. On July 6, 1918, therefore, the president summoned political and military advisers to the White House to read them a handwritten memorandum from a yellow pad. It outlined specific ground rules for intervention, of which the most important limited the total force to fourteen thousand, half American, half Japanese. The president also said that statements would be issued disavowing any intention of interfering in Russia's internal affairs, and pledging that the troops were being sent only to aid the Czechs in their fight against the German and Austrian prisoners who had attacked them.[43]

No mention was made of any role whatever for the other Allies, except for the use of available forces from vessels stationed near Vladivostok. Nor was Lansing's envisioned peace commission to be found anywhere on the yellow pad. It had disappeared, at least for the moment; Wilson was using a technique he had perfected of making the whole of his advisers' recommendations less than the sum of their parts. He had had plenty of opportunity to practice in Mexico and China.

Instructions were flashed to Admiral Knight that same afternoon directing him to land forces to hold Vladivostok safe as a base for the Czechs, *or* to provide them with a means of egress should the necessity arise. Yet the American force was not to become involved in Russian politics. The only way that could be accomplished would be for the admiral to label anyone who attacked the city "Bolshevik-Germans."[44]

Colonel House used the opportunity of the president's decision to have a friendly chat with the Japanese ambassador, Count Ishii, which turned into an indirect commentary on the meaning of Knight's instructions. If Tokyo allied itself with Wilsonian ideas and ideals, House promised Ishii, Japan would find the United States "ready to help her extend her sphere of infuence." Ishii picked up on the theme at once. The president's policy was justice for all nations, he said. In that regard, Russia had long excluded the Japanese from Siberia, even though Koreans and other Asiatics were permitted to enter. If Japanese citizens continued to be "deprived of such an outlet," he continued, Japan's position would become intolerable. House was not unsympathetic, as he candidly reported to Wilson. "It has been my opinion for a long time," he noted, "that unless Japan was treated with more consideration regarding the right of her citizens to expand in nearby Asiatic, undeveloped countries, she would have to be reckoned with and rightly so."[45]

So while Admiral Knight sat in his flagship wondering how he was to remain uninvolved in Russian politics, Colonel House was giving assurances that Japan could extend her sphere of influence. Of course, whatever had been said to Ishii did not commit the president. But Wilson had been unwilling to confront the inevitable contradiction inherent in intervention to preserve the right of self-determination. Even if he imagined that Vladivostok would turn out to be the success he thought Veracruz to have been, Wilson's Mexican experience was not yet complete. Events there were better understood as cautionary against a similar policy in Russia, especially under circumstances where American power was sure to be less effective, whether exercised directly or by restraint. Little wonder, then, that Wilson did not reply directly, but wrote only that he had been "sweating blood" over Russia, and that the situation went to pieces "like quicksilver under may touch. . . ."[46]

Lord Reading had a less than satisfactory chat with Lansing about the meaning of Wilson's decision. He received no assurances at all that intervention would include consideration for British interests, or even consultation. "Manifestly disturbed," the ambassador asked for a clarification of the matter of troop participation. Lansing repeated that it was to be limited to Japan and the United States. After all, it was merely a practical question, and any other issue raised about it was merely a false notion of "national pride and sentiment." But, protested Reading, might not the Russians conclude, wrongly, that this was a completely Japanese-American operation?

Why all this bother over a simple, straightforward statement of policy? returned Lansing. To do as Lord Reading wished would only involve everyone in a welter of military details. The ambassador was not silenced. His government would not understand, he said, why any action did not include all the Allies. Lansing was "sorry" to hear this, but the president had made his decision. Other troops might be used, if expedient, and for that reason it might be "advisable for all the powers to declare in favor of preserving unimpaired Russian political and territorial sovereignty."[47]

Somewhere in the State Department, if not in Lansing's office, John Hay's portrait smiled. So did Elihu Root's. So did Philander Knox's. For the first time the authors of the Open Door policy for China, and its new corollary in Russia, had the military force to back their demands. In London, however, to those who remembered Veracruz it now appeared that Wilson was committed too far, committed to cordoning off Siberia for his own purposes. Lloyd George was not pleased at that prospect. Moreover, he had reversed field again. On June 24, 1918, he had had his own chat with Alexander Kerensky, former head of the Provisional Government. The prime minister was not inclined to credit all that he heard from such a source, but Kerensky made an obvious impression. Enough of one, in fact, that the prime minister announced to the war cabinet that he was now ready to take full responsibility for telling the French that the Czech forces could not be evacuated from Siberia to fight on the western front. It could not be done, he said, "at a moment when the rest of their force was forming the nucleus of a possible counter-revolution in Siberia."[48]

Obviously disturbed at the prospect of being left out when the end came for Bolshevism, or when the United States and Japan made their peace with whatever Russian force prevailed, the war cabinet took immediate steps to make sure that British and French troops were not excluded. A battalion of men from Hong Kong was ordered to Vladivostok on July 10, and the French were advised that they should look after their interests as well. Lansing was not pleased about this, but it was Lord Reading's turn to suggest that this was hardly something to get upset about, merely a normal reinforcement of troops already there.[49]

Lloyd George had once talked—half seriously, it was supposed—about finding someone like Chinese Gordon for Russia. Now he was totally serious. Lockhart, in his new interventionist persona, had indicated that he was now in contact with the leaders of a "new Soviet Centre," men who needed outside financial and moral support. The "Centre" desired a military dictatorship, but only as a temporary measure. Who better to talk about that than Knox? Lockhart added that the Allies ought to send someone who could impress upon the dissidents that they had no particular political scheme in mind, but would recognize no government unable to establish and maintain order, nor could they allow a continuation of "civil and class war." Lockhart was duly informed that he could spend one million rubles to support this new "revolution."[50]

Reading warned Lloyd George, however, against any mission for General Knox. And with good reason. On July 17, the State Department issued a formal *aide-mémoire* on the president's recent decision. The purpose of this document was to distinguish that decision from military intervention, which it said "would add to the present sad confusion in Russia rather than cure it, injure her rather than help her, and . . . would be of no advantage" in winning the war. Military action, as opposed to intervention, was permissible, but only "to help the Czecho-Slovaks consolidate their forces and get into successful cooperation with their Slavic kinsmen and to steady any efforts at self-government or self-defense in which the Russians themselves may be willing to accept assistance."

Solemn assurances were required, furthermore, that no Allied government sought to interfere in Russia's internal affairs, or to impair its territorial integrity. Eventually the American government did expect to send an economic mission to Siberia to help "in every way for which opportunity may open." But nothing it would do would be allowed to embarrass or to hinder military assistance to the "westward-moving forces of the Czecho-Slovaks."[51]

As these words were read in London, Lloyd George may well have thought that no Puritan divine or Old World Jesuit had ever outdone Woodrow Wilson. What was one to make of such distinctions between military action and military intervention? And how did the sending of seven thousand troops to Siberia give Wilson the right to demand of the Allies that each come forward to the altar to promise to abide by his pronouncements? Lloyd George himself knew that the war cabinet and the French had in fact had several motives for wishing the United States to intervene: to boost morale, yes, to provide a check on Japan, again yes, and, while they might not admit it, to lend legitimacy to Anglo-French moves elsewhere against the Bolsheviks. All this was true, as was the belief that German postwar domination of Russia was a genuine peril, regardless of the question of reopening the eastern front.

But the State department's aide-mémoire, if left unanswered, laid the foundations for a "special" American role in postwar Russia that might be just as bad for European interests. It implied that America's associates had to be watched closely, that they were really only interested in establishing a reactionary, weak government in Russia. This could not go unrefuted, nor could the Americans be allowed to monopolize the proposed economic mission to Russia. Balfour agreed fully with the prime minister on these points, and recommended that His Majesty's Government propose an inter-Allied commission to monitor the situation.[52]

An inter-Allied commission was the last thing Wilson wanted. He had been misunderstood, the president explained to London. What he had in mind was not a commercial mission, but some way to employ Red Cross and educational advisers. The United States was in no position, therefore, to discuss what goods ought to be sent, or any financial arrangements.[53]

Maybe not, but it was time to plan for a post-Bolshevik Russia. Permanent Under Secretary Charles Hardinage talked of elections once the Allies reached Irkutsk. Someone else said that the Russian peasant really did not want to eliminate all large landowners, and wished also to pay for his land. Once the Germans were expelled, wrote Picton Bragge, free elections could be conducted for a national assembly. It alone would have the right to decide on a constitution, the form of government, "and the settlement of all great internal questions such as that of land."[54]

Whatever later historians might say about their motives, Foreign Office experts obviously thought that "German" domination of Russia would end only when some other kind of government had replaced the Bolshevik aberration. And that view was consistent before, during, and after the German summer offensive. Lord Robert Cecil had it in mind, as well, to appoint General Knox British high commissioner for Siberia. "We shall have to try and guide Russian reconstruction," he minuted to Balfour, "we shall have to provide relief and open up trade again: we shall have to secure Russian products and prevent their going to our enemies, besides all the military problems . . . , and the difficulty of keeping the peace between the Americans, the French, the Japanese, the Czechs and ourselves." Knox's appointment would bring a man of "authority and vigor" onto the scene. And since he was a soldier, accusations of political motivation would not arise.[55]

Whatever his previous doubts, Lloyd George, like Wilson, had made up his mind. His Majesty's Government must have its own Russian policy. Despite warnings from the Washington embassy, Balfour cabled that the United States should be called upon to urge the Japanese to send a much larger force into Siberia, and also to join with the British in an effort to persuade China to permit Japanese troop movements across Manchuria. A larger Japanese presence, of course, would have to come under Allied control, a neat way of forcing Wilson into consultations. In London, meanwhile, it was announced that Sir Charles Eliot had been appointed high commissioner for Siberia: "Sir Charles will represent His Majesty's Government in all political questions which come before the Allies, and will be in control of all British agents in Siberia, other than military or naval commands."

Balfour then smoothly proposed that Washington also name a commissioner. Wilson was furious. Whether he was angrier about the notion of an American high commissioner, however, or the fait accompli pulled off by the British was difficult to say. "We do not think cooperation in *political* action necessary or desirable in Eastern Siberia," he wrote Lansing, "because we contemplate no political action of any kind there, but only the action of friends who stand at hand and wait to see how they can help."[56]

"They are trying to scoop everything while the war is in course," Wilson complained of the Allies. Yet it seems likely, as George Kennan has suggested, that Wilson and his secretary of state "secretly hoped" that the arrival of American and Japanese forces "would elicit so powerful and friendly a reaction among the population that a pro-Allied political authority would be instituted throughout Siberia by spontaneous, democratic action. This might, in turn, lead to the prevalence of a new pro-Allied spirit in Russia proper, which in turn would either come to permeate the policies of the Bolsheviki or cause them to yield to other political forces more responsive to the political will."[57]*

Only if he led the Allies into Siberia, Wilson had finally concluded, could he lead them out again. Lloyd George feared that the path led nowhere, but he fully agreed with the war cabinet's desire to have its own Russian policy once Wilson had made his decision. Unsure of the outcome of his policy, the president had only one firm commitment. "I don't think you need fear any consequences of our dealings with the Bolsheviki," he wrote Senator James Hamilton Lewis, "because we do not intend to deal with them." To his eventual dismay, Wilson found that this attitude left the initiative to others.[58]

> *There are many more elements at work than I conjecture you are aware of, and it is harder to get out than it was to go in.*
>
> Woodrow Wilson, December 1918

Wilson could have been addressing these words to himself, instead of to a correspondent. That intervention spawned dilemmas became apparent right at the outset. The first large-scale troop landings took place not at Vladivostok but at Archangel, on August 2, 1918. Prior to the arrival of British troops under the command of General Frederick C. Poole, diplomatic agents had financed a coup d'etat against the city's Bolshevik gov-

* Kennan's language in describing Wilson's fleeting hope that Soviet behavior, if not the Soviet system, could be moderated by intervention is noticeably similar to that he used in the famous "X" article in 1947, "The Sources of Soviet Conduct," *Foreign Affairs* 25 (July 1947): 566–82. "The United States has it in its power," he wrote there, "to promote tendencies which must eventually find their outlet in either the breakup or the gradual mellowing of Soviet power." As Kennan so aptly suggests in his discussion of Wilson, those were the very goals of the Siberian intervention. When the Paris Peace Conference met, moreover, the president hoped to force the pace of his "containment" policy by arranging for a face-to-face

ernment. The new regime greeted Poole as a liberator, only to be told to take down all the red flags and banners.[59]

It was a stupid move, reported the American consul, Felix Cole. "The working class was patently absent," he went on, from those cheering the general. Poole had banned not only the Bolshevik emblem—a red flag with the letters R.S.F.R.—but the universal socialist plain red banner. The masses understood perfectly well what Poole was about, and it was certain that the Bolsheviks would exploit the general's insensitive behavior to reinvigorate their political fortunes.[60]

Had the British not blundered so, Cole complained, the United States could have tried to create a "rallying point" for anti-Bolshevik Russians. But Archangel was only an interim stronghold, a military base, for what General Poole had in mind. Before Cole's complaints reached Washington, the British had begun an advance to Vologda, four hundred miles to the south. The ultimate objective was a link-up with Czech forces and, with their help, control of rail communications lines between Archangel and Vyatka, thus forming a sort of triangle extending eastward several hundred miles.[61]

Ambassador David Francis shared Cole's doubts about British ambitions, if not their methods: "British soldiers have been colonizers for so long that they do not know how to respect the feelings of socialists." But when American forces began arriving on the scene in early September, Francis had no qualms about ordering them to cooperate fully with Poole. Nor did he imagine their mission was simply one of rescue for the stranded Czechs:

> Bolshevik success in Russia would be a menace to all orderly governments, ours not excepted, and would in my judgment impair the foundations of society itself; the guiding impulse is class hatred and it looks contemptuously on the sacredness of the family as well as the inviolability of person and property. I believe in division of land and that tillers of the soil should own it and that state should apportion same at extremely moderate compensation to present holders on easy terms but not in confiscation absolute.[62]

What Russia needed was a Homestead Act, just like America a century earlier: that was what Francis thought. Wilson feared that General Poole's

---

meeting between the Bolsheviks and their rivals at Prinkipo Island. In the twenty-five-plus years since the appearance of the "X" article, however, Kennan has steadily downgraded its importance, and reduced the scope of containment to a matter of holding the line until Europe's post–World War II economic recovery convinced the Stalin regime to abandon its extravagant demands. Whatever containment meant to Kennan, as he himself observes, it was used by his superiors to implement a policy to produce what they regarded as similar "Wilsonian" ends. Kennan and Wilson both perceived, moreover, the ultimate folly of a militarization of their recommendations.

carving out a triangle of Russia was, on the contrary, reminiscent of European imperialism in Africa. "This illustrates in the most striking way," the president wrote in dismissing an appeal for additional troops for Archangel, "the utter disregard of General Poole and of all the Allied governments (at any rate of all who are acting for them) of the policy to which we expressly confined ourselves. . . ."[63]

However much Wilson might have hoped for anti-Bolshevik uprisings, Poole's military campaign was not the way to go about helping the Russians, and it exploited the Czechs as well. "Is there no way,—no form of expression,—by which we can get this comprehended?" he asked Lansing.[64] When the secretary of state explained all this to the British, warning that American cooperation would be restricted to guarding Archangel and surrounding territory, he met with an even more baffling dilemma. How was he to respond to London's proposal for introducing two separate currencies into northern Russia and Siberia? If he said yes he would appear to be countenancing "spheres of influence." So he said no. But his words seemed to suggest that America would go along with a much more ambitious intervention: "[I]t is hoped that the assistance inagurated from Archangel and Vladivostok, respectively, may shortly effect a juncture."[65]

Short of providing all-out aid to Poole—or to some other expedition—it was hard to see how that juncture could be effected. While American policymakers squirmed, London introduced rubles printed in England to use for soldiers' pay. Another American diplomat, DeWitt C. Poole, visited Archangel and came away convinced that "any Russian government of the near future" would be compelled to mortgage its national wealth, "and it is by no means certain that nations whose losses in Russia have been more considerable than ours will find it easy to forego the opportunity of obtaining concessions or establishing spheres of influence."[66]

However little Wilson knew of Lloyd George's flirtations with the idea of a separate peace in the west at Russia's expense, and however much he had suspected that reopening the eastern front was indeed intended as a prelude to Africanization, reports now pointed to an Allied blueprint for Russia, not yet finished in detail, of course, but readily visible in outline. If these plans came to fruition, all that would have happened as a result of American entrance into the war was a shift from German dominance in Eastern Europe and Russia to Allied hegemony. Already, reported American diplomats in the Far East, the Japanese had managed to circumvent Wilson's troop ceilings. Set at twelve thousand, there were at least that many Japanese soldiers in the Chinese Eastern Railway zone, and another sixty thousand in other parts of Asiatic Russia. There were indications, said Ambassador Roland Morris in Tokyo, that the Japanese intended to introduce the yen into its occupation zones. "Recent events seem to support the statement constantly repeated that the General Staff has a definite policy in Siberia and that it proposes to pursue this policy leaving to the Foreign Office and Viscount Ishii the task of explaining after the event. I say this with great hesitancy and I hope it is not true but we must keep it in mind in watching developments."[67]

Secretary of War Newton D. Baker was not hesitant, however, in denouncing the Japanese. All that American soldiers were accomplishing, he warned Wilson, was Japan's long-term ambitions for a sphere of influence. Bolshevism's attraction mystified him, "but I have a feeling that if the Russians do like it, they are entitled to have it and that it does not lie with us to say that only ten percent of the Russian people are Bolsheviks and that therefore we will assist the other ninety percent in resisting it. . . ."[68]

The argument that Americans were there to give the Russians a chance to choose, protected from the schemes of either German or Allied empire builders, did not impress the American commander, General William S. Graves. "I think some blood will be shed when troops move out but the longer we stay the greater will be the bloodshed when Allied troops do go, . . . [E]ach day we remain here . . . we are . . . helping establish a form of autocratic government which the people of Siberia will not stand for and our stay is creating some feeling against the Allied governments because of the effect it has. The classes seem to be growing wider apart and the feeling between them more bitter daily."[69]

Whatever Ambassador Morris thought of Japanese intentions, or however many doubts plagued the War Department, Robert Lansing was loath to abandon the field in Siberia. Military progress *was* being made, he insisted to Wilson, and the adverse developments being reported only made more urgent getting on with the second-stage plan for economic succor and reconstruction. Therein rested the only way of blocking German or Allied plans for the partition of Russia, and of winning over the Russian people as well.[70]

Pulled in two directions, the president held firm. He would not order an evacuation, but he would not reply to Lansing's entreaties either. As would occur with even more fateful consequences during the League fight months later, Wilson sought to resolve his uncertainties by professing absolute certainty. In this instance he ordered the Sisson documents published under a government imprimatur, as if proving that the leaders of the revolution really were German agents would satisfy questions of policy in the future. At most, he bought a little more time.

Lansing sensed the danger. What would happen if, as many suspected, the Sisson documents were shown up as forgeries? Building the case for intervention on a dubious foundation of faked evidence was not good legal practice. Like House, the secretary sensed that Wilson's fixation on exposing Lenin, aside from its psychological implications, covered a desire to avoid discussing more fundamental issues. House pondered the matter in his diary, recording a conversation with Wilson as follows:

> I wondered why he had permitted the publication of the alleged Lenine-Trotsky documents, and whether he was satisfied as to their authenticity. He expressed himself as being thoroughly satisfied. I told him I had my doubts, and I thought their publication meant a virtual declaration of war upon the Bolsheviki Government. He admitted this.[71]

Probably only Colonel House could get Wilson to come so close to confronting himself. For his part, House was perfectly ready to see Russia partitioned. The rest of the world would feel much less menaced, he thought, if after the war there were four Russias—Siberia and three European states.[72] But while he might admit in private that he had declared war on the Bolsheviks, Wilson would never consent to allowing the liberal vision to be defaced by an agreement to parcel out Russia on shares. It no longer mattered, perhaps, what the Bolsheviks thought about American war aims or about Wilson himself, but the very existence of a liberal constituency was threatened, and with it the dimming prospects of a safe transit from imperialism to his vision of the future.

On October 10, 1918, the State Department finally announced an economic plan "to serve Russia and not to make use of her." Relief efforts were to be channeled through a specially created section of the War Trade Board. Set up initially with $5 million from the president's discretionary fund, this new agency would regulate exports and imports and seek to establish a single circulating medium for all Russia. Ambassador Francis was overjoyed. "I am impatient to know what reply our Allies will make to this proposition, especially our British cousins." But there was no turning back, he warned. If the president's plan was aborted for any reason, Russia would be easy prey for "adventurers," with deplorable results.[73]

Yes, but what would Francis recommend to implement the plan? Either one dealt with the Bolsheviks to establish the locations and logistics for the distribution of goods, and thus became their supporters by default, or one worked with their enemies and became backers of counterrevolution. Lansing was troubled, for example, by a recent Red Cross proposal to send food relief to Petrograd. Officials of that philanthropic agency told him the supplies were intended for children, and might improve America's image generally. But Lansing fretted about the consequences all the same. "Department is of opinion that Bolshevik regime has been preserved beyond its normal term by German support," the secretary cabled Stockholm, where Red Cross officials awaited his reply. "Disastrous conditions at Petrograd are appreciated but other conditions must now also be considered."[74]

American diplomats in the Swedish capital concurred. Relief supplies could be distributed only by direct dealings with the Bolsheviks. "A continuance of relief work," urged Sheldon Whitehouse from what had already been designated a "listening post" (with all that that military term implied) near Russia, "might induce the Bolsheviks to think that we do not intend to move against them and might discourage that part of the population which is anxiously hoping for us to drive out the Bolsheviks." That was enough for Lansing. "Department can not sanction any activities, however urgent and distressing the need," his order read, "which require cooperation or patronage of Bolshevik authorities."[75]

How could the president's advisers, who had pushed so hard for a second-stage plan, have missed this obvious point? They didn't. The sort of proposal they desired could be achieved only in the event of a Bolshevik collapse. By pushing for an economic plan they were really demanding a military success first. Wilson had grasped the point also. And just as he had refused to march from Veracruz to Mexico City in 1914, now he insisted that all economic plans be held in abeyance. "My policy regarding Russia," he told Sir William Wiseman,

> is very similar to my Mexican policy. I believe in letting them work out their own salvation, even though they wallow in anarchy a while. I visualize it like this: A lot of impossible folk, fighting among themselves. You cannot do business with them, so you shut them all up in a room and lock the door and tell them that when they have settled matters among themselves you will unlock the door and do business.[76]

> *We may abandon Russia: but Russia will not abandon us. We shall retire & she will follow. The bear is padding on bloody paws across the snows to the Peace Conference. By the time the delegates arrive she will be waiting outside the door.*
>
> Winston S. Churchill, 1918

How long could Wilson wait? Did he really think the Bolsheviks were securely locked up? Instead of limiting the Russian problem, intervention had expanded it. By the time the guns fell silent there were more than

180,000 non-Russian troops within the frontiers of the old empire. In addition to Allied and Czech soldiers, there were contingents of Serbs and Greeks as well as Germans. The anti-Bolshevik White Army, which depended upon foreign support, numbered more than three hundred thousand.[77]

Outside Russia the situation was even more complicated. Every issue now was saturated with fear of Bolshevism, none more so than the question of Germany's treatment. Wilson had once wanted a revolution in Germany to eliminate the military class; now he feared it like the plague. Lloyd George needed reparations as building blocks for his "land fit for heroes"; but to collect such sums from the defeated risked destroying what was left of the social order.

In early October 1918, Berlin initiated a note exchange that eventually led to the armistice. Wilson went into these negotiations wary still of German motives. Yet, he explained, "We must not appear to be slamming the door on peace." Many sincere Americans had not wanted to go to war. But now the danger was not confined to pacifists or pro-German ethnics. "The spirit of the Bolsheviki is lurking everywhere, and there is no more fertile soil than war-weariness. There is grave unrest all over the world. There are symptoms of it in this country—symptoms that are apparent although not yet dangerous." If the Germans were pressed too hard, humiliated too much, "we shall destroy all form of government, and Bolshevism will take its place."[78]

The first German note asking for peace negotiations on the basis of the Fourteen Points had been sent to Wilson from a government under the leadership of Prince Max of Baden. German democracy did not yet reign, and a German request for negotiations had been anticipated at some stage once the German summer offensive had been repulsed.[79] Obviously the thing to do was to play the prince along, hoping thereby to force the pace of German democratization while keeping in power a government that was anti-Bolshevik. As Wilson put it to the cabinet, to go into Germany "and set up a government ourselves" was unthinkable. But if the United States refused all communications, "we might witness bolshevikism worse than in Russia. . . ."[80]

A flat rejection, added Lansing in another context, would alienate large sections of Allied opinion besides uniting all German parties against the United States. "Furthermore in Eastern Germany Bolshevism is raising its abominable head, and a Germany crushed might become prey to that hideous movement. If it did, Europe might become a seething mass of anarchy. Who can tell? We must take no chance of this war culminating in such a frightful catastrophe, besides which 'the terror' of 1792 would be a happy epoch. The horrors of Bolshevik Russia must not be repeated in other lands. The doctrine is spreading as it is. It is in all the nations of Europe and is (I say it with regret) gaining a foothold in this country." Indeed, Bolshevism verged on becoming a greater danger than "Prussianism."[81]

Right at the moment, indeed, the "abominable head" was also peering into the borderlands between Germany and Russia. Roman Dmowski, president of the Polish National Committee, told State Department officials that a premature German evacuation on the eastern front would create a vacuum. As Dmowski put it,

> If all military forces are removed from Poland, the Bolsheviks will enter, with the most terrible consequences; yet, if German troops do not leave Poland when the general evacuation begins . . . they will never leave.[82]

In this delicate situation, Wilson returned a note to Berlin on October 23, 1918. All that was left in it of the revolutionary change he had wanted to see was a demand for the Kaiser's abdication. That he must have, if only because the Allies could not moderate their peace terms without Wilhelm's removal.

Prime Minister David Lloyd George and his colleagues saw the president was in a tight spot. "Wilson is in a trap," remarked Lord Reading, who was in London, "and has got to get out." The ensuing dialogue in the war cabinet was less than sympathetic to the president's plight:

> A.J.B.[ALFOUR]: One of the most humorous documents ever produced.
>
> [SIR MAURICE] HANKEY: The end of it is an encouragement to Bolshevism.
>
> A.J.B.: But Wilson is a great enemy of Bolshevism. . . .
>
> P.M.: The President did not want our armistice terms to involve enemy in undue humiliation but wanted to prevent them gaining any military advantage from the armistice. . . .
>
> I take it his theory is that all nations will be in the league. He's a curious mixture of old Bryce and Sir Arthur Yapp [General Secretary of the YMCA].
>
> [AUSTEN] CHAMBERLAIN: Nothing so humiliating as to tell them to alter their Government at his orders.
>
> A.J.B.: This is a very confused document. . . . It is inconsistent with our policy in Russia of leaving Russians to settle their own affairs.
>
> READING: Which he has laid down. . . .[83]

In pre-armistice inter-Allied negotiations, Colonel House insisted that a too rapid German evacuation in the east would only mean a Bolshevik advance. German propaganda, retorted French premier Georges Clemenceau, a trick to make the victors shiver in their sleep. Arthur Balfour was not so sure. People in those areas were vulnerable, he warned, because they lacked an army or even police security. "We therefore ran the risk of delivering them to an even worse regime than the Germans, and much as they hated the Germans, they might prefer their rule to that of Bolshevism."

The French persisted in their objections to such a course, but a final decision was put off until the matter could be discussed with a German armistice delegation. When this meeting took place a week later, the Allied spokesmen conceded two points. They permitted the Germans to retain five thousand machine guns to maintain order against a countryside "infected with Bolshevism," and they gave a favorable response to the request for a delay in evacuation timing. "The immediate evacuation of the formerly Russian territories," the Germans had warned, "would sacrifice the local population without defence to the horrors of Bolshevism." So, French protests notwithstanding, Article 12 of the armistice agreement that came into effect on November 11, 1918, was amended to read that the evacuation should take place only after the Allies decided "the moment suitable, having regard to the internal situation in these countries."[84]

One war ended, another began. Under the armistice terms Germany was obligated to turn over all captured Russian gold to the Allies. To a degree, of course, Clemenceau was right: the Germans were perfectly situated to play upon political fears in an attempt to modify Allied demands. That did not diminish, on the other hand, the genuine concern felt by leaders of the new German republic proclaimed on November 9, 1918. These men hoped for a working arrangement with the Allies in the struggle with Bolshevism. Their government depended upon it. As for the Allies themselves, their delegates had made it plain that they would not tolerate a Leninist-style regime in Germany, or even permit normal diplomatic relations between Germany and the Soviet government.[85]

Any real reduction in the severity of the actual peace terms, however, was out of the question. Immediately after the armistice, Prime Minister Lloyd George thought about bringing the kaiser to trial, a natural extension of Wilson's insistence that he abdicate. Heaping guilt on the kaiser, of course, might finesse several awkward corners that had yet to be turned. But all that such talk did was to stir emotions, already at a boil, even higher. Lloyd George opened the election campaign that fall in a conciliatory manner. "At this moment the air of Europe is quivering with revolution," he declared. The new Parliament would have to set an example to the world as well as the nation. It would have to demonstrate that democratic institutions were up to the crisis. "We cannot return to the old conditions. (Cheers.) War is like a ploughshare and a harrow. It has turned up and rent the soil of Europe. You cannot go back. If you do not sow weeds will grow. . . ."[86]

In private he worried about the "great, inflammable, industrial population" of his country, and how to prevent a spark from setting it off. He had always avowed the need for reparations from Germany, but he trapped himself during the election campaign by making them the all-important issue. What he found was that he could not be conciliatory about Europe and still meet his promise to make Britain a "land fit for heroes." Reparations would have to pay for that; the only other option was to go far beyond the prewar tax program of British Liberalism. As leader of a Tory-dominated coalition (if for no other reason), the prime minister was in no position to gamble on the latter.[87]*

Such being the case, and with patriotic fever at its height, Lloyd George promised that the Germans would be made to pay for it all. That left him with only unpleasant alternatives to contemplate. Germany would have to be "held down" in order to extract reparations at that level, and that risked shoving those noble "Teutonic peoples"—as Churchill called them now—"into the grisly gulf that had already devoured Russia."[88]

American elections in November 1918 put pressure on Wilson as well. He had asked for a Democratic majority in Congress and had been rebuffed by the electorate. Whatever the voters meant by their decision, it was clear that working with the European left would be difficult. That suited Lansing. William C. Bullitt had recommended that Wilson court the European liberal left as an alternative to confronting the Bolsheviks. The secretary agreed that there was a certain force in what Bullitt suggested, but not nearly enough to overcome the political liability and actual peril of "compromise with any form of radicalism and the unwisdom of giving special recognition to a particular class of society as if it possessed exceptional rights. . . ." Kerensky had trod that unhappy path.[89]

Wilson agreed—up to a point. He could not accept Lansing's sugges-

---

*Perhaps the most enlightening study of Lloyd George's tactics in the 1918 election is Robert E. Bunselmeyer, *The Cost of the War, 1914–1919: British Economic War Aims and the Origins of Reparation* (Hamden, Conn., 1975). By getting tough on the kaiser, the prime minister played to conservatives inside and outside the coalition, divided Labour leaders from the electorate, and set the stage for a reparations policy to float his social policies in the postwar era. On December 12, 1918, for example, Lloyd George went after the Labour party in this way: "Mr. Ramsay MacDonald and Mr. Snowden—(hisses)—are no manual workers. The Labour Party is not being run by real labour; it is being run by Pacifists and Bolsheviks. . . . If they had their way we would to-day be the slaves and bondsmen of Germany" (p. 158). One of his friends wrote Lloyd George after the election, "[T]he Coalition policy of insisting on the complete criminal and civil liability of Germany was immensely popular—this undoubtedly brought votes which would otherwise have gone to Labour" (p. 168). At Paris, Lloyd George quickly abandoned reparations in the face of the revolutionary turmoil in Central Europe, and instead sought to draw Wilson into a different kind of economic settlement that would permit him to achieve his postwar ambitions.

tion that diplomatic recognition be given to a Siberian government now functioning under Admiral Aleksander Kolchak, purely in order that *some* Russian delegation could take part in the peace conference. The secretary then proposed his own version of the Bullitt recommendation. The president should advise the Allies that America would do its best to see that Russia's interests were protected. Then he should announce that only delegates representing the Constituent Assembly would be permitted to sign the peace treaty. In the interim, however, before they could be found, "approved representatives from existing elements of order" would be admitted so that Russia's voice might be heard. Democratic socialists would not be excluded, but none of this—Lansing came back to an old theme—could mean much without a positive program of economic assistance available, "wherever we can come in contact with elements desiring to maintain democratic principles. . . . [W]hile we must set our faces sternly against anarchy and the class tyranny and terror of Bolshevism, we must at the same time cut to the root of the sore and relieve the misery and exhaustion which form such a fertile soil for its rapid growth."[90]

On board the *George Washington* as it carried the American delegation to Europe, the president proclaimed liberalism to be the "only thing that can save civilization from chaos—from a flood of ultra-radicalism that will swamp the world. . . . Liberalism must be more liberal than ever before, it must even be radical, if civilization is to escape the typhoon."[91] And as he well knew, that storm was already blowing across oceans and lands far away from Europe.

CHAPTER NINE

The Outskirts of Paris: Mexico and China

The problem is substantially the same as that of China. Only the fullest security, . . . and only a large loan can bring a solution; only substantial funds will bring about a strong government, but, just as in China, a weak government would not dare to enter upon a negotiation which, by pledging the customs house revenues, might hurt the nation's pride.

Banker Paul M. Warburg
explaining Mexico to the State Department, 1913

The Bolshevik Revolution had a lasting effect upon the way events in Mexico and China were perceived. Policymakers, following Wilson's example with the Sisson papers, invested the word "Bolshevik" with a double meaning, the second being foreign agent, which allowed them to simplify a complex historical process into two or three options. Thus they downgraded internal causes of revolution in favor of putting the blame on conspiratorial intrigues and outside agitation.

In one sense, of course, it was consistent to see the prewar "special interests" as responsible for Huerta or Yuan Shi-k'ai and the Bolsheviks behind, say, Carranza or Sun Yat-sen. To do that, however, meant sacrificing at least one half of the Wilsonian vision, and substituting for that half a compromise with the old diplomacy. Indeed, it was fear of this that caused Wilson to hesitate so long before accepting a role in the Russian intervention, and that made it impossible for him to devise a second-stage

economic program, try as he might, that would square Allied policy with
self-determination.

Yet if he could not discover the key to resolving the Russian puzzle in
some sort of updated Belgian Relief Commission, he gradually turned to
a "consortium" solution for both Mexico and China, expecting all the
while to put liberal restraints on the operations of the bankers, limits that
would conform to the standards of the new diplomacy. Although Wilson
was increasingly preoccupied with the Paris Peace Conference once the
war ended, he was perfectly aware of the unresolved trouble areas on the
"outskirts," in Mexico and China, and what it would mean if nothing
changed after the war. Reduced to an observer's role in Mexico, British
policymakers bided their time on the other side of "watchful waiting,"
anxious to know what the American president planned to do about making Carranza rejoin the world order at the proper level. In China they still
hoped to play a more active role.

> *So soon as you can admit your own capital and the
> capital of the world to the free use of the resources of
> Mexico, it will be one of the most wonderfully rich
> and prosperous countries in the world.*
>
> Woodrow Wilson to Mexican editors,
> June 1918

Wilson's pledge to the Mexican newspapermen rested upon an assumption, as he himself said, that "American" principles would prevail after the
war. Great powers would have to respect the rights of the small and weak,
all of whom were to be bound by mutual obligations to the League of
Nations. What went unspoken was the president's conviction that the
Mexicans themselves would be persuaded thereby that they did not need
to rely upon extreme interpretations of the Constitution of 1917 in order
to protect themselves from exploitation. Wilson's task was complicated,
however, by Carranza's clever shifting back and forth between xenopho-
bia (well justified in this case) and professions of support for truly revolutionary change.

In the United States' increasingly swollen government bureaucracy, a
product of the war as important as the revolutionary tide against the old
order, Wilson's Mexican policy was being reshaped with a different emphasis. The revelations of a German-Mexican connection in the Zimmerman telegram, the counselor of the State Department, Frank L. Polk, told
Ambassador Spring-Rice, would surely provide a good reason for with-

olding de jure recognition of Carranza's government and for questioning his new Constitution. "At all events there was always the possibility of having recourse to some of the exiles and other factions whose leaders were comparatively respectable; general discontent with Carranza was so great that these had good chances of easy success."[1]

At least one person took Polk at his word. British diplomat Thomas Hohler, who had challenged Wilson's policy all along, felt considerable satisfaction any time he heard American officials expressing such sentiments. If only they meant a willingness to get on with the solution, he would be overjoyed. The new constitution was "obviously impossible of acceptance," he reported to London from the United States, "as it cuts straight at the roots of most foreign rights in Mexico." President Wilson had appointed a new ambassador, Henry P. Fletcher, in an effort to ameliorate Mexican-American relations. But that could only come about if Fletcher convinced Carranza of the need for prudence. And that was an impossibility on the face of it. When, not if, he failed, the situation would become critical, because while it was possible to slur over incidents handled by consular clerks or informal agents, it could not be done when a person of full ambassadorial rank was involved.[2]

Hohler felt even more sure of his ground when he received an invitation to talk about Mexico from Colonel House. As he had anticipated, the topic was what to do if Fletcher failed. Aside from direct intervention, Hohler replied, the only solution was to find some "other party" who might be trusted to rule Mexico, some combination of exiles and anti-Carranza leaders still in Mexico. One possibility was Manuel Peláez, who ruled in the oil well areas and who could serve as a rallying point for a "new party." When the time came, House must understand, it would not be enough to give just moral support. "[P]ractical aid in the shape of money and arms would be required, and they would have to be promised with the utmost discretion lest the new party should be denounced as gringo hirelings." Deliberately causing a new revolution was an extreme remedy, but anything was better than the present situation. House expressed interest, without saying anything more except that he hoped to speak with Hohler about Mexico again.[3]

In fact, Fletcher had been sent to keep Mexican-American disagreements off the president's daily agenda, dominated as it now was by the war crisis. Oil men and other corporate interests had named a respresentative of their own, Chandler P. Anderson, to negotiate with the administration about possible ways of handling the Mexican problem. When Anderson met with State Department officials, he suggested that the best route might be to seek an article in the Mexican Constitution establishing treaties as the law of the land, and then negotiate a pact specifically protecting American interests. Initial enthusiasm for the idea faded when Anderson himself realized that a treaty would commit the United States to accepting the new Constitution, which was only Carranza's invention, and which would have no validity at all if "that faction" were overthrown. No, a much better idea, he concluded, was a simple exchange of notes.[4]

This constant talk of Carranza's weakness, his supposed alienation from the Mexican people, and his reliance on outside support helped to sustain beliefs that the Constitution of 1917 could be nullified once the war ended. After all, now that America was in the war, idealism had to give way to a more realistic policy—didn't it? Wilson did have under consideration, as a matter of fact, a rationale whereby he could allow the British to stage a naval demonstration in the event that Carranza attempted to carry out a half-threat he had made to ban oil exports. "Unfortunately," he began a note to Lansing, "the Mexican Government has, no doubt, a legal right to prohibit exports." On the other hand, the Tampico oil properties were largely British-owned, and, Wilson noted, "We have more than once allowed European governments to oblige Latin American governments to meet their financial obligations by a show of force, without deeming their action a violation of the Monroe Doctrine, because it involved no attempt at political control." Oil was "indispensable" to the British war effort, moreover, and its export would only benefit the Mexican economy. That being so, the secretary should convey this opinion through the "most direct channel available," but without quoting the president.[5]

These instructions, TR-like except for the caveat against quotation, revealed also Wilson's knowledge of the oil companies' subsidy to Peláez. "I have also understood," he wrote, "that the military commander there (whose connection with either Carranza or Villa is shadowy and hard to trace) is probably subsidized by the British owners." More realism? A definite turn to the right? Whatever it was, and however it was perceived by others, Lansing passed the word to Spring-Rice that Washington would not condemn a naval demonstration, and that while the United States would not participate directly it was also permissible to supply arms to Peláez.[6]

Carranza retracted the threat (as usual), so no demonstration took place. What had to be decided instead was the seemingly lesser question of whether Ambassador Fletcher should attend Carranza's inaugural as the first president of Mexico under the new Constitution. Chandler Anderson and Secretary Lansing both hoped Wilson would not order Fletcher to attend, or to do anything else that would add an ounce of legitimacy to the "new order" unless and until Carranza had agreed to a reservation protecting foreign rights. Wilson resolved the matter ambiguously: Fletcher should put in an appearance, but not do or say anything that would constitute de jure recognition. His assignment was to do "everything" to hold the "confidence and friendship" of Carranza. "Although it may be impossible to accept the provisions of the new constitution which are in contravention of the international obligations of Mexico, it is desired for reasons of high policy not to force an issue on the question. They will be met when they arise."[7]

Whether the president could have sustained this delaying tactic if Mexico had actually prohibited the oil sales may be doubted, but Carranza never carried out any of his dramatic threats. Oil production rose, in fact. Chandler Anderson believed that Carranza must eventually make a fatal mistake, just as the Germans had, that would force Wilson's hand. The important thing was to make sure that when this happened the issue not be protection of private interests, but "our national interests" and the outcome of the war. "[W]e were now in a position to press these considerations upon our Government as reasons for protecting foreign rights in Mexico. . . ." The British and French were sure to agree, and, concluded Anderson in a letter to a his principals, Foreign Minister Arthur Balfour had been given private assurances in person by President Wilson on the point.[8]

Exactly what these could have been is hard to say; probably they referred to the sort of measures Lansing approved in his conversation with Spring-Rice. In any event, the secretary agreed that Carranza was near the end of his rope, an oft-expressed hope by this time. His "whole purpose" now, Lansing told Anderson, was to maneuver Carranza into a position where it would become necessary for him to come hat in hand to the American Government for a loan: "[A]nd if he could be put into the position of being absolutely dependent upon a loan from us for the continuance of his government, he thought we could impose any terms which seemed reasonable and essential." Anderson feared, however, that Lansing really had no plan in mind—that matters would develop as predicted, but without careful thought being given to the right course of action. But on June 25, 1917, Carranza's confidante, Luis Cabrera, informed Ambassador Fletcher that Mexico would try to borrow money soon from American bankers. Funds were needed for railway reconstruction and for government expenses. Best of all, Mexico would make no attempt to borrow in other markets unless it failed to obtain the funds in the United States.[9]

The prospect of an American loan to Mexico was troubling to observers in London. Perhaps the real purpose of the Fletcher mission all along had been to deprive other nations of their fair share of the Mexican business. There had always been the suspicion that Wilson's idealistic exterior concealed a Yankee trader's heart. As it happened, moreover, reports about American willingness to lend money to Mexico to refurbish its railroads, where British investments still totaled more than £114 million, coincided with a perplexing announcement from Lord Cowdray that he wished to sell his oil interests to an American firm. With their pre-April 1917 "war profits" and their commanding position, British officials ruefully mused, the Americans might be in a position to buy off everybody: Lord Cowdray and Carranza at the same time.[10]

No need to worry. Despite a flurry of activity, nothing happened. Fletcher came home with Cabrera to meet the committee of oil men that Anderson represented, but what the ambassador told the committee was not enough. If a Mexican bond issue for $50 to $100 million could be floated, Fletcher said, they would be assured of lower taxes as well as continued possession of their property. Not good enough, was the reply. The committee would not participate unless the U.S. government in effect cosigned the loan, and took responsibility for Carranza's good behavior.[11]

Spring-Rice advised the Foreign Office that Luis Cabrera had been turned down flat by "New York interests," and that Fletcher had made no headway at all. The mood was all against risk-taking, at least of that sort. But when Fletcher warned his colleagues in the State Department that they could expect Carranza to retaliate by introducing legislation to confiscate the oil fields, Assistant Secretary of State Breckinridge Long shot back, "I say if necessary take fields—do not stop there—take Mexico."[12]

Wilson was talking tough, too. According to Spring-Rice, the president instructed Fletcher to warn Carranza not to put Mexico in danger of war by moving against the oil fields. A loan was out of the question. As Anderson and others had anticipated, the chance to bring Carranza to bay had arrived in the form of a question of "national interest." Over the next several months, Lansing enjoyed relative freedom from White House interference in efforts to get a hammerlock on the Mexican leader. Herbert Hoover and the wartime Food Administration were enlisted in the effort. Spring-Rice was informed that the administration could finally turn Mexican food shortages to good advantage: "Mr. Hoover intends to refuse to raise [the] embargo on food exports until [the] Mexican Government assume [a] much more satisfactory attitude."[13]

Some thought must have been given to this approach, because when Ambassador Ignacio Bonillas complained that his country could not obtain needed wheat supplies or machetes, he was told at the State Department that perhaps the United States government would prefer to help Mexico financially—with a supervised loan. But as one Foreign Office expert commented about these tactics, they had little chance of success, since the Mexican army would always get what it needed, and in Mexico the army was all that counted.[14]

Frustration produced an unusually heated exchange between Chandler Anderson and Frank L. Polk. It began when Anderson suggested that Wilson was hesitant to really do anything about Carranza because he felt responsibility for bringing him to power, and because he was anxious, Anderson implied, to be the leader of the "socialistic" camp around the world. Then Anderson hit upon a looking-glass image of Wilson's fear of the Mexican "wedge" in American politics:

> I said that I anticipated that the developments in this country and in Great Britain and France along socialistic lines foreshadowed similar attacks on property in these countries after the war, and I feared that the Administration by failing to oppose the new Mexican Constitution was likely to encourage the movement in this country. He said that that had not occurred to him; that he looked with intense disfavor and alarm upon any development of that kind in this country, and that what I had said about the relation of the Mexican Constitution to that situation was very disturbing to him, and that so far as he personally was concerned, he would be even more inclined than ever to take a vigorous stand against the destruction of private rights which the Mexican constitution represented. . . .[15]

> *Their forebearance has . . . been ill rewarded; and they have noted with surprise that the Mexican Government has committed itself deeply to schemes promoted by . . . [Germany] which practices the most autocratic rule in the world and has already reduced to chaos and disruption another country, Russia, which has also fallen a victim to its intrigues.*
>
> British draft of a proposed
> Anglo-French-American ultimatum,
> February 1918

The short lull in the chronic Mexican crisis came to an end in February 1918 with Carranza's latest oil decree, which appeared to settle the question of whether or not the Constitution would be invoked against the oil companies. The decree stated that if foreign corporations wished to continue their operations in Mexico they would have to become Mexican "citizens," under the law. Although this was the culmination of efforts that antedated Carranza and even Huerta and Madero, that had begun in Diaz's time, the circumstances under which the Constitution of 1917 was becoming operational permitted the Foreign Office to entertain hopes that a "German agent" thesis would move Wilson to action.

The American oil companies, meanwhile, sent their representatives to the State Department to deliver prophecies of ruination and paralysis. Vital industries would be left without fuel, the Allied war effort would collapse, and so on. Secretary Lansing was sympathetic, of course, and instructed Fletcher to secure at least a thirty-day postponement. The ambassador took this to mean that the United States was considering strong measures, though what these could be no one knew. On March 10, 1918, he told the new British representative in Mexico City, Cunard Cummins, to keep his eyes peeled: "Doheny [the American head of Huasteca Petroleum] would conclude that it was cheaper to throw Carranza out through supporting a new revolution than to pay his share of Carranza's taxation." Fletcher also said that he deplored the mutual suspicions that had arisen between British and American interests. Their common fate must now outweigh such petty considerations. Fletcher seemed anxious to convey "more than he put in words," concluded Cummins.[16]

What did that mean? Was Fletcher reenacting Henry Lane Wilson's shadowy role at the end of Madero's short reign, or merely hinting at changes in Washington? Cummins had other information that suggested certain Americans were planning a coup. Through his contacts with anti-Carranza leaders he had been informed that a new candidate to replace the First Chief was Alfredo Robles Domínguez. Cummins hoped that the British oil companies would get on the bandwagon, so as to keep from being left out when a new Mexican government started redistributing concessions. But meanwhile the success of the operation depended upon secrecy. Cummins even recommended against any formal consultation between London and Washington, so delicate was this business. Yet how could London operate a sound foreign policy on such a shadowy assumption? It might be a clever trap.[17]

Lord Reading must find out what Washington intended. He must undertake somehow to explain—without giving away British knowledge of any secret plot—that "while we desire to cooperate with them in any policy that may help to bring about more settled conditions in Mexico, we shall of course maintain our right to receive equally favorable treatment as the United States for the enormous British interests in that country."[18]

It was no coincidence, moreover, that these were also the weeks of London's most intense effort to get the United States involved in a common policy toward Russia. British intelligence, which had had a special place in its heart for Mexico from the time of the Zimmermann telegram a year earlier, thought it was absolutely necessary to smoke out the Americans. Admiral Blinker-Hall, the grand sachem of intrigue, went so far as to say that if the United States refused cooperation, "it remains for consideration whether we should attempt to kill the plan by a blunt exposure or to use our knowledge of its existence to demand that it should be developed in harmony with our interests also."[19]

Neither option arose, once again because of Wilson. The formal American protest against the oil decree, issued on April 2, 1918, warned that the United States might have to take steps "to protect the property of its citizens."[20] But Wilson was also moving contrariwise to ease Carranza's fears. British officials learned that the president had declared in "background" comments to White House correspondents that "Burke's idea of freedom satisfies us." Americans did not want to be charged with "butting in" to impose their own ideas everywhere. "The case of Mexico may be taken as an illustration. We in the United States aren't concerned to compel Mexicans to abolish their ideas of freedom so long as our own vital interests are not involved."[21]

Other accounts of this session record Wilson's strong resistance to "the idea of many American capitalists, . . . [and] many American public men . . . that we had a right to insist that Mexico do this and that in order that our people might go into Mexico and make money. That proposition I utterly rejected and would not stand for, and I will not stand for it. There is the acid test. . . ."[22] Wilson then ordered that restrictions on gold payments be eased, while Lansing said publicly that the State Department would look with favor upon a loan to Mexico—under the right conditions.

Many factors entered into policy calculations at this time, including, one must suppose, the problem of reconciling a decision to go into Russia with the Wilsonian "acid test" of self-determination. It simply would not do to agree to intervention under circumstances that at any level implied softening of American opposition to partition or pursuit of economic concessions from reactionary governments. For reasons of his own, Carranza postponed the operative date of the oil decree until the end of July. Several things entered into his calculations, also, not least an instinct for self-preservation. If a crisis came while the German offensive still had momentum, he might expect something much worse than a formal protest, justified as a "war measure."

Throughout the summer of 1918, Carranza and Wilson continued to zigzag around one another. On one day the First Chief would denounce American hypocrisy, contrasting Wilson's public statements with heavy-handed American communications conveyed by cable. The next day he would discuss possibilities for a loan with Ambassador Fletcher, assuring him that he still felt the only place to do such business was in the United States; would the administration be willing to open negotiations?

The Mexican-American dialogue seemed to be getting nowhere, as usual, when, on July 11, 1918, two of the most inveterately anti-Carranza diplomats, Thomas Hohler and Cunard Cummins, called on Gordon Auchinloss at the State Department. Cummins took the lead. Why, he said, should "we" continue to run serious and unnecessary risks by "permitting" an abominable pro-German government to continue in power? The regime was so hated that "we had it in our power, with merely a nod of approval and laxity in permitting ammunitions to enter that country, to permit and encourage the Mexicans themselves to depose Carranza and establish a Government composed of educated and respectable people who would be well disposed towards the Allies."

If the Mexicans wanted to change their rulers, replied Auchinloss, America had no objection. Ah, said Cummins, but the impression in Mexico was that the United States did not want a change, or at least that no movement could succeed without American approval. Surely that was an untenable position, with the German threat so pervasive. The United States and the Allies could not afford a strictly hands-off attitude. Auchinloss answered that the administration really believed that the moment had passed, if there ever had been one, for any serious plans for intervention in Mexico to develop in Germany.

Oh no, persisted the British diplomat. German aid was on its way, you could be sure of that—financial aid, for example, channeled through Argentina. Berlin would not allow its costly and well-laid schemes to go by the boards. And what of the accomplishments of Mexico's German-influenced newspapers, those purveyors of hatred against the United States? "We knew from President Wilson's words that he desired to cultivate in Central America a spirit of good will towards the United States. Nevertheless Carranza's emissaries throughout Latin America were today actively propagating ideas that preserved and fomented a spirit of suspicion and enmity towards the United States."

Equally persistent, Auchinloss replied that the United States would be able to allay this "spirit of suspicion" by manifestations of sincere friendship, such as lifting the embargo on gold and other commodities, especially foodstuffs. "[U]nfortunately," returned Cummins, "the Mexican people invariably interpreted a benevolent attitude as weakness . . . and not only would this manifestation . . . fail, but the suspicion with which every act of the United States is looked upon in Mexico would lead to suppositions and arguments regarding the probable purpose and bad faith underlying the new policy. . . ."

Finally, Auchinloss said that Wilson would not change. The "most potent reason" was obvious. "The President's public declarations of policy prohibited any change. . . . These declarations, as the world knows, have included respect of the weaker nations by the more powerful, and noninterference in the international affairs of other nations." How could the United States government now turn around and encourage the overthrow of an established government? Cummins was still not finished: "I agreed entirely but suggested that the hand of Washington behind any new movement that might be permitted to gather strength and overthrow this unfriendly Government need at no time be obvious or traceable. Even evidence of laxity in the enforcement of the regulations prohibiting the exportation of arms could be avoided."

But if what Cummins had said was true, that any movement opposing Carranza needed American approval, then activity of this sort was sure to be laid at Washington's doorstep. So spoke Auchinloss, with an air of exasperation. But Cummins would not leave without a parting shot. "My regret," he concluded to Auchinloss, and in his report to London, "was accentuated by the fact that if the situation were wisely handled not only could we destroy the hopes of Germany through the instrumentality of Mexico but once and for all dispose of the Mexican question and all its dangers. The difficulties of solving the Mexican situation had been greatly exaggerated. Not only could an intelligent and honest government, well disposed towards us, be established in that country within two months, but by the same measures revolution could be stamped out for all time."[23]

That was the crux of the argument, of course: what it would take to stamp out revolution. Mexico was only one place, but both sides in this exchange thought that what was applied to one place had to work everywhere. After this heated conversation, which burdened Auchinloss's loyalties to Wilson's policy, came welcome confirmation that Carranza was serious about a loan. Henry Bruere, a financial expert who had recently returned from Mexico, was the messenger. After studying Mexican finances at Wilson's request, Bruere and a colleague, Thomas Lill, had concluded that a loan would speed reconstruction and the reestablishment of Mexican credit. And like political experts who had studied the situation, Bruere and Lill also concluded that a loan was the only alternative to a sequence of events—taxation and confiscation, ultimate collapse and intervention—that would be much more "costly both in funds and principle." "It is of first importance," they reported, "that America's voice should be preponderant in influencing the future economic development of Mexico, in so far as that development will rest upon outside financial aid."[24] Changing Carranza for another man would not ease America's Mexican problem one bit. Carranza might have to be dumped at some point, true, but that would not solve the revolutionary issue. What was needed was a "quiet" period, just as Wilson had proposed, to allow things to settle down.

But Cummins's report had apparently set in motion an approach at a higher level. On August 17, 1918, Balfour cabled Colonel House straight out that he was willing to cooperate in a plan for aid to Carranza opponent Robles Domínguez. Wilson was furious, perhaps not least because of the opening he himself had apparently given for such proposals by the recent decision to use troops in Russia. House replied for the president that the offer was appreciated, but that it was hoped His Majesty's Government would refrain from aiding counterrevolutionaries, either directly or indirectly. The guiding principle of American policy was noninterference. No one was happy with Carranza's attitude, but the situation seemed to be improving. "The United States hope that economic assistance will help Mexico to recover her stability. . . ." Balfour could rest assured that the president would deal with the oil supply matter in accordance with the "recognized principles of International Law and the rights of foreign nations." However little he may have credited this renewed promise, Balfour informed British representatives in Mexico City that American objections ruled out British aid to counterrevolutionary schemes.[25]

A few weeks later, on October 4, 1918, Fletcher and Secretary Lansing met with Thomas Lamont of J. P. Morgan & Company. It was agreed that the first step must be to create an international committee, on which American bankers would predominate. Carranza must be made to see that this was the one group "capable of dealing with the situation as a whole." The Huerta situation must not be allowed to repeat itself; Carranza must not get an opportunity to play off one set of creditors against another. Equally important, the Europeans must not create for themselves opportunities to disrupt the needed process by offering special inducements. French and British members of the committee would have to agree that the "policy of the United States Government regarding Mexico [will] be the dominating influence in the operations of this group."[26]

Unhappy at the prospect of being ordered around in this manner, the Foreign Office did not exactly encourage British bankers to rush into an agreement. The view expressed there was that the more specific the negotiations got, the less likely anyway that Carranza would bite.[27] Yet the oil crisis seemed to be easing. On November 22, 1918, furthermore, Carranza asked the Mexican Congress to exempt from nationalization lands under development prior to May 1917. Full legal title to such properties would have to be exchanged, however, for government licenses that would be revocable should the companies fail to pay their obligations to the government.[28]

Loopholes. Carranza always left himself plenty, and that worried those who might have been encouraged to believe that the First Chief was leading his people along the path of righteousness. With the war over, Thomas Lamont wrote Fletcher on December 6, 1918, everyone wanted to settle up outstanding business affairs. There was always the danger that various interests, say the railroads or the utilities companies, would seek their own private arrangements at the expense of the common good.[29] A few days later Thomas Lill reported that he had persuaded Carranza to send an emmissary, Rafael Nieto, to New York to discuss terms for redeeming Mexico's outstanding debt. Undue optimism was not warranted, said Fletcher, but Lamont should get on with an announcement of the formation of an international bankers committee.[30]

In London there were as many frowns as smiles at this news. Too hasty, it was said and, with arched eyebrows, too obviously designed to insure Americans the role of lord of the manor. As it happened an expert on banking views, J. P. Morgan himself, was in London for meetings, and at dinner a second-level Foreign Office man heard the inside story. Morgan was sure that the formation of an international committee was a step in the right direction. If Carranza "was maintained in power," as Morgan put it, he would need a large loan. Carranza was without money or any real prospect of getting any, save by confiscating private property. Understandably, Mexico was a very sore subject for President Wilson. If one wanted to go down another road (a shorter one than the committee route, but also a dangerous one), the best approach would be for the British and French to say that they intended to take steps to obtain redress for injuries suffered to life and property. "Mr. Morgan thought that a proposal to intervene would be particularly effective if based on the murders and outrages (which should be given in detail) committed under the Carranza regime." Popular feelings ran high in the United States on that subject, the banker concluded. In about six months, he predicted, after the peace conference had done its work, that would be the moment to press Washington to act.[31]

Meanwhile, Rafael Nieto came to New York. So far as the bankers were concerned he might as well have stayed home. His one piece of encouraging news was that the Mexican Congress would accede to Carranza's request that the Constitution of 1917 not be made retroactive. As for a loan, there must be a misunderstanding. Mexico did not need a new loan; he had come to confer about interest payments on old debts. Commerce was now flourishing, disorder coming to an end. His government had put a hundred thousand troops into the field, supplied with the most modern equipment.[32]

Only Henry Bruere thought something might still evolve from these negotiations. Regardless of what had been said, he told Washington, Nieto had instructions to "follow our leadership." The heart of the plan the bankers had worked out was that Mexico and the United States should sign a treaty spelling out mutual obligations. "It is proposed that the State Department of the United States Government be requested to draft a tentative treaty, taking into consideration the new Mexican Constitution, which will provide a satisfactory basis for the operation of business enterprises in Mexico by the nationals of other countries."[33]

This proposal, said Bruere, was the culmination of everything that had hitherto been tried since 1910. "[I]f it is successfully consummated we shall have worked out the only possible alternative to a very much more drastic procedure with regard to Mexico than has heretofore been contemplated...."[34] As a sop to Carranza's pride, the State Department ordered a further easing on exports, including a large shipment of cartridges and rifles. When Lord Reading questioned the wisdom of this step, Frank Polk explained that it was very difficult to berate the Mexican government for failing to protect life and property and then deny it the means to do so. Almost simultaneously, though, Polk was forwarding to the White House two memoranda, one from Fletcher, the second by Consul General George A. Chamberlain. Both predicted failure. The ambassador was particularly exercised about Carranza's anti-Americanism. Indeed, argued Fletcher, Carranza would have welcomed a German victory as revenge for " '48" and a final end to the Yankee menace. The proof was the First Chief's refusal to accept a loan. Mexico's debt approached $350 million, but Carranza displayed absolutely no interest at all in honoring his country's obligations. Nieto was a smokescreen. If Carranza was not soon brought to book, Mexico's next generation of leaders would come to power with an entirely wrong impression and accomplish even more unimaginable evils. Mexican unregeneracy would afflict all the world. "Carranza considers himself the bulwark of Latin America vis-à-vis the United States...." Either now or later, he ended, Washington would have to face up to the inescapable task of putting "Mexico in her proper place in the family of nations." George Chamberlain focused on the narrow issue of commercial losses. Like the ambassador, however, he believed the only remedy was an international "ultimatum" calling upon Mexico to "accept a controlling commission to put its house in order, or, in the event of refusal, face an absolute commercial embargo as an outlawed nation."[35]

While Carranza trifled with the bankers, Mexican foreign secretary Alberto Pani had traveled to Paris. He was there, he told reporters, to announce the "Carranza Doctrine." This doctrine proclaimed that henceforth no nation had a right to interfere in the internal affairs of another country for any reason, even when property rights were at stake. It also affirmed the right of any nation to alter its constitution so as to take whatever properties were necessary as government and national welfare might require. Nieto might be promising restrictions on Article 27, but Pani was seeking to extend its scope to include the world. Pani's presence in Paris as spokesman for the Carranza Doctrine was embarrassing to the Americans, either as evidence of unfinished business or of Wilson's folly in promoting revolution. The peace conference would be difficult enough without his intrusion. But as it soon became clear, Mexican affairs were world affairs.

> *We are coming to the parting of the ways, when we must decide definitely between Japan and America, whose aims and policy in this country are diametrically opposite.*
>
> Sir John Jordan, Minister to China, November 1918

For Britain, working with America in China was even more difficult, in some ways, than achieving harmony in Mexico. Robert Lansing's immediate goal in the latter country was to get Carranza safely corralled with a loan. The China policy was more complicated than that, and when he explained it he often left a trail of confusion in his wake. As in Mexico, there were always the Wilsonian boundaries to consider, but in China there was also the complication of a third power: Japan. Nevertheless, Lansing had in mind a bold initiative by which he would convert the Japanese thrust onto the Asian continent into a diplomatic gambit to deprive the European powers of their "spheres of influence" after the war. Having accomplished that stroke, he imagined, then he or his successors could turn back to Japan. And China, meanwhile, would have been liberated, free to accept the sort of disinterested foreign aid and advice that Paul Reinsch (and others before him) had been talking about for so long, free also to pursue a liberal path of political development.

When Arthur Balfour visited Washington in the spring of 1917, Lansing had hinted at certain aspects of his proposed China policy without revealing the whole. He wanted to push Japan out of China proper, said the secretary of state, "and confine her to Manchuria, where she was bound to clash with Russia." In that way both of the "troublemakers" in Asia would be given a check to their expansionistic ambitions.[36] On the other hand, as he told Paul Reinsch, Lansing would not say that Japan had gained an exclusive "sphere of influence" in Manchuria, and while he would not push American railroad interests there the way Philander

Knox had done, business interests were not to be warned off. His words should be understood only to mean that Washington recognized certain specific concessions belonging to Japan, and to provide an assurance that the United States had no desire to crowd Japan in Manchuria.[37]

What the secretary hoped to do with this Manchurian wedge soon became clear. On May 1, 1917, the French ambassador met with Lansing to complain about an American infringement of its traditional sphere of influence. Lansing was unresponsive. The French claim was based upon a supposedly secret assurance, obtained without any quid pro quo for China. Such unequal arrangements were at the heart of China's modern difficulties, Lansing believed, and simply could not be tolerated any longer. "I should regret exceedingly," Lansing concluded, dismissing his visitor, "to find our Governments at variance on this question of the policy of the open door in China in regard to which hitherto they have been in such hearty accord."[38]

The assault on spheres of influence broadened a few weeks later when Lansing sent identical notes to London, Paris, and Tokyo requesting that they all join in an American-originated representation to Peking. The proposed communication expressed regret at the worsening factional discord there, and informed the Chinese that their entrance into the war was "of quite secondary importance as compared with unity and [internal] peace . . . so essential to China's welfare." Lord Robert Cecil thought the note would only make the Allies look foolish and meddlesome. "Draft an exceedingly courteous and conciliatory (and rather wordy) refusal," he instructed his Far East experts.[39]

Japanese reactions were much stronger. Newspapers denounced American presumption. The formal response made the point in somewhat less strident phrases. "Japan possesses paramount interests both political and economic in China," it began, but Tokyo had scrupulously refrained from making representations of the sort Washington suggested. Handing over the note, Ambassador Sato Aimaro reminded Lansing of William Jennings Bryan's March 13, 1915, statement recognizing, he said, Japan's special position in China. Lansing denied Bryan had done that; all that he had said was that territorial contiguity created special relations between Japan and the "districts of Shantung, Southern Manchuria and East Mongolia, but he did not admit that the United States might not in the future be justified in expressing its views in regard to Chino-Japanese relations involving even these districts."[40]

The focus then shifted back to the French and British holdings. Notes were dispatched to Paris and London on August 24, 1917. To the French, Lansing expressed the "sincere belief of the American Government" that the surest way to preserve China's territorial integrity was for all powers to join in supporting equality of opportunity "in all parts of China without exception." The British were told that claims for monopoly privileges in one region would produce demands for similar privileges elsewhere, thus making a mockery of the Open Door policy. American and British interests were identical, this note concluded, and required an "interpretation of the 'open door' policy . . . that will protect bona fide contracts and still preserve equality of commercial opportunity."[41]

Thomas Lyons spoke for the Foreign Office in dismissing the American note as "very idealistic and impractical."

> They maintain that, since we have not formally recognized the existence of French, German and Japanese spheres we are placed in much the same position as the U.S. Govt with regard to the question of the "open door."
>
> In point of fact there is no similarity between our positions. . . . [W]e have tacitly recognized the existing spheres.

True, in theory a general renunciation of spheres of influence would suit British interests. Perhaps the Americans had some hidden reason to believe the Japanese were prepared to yield to their wishes. But British policy could not proceed on such an assumption. Balfour fully agreed with his adviser, noting in passing the he himself had probably been responsible for initiating British policy in regard to spheres of influence back at the turn of the century.[42]

Between the lines here was evidence of a growing concern in London that if a Japanese-American initiative *were* successful in dismantling spheres of influence, only those two successor states would receive the advantages. As they had throughout the war, two forces pulled against each other: concern about Japan's ambitions versus a desire to settle with a power along familiar sphere-of-influence lines. Ironically, it had also been Arthur Balfour who suggested to Lansing a possible way of jockeying the Japanese by threatening a steel embargo. He had done so while in Washington in the early days of American participation in the war, however, simply because London desired a greater effort from Japan on behalf of Allied shipping needs. The idea was picked up by Assistant Secretary of State Breckinridge Long, who told Lansing that "aggressive use" of such a threat would also insure a satisfactory settlement of the political issues.[43]

Lansing suspended judgment while he awaited the arrival of Special Ambassador Viscount Ishii Kikujiro. The Japanese had always planned to send a special mission to the United States, as the other Allies had done once war was declared by Congress. But its importance was increased by the flood of correspondence that Lansing had authored on China over the summer months of 1917. In his *War Memoirs*, the secretary would write that he was hampered as these talks began by Bryan's March 13, 1915, statement. That note could not be repudiated outright; hence it was up to him to reduce it to an anodyne expression of goodwill, and proceed from that basis to accomplish an entirely different end.[44]

The talks began on September 6, 1917, with Lansing asking for a mutual reaffirmation of the Open Door policy as a fitting statement of principles for nations joined in a struggle with German imperialism. Ishii replied that Japan now had a special position in China; therefore a bare reaffirmation of the Open Door policy would not do.

The opening moves thus accomplished, Lansing proceeded swiftly to the middle game. The United States did recognize that Japan had a "peculiar" interest in China, he said, a "natural thing" that arose from geographic proximity. But if they were to give that "peculiar" interest a place in a statement reaffirming the Open Door, it might be misunderstood as a "peculiar political interest." Indeed, he went on, Japan's best interest would be served, given its geographical advantage, by preventing "those who want to go back to spheres of influence after the war" from having their way. Looked at from a narrow point of view, the United States should opt for spheres of influence for the same reason. But such an approach was contrary to American policies and principles.[45]

Reviewing his discussion with Ishii for Sir Cecil Spring-Rice's information (and instruction), the secretary added that he had compared Japan's situation vis-à-vis China to the Monroe Doctrine, pointing out that America had not asserted its control over the hemisphere, only a "hands-off policy addressed to all the world," and that it had received "no formal or diplomatic acceptance from other Powers." The distinction may have puzzled Sir Cecil, but Lansing seemed very sure that he would soon have Ishii talking the same language. He had gained the impression, noted the secretary, that all the Japanese wanted out of the talks was to "get something written" for public consumption. It had been left that Ishii would contact Tokyo about the American request for a simple reaffirmation of the Open Door policy.[46]

Lansing had good reason to emphasize any sign of Japanese agreement with his views, because the main topic of this conversation was not what Ishii had said, but the British response to the American note of late August. Sir Cecil had brought it with him. His Majesty's Government, it began, would prefer it if the situation were as the United States Government had stated it to be. Unfortunately, with Japan so deeply ensconced in Manchuria, Great Britain could not throw open the only area where it still had an advantage. If American funds were available for building Chinese railroads, Britain would welcome cooperation anywhere, but it could not surrender its concessions outright, nor see the Yangtze region thrown open to the highest bidder.[47]

Lansing read the note and said only the he would reply later. This turned out to be very soon, even before the secretary met for a second time with Ishii. American business interests wanted no ticket of admission to a British—or any other—sphere of influence, he told London. "With considerable interest," his response began,

> is read the statement in the memorandum of the British Embassy that, "in the view of His Majesty's Government, it is a cause for regret that a regime whereunder specific areas are earmarked for the enterprise of specific countries has gradually taken the place of a regime of free railway construction."
> The American Government would fully share that regret did it feel compelled to recognize that such a change had actually taken place. This the Department of State does not admit.

Neither did it admit that Great Britain had ever really recognized the existence of spheres of influence. Yet as matters stood, nations with the resources and ability to develop China were debarred from entering reserved areas. If the American position prevailed, on the other hand, China would enjoy more uniform development. All would benefit. "There could be a friendly co-operation between the citizens of any Powers for their mutual good and to the lasting benefit of China—a condition which is now hardly possible except as such polite invitation as is suggested in the memorandum of the British Embassy. . . ." Nations friendly to China owed to themselves, and to one another, as well as to China "the duty to assume that attitude among themselves and towards China which will better enable her to meet the economic demands which will increasingly be made upon her."[48]

This last sentence was the only hint that the American attitude also encompassed an understanding of China's internal turmoil—described, significantly, in terms of outside pressures. The lecture did not go down well in London.[49] But Lansing kept after his main goal: a reaffirmation of the Open Door policy, however qualified. And if he could avoid condoning a wholesale transfer of former German leaseholds in Shantung in his talks with the Japanese ambassador, he would obtain the lever he needed to pry out all the others.

Ishii met Lansing again on September 22, 1917, to report that the imperial government had replied that it did not wish to reaffirm the Open Door policy at this time. Lansing retreated tactically, offering to recognize not a "paramount" Japanese interest in China but one based on geography, coupled with a statement that the United States fully understood Japan's population and industrial problems and the need to resolve these in Korea and Manchuria. Ishii still demurred. Japan did not want to possess Manchuria, he said. The secretary sensed an advantage and pressed forward. "My view was that in China foreign commerce and trade should be entirely unhampered." And he gave examples. With some hesitation, Lansing noted carefully, Ishii gave his assent. He seemed desirous of avoiding specifics. Actually, so was the secretary, for he could not really go beyond generalities in offering economic cooperation for Japanese restraint.[50]

Specifics were also successfully avoided in the final version of the Lansing-Ishii Agreement published on November 2, 1917. In the agreement, actually a letter from Lansing to the viscount, the two governments formally recognized that "territorial propinquity creates special relations between countries." But while Japan had such interests in the part of China closest to its possessions, the next paragraph said that China's territorial integrity remained "unimpaired." The United States was confident, moreover, that Japan's "repeated assurances" of nondiscrimination in economic matters, even in areas of geographical proximity, were sincere.

Then came Lansing's desired reaffirmation of the principles of the Open Door policy. There was also an unpublished protocol that pledged the signers not to take advantage of the present turmoil in China to seek special rights or privileges that would in any way abridge those of citizens of friendly states. All told, in fact, there were three such reaffirmations of Hay's Open Door policy in the document. But Lansing was not unhappy with the cloud of ambiguity that swelled up immediately upon publication of the agreement. Indeed, apparently to soften Ishii's burdens the secretary had suggested that the phrase "special interest" would leave "ample room for suitable interpretations on both sides."[51]

The Chinese complained, on the other hand, that the Lansing-Ishii Agreement left them no room. When the Chinese minister attempted to set forth Peking's objections and caveats, Lansing treated him in an almost cavalier manner. China did not offer the same attractions to American capital that it once did, he said bluntly. Japan and the United States were the only two nations with money to invest, but American capitalists would not risk their money in China until the political atmosphere cleared. "The time had passed when China could play off the United States against Japan. . . ." These were harsh words, made all the more so by Lansing's curt question: would China be better off if the United States simply dropped out of Asian affairs? The plain fact was that fear of Japanese opposition could freeze out any American loan proposal. Besides, it was axiomatic that nations had special interests in the affairs of their neighbors. Surely it was desirable to concede that truth in exchange for the declarations Japan had made.[52]

Lansing seemed very sure of himself.

> *By frankly denouncing the evil influences which have been at work, by openly proclaiming the policy of Japan is not one of aggression, and by declaring that there is no intention to take advantage commercially or industrially of the special relations to China created by geographical position, the representatives of Japan have cleared the diplomatic atmosphere of the suspicion which had been so carefully spread by our enemies and by misguided or over-zealous people in both countries.*
>
> Committee for Public Information press release, May 26, 1918

Wartime press releases—what a fanciful portrait of reality they are obliged to offer. Examined by British critics, however, the Lansing-Ishii Agreement had all the charm of a Venus's-flytrap. Inside the Foreign Office it looked as if Japan had obtained from a naive State Department a license to demand entrance to the Yangtze while neatly tucking away both Manchuria and Shantung. Balfour thought it would develop as follows:

> a Note which (a) proclaimed the "open door," and (b) said that notwithstanding the "open door" Japan had special rights in parts of China; and (c) *omitted* to say that we also had special rights in parts of China (viz. the Yangtze Valley) could not be formally accepted by us without, by implication, making a surrender of our rights.[53]

The perception was close to the truth. Washington's trumpeting of the Lansing-Ishii Agreement also made it appear that Japan had confessed to its imperialist sins and started on the path to redemption. Of course, it was implied, the Japanese were not really responsible for the evil—the Germans were. Since Britain and France were also at war with the same evil, all the more reason for them to confess too.

The sudden outpouring of supposed Japanese-American friendship, viewed in this light, confirmed suspicions both of America's ineptness at diplomatic handicraft and of its unabashed cupidity. At a banquet honoring the Japanese special mission, Judge Gary of U.S. Steel even criticized the Chinese for continuing to believe that Japan posed any peril to their interests. The British consul general in New York was present for these remarks, and reported to Spring-Rice that an official of the Guaranty Trust Banking Corporation had leaned over to him and whispered, "This sounds rather like 'hands off China' to every other nation."[54]

No one in London really believed that the Japanese-American alliance had much chance of lasting, but they were pretty well on to Lansing's game. For that matter, three could play as well as two. Lansing, meanwhile, was anxious to learn what had developed with the bankers. Even though the president had severed all official connections with the "old group," the consortium bankers still behaved as if they enjoyed a special sphere of influence over China loans. The lack of teamwork in the American financial community had been a problem for the administration since 1913, and had yet to be resolved. Suggestions that the American group be reconstituted and enlarged had always run into difficulty and collapsed. Independent loans had not proved feasible.

Even if the Lansing-Ishii Agreement dispelled fears of Japanese intransigence and opened the way to Chinese stability (admittedly two very big ifs), nothing would come of the effort without equal progress on "internal" weaknesses in the China policy. It especially grated that the consortium now seemed obsessed with recouping earlier losses to the detriment of larger issues. The bankers always responded to this accusation by pointing out the need for investor confidence. Was the U.S. Treasury prepared to stand behind China bonds in the same way it guaranteed the Liberty Loans to finance the war?

What had happened in March 1917 was a perfect example. The old consortium group approached the State Department during that month to advise it of a Japanese invitation to participate in a new loan to China. The bankers professed only a mild interest in the proposition, even though it did appear to offer "an exceptional opportunity again to promote the legitimate commercial aspirations of our country in the Far East." During the course of the negotiations "it might be arranged," said the American group, "that the securities of the Hukuang Loan . . . would be made more definite by the Chinese Government for the better protection of the American bondholders. . . ." Japan was offering, in other words, to see that the bankers got paid off for cooperating in their China policy.[55]

That was too crude, of course, but the request for administration blessing made it clear that unless something was done, and soon, the temptation to say yes to such an offer would grow until finally commitments were made that would be next to impossible to undo. What good would it do for Lansing to succed in disengaging the machinery of the old diplomacy, if then the bankers got enmeshed in a financial trap? Hence the secretary stalled his response until he could work out a strategy parallel to that he would use with Ishii, one that would go down well with Wilson and would give the administration greater control over the American financial moguls, who had yet to acquire the congenial habits of behaving like quasi-official "public servants" as did the financiers of rival industrial powers.[56]

Using the medium of an exchange with a Belgian diplomat assigned to China, Lansing drew up a list of arguments for a new consortium to give to the White House. The principal reason was that under present conditions, Japanese-American competition meant Tokyo's predominance in the China loan market, not least because the Japanese government and its bankers always worked hand in hand. A new international banking organization, the secretary wrote Wilson, was really the only way to take advantage of the changed attitudes wrought by the war, and to make them permanent. "My own view is that the whole question, being of so much importance to our future relations to the Far East, ought to be considered with little regard for the past."[57]

While they waited for presidential approval, Lansing's aides set down the criteria for a new consortium. The two most important conditions, said Assistant Secretary Long, must be first, that no loan could be undertaken unless at least three powers agreed to its terms, and were ready to cooperate; and second, that American membership be expanded so as to include bankers from all sections of the country. This last, by preventing any one group of individuals or firms from exercising a dominant influence, would therefore oblige the consortium "to operate under the approval, and, if necessary, under the direction of the Secretary of State."[58]

It now appeared that the secretary might have taken too long to launch his campaign. Word came from Minister Paul Reinsch that the Chinese were about to open negotiations for a $100 million loan from the old consortium, sans Germany of course. The British were as alarmed as their American counterparts, however, and the Foreign Office view was that such a proposition meant Japanese control. If the negotiations could not be prevented, asked the British, would the United States consider forming an American group on an ad hoc basis, if necessary, to participate?[59]

Backed into a corner, London had called for help. That was no doubt gratifying to know, but instead, Breckinridge Long called in the Chinese minister to offer him a substitute, a $25 million loan from the American government. It might be arranged, said Long, provided that Peking agreed to strict controls over its expenditure and promised to spend the money in the United States. When he received a positive response from the minister, Long inquired if the consortium negotiations had been suspended, because of course the American loan was to be a substitute. If the loan was made, moreover, Washington would wish to send a commission of experts to China. On top of all this, Long specified other requirements and obligations that China must fulfill to be eligible for this aid, a complete program, in fact, that would "make her less dependent upon foreign help and less torn by factional fights within."[60]

Not surprisingly, the weight of all these conditions sank whatever prospects there were for the loan. It seems most likely that everyone connected with the idea was just as happy not to have to go on with the project. The success of Lansing's negotiations with Viscount Ishii claimed all the attention of policymakers at the moment, anyway, coupled with the president's decision of November 9, 1917, that as a "war measure" the United States would try to construct a new consortium for China.[61] Paul Reinsch, who had fought so hard to make Wilson's Open Door policy work, and who had been so frustrated earlier, gave Lansing his congratulations. China could well become "one of our greatest natural assets," the minister wrote the secretary on December 20, 1917. Lansing replied that there was no lack of will to aid China but added, "The nations warring against Germany must . . . work in concert; the United States cannot act alone."[62]

With the triumph of the Bolsheviks in Petrograd, Lansing's words took on special significance.

> Out here in this ultra-Autocratic Empire, where the Throne has been regarded with something like idolatry, and where the Japanese Parliament or Duma exercises little if any control over the Government, the sudden sweeping away of a somewhat similarly-run Autocracy only a few hours distant from Japan has had a dazzling effect.
>
> Sir Conyngham Greene, May 1917

Declaring himself the only legitimate successor to the republic "betrayed" by Yuan Shi-k'ai, Sun Yat-sen established a rival government in Canton in September 1917. Sun's activities were a disturbing indication to Washington that policymakers had been right to fear what entry into the war would do to Chinese politics. Reinsch, of course, had insisted that it would be China's salvation, a unifying force that would transform an Asian scene, outwit the Japanese, and align China with the Progressive elements at the peace conference. Instead, it was now feared, China would be more divided than ever because of the added stimulus to radical nationalism.

The Kuomintang party, which Sun led, was the most serious nationalist movement to emerge thus far out of the Revolution of 1911. Itself an amalgam, Sun's organization openly welcomed support from both the disgruntled warlords and Soviet Russia. And Sun even flirted with an arrangement with Japan over Manchuria. Wilson thought him an adventurer. "I do not like to correspond directly with Sun Yat Sen," he wrote Lansing, "much as I have sometimes sympathized with his professed principles and objects."[63]

Whether Sun was to be China's leader or not, however, the Western powers and Japan were agreed that postwar relations with China would have to be put on a new basis. "A great deal of trouble and embarrassment will be avoided," Wilson also advised his secretary of state, "if we can draw China into the best possible cooperation and give her a more definite set of international connections in the common cause."[64] But the requirements for big power cooperation in China, however skillfully managed, were bound to collide with the rising force of Chinese nationalism, whoever finally dominated the movement.

On June 20, 1918, Lansing told the president that the Treasury now agreed the financial requirements of the European war had abated enough to permit loans to China. Hence he wanted to call together representatives of the old group and others interested in Far Eastern loans to discuss an enlarged American group. Various projects might be undertaken, but the most pressing need was to break Japan's grip on Chinese currency reform. In the interim between the Lansing-Ishii Agreement and this letter, much had happened. And in other respects much had not happened. The British, who were not content to be saved by endorsing the Lansing-Ishii rhetoric, were nevertheless disappointed at the gap between State Department announcements that the consortium was to be reconstructed and actual performance. Lansing's surprisingly laggard pace also alarmed Paul Reinsch, always alert to Japanese schemes. While Washington delayed, he reported in April 1918, the recently installed currency adviser in Peking, Japan's Baron Sakatani, had put out a claim to control all foreign loans and domestic bank note issues. The Chinese were resisting, but time was short. "I have the honor to urge the necessity of prompt action." How many times had he sent that message? "The power to maintain our position in financial and industrial work in China will be a prime necessity for American industry after the war."[65]

In reply to Lansing, Wilson suggested a halfway covenant with the bankers. There could be nothing like the "unconscionable arrangements" contemplated by the old consortium, he said, and he worried that China was even more vulnerable than it had been earlier. The bankers also had conditions. They wanted to be assured against "wildcatters," and they wanted all current loan projects surrendered to their control. But they did not demand a government backup to protect them against untoward Chinese behavior, a point whose absence should have alerted State Department planners at the outset that the goal of an international consortium had different meanings for political advisers than it did for the bankers. At this early stage, however, it was enough just to cope with the problems of organization.[66]

Even so, it was impossible not to look ahead sometimes and speculate on what might be. Assistant Secretary Long, who was put in charge of consortium affairs, was interested in what Colonel House saw in the future. "He thinks China's only salvation is government under and by a commission of the big and interested powers. I suggested that if the consortium materialized into a international group that the representatives of the group, controlling China's purse, and working in close cooperation with the Legations, might be the power he had in mind."[67]

If that in fact happened, the bankers would not need "gunboat" diplomacy to protect their loans. Near the end of the war, Sir John Jordan, long-time British minister to China, reviewed the situation from his perspective. He noted that those who had hoped that China's entrance into the war would cure both internal and external problems had been sadly disappointed. Instead, because of internal divisions, Japan seized the opportunity to establish its position under the guise of supplying war loans. All under the pretext of cooperation with the Allies, the northern warlord regime had waged civil war against the south, keeping China in a state of turmoil. China's debt to Japan, Jordan continued, was already considerably larger than the indemnity it had been forced to pay after the Sino-Japanese War of 1894–95. Eighty percent of the "intelligent" Chinese would prefer international financial control to Japanese dominance, he estimated. There was no third alternative. "104,000,000 yen purchased Corea," a prominent Chinese had told him, "a billion will seal the fate of China, and Japan is only too anxious to provide the money."[68]

Jordan was also especially interested in what a new China hand, Woodrow Wilson's friend and former political patron Charles R. Crane, was saying on his fact-finding tour through China gathering materials for the peace conference. Crane was openly putting it about that the League of Nations was to be "an Anglo-Saxon combination," one that would "control militarism in the Far East, and insure that resources of China are developed, not for the aggrandizement of any particular nation, but for the common benefit of all. The idea roughly is, that the Powers should disclose their concessions, put all their cards upon the table, agree to make no further secret arrangements, and come to an understanding on the whole subject." Sir John knew full well that *if* this was Wilson's policy—

and the parallel with what was happening on the Mexican front suggested that it might be —then His Majesty's Government faced some hard decisions in the near future, perhaps during the peace conference itself. "[W]e are coming to the parting of the ways," Jordan wrote, "when we must decide definitely between Japan and America, whose aims and policy in this country are diametrically opposite."[69]

After consideration had been given to Jordan's recitation of what he supposed American policy to be, and the need for standing side by side with Wilson, the task of devil's advocate was given to Ronald Macleay, who was to make the case for continuing Sir Edward Grey's policy of spheres of influence. To begin with, said the Foreign Office expert, the United States would have to demonstrate that it was in China to stay, and not just off on another flier. Only then should "we commit ourselves to the acceptance of the new American policy in China. . . ." Else His Majesty's Government would only succeed in placing itself in double jeopardy. It would be very easy, in fact, to antagonize Japan by demanding access to Manchuria, while having to give up claims to special rights in the Yangtze. Was it likely, on the other hand, that public opinion in China was ready to accept international control of the country's finances? Certainly the "more advanced" political thought in Sun Yat-sen's movement would not stand for any such thing. Sun had no conception of his limitations, but was confident he could manage China's affairs without foreign advice. Had Sir John, finally, taken into account the strong sentimental strain in American policy that might cause Washington to end up siding with the southern Chinese radicals against all rational calculation of Western interests in China?[70]

Balfour ruled in favor of Macleay. Dangerous pitfalls awaited the unwary. Under no circumstances, it was decided, should British negotiators at Paris advocate formal supervision of China's finances, at least not until it had been ascertained what American intentions were and, indeed, what the Japanese intended to propose. Valued as his opinions were, Sir John Jordan's "very radical proposals" could not provide the basis for any British initiative. Wilson would have to put the ball in play.[71]

The president's advisers were, in fact, gearing up for a major effort. Anarchy and division would soon disappear, the enthusiastic Charles Crane reported to Wilson, if the peace conference abolished spheres of influence. "Indeed the cause of Christianity in Asia is largely tied up with what you advocate at the Peace Conference and what it does," Crane told the president. He did not repeat here what he had said to Sir John Jordan, but Crane's full-blown vision suggested that the Foreign Office was right to be cautious. His idea seemed to be a sort of philanthropic protectorate over China, which in one version would be dominated by the

Board of Foreign Missions of the Protestant Churches of America, and in another by an interlocking board of directors of an Anglo-American banking combine. Compared to this, even Frank L. Polk's elaboration on Lansing's China policy goals seemed modest. If the president could take time during his preconference visit to London to line up the British, then France and Italy would follow along. An understanding on the need to eliminate spheres of influence would strengthen the hands of the "liberal elements" in Japan. Wilson need only make the American position clear.[72]

Such optimism was unwarranted, as the British knew. But the raised expectations, born in part as a result of Wilson's taking unto himself the armistice negotiations with Germany, also reflected a sense that finally, after nearly six years, the time for decision had arrived. No more gestures, no more clever evasions. But did Wilson and his close advisers know what they were really after: a China set free to determine its own future, or a benevolent protectorate? And what did they want for Mexico?

In Mexico's case, the enunciation of the Carranza Doctrine at Paris had caused great consternation. Inklings of a similar difficulty with the Far Eastern initiative had begun to appear as early as mid-November 1918, when Ambassador Roland Morris cabled that he had learned Japan intended to introduce a declaration of racial equality at the peace conference. Discussions were already under way, he said, with China so that the Asian nations could present a united front, while Japanese publications were stressing the nation's obligation to take the lead in representing the yellow race.[73]

In recent weeks, moreover, Tokyo had welcomed Peking's overtures for north-south negotiations to end the civil war, much to the puzzlement of Western diplomats. But now the reason was apparent. Japanese strategy, Polk advised Secretary Lansing on January 5, 1919, was to encourage China to insist upon abolition of extraterritorial rights (the crux of the Western position in China since the Boxer Rebellion and the symbol of Western rule and "legitimacy" in Asia) and control of the tariff (the complementary financial authority)—demands the white powers could not meet. In exchange, Tokyo would expect China's support for a strictly bilateral settlement of the Shantung issue. "All general provisions made by the Peace Conference for the protection and salvation of China would be futile if Japanese special right in Shantung should be acknowledged," Polk warned.[74]

While that was so, Shantung was far less important than the mischief such a strategy would accomplish by planting seeds of doubt about the West inside China. The world had become, as Wilson would say, one huge whispering gallery, and that was true from the outskirts of Paris to Central Europe, and back again to Mexico and China.

III

A WORLD MADE SAFE

*If America fails now, socialism rules the world and if
international fair play under democracy cannot curb
nationalistic ambitions, there is nothing left but socialism upon which Russia and Germany have already embarked.*

Joseph P. Tumulty to Woodrow Wilson,
December 31, 1918

*If we seek to impose hard terms on the enemy, we
shall almost inevitably produce Bolshevism in the enemy countries, but temporarily at any rate we shall
satisfy . . . and prevent anarchy in the Allied countries. If, on the other hand, we seek to impose moderate, liberal terms of peace, we may be too late to save
the enemy countries from Bolshevism, and we may
through disappointment, produce Bolshevism among
the Allies.*

Robert Cecil to Colonel House, 1919

CHAPTER TEN

Wilson and Lloyd George
in Paris

We are sitting upon an open powder magazine . . .
Colonel House, March 1919

If the Russian situation was not resolved, Winston Churchill warned Prime Minister David Lloyd George in early 1919, "we should come away [from Paris] . . . rejoicing in a victory that which was no victory, and a peace which was no peace. . . ." In a few months' time the Allies would be compelled to gather their armies again. His idea was to say to the various Russian factions: Come together, and we will help you. But he also advocated being prepared for a refusal and standing ready to "use force to restore the situation and set up a democratic Government."[1]

The war over, new justifications were needed to continue the intervention and to forestall the question of Russia at the peace conference. Lloyd George had a very different solution in mind, although it built upon Churchill's idea. His hope, the prime minister told the war cabinet, was to bring together representatives from each of Russia's contending factions to see if their differences could not be resolved. But no more troops. "To send our soldiers to shoot down the Bolsheviks would be to create Bolsheviks here," Lloyd George insisted. The war cabinet went along, but stipulated that in the event of a Bolshevik-sponsored attack on Poland and Rumania, His Majesty's Government would have to come to the defense of those countries.[2]

Churchill was satisfied. It was only a matter of time until the Bolsheviks went on a rampage. When that happened the War Office would be ready. "Naturally it followed that we should try to combine all the border states hostile to the Bolsheviks," he wrote later, "into one system of war and diplomacy and get everyone else to do as much as possible."[3] And just over the horizon, he thought as well, was a hard decision "to bolster up the Central Powers . . . in order to stem the tide of Bolshevism."[4]

Also in preparation for Paris, President Wilson had sent a secretary of the American embassy in London, W. H. Buckler, to see what might be gleaned from the Bolsheviks themselves. Buckler was to meet in a "neutral" city with Maxim Litvinov, a Bolshevik diplomat who had lived in the West much of his life. "What I am at present keenly interested in is in finding the interior of their minds," Wilson explained to Robert Lansing, adding, "The real thing with which to stop Bolshevism is food." A day earlier, in fact, on January 9, 1919, the president had sent an urgent request to Treasury Secretary William Gibbs McAdoo to speed aid to Rumania. An extremely dangerous situation existed there, "which must be relieved in the next few days and one which, if cumulative, with others, may necessitate increased military effort on our part."[5]

> *Very near to Prinkipo lay another island to which the Young Turks had exiled all the pariah dogs which had formerly infested the streets of Constantinople. . . . To Bolshevik sympathizers the place seemed oddly chosen for a peace conference. To their opponents it seemed not altogether unsuitable.*
>
> Winston Churchill,
> *The Aftermath,* 1929

Wilson's mind never came to rest on a solution for the Bolshevik puzzle, and he infuriated both sides in the debate at Paris. At preconference discussions on January 19, 1919, the French proposed the first of several military options for resolving the issue. Given an opening (actually, he would have taken a mouse hole if necessary), Lloyd George stepped in with his plan for a general conference.[6]

Did he want to strengthen the already "truculent World Bolshevik propaganda," challenged French foreign secretary Stephen Pichon? It would be much better (and safer) to hear the opinions of Russians in exile in Paris. That would solve nothing, returned the prime minister. The Allies had got themselves in a fix over Russia because they lacked a policy, and the men Pichon wished to have heard represented every opinion except the prevalent one. "It was prevalent in some respects," cautioned Wilson, finding it difficult to say what American policy was beyond waiting.

Lloyd George barely paused. "He feared," Big Four minutes recorded, "that the fact that it was prevalent must be accepted. The peasants accepted Bolshevism for the same reason as the peasants had accepted it in the French Revolution, namely, that it gave them land." No getting around it, either, the Bolsheviks were the de facto government. "We had formally recognized the Czar's Government, although at the time we knew it to be absolutely rotten. Our reason had been that it was the *de facto* Government. We recognized the Don Government, the Archangel Government and the Omsk Government, although none of them were good, but we refused to recognize the Bolshevists. To say that we ourselves should pick the representatives of a great people was contrary to every principle for which we had fought." Let his colleagues consider a final point. "The British Government made exactly the same mistake when they said that the *émigrés* represented France. This led them into a war which lasted about twenty-five years."[7]

After this dramatic recital, the proposal itself seemed an anticlimax. All the different governments now at war inside the old Russian empire, said Lloyd George, should be summoned "to a truce of God"—"somewhat in the way the Roman Empire summoned chiefs of outlying tributary states to render an account of their actions." What did the others offer? The idea of crushing Bolshevism by military force was "pure madness." There was no one to occupy Russia's vast interior. A blockade, then? That would only cause additional deaths, women and children, friends of the Allies. He had heard it said that if the Bolsheviks were allowed to come to Paris, they would convert France and England to their abominable creed. "If England becomes Bolshevist, it will not be because a single Bolshevist representative is permitted to enter England. On the other hand, if a military enterprise were started against the Bolsheviki, that would make England Bolshevist, and there would be a Soviet in London."

Still not entirely convinced—and perhaps wondering what had caused this dramatic change in British policy from a year earlier, when all he had heard from London was "intervention"—Wilson stated his agreement with certain of the prime minister's ideas. In America considerable progress had been made in checking the power of capital, yet even there labor and capital were not friends. "Unless some sort of partnership between these two interests could be obtained society would crumble." Sending troops to Russia was a sure way of destroying progress at home. Indeed, not even wealthy Americans thought in those terms. "We should be fighting against the current of the times if we tried to prevent Russia from finding her own path to freedom." If the Bolsheviks refrained from invading neighboring states, he would be prepared to see them—and all other groups that wished to be heard.[8]

French objections continued, however, forcing Lloyd George to offer a compromise. The proposed meeting could be held someplace else, as far away from Paris as his colleagues liked. Wilson liked the "Truce of God" format, probably because it reminded him of his own notions of how to deal with the Mexican Revolution. He also agreed, however, with French prime minister Georges Clemenceau that such a conference ought not to be held in Paris, but at a distance, somewhere "convenient of approach."[9]

The apparent agreement between Wilson and Lloyd George was just that, apparent and nothing more. At a general conference of the sort the president had in mind, the moral force the Bolsheviks had exerted as defenders of Russia against the invaders (German and Allied) would dissipate. Whoever represented the Leninist regime would have to put all the cards on the table. Once exposed, the Bolsheviks would not dare withdraw. They would have to come to terms. An isolated location, therefore, was essential in the Wilson version.

To Lloyd George, on the other hand, the "Truce of God" was only preliminary. Probably he favored some form of partition, but not in the same way Africa had been parceled out. What he hoped was that the Bolsheviks themselves would accept limitations on their "Russia," and allow other "Russias" to go their own way under new names—Latvia, Lithuania, Siberia, Poland, the Ukraine, and so on. That might seem best, after all, for future world peace.[10]

At one point Wilson turned to the Japanese delegate, Baron Makino, to ask his opinion. Makino asked a question neither Lloyd George nor Wilson wished to explore. Suppose the Bolsheviks accepted the invitation, he mused, but then refused to negotiate anything but the surrender of the anti-Bolshevik opposition? The president's answer was instructive. The Allied emissaries would, in that case, merely report back what had been encountered. Clemenceau perceived that there really were two proposals on the floor, that Lloyd George's contemplated recognition, and that Wilson would go no further if the Bolsheviks followed Makino's scenario. To be sure which he was voting for, Clemenceau asked Wilson to draft the invitation.[11]

Wilson gladly complied. His draft promised the Russian people an absolute right to self-determination. "It is not their wish or purpose," it said of the Allies, "to favor or assist any one of the organized groups now contending for the leadership and guidance of Russia as against the others." The place chosen was Prince's Island (Prinkipo) in the Sea of Marmora off the Turkish coast. What recommended this location was that

Bolshevik delegates traveling to the meeting would not pass through any European country.[12]

The Prinkipo conference was doomed from the outset never to take place, thanks to opposition from all sides. News of the conference proposal sent shudders through anti-Bolshevik redoubts both inside and outside Russia. At Admiral Kolchak's headquarters in Siberia, reported General Alfred Knox, there was a feeling of betrayal: "[S]uddenly the whole of Russia is informed by wireless that her Allies regard the brave men who are here fighting for part of civilization as on par with the blood-stained, Jew-led Bolsheviks." From Washington, Frank Polk, the acting secretary of state, reported the widespread view that the call for a conference undermined the morale of all anti-Bolshevik parties. Kolchak's government should be recognized as soon as possible, Polk asserted, to give it the moral support necessary to "withstand the crisis created by the recent action of the Peace Conference."[13]

The official Soviet reply to the Prinkipo invitation repeated an offer Maxim Litvinov had made to William H. Buckler, one not previously countenanced by Wilson. Dated February 4, 1919, it offered to purchase an agreement with the capitalist powers. The only reservation was that the "future development of the Soviet Republic will not be menaced." There were no internal enemies of the regime, it argued, only Allied fictions. What had to be settled, therefore, pertained only to Allied-Soviet relations. Litvinov promised attractive terms. The Bolsheviks would repay loans, deliver raw materials, grant concessions, and even give up territory. As for the frequent complaints about revolutionary propaganda, the Russian government would undertake as part of a general settlement not to intervene in the internal affairs of Allied nations, but it could not limit the freedom of the revolutionary press.[14]

Clemenceau was delighted by the response. It proved what he had been saying all along. Any attempt to deal with the Bolsheviks would be turned to a propaganda advantage; even this offer of concessions sounded like an indictment of capitalist misbehavior and greed.[15] Called home to deal with labor unrest and the perennial Irish question, Lloyd George met similar criticisms of Prinkipo with a frank statement of what had been tried and failed in efforts to unseat Lenin. In addition to financial support, he told the House of Commons, the Whites had been given ammunition and guns. "Pretty much the whole of their equipment—at least a good part of it—has been supplied by the Allies. . . ." Who was ready to do more? Who was now willing to send troops? Not the United States. "America will send neither men, money, nor material. . . . Has anyone calculated the cost?" Would the Honourable Members, he ended, "turn their minds occasionally from the newspapers . . . just to read up the story of the French Revolution."[16]

What a pity Prinkipo failed, Lloyd George subsequently wrote his private secretary, Phillip Kerr. It was the victim of silly maneuvering between the French and the émigré community. "Now you can exact some terms which would guarantee better government in Russia; a few months hence [the] Bolsheviks would [sic] may be triumphant and absent."[17]

> *What we were seeking was not a* rapprochement . . . , *but clear information.*
>
> Woodrow Wilson, February 1919

In his *War Memoirs,* Lloyd George wrote that Winston Churchill "very adroitly seized the opportunity" of the failed Prinkipo initiative to push his own views at Paris. More likely, Lloyd George guided the whole business in an effort to see how Wilson would react to an out-and-out interventionist proposal. Sending Churchill was a controlled experiment, but that did not mean it was foolproof.[18]

An interesting setting awaited the former first lord of the Admiralty, now secretary of state for war. Clemenceau had just indicated to press interviewers that France had a great stake in Russia. "France has something like twenty billions invested in Russia, two-thirds of that sum in Russian Government securities, and the remainder in industrial enterprises." Other billions had been lost in recent years in Mexico. Now there were war debts to pay, along with other obligations. Germany had been defeated, yes, but there remained for the "Teutons" a "chaotic, yet fruitful Russia." France was determined not to lose in Russia what it had won in the West.[19]

Wilson's public reflections on Prinkipo again stressed concern for Russia. Unhappily, he told reporters, only the "least desirable" elements had responded to the invitation, "to the exclusion of those who might restore order." The Soviet reply was insulting, moreover, and "revealed the Bolshevik desire to split the loot between them and buy recognition."[20]

In a sense, Lenin had played into the president's hands. Now Wilson could associate the Bolsheviks, if not with the German military cause, then with the "special interests" he had been fighting since 1913 in Mexico and China. But if that was so, he also offered Churchill a very large opening. Sitting in for the prime minister, the secretary of war asked if Prinkipo was to be pursued further, or if some other policy had been adopted. Wilson backed away from that challenge with an anti-interventionist statement, which, however, trailed off with the remark that he was about to depart for the United States to fulfill his constitutional obligations. He did not have time to elaborate, but he was for sending informal representatives to talk with the Bolsheviks. When Churchill pressed for a decision to arm anti-Bolshevik forces, Wilson appeared to waver. "President Wilson said that he hesitated to express any definite opinion on this question. He had explained to the Council how he would act if alone. He would, however, cast in his lot with the rest."[21]

Whatever Wilson intended by these words, Churchill thought he had been given a green light. "Wilson's last words," he wrote to Lloyd George, were that "while anxious to clear out of Russia altogether and willing if necessary to meet the Bolsheviks alone at Prinkipo, he would nevertheless if Prinkipo came to nothing do his share with the other Allies in any military measures which they considered necessary and practicable to support the Russian armies now in the field. I considered this a very satisfactory note for him to end on. . . ."[22]

The next day Churchill presented his case for an ultimatum to Moscow. The Bolsheviks were to be given ten days to agree to a cease-fire in the civil war. If they did, and only if they did, the Whites would be asked to do the same. After that, some sort of talks could begin. Churchill was vague about that point because he could not really believe the Bolsheviks would accept. He was seeking only a clear conscience to display to the world. What he imagined would unfold was the formation of a Allied Council on Russia, followed by the development and execution of a military strategy. Unless Russia "formed a living part of Europe," he prophesied, "unless she became a living partner in the League of Nations and a friend of the Allied Powers, there would be neither peace nor victory."[23]

Clemenceau had been waiting to hear such sentiments from an English-speaking ally, and declared himself ready to build "a barrier around Russia" at once. Balfour and Colonel House, who was sitting in for Wilson, feared prophets of this kind, ready to sacrifice everything— certainly readier than the Bolsheviks at this point—for an ideal. Further discussion was necessary, they said. Nothing more should be done besides sending a telegram to the Bolsheviks asking for a cease-fire. But Churchill sent orders anyway to British forces in northern Russia, instructing them to prepare for an "active defensive on the Dvina River."[24]

It was time to call a halt to this experiment before it exploded in everyone's face. Lloyd George sent word that there could be no "expensive war of aggression against Russia." An impeccable source—Austen Chamberlain, chancellor of the exchequer and a leading Tory besides— had told him that it was financially impossible. Beyond that there was the labor position. "Were it known that you had gone over to Paris to prepare a plan of war against the Bolsheviks it would do more to incense organized labor than anything I can think of; and what is still worse, it would throw into the ranks of the extremists a very large number of thinking people who now abhor their methods."[25]

Little more than a year before, Lloyd George had dealt Ramsay Mac-Donald a devastating blow in the debates over the abortive Stockholm conference. He had no doubt hoped to make the Churchillites equally vulnerable, but he had not anticipated Wilson's response. He soon felt relieved, however, because the president informed the peace conference that he had only meant to say that he would not take any hasty action by himself. Whether or not these were second thoughts, Wilson no longer supported the Churchill plan, saying, "It would be fatal to be led further into the present chaos."[26]

As always, it was easier to say where Wilson would not go than to pin him down to a positive course. Even Colonel House was misled by the president's random comment that he wished to send informal representatives to the Bolsheviks, and proposed that William C. Bullitt be sent to see if a truce was not possible. Lloyd George was all for the idea—at the outset. As always, the P.M. was looking for some way to force Wilson to decide; besides, something had to be done to head off yet another French proposal to unloose "the whole of Eastern Europe, the Finns, the Esthonians, the Poles, the Roumanians, and the Greeks" on Russia. It was a crazy scheme, insisted the British prime minister, because the only party inside Russia that had ever promised self-determination to these various groups was the Bolsheviks.[27]

Afraid, after the reactions to Prinkipo, that publicity would destroy Bullitt's mission before it got started, House told Lansing that he was sending the young liberal to Russia to "cure him of Bolshevism." Lansing knew better. He knew this was more than a fact-finding expedition, and he also knew that no one was being sent to the White governments.[28] Using Phillip Kerr as a sort of intermediary, Lloyd George had spelled out in some detail what he expected of the mission:

> [i]f we could negotiate a settlement which would secure to Kolchak, Denikin, the Archangel group and the small nations on the Western border of Soviet Russia the free control of their own affairs and at the same time allow Allied agents to penetrate European Russia with full guarantees for life and property, we should have amply fulfilled our obligations and at the same time have struck a deadly blow at the more violent and abominable forms of Bolshevism.[29]

Something more was on the prime minister's mind, a concern that with war's end America was no longer really committed to Europe. For all his talk about the League of Nations, Wilson seemed distant and, worse, unconcerned about economic recovery. If Europe was to find its way back to anything approaching prosperity, the Russian question had to be settled. Lloyd George saw in the Bullitt mission a way of convincing British conservatives that the Americans were just as anxious as he for peace with Russia.

An uncommitted America was as unsettling to Europe's future, thought Lloyd George, as Lenin's untamed revolution. Since he recognized that intervention was folly, Wilson should also understand the futility of continuing a "watchful waiting" policy. Russia was not Mexico, in other words, but such an approach could produce many Mexicos, or situations much worse. Put still another way, if Lloyd George could reconcile Conservative opinion by demonstrating that a major push for liberal solutions (on a spectrum of questions, not just Russia) originated *outside* of Britain, and therefore outside of domestic political control, he could also demonstrate to the left that Wilson had a full share in all policy decisions that were less than ideologically perfect from that point of view.

Bullitt arrived in Moscow in time to witness the First Congress of the Communist International. Although revolutionary zeal ran high, the theme was not the immediate overthrow of the Western capitalist governments but united action to force an end to the anti-Bolshevik intervention, diplomatic recognition of Soviet Russia, and establishment of commercial relations.[30] His talks with Soviet officials went well, the latter insisting only that any agreement be reciprocal; for example, if Allied citizens were to have the right of free entry into Russia provided they did not interfere in domestic politics, Soviet citizens must be accorded the same privilege in the Allied nations.[31]

Making the conditions reciprocal did alter the proposal from a "cooling-off" attempt to one that stressed the dynamic nature of the situation. While Bullitt negotiated, Lloyd George sought American aid in another related endeavor (which was perhaps at the heart of his Russian policy since the armistice): a quick settlement of the reparations issue. House recorded the overture and his impressions of Lloyd George's predicaments:

> By helping him out, he meant to give a plausible reason to his people for having fooled them about the question of war costs, reparations and what not. . . . He wanted the amount named to be large, even if Germany could never repay it, or even if it had to be reduced later. He said it was a political matter in which the English were greatly interested and he did not want to let the Conservatives "throw him" on a question of such popular concern.[32]

Wilson returned to Paris, meanwhile, impressed with the need to arrive at a final draft of the peace treaty as soon as possible, but wary of what had been done in his name during his absence. On board the *George Washington*, Wilson had been handed a news bulletin describing the new German government's concession to "soldiers' and workers' " councils in order to end a general strike. It upset him:

> [T]his looked bad; that if the present government of Germany is recognizing the soldiers and workers councils, it is delivering itself into the hands of the bolshevists. He said the American negro returning from abroad would be our greatest medium in conveying bolshevism to America. For example, a friend recently related the experience of a lady friend wanting to employ a negro laundress offering to pay the usual wage in that community. The negress demanded that she be given more money than was offered for the reason that "money is as much mine as it is yours."

Bolshevism was bound to have an impact on the way business was done in America, he added, and businessmen might have to adjust to having workers on their boards of directors.[33]

Wilson was not ready to adjust to what Bullitt brought back from Russia, on the other hand. He looked worried and tired, observed House. And when the proposed military terms of the treaty were read to the Big Four, he sought refuge in a "containment" shelter:

> President Wilson asked to be assured that the exterior dangers from the Bolsheviks and so forth, which the Germans might have to meet on their eastern frontiers had been considered by the military experts in fixing the total number of effectives to be allowed in Germany.[34]

The president also made a connection between the Russian question and Germany similar, at least on the surface, to what Lloyd George had discussed with House. Astonished at French insistence upon astronomical sums for reparations—seemingly with no upper limit at all—Wilson summoned his energies to resist Clemenceau. The Germans would never accept a burden that would "grind them down for fifty years, and then be a legacy to be passed on to their children. Rather than do that they would turn to anything—Bolshevism, or something which would promise them relief."[35]

> *This plan does not involve any recognition or relationship by the Allies of the Bolshevik murderers. . . .*
>
> Herbert Hoover, April 1919

It was now possible to see where Lloyd George had been heading all this time. British Conservatives would not stand for a policy that let Germany off the hook and appeared to allow Russian Bolshevism free rein throughout the "civilized world." They would not tolerate such double leniency for the very good reason that the only way commitments to the country's laborers and returned soldiers could be fulfilled without radical social change was by reparations. That had been Lloyd George's old position. Few agreed with him now when he asserted that Russia offered a way out of the bind, even if it did not mean allowing Lenin's agents to come to England in the critical postwar transition period.

Lloyd George was reading an attack on his "pro-Russian" policy when Bullitt came to breakfast with him on the morning of March 27, 1919. The London *Daily Mail* painted a lurid picture of anonymous "tempters"—as infamous as those who had "preached peace with profitable dishonor in July, 1914"—holding out as a solution to British economic problems an arrangement with Lenin, a man dedicated only to destroying "ordered democratic civilization."[36] Little wonder Lloyd George told House that if the Bullitt contacts were to come to anything, Wilson would have to take the lead. The president did not even see Bullitt, excusing himself from an appointment House had made by pleading a headache. When the pain passed, Wilson did not reschedule the appointment. For the president, as for Lloyd George, the pressing business was the German treaty. But as the prime minister knew, that was no reason for thinking that Europe could go on forever ignoring its Russian problem.[37]

Big Four negotiations on the general peace treaty now centered on Lloyd George's March 25, 1919, "Fontainebleau Memorandum," which made the case for a moderate peace and a reparations burden that could be managed in one generation. Temporarily (perhaps permanently) blocked on the Russian avenue (wherever that led), the prime minister had rethought the reparations question. Speaking to the others on March 27, he began his presentation with a dire reminder that the "whole existing order" had been put in doubt by the war. What impressed him most about Russia—he could not talk about Germany without mentioning Russia—was that despite the almost total destruction wrought by war and revolution, the Bolsheviks had succeeded in building an army, which might very soon be the only one eager to fight, "because it is the only army that believed that it has any cause to fight for."[38]

Imagine, he continued, a vast Red Army, perhaps as great as three hundred million, organized under German instructors, equipped with German cannon and German machine guns, ready to renew the attack on Western Europe. No one could face such a prospect with equanimity, said the prime minister. And now revolution was brewing in Hungary. Lloyd

George had chosen the grounds; Clemenceau would meet him there. What would be the result, the French leader said, if the citizens of France and Great Britain felt betrayed after all the blood sacrifices of the war? Lloyd George pounced on this. Yes, he would have trouble in Parliament selling a moderate peace, but not from the working class. "The English workman has no desire to overwhelm the German people with excessive demands. It is rather in the upper classes that an unbridled hatred of the Germans will be found."

Lloyd George could play many roles. Here he professed to be afraid of the upper classes' hatred for Germany; elsewhere he had acknowledged that their interest in reparations had a more sophisticated reason: avoiding social upheaval and providing money for welfare schemes. However that may be, Clemenceau repeated his call for a military solution. If the Allies feared a connection between Germany and Soviet Russia, then do something about it—destroy the Bolsheviks. Marshal Ferdinand Foch was ready with a new variation on the standard French theme, this one using Polish and Rumanian troops to establish a *cordon sanitaire*. Once that had been accomplished, it would be an easy matter to "clean up places in the rear, which, like Hungary, may be infected."

This drew Wilson out of his shell of indecision:

> We hear the expression "clean up Hungary," which means, in other words, to crush Hungarian Bolshevism. If this Bolshevism remains within its own frontiers this is no business of ours.[39]

The president's firm resolve against large-scale military intervention now gained the substance of a concrete alternative. Writing to Wilson on April 3, 1919, Herbert Hoover warned that a military venture in Central Europe would mean years of police duty, and a close alliance with the most reactionary classes in the whole world. It meant going against "our fundamental national spirit." Under such circumstances, American soldiers could hardly be expected to resist Bolshevik infection. The best way to deal with the problem was to ask someone from a neutral nation to undertake a food relief plan, provided, of course, that the Bolsheviks agreed to cease all military action across international borders and the subsidizing of disturbances abroad. "This plan does not involve any recognition or relationship by the Allies of the Bolshevik murderers. . . ."[40]

About two weeks later Hoover went into action. The American food expert wrote Wilson on April 15, 1919, that food supplies should be shipped to Hungary for purely humanitarian reasons, and that this would not imply support or recognition of Bela Kun's communist government. Hungary would be put on close rations. "If we put Hungary on precisely the same food basis as the other states," he said, "we shall lose control of the situation in the surrounding states." Food supplies would be closely monitored so that anti-Bolshevik elements in Budapest would not feel betrayed. "[W]e are maintaining a thin line of food to show that we stick to our engagements." The president approved the request without comment.[41]

Operating for once without Allied constraints, the American relief expert moved about Central Europe shoring up anti-Bolshevik defenses with his "thin line of food." Hearing of a conspiracy to stage "a serious outbreak on May Day" in Austria, he moved swiftly to take the offensive. "With the President's approval I authorized the Austrians to placard Vienna with a statement from me to the effect that any such action would jeopardize the city's already sparse food supply. No disturbance took place."[42]

It galled Americans that Hoover was criticized in the French press for supposed pro-Bolshevism. Much of this comment originated, of course, as a reaction to Hoover's well-known opposition to continuing the food blockade against Germany until the treaty had been signed. But Hoover stood fast, unshaken by such blind failings. "While I regard the parlor operators who are coquetting with this fire [Bolshevism] with contempt," he remarked to Colonel House, "I do realize that we stand to further the forces of disorder in the United States if we stand still."[43]

Even more than press criticism, however, Americans resented what they believed was a smokescreen to cover the same old diplomatic games. They believed that France wanted to crush Germany, install itself in Germany's place economically and politically throughout Central Europe, and, most obnoxious of all, use American money to promote all these schemes.[44] If that was the way France attacked Bolshevism, Wilson's advisers wanted none of it. Of course, sitting atop the world as they were economically, it was easy for Americans to say that France's eastern policy was a narrow negation of Wilsonian ideals. But without a Russian policy of his own, even granting Hoover's successes in recent days, the president was actually being driven to reconsider the very fundamentals of a League of Nations. Hoover, for example, insisted that it could not be built upon the foundations of wartime Allied cooperation, and he cited the current French agitation for a common policy in Eastern Europe. If America remained engaged (entrapped, really) in the wartime Allied commissions, he wrote the president on April 11, 1919, the connection might lead to the destruction of the League. He explained this seeming paradox in three ways:

    1. To continue the commissions on Allied terms would place American political and financial power at the beck and call of the Allies, a situation repulsive to the nation's self-interest and self-image.

2. To use them to force a peace treaty on strictly American terms, on the other hand, would make the United States appear to be a defender of the recent enemy states.

3. Faced with the sole responsibility for their actions, the Allies will not attempt what they sought under American protection.

Then came an eloquent statement of a Paris-chastened Wilsonian credo:

This whole matter has a very practical relationship to the League of Nations. If we can bring to an early end our whole relationship to these political combinations in Europe, which grew up before and during the war and can lend our strength to the League of Nations, that body will gain a stability and importance which it could not otherwise attain. As the Central Empires and Russia will not be for some years admitted to the League, and if we continue in what is in effect an armed alliance in Europe dominating these empires, the League will become simply a few neutrals gyrating around this armed alliance. It will tend to drive the Central Empires and Russia into an independent League. . . .

I have the feeling that the revolution in Europe is by no means over. The social wrongs in these countries are far from solution and the tempest must blow itself out, probably with enormous violence. Our people are prepared for us to undertake the military policing of Europe while it boils out its social wrongs. I have no doubt that if we could undertake to police the world and had the wisdom of statesmanship to see its gradual social evolution, we would be making a great contribution to civilization, but I am certain that the American people are not prepared for such a measure and I am also sure that if we remain in Europe with military force, tied in an alliance which we have never undertaken, we should be forced into this storm of repression of revolution, and forced in under terms of co-ordination with other people that would make our independence of action wholly impossible.[45]

Wilson wrote Hoover that he was "very much impressed with this letter . . . and am ready to say at once that I agree with you."[46] Looked at from Lloyd George's perspective, of course, such an attitude could also produce a fatal blow to prospects for European recovery. No more than Hoover did he want the Americans to undertake a military protectorate, however. He wanted Wilson to take the lead in another policy.

His latest idea had been supplied by a Treasury official, John Maynard Keynes, who had come up with an ingenious plan for transforming German reparations from a dead weight that could sink the continent beneath a sea of misery into an economic stimulus that would lift the world. All this was to be accomplished by simply having the enemy states and those of "new" Europe (meaning the countries carved out of the fallen empires) issue bonds that would be accepted in payment for all intergovernment debts. Of the proceeds, four-fifths should be applied to reparations, the remainder to the purchase of raw materials. Noting that it had been Mr. Hoover who pointed out to the Supreme Economic Council that even before the war Europe's four hundred million people had just managed to feed, clothe, and house themselves, with scarcely six months' capital on which to live, Keynes reminded everyone that this slim reserve had vanished during the war:

> If free movement were possible and other countries could absorb it, there would inevitably be a vast emigration from Europe, until an equilibrium were established between the numbers of the population and the means of livelihood. As that is not possible this equilibrium must be reached in some other way. In Russia it is being reached, it appears, by reduction of population by starvation, and by drastic change of occupation, e.g. by the town population being forced out on the land as laborers.
>
> To what extent the same conditions spread over the rest of Europe must depend largely on whether or not the obstacles to the resumption of production can be rapidly overcome. . . . A proposal which unfolds future prospects and shows the peoples of Europe a road by which food and employment and orderly existence can once again come their way, will be a more powerful weapon than any other for the preservation from the dangers of Bolshevism of that order of human society which we believe to be the best starting point for future improvement and greater well-being.[47]

The immediate advantage to Americans, Keynes told members of the Washington delegation, was that the United States could collect on the war debts at once simply by accepting up to 50 percent of the bond issue. But since the bonds were to be valid for paying *all* intergovernment debts, it soon became obvious to Wilson's advisers that the Keynes plan would put the United States in an impossible position. Either it became the chief reparations collector, both directly and indirectly, or it forsook ever being repaid for the war loans. When the plan was forwarded to Washington for Treasury comment, the reply was swift and negative. Secretary Carter Glass and his associates deemed the Keynes plan "indefensible" on any grounds. Their objections went beyond reparations and war debts. The plan would continue the baleful practice of huge government loans. It would create a stupendous inflation in America. By maintaining an exaggerated role for governments in the international economy, it would produce greater world unrest. Congress would never approve. And so forth.[48]

The American delegation hastened to reassure Washington that neither the president's advisers nor Wilson himself had given any encouragement to the prime minister in regard to the Keynes scheme. Delegation members were more sensitive, however, to the less self-evident issues at stake. Between Hoover's argument against commitment to Allied agencies and the the Keynes proposal rested a whole collection of issues. These could be summed up, however, in two words: aloofness and engagement. After discussing the situation, the president and his advisers decided nothing could be done until he returned home. Then he would consider whether to present an appeal to Congress for loans to Europe at the same time that he submitted the peace treaty to the Senate, or wait until the ratification hurdle had been passed.[49]

It was agreed, nevertheless, that whatever steps were decided upon, the sine qua non of any plan must be an early return to private channels. Wilson had great difficulty with this conclusion, and with the deeper confusions about America's new role it implied. Bolshevism, he had insisted (as had Hoover), was a protest, however misguided, against the way the world had worked. Now he was being told that the only way to avoid being chained to reactionary Allied designs and their inevitable results was to insist upon a return to the prewar international economic system. True, this system would have been purged of political error (imperialism, secret alliances, etc.) and would be conducted according to a new set of rules laid down by the League of Nations. But Wilson's mind was not easy. Many thoughts were churning.

He clung to the belief, expressed again in a short speech to the International Law Society in Paris, that the League itself would eventually come to represent more than a set of rules, that it would be a community of both men and nations. But that would take time. "May I say that one of the things that has disturbed me in recent months is the unqualified hope that men have entertained everywhere of immediate emancipation from the things that have hampered them and oppressed them. You cannot in human experience rush into the light. You have to go through the twilight into the broadening day. . . ."[50] If anyone had encouraged "unqualified hope," however, it had been Woodrow Wilson.

President Wilson said that Kolchak's program was all right viewed in the background of M. Tchaikowsky's mind. What, however, did it look like, he asked, viewed in the background of Admiral Kolchak's mind.

Big Four discussion, May 1919

The Big Four agreed to give Hoover's idea for reaching inside Russia a try. He had suggested that the Norwegian humanitarian and explorer Fridtjof Nansen be put in charge of a food relief plan. Signed by the Big Four, Nansen's offer stipulated that "existing local governments of Russia" would have to cooperate. That meant the Soviets would have to permit contacts between the Allies and the Whites; otherwise the onus for continuing to allow the "stricken peoples" of Russia to suffer would fall upon the Bolsheviks.

Also included was the requirement that the Bolsheviks agree beforehand to a cessation of hostilities against their opponents, as well as a suspension of all troop movements and transfers of military material "within Russian territory." The relief workers, on the other hand, were to enjoy free movement in all parts of the country, and freedom to deal with whom they wished. "The people in each locality should be given, as under the regime of the Belgian Relief Commission, the fullest opportunity to advise your Commission [Nansen's] upon the methods and the personnel by whom their community is to be is to be relieved." According to Big Four rules, in other words, areas controlled by the anti-Bolsheviks could be serviced under the aegis of the local government, while in other areas anti-Leninist distributors might be found.[51]

The list of conditions did not end there, but went on to stipulate that all "expenditures in the purchase and transportation of supplies must be met by the Soviet Government." The Soviets were thus expected to pay for the provisioning of their enemies. Even slanted as it was, however, the Nansen plan brought a storm of protest from dedicated anti-Bolsheviks in the Allied countries. Churchill complained, for example, that the territories Kolchak controlled had suffered no food shortages, so that no matter who did the distributing, it was the Bolsheviks who would benefit by having their areas provisioned.[52]

Having moved their capital to the safety of Moscow, the Bolsheviks offered to sit down and discuss the Nansen plan. They would pay for the foodstuffs. But they wanted to remind the world that they had also accepted Prinkipo, and had received the Bullitt mission. Nothing came of these because the Allies really wanted to deal with the so-called Kolchak and Denikin governments, where "all power belongs there to the wildest adherents of Tzarism.. . . ." Nansen did not object to a conference in Moscow, but was stopped by a cable from Paris telling him that negotiations with Lenin's people were out of the question. Wilson, for example, looked at Moscow's reply and commented that "he did not feel the same chagrin that he had formerly felt at having no policy in Russia. It had been impossible to have a policy hitherto." And now dismissing the Bolshevik response—and indeed everything the Bolsheviks had said since the

peace conference began—was easier for the Big Four, as even the president's comment implied, because of Admiral Kolchak's recent string of
military successes in Siberia.[53]

The prevailing view in May 1919, as expressed by Clemenceau, was
that "the Bolsheviks were now going down hill." Kolchak's improved fortunes produced a demand that he be recognized as the lost heir to the
Provisional Government. But Wilson's pledges to Russia now began to
catch up with him back in Washington. The continued presence of
American soldiers in Siberia after the armistice had stirred not a demand
for Kolchak's recognition, but criticism from liberals, many of them dedicated Wilsonians, as well as an "isolationist" backlash in Congress.

Informed of this growing restlessness, the president had replied from
Paris that the State Department should supply critics with details about
recent successes in obtaining promises from Japan about troop withdraw-
als, and of the world service being performed in protecting the Trans-
Siberian Railway, which gave "practical effect to the principle of the open
door." It would not hurt, either, to point out the "potential value of this
railroad as a means for developing American commerce particularly from
the west coast of the United States. . . ." But the key theme must be
Japan's undisguised ambition to dominate Siberia, and the consequent
danger that if Congress failed to support Wilson, not only the open door
to that area but access to European Russia would be closed.[54]

For several months Wilson had rejected Anglo-French arguments that
intervention in Siberia would restore the eastern front; his own efforts to
suggest that American forces in Siberia somehow insured access to Russia's eastern regions parodied his criticism of Allied motives—and did not
go down well in Washington. Acting Secretary of State Frank Polk was
quick to return a warning that while what the president said was undoubtedly true, it would not suffice. That sort of appeal was asking for trouble.
Critics would not be silenced, he cabled, until they could be assured that
the administration had good and sufficient reasons, not just the Trans-
Siberian Railway, for risking the lives of American soldiers.[55]

Not just Congress, but the War Department wanted to know. From
mid-March 1919, General Graves had been protesting that his men were
being forced to take sides in a civil war that was none of their business.[56]
The president could not simply ignore his own military advisers. General
Tasker Howard Bliss put it straight out: If American forces were ordered
to make war on the Bolsheviks, they would come under the command of
the Japanese. (And even if they did not, they would be doing Japan's
work.) "I do not think that this under any circumstances should be permitted." If, on the other hand, the United States sent in a larger force, to
assure its "independence," Bliss added, "in all certainty the Japanese will

send a still larger one in order that they may keep the upper hand." Secretary of War Newton D. Baker also insisted that things could not go on as they were. "Either General Graves should be directed to cooperate with the Kolchak Government or he ought to withdraw." Baker's choice would be to get out. Buffeted from all sides with conflicting opinions, Wilson retreated once again into the false security of indecision. He would let the Big Four present whatever arguments they wished for providing military support on a continuing basis to Admiral Kolchak, though admonishing them that he had always wanted to get out, "and leave it to the Russians to fight it out among themselves." That was a strained interpretation of his efforts since July 1918, true only in the sense that he had not wished to intervene with the Allies but, as he imagined it, against their schemes.[57]

Such a distinction, if valid at all, was now about to disappear as the Big Four's attention shifted from events in Central and Eastern Europe back to Siberia, where it was proposed to grant Admiral Kolchak diplomatic recognition as well as military weapons and advice. If General Graves remained, would he, as Secretary Baker and others feared, merely lend the stars and stripes to those who wished to use an American banner to disguise their own aims? If Kolchak survived, on the other hand, what were the consequences of withdrawing the Graves mission? It was always the same dilemma, and Wilson had no real answer still.[58]

Lloyd George's military adviser in Siberia, the never-doubting General Knox, wished that Graves would be sent home, the sooner the better. The American general's "neutralism" only aided the Bolsheviks, he charged. Writing from Kolchak's headquarters, Knox suggested his own solution. First, the Bolsheviks should be told that they could never qualify for membership in the League of Nations. That in itself would undermine Lenin's precarious authority. Then attack the Bolshevik bastions of power, Petrograd and Moscow. The Japanese would march from Siberia, and "subordinate commanders would be instructed to obey without haggling." There was no place for hagglers like Graves and, for that matter, Wilson:

> It is by Jews most of whom talk American and German better than Russian that Russian Bolshevism is kept alive. The effectiveness of Allied action in Russia is being paralyzed under purely Hebrew influence by the power which has least financial and material interest at stake in Russia and knows least of the country.[59]

Although he did not join in Knox's vitriolic condemnation of "Hebrew influence" apparently originating in America, the views of Sir Charles Eliot, British high commissioner for Siberia, were otherwise identical. Kolchak must be recognized, he wrote Balfour on April 5, 1919, if only to force the Americans to play the game as it should be played. As matters stood, he stated, the Americans did not even "prevent peasants from avoiding conscription and forming armed bands."[60]

The alliance of War Office and Foreign Office in Siberia carried over to London. The general staff, under Churchill's constant prodding, put it as their view that recognition of Admiral Kolchak would improve the military position at Archangel. "It is not too much to hope," the general staff asserted, "that in such circumstances a real and permanent junction may be effected between the Siberian and North Russian forces, which will enable the Archangel Government to stand alone after the withdrawal of the Allied troops."[61]

Despite the War Office's confidence, the Foreign Office could never quite bring itself to think of Kolchak, by himself, as Russia's savior. The most important thing was to engage the Americans. If it appeared that the Russians were rallying to the admiral, or if it appeared that there was growing outside support for him, something might take shape. And if that were the case, it might also be possible to bring the prime minister around. On May 1, 1919, Churchill attempted to move things along that path via Canada. Writing to Sir Robert Borden, head of the Canadian Delegation to Paris, he pictured Kolchak as on the verge of a final campaign to take Moscow. He could not help but feel sorry, the secretary of war went on, that Canada had so far not been able "a little to help us in bringing about these good results." He understood Sir Robert's desire to withdraw the Canadian contingent from the empire forces at Vladivostok, but it was not possible to have a few volunteers to cooperate with "our various missions to the loyal Russian armies?"

The officers he had talked with, wrote Churchill, "spoke to me of their desire to volunteer for service in Russia against the Bolsheviks," but were inhibited by military regulations. "Even a few hundred Canadian volunteers would be of great assistance and would make a name for themselves in this most righteous crusade." The Russians had lost faith in the Allies— all but Great Britain. "Japan they always feared and distrusted. America has made herself indescribably hated in Siberia. The French have lost all credit at Odessa and in the Crimea. But Britain has never failed." At every point where "we have assumed any degree of responsibility the Russians are either holding their own or prospering." It might well be that future relations with a regenerated Russia, "with all its immense commercial and military possibilities, may depend upon action taken now." If Canada stepped forward, Australia was bound to follow.[62]

In war cabinet discussions Churchill was equally given to hyperbole, declaring that every available officer must be sent at once to Russia. Kolchak's victories were being won in British uniforms and with British weapons. "It was quite possible that the Bolshevik regime would crumple up, and we should get a civilized Russia friendly to us above all other powers. . . ."[63] Lloyd George reminded his colleagues that chances were better than even that instead something worse would appear. Balfour spelled that out. Having created a series of new states on Russia's borders, some of them from old Russia, the danger now existed that the "new Germany and the new Russia [might] combine to dominate or destroy them. . . ." In that event, Kolchak might prove to be a curse rather than a blessing.[64]

Back in Paris it was decided to hear a representative of the Archangel government who was reputed to know Kolchak's mind on such questions. Could he be trusted not to cooperate with Germany, for example? Wilson was unsatisfied with this proposal, and announced that he would send Ambasador Roland Morris from Japan to find out more. Meanwhile, it took the Big Four nearly three weeks to agree upon a letter to Kolchak outlining conditions for diplomatic recognition. Like the Nansen letter, it was heavily loaded with requirements: he would have to resummon the 1917 Constituent Assembly, hold free elections, abandon the former land ownership system, recognize an independent Finland and Poland, join the League of Nations, and recognize Russia's pre-Bolshevik debts.[65]

Self-determination was a forgotten issue. But General Knox aided Kolchak in the writing of his reply, so that the liberal canon was at least given lip service. In due course, Kolchak was advised that he was eligible to receive material support, but nothing was said about diplomatic recognition—another indication of Allied unwillingness to go out on a limb without gilt-edged assurances, or full-scale American cooperation.[66]

> *They will . . . put in dummy social democrats, and dummy democrats of all kinds in their Government. They will then hold an election. . . . The wretched people . . . who have suffered frightfully under Bela Kun's regime will probably vote for peace and order at any price.*
>
> Herbert Hoover to Phillip Kerr,
> August 1919

A salutary lesson about what might happen to Russia under Kolchak's rule was offered by the unhappy outcome in Hungary. Yet in another way the Hungarian situation also propelled the Big Four toward more desperate measures against the Bolsheviks. Even Hoover got caught up, for the one and only time, in schemes for using military force to combat the Bolshevik peril.

At first Hoover had insisted upon neutrality in regard to Bela Kun's communist government in Budapest. So long as he did not attack his neighbors, Hoover was prepared to wait him out. From mid-April on, however, that stance seemed less and less viable. The issue was forced, much to the disgust of Americans, by a Rumanian military attack on Hungary. Once begun, unfortunately, the conflict threatened to spread Bolshevism to Germany itself. In a Big Four discussion, Wilson placed the dilemma before the Allied leaders. "The Rumanian advance had increased the disorder," he began, but now "the failure of the Rumanians to continue their advance had again caused further disorders and attacks on the alleged counterrevolutionaries." What were they to do?

Clemenceau's ardor for military heroics cooled when it was then pointed out that French troops were the closest to the scene and would have to bear the brunt of an attack on communist leader Bela Kun. He would study the problem, he said. Wilson declared that he did not trust the Rumanians, and doubted whether a military advance would be wise. But successful Hungarian counterblows, and the outbreak of Hungarian-Czech hostilities, could not go ignored. A cable was sent to Budapest warning of "extreme measures" if a cease-fire was not accepted within forty-eight hours.[67]

Hoover's agents on the scene warned that the Hungarians had been made arrogant by their successes, and were now marching Czech prisoners up and down the streets of Budapest. Worse, their leaders were "constantly welding closer and closer the nationalist spirit and the Soviet government." Waiting Bela Kun out was no longer possible:

> It would do as much as millions upon millions of dollars worth of food and effort, . . . can you not again put whip and spur to jaded steed and nose out this race with the Bolsheviks in Central Europe.[68]

All his previous proscriptions against force notwithstanding, Hoover was willing to make the running. Unless something was done at once, he advised Wilson, "the adjacent orderly governments will fall into chaos. As much as I dislike to suggest it, I can see but one solution and that is for the French troops which are now in Jugo-Slavia to advance on Budapest without delay. Otherwise, it appears to us, that both the Czechoslovakian and the German-Austrian Governments will surely fall." Yet again Wilson demurred. "It might be very imprudent to send the forces of neighboring countries into Hungary," he remarked. He managed to stall the situation until Bela Kun himself alleviated the crisis by accepting a cease-fire, although the Rumanians continued their attack.[69]

After the president left Paris for the last time, Hoover took part in Allied plans to foment a coup designed around the Hungarian army. If it worked it would be possible "to crush Bela Kun . . . without the Allies being called upon to strike a blow." On July 26, 1919, these plans were set in motion with a Supreme Economic Council statement that food promised to Hungary would be delivered as soon as a representative government was formed. In the past such appeals had not borne fruit in Hungary, but this time the combination of internal difficulty, Rumanian military pressure, and the economic blockade forced Kun to relinquish power. And on August 1, 1919, he fled to Moscow.[70]

But with Bela Kun gone there was no one to mobilize the Hungarians to resist the Rumanian advance, which, warned the same men who had just gotten over one fight, would be bad for Central European stability.[71] Rumanian reparations claims against Hungary outraged Wilson. The Rumanians should be put on notice, said the president back in Washington, that the United States would oppose their every claim to territory or sovereignty anywhere if they persisted.[72]

But the affair was turning into an object lesson for Americans about how little influence they really had on events in Central Europe. The Rumanians kept coming, joined by Hungarian counterrevolutionaries, and both were backed by British and French forces. With allied machine guns trained on the Hungarian ministry buildings, a counterrevolution at last materialized in the streets, setting a precedent, ironically, that the Russians would emulate nearly four decades later, in 1956. It was not what the Americans had anticipated, not at all. The Archduke Joseph was put into power; the ancien régime, the Hapsburgs, was back in business. From Moscow, the Bolsheviks charged the Allies and America with reestablishing "reactionary government in its worst form." Hoover was stunned by the dramatic truth of his own recent predictions and by the denouement of Wilsonian dreams, and chastened by his role in the proceeding. Acting almost single-handedly, Hoover forced Joseph's resignation. But he could not prevent the White terror that succeeded the Hapsburg Brumaire, nor the dictatorship of the right that emerged under Admiral Horthy.[73]

Hoover in fact predicted a long struggle:

[A]lready all the reactionaries are rushing to Hungary from Switzerland, which will stir the German militarists to renewed hope, and the argument is already being used and broadcast in Bolshevik Russia that the obvious intention of the Entente is to restore the Czar because they have already restored a Hapsburg in Hungary.

At bottom, concluded Hoover in a talk with Phillip Kerr, the trouble was that Allied representatives in Budapest—along with their American counterparts—were "really in with the ancien regime." "It is not . . . that they are not really trying to carry out their orders, but that being 'officers and gentlemen,' they naturally dislike the social democrat type of person, and associate much more easily and freely with people of their own class."[74]

Fortunately for the Wilsonians' peace of mind, Kolchak fared less successfully than the Central European right. During the admiral's brief moment of glory, Churchill obtained Lloyd George's approval for a military strike southwards. General Ironsides, the British commander in north Russia, was sure that all it needed was one strong push to topple the Bolsheviks. The plan was presented, however, as merely a means of "relieving the situation" preliminary to withdrawal. The chief of the general staff enlightened the war cabinet as to what that meant: "If once we could establish connections, we would hand over control of the operations to Admiral Kolchak, and proceed ourselves to withdraw from Russia."[75]

Doubters were silenced by Churchill's comment that the strike was consistent with the impending recognition of Kolchak and the sequel, which was to be American and Japanese willingness to play a greater role. Had Kolchak done well in his next battles, that might have turned out to be the case. The strike from Archangel was scheduled for early July, but in mid-June reports arrived that the admiral had suffered serious reverses at the hands of a much smaller Bolshevik force. This prompted Lloyd George to cancel the strike. Never daunted, Churchill protested that General Denikin in the south had gained more territory than Kolchak had lost. The war cabinet refused to hear more. No one wanted "the additional stigma of failure" attached to the far-from-glorious record posted in Russia thus far.[76]

A few days before he left Paris, Wilson discussed Russia with his advisers. The president agreed, one adviser recorded in his diary, that he would have to go before Congress and tell "the whole story" of how funds were needed to support "a great constructive program" for aiding Russia through the Trans-Siberian Railway and keeping Japan from creating a sphere of influence.[77] He went so far as ordering Ambassador Roland Morris to complete his once-aborted mission to Kolchak. But despite the latter's agreement that America was the only power that could take the lead in Russian reconstruction, nothing came of Morris's optimistic reports.[78]

Kolchak's rapidly declining fortunes once again saved Wilson from confronting the issue squarely. His remaining energy went into a fight for a League of Nations that he had once dedicated to the principle of self-determination. It was not a happy assignment, for Wilson or for disappointed liberals. In speeches delivered on his final cross-country crusade, Wilson fell back on the threat of Bolshevism as an argument in favor of the peace treaty and the League. It was a sorry ending for the dialogue begun with hopes so high in January 1919.

CHAPTER ELEVEN

At Arm's Length and Beyond

If possible, certainly, we desire American co-opera-
tion, and I would even say American leads, but if
not, if the United States decides not to take part in
this great international effort, then we must go on.

Lord Robert Cecil, November 1919

After Paris the world waited for the United States to make up its mind. Everything was in limbo. "The League, I am sorry to say, is a failure." When he said this David Lloyd George was not, however, talking about the Senate debate. He was responding in this instance to a suggestion that the new world organization could now take charge of the Russian question, along with the other business of upholding the Versailles Treaty. Disturbed by Wilson's unwillingness to consider his plans for European economic recovery, which, more and more, required a settlement of the Russian problem, the prime minister thought little of the League's future. "The League is to apply to every nation but America. The League is not to interfere with American affairs, but America is to have a voice in the affairs of Europe. A strange position!"[1]

He would not have thought it so strange, of course, if the American president saw eye to eye with his proposals. That was often hard to do, because Lloyd George could look different ways at the same time. Yet the very arguments that Wilson made for American participation in the League drove him farther from what Lloyd George had in mind in regard to Russia. And when the president fell ill, the lines of communication between London and Washington went slack at the most critical moment.

Even a serious delay in the adoption of the League will do much to institute anxiety throughout the world, not excepting Europe, and I know of what significance it will prove to be that you should lend your great influence to prevent giving even an added opportunity to the forces of disorder and evil.

Wilson to Cardinal Gibbons,
July 25, 1919

On June 4, 1919, as Wilson was winding up his affairs in Paris, his personal secretary, Joseph Tumulty, alerted him to the bomb attack on the home of Attorney General A. Mitchell Palmer. "What happened in Washington last night in the attempt upon the Attorney General's life is but a symptom of the terrible unrest that is stalking about the country," Tumulty told the president. If not checked, that unrest would swell into a monstrous assault "upon everything that we hold dear." Just as soon as he got back, Tumulty urged, the president should summon a national industrial conference to develop a national plan for resolving labor disputes. Past wars had been caused by balance-of-power politics and the attempt of the strong to exploit the weak. And domestic politics had in the past mirrored the international scene, as "capital got the apple and labor the core." "It is either a League of Nations or a final war; Europe paralyzed; Bolshevism spreading throughout all the European countries."[2]

Thomas Lamont, who had emerged as one of Wilson's principal economic advisers at Paris, carried a similar message to the financial and business community. Republicans were right to criticize the failings of the administration, he said, and to wish that Paris had produced a better treaty. "But when it comes to the final analysis, none of us can stand out against the great and overwhelming fact that the rejection of this Treaty means continued unsettlement, means a revival of Bolshevist effort throughout Europe."[3]

Lamont and other pro-League Republicans tried very hard to find a way for the president and their party's leaders in the Senate to compromise. That would not be easy. The president's long-time antagonist, Republican Senator Henry Cabot Lodge, who had dogged his path from the days of "watchful waiting" in Mexico, himself waiting for an opportunity to expose all this Wilsonian nonsense about foreign affairs, now stood in a position to act. As the new chairman of the Senate Foreign Relations Committee, the peace treaty was his to deal with. He promised the fullest hearings; every page, every paragraph, every word even, would receive proper scrutiny. For each of Wilson's Fourteen Points, Lodge had a reservation to attach to the treaty. Wilson's refusal to accept the Lodge reservations, Sir William Wiseman told London, was not born of stubbornness. Besides the impasse this struggle promised in the United States, Wiseman reported, the president had told him that the senator's actions would set a dangerous precedent. The newly created states, none of whom was really satisfied with the treaty, would insist on likewise coming forward with their objections. And then what? "[U]nless all the great Powers including the United States," Wilson told Wiseman, "unite to support the Treaty and the League there is a grave danger that Bolshevism may over-run Europe."[4]

If he could not persuade the Republican senators of this danger, Wilson concluded, he would set out on a tour to mobilize the people. Sir William thought the president would win. From other sources, moreover, Wiseman had learned that "big business interests have warned Senators not to delay this treaty." Secretary of State Robert Lansing also had no doubts that "economic interests" favored ratification. At the moment, unfortunately, personal and party animosities gave treaty opponents an undue influence. "Most of the opposition would deny this, and probably deny it honestly, but there is no getting away from the fact that they are simply saturated with hatred of the man rather than the treaty. It is something like the feeling against Andrew Jackson."[5]

For his part, Lansing feared that neither the president nor the opposition was really concerned enough about the impending stalemate. "The time has come when the thinking men of this country must forget their political differences and band together to meet the coming storm, for revolution is in the air—it may even be a bloody revolution. . . . We ought to forget our political quarrels, which seem so puerile in the face of the great peril to American nationalism which is approaching, and unite with all our vigor in a supreme effort to check the present movement."[6]

Tumulty and Lansing worked together to get Wilson to make anti-Bolshevism a major part of the fight for the treaty. "I think it is time for this Government," wrote the former, "to take a very definite stand since there is growing up a propaganda in favor of classism in contradistinction to nationalism which seems to me to menace our present social order." As the principal leader of the world Progressive movement, Wilson was himself the most effective agent to check this dangerous trend.[7]

In reply, the president informed Lansing that he would use his Labor Day proclamation to warn the nation against Bolshevism "in some way that may attract attention."[8] And when Wilson wavered about keeping antiwar leader and Socialist candidate for president Eugene Debs in prison, he was warned by Attorney General Palmer that freeing Debs would damage the fight for the League:

When we release Debs, we shall have to release also two or three
other leaders of the same class. Their release now would be used
by many opponents of the peace treaty as evidence of too great
leniency toward law violators of the radical element in the labor
classes, in a way that would prejudice many people against the
liberal labor provisions of the treaty.[9]

"I entirely agree," Wilson wrote back, and set off on his tour to make
the rest of the world safe for democracy.[10]

At Des Moines, Iowa, on September 6, 1919, the president told his
audience that when the Constituent Assembly in Russia was dispersed in
January 1918, power had been seized by a tiny group every bit as ruthless
and pitiless as the tsar himself:

And in other parts of Europe the poison spread. The poison of
disorder, the poison of revolt, the poison of chaos. And do you
honestly think, my fellow citizens, that none of that poison has got
into the veins of this free people? Do you know that the world is all
now one single whispering gallery. . . .

And money coming from nobody knows where is deposited in
capitals like Stockholm to be used for the propaganda of disorder
and discontent and dissolution throughout the world, and men
look you calmly in the face in America and say they are for that
sort of revolution, when that sort of revolution means government
by terror, government by force, not government by vote.

So long as the world was kept waiting for peace, and the guarantees
behind it—he made the connection—the poison would spread more and
more rapidly until even America, "this beloved land of ours," was
enveloped.[11]

Evaluated later, the president's tactic seems questionable indeed. The
greater fear of those he was trying to reach beyond the city limits of Des
Moines was that American participation in the League would mean an
increase in contacts with the poison-infected areas of the world, not a way
to escape the menace.

Lodge and his Republican allies found a common theme for the "truth
squads" that they sent into the cities Wilson had visited in this final crusade. Wilson gave it to them by his insistence upon making Bolshevism a
key issue in the debate. Conservative Republicans, like the senator from
Massachusetts, could now give full expression to their fears of radicalism,
while the old Progressive contingent, led by Senator William Borah and
others, could point to Wilson's interpretation of the League's role as proof
that it was designed by Old World Machiavellis to preserve the status quo.
Brooding outside the partisan debate were figures like Herbert Hoover,

whose unmatched firsthand experience in Central Europe now caused him to wonder about all great efforts to make the world safe for democracy. Postwar isolationism was not the product of some primeval yearning for a simpler life, a Midwestern curse upon the nation; it was born here, in this debate, and combined many elements and modes of thought, including, it should be noted, what Wilson himself was close to saying as he expended his last energies on the lost cause.

The dramatic labor disputes of the era were almost always blamed on foreign-influenced radicals, anarchists, and recent immigrants. Yet after the president was taken ill on the West Coast, Tumulty kept pressing the Bolshevism issue. The cabinet ought to take up the matter of another public statement, he wrote Lansing on October 28, 1919, as Wilson lay gravely ill in the White House. The Bolshevik threat must be treated as a contagious disease new to the medical profession, and dealt with as the Public Health Service would deal with it. "In other words, the thought of the country, conservative as well as liberal, ought to be concentrated on what Bolshevism seeks to do and what it has done in Russia."[12]

Lansing reassured him that the cabinet had been discussing the problem, but he now felt "everybody is weary" of the whole treaty struggle. He himself believed that the first order of business was to put down the revolution at home. Upon hearing of an IWW "agitator" named Wesley Everest, a war veteran who had been jailed after shooting into an Armistice Day parade, then dragged from jail, castrated, and murdered by a mob, the secretary wrote a memorandum to himself:

> The leaders of Bolshevism and anarchy regardless of their nationality must be shown in no uncertain way that they cannot organize or preach against government in the United States. Too long we have permitted these fanatics to enjoy the liberty which they now seek to destroy. If not traitors to the Republic, they are traitors to civilization and to mankind. Deportation, imprisonment or execution should be their portion according to the heinousness of their crimes. It is force which they fear. Let it be exerted without mercy but with impartial justice.[13]

Wilson had not conjured up the "red scare" by his use of anti-Bolshevism as an argument for the League, but nothing he had done either in response to the Russian Revolution or in his campaign for the treaty had armed him with positive means to overcome its impact. Perhaps there was nothing he could have done. On November 19, 1919, with most Democrats following their stricken leader's order to refuse any modifications or amendments, the Senate rejected the Versailles Treaty.

I dread wild adventures in lands whose conditions are unknown, and where nothing but catastrophe has awaited every Empire and every Army that has ever invaded them.

David Lloyd George, November 1919

Looking back a decade later, Winston Churchill pronounced British policy toward Russia in 1919 a great success. Discovering here too the foresight he so often attributed to himself, he wrote that the Bolsheviks had been kept busy with Kolchak and Denikin at their heels. "Their energy was turned upon the internal struggle," and thus a breathing space was purchased for the border countries. During these precious months also, Socialists in France, Great Britain, and Italy finally became aware that Russia had frozen over into an "indefinite winter of sub-human doctrine and superhuman tyranny."[14]

If Churchill had had his way at the time, however, no one would have had any breathing space, and the splits caused by an outright interventionist policy might well have been irreparable, especially with the internal disputes leading to the 1926 General Strike. "What Labour did between 1919 and 1924," writes Cambridge historian Maurice Cowling, "was to create an atmosphere which no politician could ignore. What the Conservative leaders did was respond, not resentfully like the Liberal party toward a prodigal son, but with a coolness which implied reasonable disagreement about the best way to achieve objectives that were held in common."[15]

In this view, Churchill was still (and probably forever) a Liberal, while David Lloyd George emerges in the end as the most enlightened Conservative of his day, on either side of the Atlantic. The trouble was, accepting this framework, that too many of the Conservatives in the Lloyd George coalition opted to follow a Liberal, Churchill, on a path to confrontation with Russia because it was also the way (supposedly) to force Labour to renounce class politics at home. As he said of himself, Lloyd George feared adventures in strange far-off places, and dreaded the glint in the eyes of adventurers at home. Though fully prepared to demonstrate to the coal miners, by whatever means necessary, that they could not win a major strike in 1919, the prime minister sought to turn the red scare in England to his own advantage. What worried him more than the threatened strikes, he told the cabinet in August, was continuing low productivity. "The men were not working well." And why was that? There was a lot of "false political economy" going round, fostered by a formidable body of young men who wished to destroy the present industrial and parliamentary system. They had made headway because labor felt too little attention was being paid to its needs. "Cromwell had the same ideas in his conflict with Sir Harry Vane, and one found exactly the same spirit in his speeches as in the appeals of the Bolsheviks, where the futility of talk was contrasted with the value of action." One could not take "risks" with labor, he went on. "If we did, we should at once create an army within our own borders, and one which would be better provided with dangerous weapons than Germany. We had in this country millions of men who had been trained to arms, and there were plenty of guns and ammunition available."[16]

Churchill, of course, always took the position that there was no reason to apologize to laboring men, or the Labour party, for the government's Russian policy. The triumphs of White leaders, made possible by British aid, heralded the rebirth of a truly democratic Russia. Failure would come only if His Majesty's Government wavered at this critical time and its moderating influence was removed.[17]

Starting in late July 1919, Lloyd George began trying to lead Churchill, and the interventionists in general, along a circuitous path to a Russian policy based on traditional definitions of national interest. The first step in this plan was to refocus his colleagues' attention by directing it away from the Baltic area and Siberia to south Russia. His idea, it can be surmised from what followed, was that while the larger interventionist schemes, based as they were on ideology, centered on military initiatives in those areas, a definite plan of military aid to Denikin in south Russia would be self-limiting, and bring to the fore questions of British national interest as opposed to ideological adventurism. But, of course, the plan must be presented in the strongest anti-Bolshevik terms possible. Thus, Lloyd George said to the cabinet, what would draw the Bolsheviks most, draw them like a magnet? The mineral riches of south Russia, he answered himself. British policy, then, should be to give Denikin a good chance to defend himself.

It never bothered Lloyd George, it should also be remembered, to think about several new "Russias" that might spring up out of the wreckage of the Romanov dynasty. In any event, Churchill bit. The war cabinet decided on August 12, 1919, to send General Denikin a last "packet" of aid; the whole situation could then be reassessed at some later date. The only serious dissent came from Austen Chamberlain, chancellor of the exchequer. And how it must have pleased Lloyd George to hear Chamberlain put all the objections he himself felt. Why, asserted the chancellor, with one eye on Lloyd George and the other on Churchill, was it suddenly being assumed that a non-Bolshevik Russia would be any less prey to Germany? Or why, on the other hand, should it taken as fact that a strong non-Bolshevik Russia would be any more friendly to Great Britain? Where were these schemes moving or, better put, drifting? Chamberlain could see many dangers ahead, and adding Deniken to the list of clients did not help the outlook for either the budget or British welfare.

Exactly, said the prime minister. He asked the war cabinet to look at it this way: Forget about the Baltic, Germany would control that area for quite some time. For that matter, it was against British interests to block Germany there. How else would Berlin obtain the revenues to pay reparations? "We certainly cannot go to war again in order to place a customs barrier between Germany and Russia." If Denikin managed to survive, on the other hand, but in not too strong a position, things might work out well all around. Then His Majesty's Government should seek peace with Lenin. If both sides were fairly strong, he concluded, then Lenin would have to say, well, Denikin is powerful enough to prevent me from getting coal. And Denikin would have to say, so, Lenin is powerful enough to prevent me from getting to Moscow. At that point serious negotiations would become possible.[18]

Lloyd George's full purpose became clear, to Churchill's surprise, on the night of the prime minister's traditional Guildhall speech in honor of the Lord Mayor of London. "If the Russian people wish for freedom," he said on that occasion, November 8, 1919, "we can always say we gave them the chance. . . ." With winter now upon Europe, perhaps it could be agreed that the time had arrived to see if the great powers could not promote peace and concord in Russia. Looking about him, the American ambassador, John W. Davis, saw a look of astonishment on Churchill's face. Despite later disclaimers, the prime minister had opened the door to formal negotiations with the Bolsheviks without bothering to inform his colleagues. "Victories are usually won in Russia," the speech ended, "but you sink in victories; and great armies and great empires in the past have been overwhelmed in the sands of barren victories. . . ."[19]

Once a firm advocate of intervention, Robert Cecil had been converted by Lloyd George's preaching. A few days later in the House of Commons, Cecil delivered the ritual denunciation of Bolshevism, but ended with a call to abandon the effort to force another form of government on Russia. Above all, he warned, His Majesty's Government must speak with one voice. "I could not help when I heard him last week having a picture of my right hon. Friend [Churchill] riding at the head of Cossacks making a triumphant entry into Moscow," Cecil said. "That was the kind of tone and platform from which he spoke." But there had followed the prime minister's speech at the Lord Mayor's banquet. Which, asked Cecil, represented British policy?[20]

Lloyd George could not have wished for a better cue. The history of the Russian Revolution was a sad affair, he said. "The chariot of Bolshevism is drawn by plunder and terror." But where did intervention lead? It led to financial ruin, as it had in prerevolutionary France. "[W]e would sink this country in the same morass as Russia is in now." One object of intervention was said to be Russian unification. "There was a very great Statesman, a man of great imagination, who certainly did not belong to the party to which I belong, Lord Beaconsfield, who regarded a great, gigantic, colossal, growing Russia rolling onwards like a glacier towards Persia and the borders of Afghanistan and India as the greatest menace the British Empire could be confronted with." If Russia was weak and divided under Lenin, he seemed to be saying, all the better for Great Britain. Neither did Lenin's ideological power require his destruction. Paying heed to legitimate social complaints at home would do more to destroy Bolshevism. "If we do that, I have no fear of revolution. . . ."[21]

The prime minister then sought to introduce national interest back into the debate in economic terms, contrasting the benefits of restoring normal commerce with the dangers of risking huge sums to overturn Lenin. Reactions were not long in coming. Moscow broadcast a message affirming its belief in satisfactory economic relations between opposing social systems. "We are ready even to make sacrifices for the sake of a close economic connection with Britain," the Bolsheviks announced.[22] The American reaction was an expression of displeasure. To this, Lloyd George returned the perfectly candid response that he sought agreement with the Soviets on economic matters, and hoped to thereby encourage Russia's division into a number of smaller independent states, none of sufficient size to threaten the peace. Ambassador Davis was not content to let this pass. Industrial unrest in America had heightened anti-Bolshevik feelings, he remarked, implying a belief that hard times in the capitalist world could be overcome only when workers were not distracted by, and did not distract employers with, the Soviet Union. It also implied that economic isolation was the way to destroy Bolshevism.

Lansing then made it plain that what was indeed Washington's position. It was simply useless, he urged Davis (who needed no stimulus), to seek an understanding with Lenin, as "has been demonstrated by past experiences." What past experience was Lansing talking about? Prinkipo? The Bullitt mission? The Nansen offer? Lloyd George must have wondered. But the secretary's stricture had hardly begun. "The ultimate aims of the Bolsheviki are hostile to all existing governments and any apparent compromise which they make with these governments is vitiated by their avowed opportunism," he warned. If that were so, Lloyd George had answered critics in his own country, why not make things more difficult for Lenin by recognizing the independence of the border states once part of the empire? And why not concentrate on an equally opportunistic policy of trading with Russia so as to restore the domestic economies of Europe? Lansing replied to this argument that premature recognition of the border states would impede the progress of anti-Bolshevik forces within Russia. The American government could not countenance the view that it was right, or even wise, to encourage Russian dismemberment to remove the menace to Europe. "It is my belief that if Lloyd George seeks to reach such an understanding he will incur serious moral responsibility as well as make a great tactical mistake."[23]

A Lansing–Lloyd George dialogue of this sort never actually took place. The prime minister's responses to critics were given in the House of Commons, and Lansing's comments came in cables to Ambassador Davis. Apparently thinking himself challenged to reaffirm the American approach, Lansing sent a nineteen-page memorandum to the White House, based on assumptions identical to those put forward by Lloyd George as his starting point: Russia was a vital contributor to the "complicated system of production and distribution by which the world is clothed and fed." World recovery was impossible without Russia's resources. But nowhere did Lansing agree with the prime minister about coming to some agreement with the Bolsheviks. The "adventurous revolutionaries" who were, unhappily, in control of Russia thought only of destruction, he wrote.

> Events must take their course; but it lies within the right and interest, if not within the duty, of the United States and other enlightened nations of the earth to encourage by all available means the creation of a situation favorable to the rapid movement of events through the natural channels marked out for them by the interplay of purely Russian factors toward the establishment of a Russian government resting on the collective will of the Russian people and concerning itself with Russian affairs.[24]

Bold words, indeed, but just as Wilson had never been able to put together the pieces of a positive program, so Lansing's recommendations fell short of anything close to a plan for establishing a government "resting on the collective will of the Russian people." There were hints at a plan to get in touch with the so-called Green armies, made up, it was said, of disaffected peasants who hated both the Reds and the Whites. There was a strange recommendation for cooperating with Japan to maintain control of the Siberian railways in order to initiate large-scale commercial transactions with Russian cooperative societies, and to that end it was proposed that a Russian Bureau be established with a revolving capital of $100 million. But that was it.

Less than three weeks later, moreover, Lansing urged that American troops be withdrawn from Siberia, to avoid contact with the advancing Red Army. Wilson agreed. All that was left was a moral and diplomatic embargo, which did little more to keep goods out of Russia but became a source of much bickering and complaint against the nation's recent allies, and especially, of course, against Prime Minister Lloyd George.

> *There really is no blockade against Russia. That's an*
> *incidental part of the German blockade.*
>
> Woodrow Wilson, June 27, 1919

In anticipation of a White triumph, the Supreme Economic Council had decided to lift the blockade against trade with Russia simultaneously with the lifting of the blockade against Germany. Confronted by reporters, Wilson had dodged the issue with his June 27, 1919, statement that no formal blockade had ever existed. "Theoretically," it went on, "Russia is free to trade now, but there is nobody to trade with. The real difficulty is the uncertainty of credit."[25]

When the anti-Bolshevik victory did not take place, new rationalizations were needed. Despite its conviction that Russian recovery was essential to the world economy, the State Department insisted that trading with the Bolsheviks was suicidal. Business inquiries about the blockade were handled by a standard reply that export licenses were not being granted. The money the Soviets intended to use to pay for imports, one senator was told, had been seized illegally from the "Russian people." "It is believed by the Department that it would be most unwise for the Government of the United States to sanction or permit what might prove to be the exploitation of the resources of the Russian people."[26]

In areas controlled by Admiral Kolchak, on the other hand, the department was determined to meet Allied competition. For example, Admiral Mark Bristol, the American commander in the region, reported on November 11, 1919, that he had issued general orders to encourage trade, and he was engaged in having his flotilla show the flag in all possible ports of south Russia.[27] Generally, however, concern either for European recovery or American trade took second place to ideological considerations, at least until it was clear the Bolsheviks could not be overturned. The case of one businessman's attempt to trade with Russia illustrates the tenor of American policy. How was it consistent with the President's Fourteen Points speech, asked E. P. Jennings, president of the

Lehigh Machine Company, to continue the trade embargo, or in the national interest to deny Americans a chance to obtain Russian trade? Jennings enlisted Attorney General Palmer, of all people, to intercede for him at the White House so that he could ship a thousand printing presses at a total value of $4.5 million. Russia's new rulers, argued Jennings, were trying to improve the intellectual life of their country, importing millions of copies of Charles Dickens's novels. Addressed to the president through Palmer, Jennings's letter wound up back in the office of the foreign trade adviser at the Department of State. His recommendation was against allowing the sale, as printing presses were the very weapons that would most help the Bolsheviks in their campaign against civilization.[28]

All this time, from Wilson's return from Paris until after he took ill, the search continued for a policy that would be not only consistent with the Fourteen Points speech, but workable. The "alliance" with Japan in Siberia was embarrassing. Admiral Kolchak's recovery from a series of military setbacks made the pursuit of a coherent policy even more perplexing. When his cause had been given up for lost in early September 1919, Lansing had cabled a suggestion that the admiral agree to put his gold in the American legation in Peking for safekeeping—so that it could be returned to the Russian people as soon as there existed a stable authority to receive it. Kolchak was not interested in the idea. A few weeks later, on the other hand, when the admiral was enjoying a string of military victories, Lansing told bankers that the administration favored loans to his Siberian government and was committed to supporting him.[29]

Ambassador Morris wondered why, then, the administration did not simply support Japan's efforts to restore order in Siberia. "[W]e cannot be placed in the position of seeming to stay the hand of Japan, while failing to offer any alternative plan of relief."[30] The American boycott was hopelessly inconsistent and tangled, and worked against everyone's best interests. It would produce only ridicule, shut out only common sense. Lansing took the point. Despite Kolchak's varying fortunes, he instructed Morris, it was highly important that he continue to head the Siberian government. Even surrounded as he was by reactionary elements, the admiral's presence validated the "democratic assurances" he had exchanged with the heads of government during the Paris Peace Conference.[31]

Doing his best to make the policy consistent, Lansing denied the petition of the Lithuanian National Council—presented as an example of self-determination—for United States support of the independence of the Baltic states. The United States could not follow Britain's lead in recognizing the independence of those "provinces," he said. "As you are aware," the secretary wrote its chairman, "the Government of the United States is traditionally sympathetic with the national aspirations of dependent peoples. On the other hand, it has been thought unwise and unfair to prejudice in advance of the establishment of orderly, constitutional government in Russia the principle of Russian unity as a whole."[32]

Lansing was at a dead end. If the Whites triumphed in the civil war, as he wished, what future was there for the Baltic states or any other "province" that had separated itself from the old Russian empire? From the broad avenues where it had originated as a principle of the new liberalism, self-determination had marched steadily into narrower and narrower alleys that had twisted and turned into this final cramped place. It was not possible to simply turn around, go back to some selected place, and choose another route. Such an escape did not exist. Only if the Bolsheviks triumphed, paradoxically, could self-determination be resurrected, not because of any wish on Lenin's part to promote nationalism, but simply because he wished to buy time for the Soviet system to survive. But to Americans, of course, that would mean participating in a corrupt deal. If Lenin wished to "sell" the Baltic states or some other part of Russia, to "buy" them would be to purchase a forbidden fruit. Lloyd George read his bible differently, paying close attention to passages that enjoined the Lord's servants not to bury their talents in the earth, but to profit from its bounty.

> *Russia is one of the great resources for the supply of food and raw material. The present condition of Russia is one of the contributing causes to the prevailing high prices, and high prices are undoubtedly in all lands the most dangerous form of Bolshevik propaganda.*
>
> David Lloyd George in Commons,
> November 17, 1919

Although it has been generally overlooked in later discussions of John Maynard Keynes's indictment of the Versailles Treaty, *The Economic Consequences of the Peace*,[33] Keynes reserved some of his sharpest comments for the unwritten clauses pertaining to Russia. "The blockading of Russia lately proclaimed by the Allies is therefore a foolish and short-sighted proceeding; we are blockading not so much Russia as ourselves." The same people who had expressed such great fear of a Russo-German union, he went on, were "even more afraid of the success of Bolshevism." They lived in constant torment because the only forces capable of fighting the Bolsheviks would, given the opportunity, align themselves with German reactionaries. "Thus the advocates of intervention in Russia, whether direct or indirect, are at perpetual cross-purposes with themselves."[34]

Lloyd George probably wished he had other allies, less controversial ones than Keynes. He had tried to work with the Americans, but the latest word from America—for example, Lansing's efforts to reconcile support for Kolchak with a refusal to grant recognition of the Baltic states— suggested nothing so much as a Gordian knot. And Wilson was not able, even if he was inclined, to untangle the mess. Preposterous as it was under these conditions, moreover, a State Department official would try to warn off Lloyd George by asserting to the new ambassador, Sir Auckland Geddes, that the president still "regarded America as being in [the] position of trustee for Russia so long as she was unable to look after her own interests."[35]

What was one to say to such pretensions, in terms either of Wilson's personal capacities or America's turn inward away from Europe's political problems? Lloyd George had also sought a new beginning with Clemenceau. The premier had given him a small opening by stating that "on the whole" he was rather relieved that the United States had dropped out of the peace settlement. As for the Russians, well, they were " 'Orientals' who thoroughly enjoyed fighting among themselves with all their tortures, and so on," and he had come to think that a mistake had been made in interfering. Yes, agreed Lloyd George readily, and he was pleased to see that a recent French election had appeared to demonstrate little fear of Bolshevism spreading. Clemenceau shied, however, when the prime minister pressed for a meeting with Russian leaders. France had spent 750 million francs fighting the Bolsheviks, he said, and the public was still against dealing with Lenin.[36]

At home, the prime minister's critics went after him because of his claims that Russian warehouses were bulging with grain for export. And he did overstate the economic case, to his subsequent embarrassment. But that mattered little, he thought, compared to the value to be gained from reengaging Russia as much as possible along prewar lines. Like Wilson, Lloyd George did believe ideas counted. Reengaging Russia, no matter what critics said, would have obvious benefits over the long run to the health and well-being of the European economy—which was essential to the proper functioning of the British export economy. No less important, however, would be the ideological return from demonstrating the vitality of liberal democracy by dealing with the Bolsheviks face to face. In other words, it would reengage his fellow countrymen in the effort to make their own institutions work, an impossible task if capital or labor came to feel that Britain could not cope with revolution. Britain could not afford what the United States apparently preferred, the ideological extravagance of isolation. Lloyd George's countrymen required a higher level of exports, and they were less sheltered from European politics.

At the first post-Versailles conference of Allied leaders, Lloyd George produced representatives of the Russian cooperative societies, presumably non-Bolshevik organizations, who nodded vigorously when the prime minister declared that increased trade was "the most effective way of striking a blow at Bolshevism."[37] After they left, Lloyd George continued to make the case, pointing out to Clemenceau and Italian Premier Nitti that wheat imports into Europe from America were at abnormally high levels. If that continued, Europe would be left at the mercy of the unpredictable Americans. Resuming trade with Russia, on the other hand, would bring down wheat prices and destroy Bolshevism. "The moment trade was established with Russia, Communism would go."[38]

An Allied committee headed by E. F. Wise (whose leftist sympathies informed his agricultural expertise, according to his critics), reported in favor of opening trade with the cooperative societies. A press release asserted that no change in policy had taken place, but Soviet regimentation of foreign trade meant that Moscow had had to have given its approval. And the decision did mean the lifting of the blockade.[39]

Back in London, Lloyd George's critics awaited him with new charges of Soviet subversion directed at Persia and India. Surely it was out of the question, replied the prime minister, to send three divisions to the Caucasus region, the latest scheme of the interventionists, unless the French came along. He had gleaned from the Industrial Unrest Committee—which he pitted against all the conclusions of the various Russian study groups—that there were hardly enough troops to maintain domestic order. The only attacks the Bolsheviks had launched were words, propaganda, and what good were troops against that? "It was true that in the United States of America military methods had in a sense been adopted, that is to say, the rounding up and banishment of the Bolsheviks." But the Palmer raids in America were hardly models for Great Britain to emulate. And all that had been accomplished by the interventionists in terms of influencing Russia was to make the Red Army the most "formidable power in the world, since all the other armies were demobilized."[40]

There were some loose ends to this argument, but it had the effect of contrasting the futility of the American response to the revolution to what Lloyd George offered. The decision to resume trade, taken as it was without consultation with Washington, brought an angry State Department response. And Washington's anger was increased by the way the Bolsheviks were boasting about their ability to pay gold for imports and their willingness to grant concessions. The nations that first opened trade relations, said Maxim Litvinov in a newspaper interview, would be the ones to reap great advantages.[41]

These constant appeals to capitalist cupidity were infuriating, particularly to the Americans, who had not yet got the knack of Old World diplomacy even as well as the Bolsheviks had. Nevertheless, the Allied decision prompted American reassessment of the situation. Trade adviser Julius Lay asserted that it was time to admit that military and economic intervention had failed. It was no longer sufficient to put off reopening trade on the basis of some abstract hope of Lenin's overthrow, or because it would supposedly advantage the Bolsheviks. The key consideration must be European recovery. As for the tainted gold Litvinov offered, what better way was there to drain off a potential source of funds for revolutionary propaganda? Herbert Hoover agreed, it was said, that Lenin could not reap any great ideological advantage from trade. Instead, "the unsoundness of the Bolshevik communistic theories will stand forth increasingly apparent." A final point for consideration was that the expected boon to American trade ought not to be foregone.[42]

News of Kolchak's execution brought other voices into the debate. Prominent among these was John F. Stevens, previously a steadfast supporter of intervention. Now all that was being accomplished, insisted Stevens, the head of the American Railway Commission to Russia, was Japanese domination in the Far East. Exasperated by official silence, Stevens traveled seven hundred miles to talk to Thomas Lamont when the banker came to China to complete the consortium negotiations. They dined together while Stevens told his story. For nearly three years he had been on the "front line," Stevens said, battling both the Bolsheviks and the Japanese, in the effort to assure a "neutral" regime for Russia's Far Eastern railroad system. Japan must be stopped, he said. "We need foreign markets badly and that [Siberia] is the very best of them all—the richest, most prosperous, most able to pay. . . . I tell you it is a situation for misgiving and prayer, not for ignoring it as our State Department seems to do." Recently he had received an offer from the Bolsheviks: gold for railroad cars and locomotives, sewing machines and harvesting machinery. He had forwarded this to Washington and heard nothing. What was happening?[43]

And from Copenhagen came word that Litvinov wanted to visit the United States. Pressure was building in Europe, cabled the American minister in that city, for a complete resumption of trade. "I do not know whether complementary pressure is growing in the United States," added Arthur Schoenfeld, "but the thought suggests itself that British tendency seems to be to press every British advantage in this direction in the face of a more or less active Russian desire to broaden trade relations with the outside world." Litvinov had told intermediaries that the Soviet government did indeed control the cooperatives, but it also opposed awarding Great Britain a trade monopoly. Russia needed locomotives and agricultural machinery. It would pay gold. Europeans sought raw materials, but Litvinov and his government knew that Americans had no need of those and would prefer gold. Like so many other communications, for example that of John F. Stevens, Schoenfeld's report was forwarded to the White House—and disappeared.[44]

Meanwhile, State Department officials mulled over yet another communication on Russian trade. Ellis Loring Dresel in Berlin had mailed a copy of a recent article by Karl Radek, the Bolshevik "representative" to Germany who was now in prison awaiting deportation. German authorities had kept the "proletariat" away from Radek, but they had admitted a steady stream of German industrialists to his cell, which became temporary headquarters for Russo-German trade talks. Radek's article made one simple point. To save themselves from economic disaster, the Allies would soon have to come to terms with the New Russia. Why, then, should Germany be left out? "I am not diplomatist enough to pretend that I believe in the longevity of the German situation today," he wrote. "The German Bourgeoisie does not believe in the longevity of our Bolshevistic existence. In other words, we are of the same opinion. But why should we not exchange linen for medicaments, wood for electric apparatus? Does the German Bourgeoisie demand a certificate of immortality from people to whom they sell underdrawers?"[45]

"I believe the trading is inevitable," Frank Polk wrote the president, "and it would be just as well for us to declare our position so as not to appear to the world as an unwilling follower rather than a leader." Those who recommended lifting the official ban on trade noted that there need not be political relations and that Bolshevik trade commissions would not have to be admitted to American soil. In other words, removing the embargo would change practically nothing, while it would permit the administration to deny accusations that it wanted to starve out the Bolsheviks.[46]

Thus reassured, Wilson approved a formal announcement of the new policy on March 20, 1920. Issued only because the administration did not wish to appear an "unwilling follower," the announcement exuded resentment and suspicion. A few days before the ban was lifted, Polk informed Wilson that the League of Nations was planning to send a commission to investigate conditions in Russia. It was hoped that an American would go along to observe. Polk had prepared a list of possible candidates for such a mission in case the president was interested. Wilson was not.[47]

Nearly eighteen months had passed since the armistice, and the administration still lacked a Russian policy, still waited for the true Russian

democratic spirit to make its appearance and drive away the Bolshevik
impostors. The resentful suspicion grew that it was Britain that blocked
the way.[48] Every dark shadow that flitted across Central Europe became a
British plot. For instance, on hearing of the Kapp Putsch, which briefly
brought a right-wing government to power in Berlin, Assistant Secretary
of State Norman Davis wrote Lansing's successor, Bainbridge Colby, that
he was sure London was in close touch with the conspirators. "That the
British are now engaged in developing a big project for the commercial
control of Russia is another fact which had been brought out," he continued. "This they are trying to do by the development of German commercial groups."[49]

Stranger things had happened, no doubt, and it may have been satisfying to believe that the Russian Revolution, if not caused by agents of
reaction, as had once been thought, was responsible for revitalizing the
most objectionable features of the old diplomacy. At any rate, Wilson
demanded a full investigation. When it was pointed out that London or
Paris stood to lose the most from a reactionary regime in Berlin, the
president conceded the point. But he felt certain, he said, that the British
kept a "watchful lookout for any material advantage of any kind that they
can get out of the situation in Germany or the situation in Russia. . . ."
Stay on their track, he admonished, so we "know exactly what they *are*
doing."[50]

Something "extraordinary" was going on, agreed Secretary Colby: a
high Bolshevik official, Leonid Krasin, had been invited to London to
negotiate on behalf of the cooperative societies. Americans had been
skeptical about the imaginary bulging warehouses of Russian grain from
the outset. Maybe Lloyd George was honestly looking for lower food
prices, but he also wanted to be there when industrial concessions were
being passed out. And that would explain also Krasin's mission: he had
once been a director of a vast German subsidiary in Russia.[51]

> *My object is peace . . . an end to all this bloodshed
> and conflict. . . .*
>
> David Lloyd George, July 1920

The prime minister was making definite headway with his Russian policy
in early 1920, much to the chagrin of a variety of opponents: the French,
the Americans, and half of the cabinet. On February 6, 1920, Arthur
Balfour, who generally sided with Lloyd George, put the Russian policy
into a context they both understood best: "In substance what the coalition

stands for is Reform versus Revolution." They must all stand together in defense of that position. Balfour's support was conditional, therefore, upon Lloyd George's not trying to go too fast in any direction. The prime minister understood, and wrote in reply, "The general line of demarcation between the contending forces is clear, and becoming clearer every day. It is embodied in our formula of reform against revolution. . . . The Socialist movement has behind it most of the organized labor of the country. A more serious development, however, is the extent to which it is attracting the lower middle classes; and unless there is a concerted effort made to arrest this tendency very grave consequences may ensue to the whole order of society."[52]

The reengagement of Russia was high on the list of concerted efforts needed, and was the reason for Krasin's invitation to London. In preliminary discussions the Russian had made it clear that his country wanted locomotives—thousands of them—and financial aid in the form of credit. The Soviets also expected the Allies to force the border states to stop fighting. After all, said Krasin, this was only reasonable, since economic recovery depended upon peace; otherwise sufficient transport and labor resources could not be devoted to trade. The sole reason the Poles were not willing to negotiate, he insisted, was Allied refusal to cut off support.[53]

In late 1919 Poland occupied a swath of territory some two hundred miles to the east of the last proposed boundary line. General Josef Pilsudski, whose political and military ambitions rivaled those of past kings, held his position and awaited word of Denikin's fate—and Allied disposition. Throughout December and January, Moscow offered peace negotiations. Lloyd George's carefully worded warning to Poland's Foreign Minister Patek not to jeopardize the trade negotiations indicated where the prime minister stood, but soon after this Patek traveled to Paris, and there heard a different version of Allied concern. The French emphasized their willingness to protect the Polish front line against attack from the Red Army, and there was much talk about military supplies for "operations in the coming spring."[54]

Sir Horace Rumbold, British minister in Warsaw, felt a deepening unease about Pilsudski's rumored desire to make Poland the leader of a group of "buffer states" in Central Europe. Far from desiring peace, the Poles believed themselves to be warriors performing services vital to the world, services that entitled them to ask for five squadrons of Bristol fighters. The thought of giving Pilsudski a fleet of airplanes to carry on such work raised goosebumps in Whitehall, where even the bravest anti-Bolshevik shuddered at being involved in Polish plans to serve the world in this fashion. Even those who wished Lloyd George no success with his Russian game did not want to see Poland emerge as the balancer in

Central Europe. That might endanger the British position in the Baltic, whose states offered a great potential base, some hoped, "for a controlled experiment in the reconstruction and development of Russia . . . ," Rumbold reported. Former parts of Russia, such as Latvia, Lithuania, and Estonia, could become a showcase for anti-Bolshevik methods; besides, if Poland became too powerful, then the only alternative for Britain might be closer relations with Russia![55]*

"Let us keep clear of the Polish business," said Balfour's successor at the Foreign Office, Lord Curzon. "If it succeeds we shall get better terms. If it fails ours will not be the blame." Perhaps the Polish offensive would succeed well enough that the Bolsheviks would have to negotiate with Denikin's successor in the Caucasus region, General Piotr Wrangel. Plans were made for sending a British officer to make sure the empire's interests were considered, if that eventuality developed. In the excitement of the moment, it was all but forgotten that negotiations, even under those conditions, would imply recognition of the legitimacy of the Soviet regime.[56]

As the time for Krasin's arrival approached, the Foreign Office began to calculate the pros and cons of the prime minister's latest venture. Owen O'Malley set out the framework: "[W]e must decide which of two factors is most dangerous to the existing order of society in Europe and to the security of the United Kingdom, namely virtual recognition of the Soviet Government or starvation and disease on an unprecedented scale."[57]

A surprising convert to Lloyd George's position was O'Malley's minister, Lord Curzon. Interested always in the traditional Eastern question, Curzon saw Bolshevism as only a new face on an ancient rivalry. Bolshevism was at war with peoples and states in whom His Majesty's Government had a direct interest, Curzon explained to the cabinet, instancing Moscow's efforts in Afghanistan, where the Russians were trying to negotiate an alliance aimed at supporting insurrection on India's northwest frontier. Similar occurrences were evident in the Caucasus region, with Persia the ultimate goal.[58]

Negotiations offered an opportunity to put the Russians straight on what His Majesty's Government would, and would not, tolerate. On the eve of Krasin's arrival, accordingly, the war cabinet resolved that the Russians would have to agree to put an end to propaganda and subver-

---

*What a dramatic prophecy that turned out to be in 1939, when, as Lloyd George feared, Neville Chamberlain would have to make a choice, or series of choices, between Russia and appeasement. In the interwar era, Great Britain became the reluctant guardian of the Baltic nations' independence. Chamberlain could not make a choice against appeasement without appearing to endanger the relationships that had grown up in those years. The peril of leaving Russia unengaged in 1919 thus increased manyfold over the next twenty years. But of course prophecy is a gift usually ignored for practical reasons.

sion outside Russia and recognize in principle Russia's prerevolutionary debts. But at the same time it also resolved that French criticism about receiving Russian gold was not to be allowed to deter an agreement. If locomotives were to be sold to Russia in order to provide transport facilities for the grain trade, gold was the only way to set the process in motion.[59]

Lloyd George was in a mellow mood. How foolish the Poles were, he told the bishop of York over breakfast. "Very like the Irish," quarreling with all their neighbors, he rambled on. How foolish, too, the French. They would never see any of their gold as matters stood. The only way they could ever be paid back was in goods, and that meant enabling the Russians to develop their resources.[60]

At the opening session of the Anglo-Russian talks, Krasin impressed Lloyd George with his businesslike demeanor. It was almost as if the revolution had never taken place. But it was too soon to celebrate. Krasin's willingness to meet British demands about propaganda was his own idea, not Moscow's order. Indeed, as intelligence intercepts revealed, Foreign Affairs Commissar Georgi Chicherin had specifically warned against any promises to shut down the revolution in the East. "The situation that has been created in the East is a difficult one for England. In Persia they are almost helpless in the face of the revolution. Disloyalty is increasing amongst the Indian troops."[61]

Meeting privately with the prime minister on June 16, 1920, Krasin confirmed the accuracy of the intercepts, though in a backhanded fashion to be sure, and tried to explain away the contradiction. There were extremists on both sides, he confided. Those in Russia preferred world revolution to world peace. Fortunately, they were a minority. The Allied extremists preferred war with Russia to peace with the Soviet government. Perhaps that was so, but Lloyd George pointed out that his own position, already vulnerable to attack on several sides, had been made worse by publication of a Lenin letter to British workers. It was an insane document, the prime minister told Krasin: things might really come apart unless a speedy agreement on debts and propaganda could be arranged. Those who opposed settlement could get the upper hand, as had happened after the French Revolution. "The consequences had been twenty years of bloodshed ending in a Napoleonic despotism in Europe," he reminded his visitor.[62]

When formal talks resumed two weeks later, Krasin stuck close to the Moscow line: a truculent defense of Soviet behavior as a necessary response to Allied provocation, coupled with the assertion that Britain had no right to insist upon restraint anyplace but in Britain itself. If an agreement to resume trade was forthcoming, Moscow would be willing to exchange pledges of nonintererence in internal political affairs.

The Chicherin intercepts, on the other hand, implied very clearly a desire if not to cause a revolution, then to bring pressure on London. That was infuriating. Krasin's position on the debts was also phrased in what seemed to be deliberately insulting fashion. If debts were to be considered, he argued, then first priority would have to go to Allied obligations to the "hundreds of thousands of widows and orphans . . . whose relatives have died through British and French bullets and shells during the so-called intervention. . . ." So much for the private debts. As for government loans to Russia, as far as the Soviet government was concerned these too had been erased by the intervention and the economic blockade—"the last in order to compel the Russian people through hunger and privations to deny those forms of State life which that people chose for itself after it overthrew the autocratic Czarist Government." So long as the Soviet government remained unrecognized, there could be no question of its being held responsible for debts contracted by its predecessors. Should the British still wish to go ahead with the negotiations for a comprehensive settlement on those terms, the Soviet government was ready. But the reopening of trade was a simpler matter to arrange, requiring only that the blockade be lifted and the necessary papers issued.[63]

The "lecture," as Lloyd George would call this tirade, lessened hopes for an early agreement. Krasin seemed almost equally uncomfortable with his role in the drama, which reflected Soviet ambivalence, uncongenial to his experience as well, about entering into the traditional diplomatic bargaining process, and a preference for already shopworn adversarial encounters as at Brest-Litovsk. Krasin dropped hints to this effect by suggesting that the best way to proceed would be for him to return to Moscow as soon as possible with a list of specific British demands requisite to reopening trade.

Lloyd George offered Krasin a ride on a speedy British warship bound for Russia, and an admonition to convey to ideologues too comfortable with their abstractions and slogans: "If these negotiations broke down, the position would be worse than if the negotiations had never taken place, but in any case he wished to know definitely, without further delay, where he stood." Lloyd George could hardly have made it any plainer: he wanted to know where *he* stood, and the Russians should be concerned as well if they understood anything about the "crisis" other than the dialectic. Passage booked on a warship should make the point emphatic.[64]

The answer, such as it was, came from Chicherin: Why not treat the current situation as an armistice preliminary to a final accord? Lloyd George made the best of that he could, telling French Premier Millerand that his object was peace, for "attacks upon Bolshevik Russia were simply strengthening not merely the Communist Government but the Communist elements in the Government, and . . . as soon as Russia was at peace Russia would disintegrate."[65]

No help for Lloyd George in handling the French could be found in the United States. Wilson's advisers assured the president that while American businessmen were eyeing the British negotiations with some concern, no groundswell had arisen at home for undertaking similar talks. Secretary of State Bainbridge Colby, moreover, kept insisting that the Bolsheviks were at last on the verge of a final collapse. Two months at most he gave them. If that were so, wondered the British ambassador, Sir Auckland Geddes, what sort of government did the secretary foresee arising out of the ashes? Colby retreated a step or two when thus challenged. Well, he said, the absence of an alternative probably did make the inevitable downfall somewhat less than imminent. But what, he wanted to know, were the true British "motives" for pursuing the Krasin negotiations so avidly?[66]

Geddes could not but marvel at the contradictory attitudes he found in America. Ah, if only the Irish situation could be painted as Bolshevik-inspired, he wrote Lloyd George privately; American feelings about events there would change overnight. "There is nothing that I know of that this country is so frightened of as Bolshevism. They have got a very large unassimilated foreign population that responds to Bolshevik and Socialist propaganda."[67] The red scare of recent months had abated by this time, but Geddes was right. "Revolution is everywhere," the president told Democratic chairman Homer Cummings at the end of May 1920, then sank back into the lassitude his illness had caused.[68]

Although Lloyd George's Russian policy drew no response from the icebound postwar Wilson administration, it responded with surprising vigor to an appeal from Samuel Gompers, president of the American Federation of Labor. A staunch Wilsonian, Gompers was an even more dedicated anti-Bolshevik. Early in June 1920 he asked for Colby's aid. He needed a full statement of the reasons for America's continued aloofness from any dealings with the Russians. It was required, Colby reported to the president, in order to quiet rumblings within the AFL membership ranks—complaints, interestingly enough, that official policy was not "enterprising or sagacious from a commercial point of view." Colby's letter instead took direct issue with British arguments. All European efforts to restart the Russian trade, it said, had floundered because of the Soviet demand for diplomatic recognition. The United States had no desire to interfere with Russia's internal affairs, but recognition of the "existing regime" would deprive an overwhelming majority of the right to self-determination. That was always an awkward corner for the Wilsonians, of course, but once around it Colby had easy sailing. The Soviet regime's behavior toward other governments had violated every principle of international relations, he charged, every convention that underlay the structure of international law.[69]

Meanwhile, Lloyd George took on his opponents on the floor of Commons. Colby might have been sitting on the bench opposite as he spoke, impatiently waving his letter to Gompers. England had traded with the tsar, began the prime minister, done business with his corrupt government, dined with the authors of the pogroms, and signed treaties with those responsible for "scores of thousands of innocent people massacred." Indeed, British traders had sold goods for hundreds of years to cannibals, whether in the South Seas or in Africa. The Turks had committed more atrocities than the Bolsheviks, yet no voices were heard demanding immediate cessation of that trade. It would be pleasant, to be sure, if the world were so ordered that one could avoid contacts with such governments and such peoples. "But we cannot indulge in these things; they are a luxury. . . . We must take such governments as we find them, and thank God how very happy we ourselves are here."

Colby remained unimpressed. Besides constant reminders that Lenin's days were numbered, the secretary of state thought he ought to point out that despite the prime minister's view, it could be dangerous for imperial well-being to sell locomotives and railway equipment to this particular band of fanatics. Had the Board of Trade really considered, he asked Auckland Geddes, what difficulties would be added to future defense to gain a few pounds sterling?[70]

Bad enough that the Bolsheviks should keep heaping coals on the fire. To hear similar taunts from Washington about British greed, passed along with a sanctimonious concern for the empire, hardly presaged an era of cooperation—except on American terms. And worst of all for Lloyd George, although Colby did not sit in Commons his words gave sustenance and inspiration to all those who prayed for the prime minister's schemes to fail.

CHAPTER TWELVE

The Shape of Things to Come

The Mexican Government has not recognized nor will it recognize . . . [the Monroe] doctrine, nor any other which attacks the sovereignty and independence of Mexico.

Mexican communication to the State Department, April 1919

We no longer look to the Western Powers. Our faces are turned toward Russia.

Sun Yat-sen, December 1923

Neither the International Bankers' Committee for Mexico nor the new China consortium ever succeeded in resolving the problems they were created to deal with, although both were useful in reconciling differences among the industrial nations. For eight years Woodrow Wilson had wrestled with the "special interests," drawing from the Mexican and Chinese experiences lessons he thought applied to Russia as well. In the end it was beyond his capacity to apply them anywhere. America had changed profoundly.

Off to one side during the domestic fight over the League, Mexico and China came back to center stage at the end of the Wilson years. Wilson would fire Secretary of State Robert Lansing for plotting with the cabinet behind his back to overturn his Mexican policy. He would also predict that the Republicans would go to war to put an end to the Mexican disorder. But the truth was that instead of a Mexican policy, at the end of the administration there was only a replica of the Russian nonpolicy. As in the Russian instance, moreover, the paralysis was not primarily because of Wilson's illness, but was the result of a more general condition.

China was put into the hands of the bankers with the expectation that a new consortium could work wonders if only the Chinese were made to understand that Japan had been brought into harness. Instead of what the State Department wanted, however, the bankers went their own way. And, in effect, China was partitioned. "There is nothing in South Manchuria and inner Eastern Mongolia," consortium negotiator Thomas Lamont had concluded, "that would lead us to want to put money there unless Japan desires to go along."[1]

The administration's willingness to accept Lamont's evaluation, and seek no more to rectify wrongs done to China, was the product of many factors, not least simple exhaustion. Ennui also accounts for much of the hardening attitude toward Mexico. Had there been no war, it has been argued here, Wilson would have had to abandon "watchful waiting" much sooner: he would have had to either join with the industrial powers, or act on his own. But the war, which was supposed to give new life to liberalism, had instead left in its wake the Bolshevist plague. The prevailing mood in the State Department, said British Ambassador Auckland Geddes, was a rigid determination to force on the Mexicans an agreement that would "enable America to occupy a position towards Mexico very similar to that which she has now towards Cuba."[2]

But exhaustion and ennui are appropriate terms for explaining the shifts in mood, not for other changes. The most important of these was the growth of an "institutional" foreign policy that by war's end had completely altered the functions of the president and the professional bureaucracy, increasing the latter's power. Disabled as he was, Wilson understood the change. So would his successors, Herbert Hoover and Franklin D. Roosevelt, both of whom sought to find a new definition for liberalism that went beyond Wilsonian concepts yet retained their spirit.

Something of what was happening in these last months can also be explained, finally, by referring to Lloyd George's problems in finding a constituency for his Russian policy. Where the prime minister needed American help for that initiative, Wilson needed help from the British for his policy in Mexico and China. Neither got what he wanted. Instead, Lloyd George saw his opponents look to America for ideological support, and Wilson saw the State Department become more like the Foreign Office in dealing with the world outside Europe.

> *We cannot be too careful not to serve these predatory interests, because they intend the demoralization of our own politics and the control of Mexican politics.*
>
> Woodrow Wilson, November 1920

To the end, Wilson feared the impact of the Mexican Revolution on American politics. His final comments on Mexico often appear to be written for the historical record, a legacy to future liberals. Where he had once been determined to make policy fit his public statements, it was now the opposite. He had vowed that while he was president no one would attempt to rearrange Mexico's internal affairs by force. He had kept that promise. Neither the Veracruz landings nor the Pershing expedition ended with a march on Mexico City. But beyond that point he was stymied.

Hopes had been raised that Carranza would accept the offer of the bankers, but as the Paris Peace Conference came to an end, these hopes were dashed. "I find something that I am going to state to you frankly," wrote Luis Cabrera, a Carranza aide, to banker Henry Bruere, "and it is that in view of the general conditions of the world all the nations have their financial situation pending of resolution and I consider it would be worthwhile to wait for some time before we can make an arrangement for our debts, at least until we know the general rules that the principle countries will adopt for that purpose."[3]

What Cabrera was saying was that if the great powers forgave each others' war debts, Mexico had as good a claim as any European nation to be treated the same way. It was not a protectorate of the United States, or a colony under League mandate, or a ward of the international bankers. After considering his reply for several days, Bruere finally wrote that Mexico would need economic cooperation from the outside world. "I can only say that I am greatly disappointed that there should be further delay and trust, in the interest of Mexico's welfare, that the delay may be of very brief duration."[4]

New decrees aimed at forcing the oil companies to comply with the Constitution and petroleum legislation under consideration by the Mexican Congress prompted Ambassador Henry Fletcher to exclaim that what Carranza demanded "strikes at the very heart" of current discussions between Mexico and the United States.[5] One oil man, Harold Walker of Huasteca Petroleum, summed up the feelings of them all. It was immaterial who was president of Mexico, he wrote Fletcher,

> so long as what we bought and the industry we created remains ours. . . . I cannot forget your words the first time I had the honor of meeting you, "The sole point with these people is to make them live up to their international obligations." You said the whole thing there. That is the solution of the Mexican problem. That solved it from 1878 to 1911. It is our hope that such attitude will solve it for another thirty years.[6]

Walker's calendar looked backwards; 1911 was already a hundred years ago, only he could not see it. Time and space had rushed together. Already the clock had been set ahead in Colombia. Since 1914 the Senate had had under consideration a treaty that promised Bogota $25 million to bring an end to bitterness of the Panamanian "affair." What held it up now was a fear that the Colombians were planning to follow Mexico's course in dealing with foreign oil companies.[7]

Unfortunately, Secretary Lansing informed the American minister in Bogota, Mexico's actions had started a trend. "With the passage of time this tendency seems to have crystallized into policy, and the complications growing out of Mexico's policy not only threaten the confiscation of vested rights in oil properties but also include the essential principles upon which amicable international relations are founded. . . . In these circumstances it is but natural that this Government should look with grave concern upon an effort by Colombia or any other Latin American country to adopt a nationalization policy, injurious to American citizens, similar to that now being attempted by Mexico."[8]

As the effort was being mounted to contain a threatened epidemic of the Mexican "disease," plans were also going ahead for constructing a rationale for intervention at the source, based upon Carranza's disregard for human life. On July 21, 1919, Acting Secretary of State William Phillips instructed the chargé in Mexico City that he was to issue a public statement about the shooting death of one Peter Catron, killed by bandits. "You will . . . state that should the lives of American citizens continue to remain unsafe, and these murders continue by reason of the unwillingness or inability of the Mexican Government to afford adequate protection, this Government may be forced to adopt a radical change in its policy with regard to Mexico."[9]

Foreigners were safe in populated areas, retorted the First Chief. When the oil companies insisted upon sending a paymaster out alone into a remote area, such incidents were bound to occur. It was even possible that the companies were in league with the rebel bandits. "[T]he menace embraced in your note has surprised the Mexican Government, all the more so since it seems strange that it should be expected that even in depopulated regions human life should be protected in a more perfect manner than in the most populous cities of the most cultured countries where bloody crimes often occur without the governments thereby becoming the object of severe observations."[10]

As he had often done in the past, Wilson moved to head off a crisis. Appraised of Carranza's insolent reply, and of other recent transgressions committed by the First Chief, for example his authorization of "thoroughly anti-American" writings, the president had a surprising recommendation:

This is all exceedingly serious. Do you not think it would be best for Mr. Fletcher to return at once to his post at Mexico City? I fear that there is not sufficient influence upon Carranza in his absence, and that there is a possibility that he may feel freer than he would feel if Mr. Fletcher were there, to express publicly his outrageous attitude.[11]

Ambassador Fletcher's return from a political "vacation" would signal that the administration had not deviated from Wilson's noninterventionist stance, and indicate to the ambassador that he should occupy his time with tasks other than gathering evidence of Carranza's misdeeds.

Carranza may have missed the nuances, but he was aware of general developments. On September 1, 1919, he informed the Mexican Congress that an oil company campaign was under way to force intervention, "in order that our laws may be in accord with their personal interests. . . . [T]hey present as a reason for intervention the lack of guarantees which they claim prevails in our territory, this being a most effective means of impressing public opinion." He then took pains to refute all charges, instance by instance, and to detail what had been done to maintain order.[12]

Mexican officials were also at pains to remind the American government that the proposed new law exempted all properties in operation on or before May 1, 1917. All that meant, reiterated chargé George Summerlin, was that nationalization would not be complete for twenty-five years, when the old wells ran dry. New wells in Mexico and, increasingly important in Washington's view, new wells in places like Colombia, where exploration had only begun, would be possible under terms outlined in the Mexican Constitution and those elsewhere that it spawned. And besides, what assurances were there that sometime later Carranza or his successors might not introduce still more drastic legislative measures? The continuing impact of Mexico's "constitutional socialism" promised a never-ending series of confrontations.[13]

In October, Consul William O. Jenkins was kidnapped by an antigovernment band led by a subordinate of Manuel Peláez, the Mexican "warlord" who controlled the oil fields. The kidnappers announced that their purpose was to demonstrate Mexico City's inability to protect foreign nationals. Ransomed by private sources, Jenkins was promptly arrested by government officials and charged with criminal collusion. On November 18, 1919, Lansing summoned the cabinet on his own account to take up the Jenkins case. At this meeting, and at two others he summoned, Lansing played a very cool game, siding with the moderates.[14]

Then, on November 27, Mexico City formally rejected an American protest note on the Jenkins case. Lansing called Ambassador Ignacio Bonillas to his office and reminded him of what had happened to Germany when it had attempted to overturn the code of civilization. He had only wanted to shock Carranza out of his belief that he could go on and on with such insults, Lansing wrote in private notes. The Jenkins case was only one incident, but, he added, he was not at all sure that the "issue between this country and Mexico might as well come now as at some later time."[15]

In public, however, he continued the moderate's role. When Senator Albert Fall's "smelling committee" (Wilson's name for it), otherwise known as the Special Committee Investigating Mexican Affairs, called upon the president in his bedroom on December 5, 1919, Lansing telephoned ahead to say that Jenkins had been released. He had previously written, moreover, to assure the president that the State Department could handle the case without a crisis developing. But thought had to be given to a long-range plan of action, lest Congress draw its own indictment against Carranza which would "appeal very strongly to the people and arouse a very general indignation."

Lansing's concern to keep Congress from seizing the initiative was no doubt genuine, but it was also the feint he needed to make to persuade Wilson to go along with his developing plan. Wilson had appointed Lansing in 1915 because, the president had confided to House, he was a good note drafter who would not try to become a policymaker. He had underestimated his man. The secretary had moved Viscount Ishii around on his chessboard and, also in regard to China, had got the knack of appealing to the president along Wilsonian lines. The secretary overplayed his role now, however, suggesting to the president that he had fashioned the Jenkins note in such a way as to divert anger from general issues into a narrow dispute that, he said, he "knew could not possibly result in a rupture between the two Governments."[16]

What he kept secret was that both he himself and the State Department had in fact encouraged popular outrage over the Catron and Jenkins cases. Where the president had skilfully used public diplomacy to set limits on what the U.S. government could do (as in the instance of Frank Polk's response to British appeals concerning the Robles Domínguez conspiracy a year earlier), Lansing was using it to engender support for an interventionist policy so that Wilson would be forced to act. In this instance he failed, but it was another sign of the altered balance.

Lansing did not deny to the president that the oil controversy was at the center of the current dispute, as his plan unfolded, while insisting that the Mexican Constitution raised the broadest issues. "The limits of diplomatic pressure in regard to this whole matter," he wrote Wilson on December 19, 1919, "seems to have been reached." Carranza would force a break rather than yield a single point. If the United States acquiesced in a procedure whereby the companies had to accept the new petroleum code in advance of its actual passage, what would happen to the rule of law? Besides the great damage this would do to American prestige, the outlook was for oil shortages and general harm to industry. He awaited the president's instructions.[17]

While he followed his own "watchful waiting" policy, the secretary instructed Ambassador Fletcher to prepare a final offer. Lansing presented this to the president as his own plan on January 3, 1920. Fletcher was to return to Mexico City, but only to deliver an ultimatum. It consisted of four demands. First, Carranza must pledge to provide effective protection of life and property. Next he must agree to a joint Mexican-American commission, perhaps with a third-party umpire, to adjudicate all claims. Third, he would have to agree to accept the Hague Tribunal as an arbitrator to decide the legality of all decrees, laws, and regulations issued under the Constitution of 1917. Finally, while all this was being decided, he would have to suspend enforcement of recent Mexican petroleum laws. Carranza would be given a last warning at the end of four weeks. If he had not complied with the ultimatum in another seven days, Fletcher would ask for his passport.[18]

Lansing admitted that some might say that intervention would follow as a matter of course if the United States thus broke off relations. That was not necessarily so, however, he argued; Fletcher's asking for his passport might shock Carranza back to reality. It was also possible that severing relations would shock the Mexican people into eliminating Carranza themselves. If this happened (or even if it did not), breaking relations offered a chance to begin afresh with a new Mexican president, if the promised elections produced a decent successor. "I understand that candidates for the Presidency are in practically all instances convinced that the Carranza attitude toward the United States has been disastrous for Mexico and many patriotic Mexican people believe that the novel provisions of the new Constitution are a great obstacle to economic progress to Mexico and her credit abroad, and that the new Constitution will be amended."[19]

As a final touch, the secretary assured Wilson that the plan he was submitting would not meet with cordial approval from the oil men, who, for reasons left unclear, would be outmaneuvered. Wilson was not to be finessed in such a manner. Almost immediately, the president asked for Lansing's resignation. Mexican policy was only part of what was involved; the cabinet meetings Lansing had summoned and presided over were probably more important. But they too were symbolic not only of Wilson's semiparalysis, but of a struggle between two forces within government.

With the secretary's removal, and Carranza's well-timed agreement to refer several Mexican-American issues to a mixed claims commission, relations settled into a period of uneasy quiet.

This is not the opportune time for negotiations, anyway.

Woodrow Wilson, November 1920

In the remaining months of his administration, Wilson took satisfaction from having removed Lansing's baleful influence. The more he exaggerated that influence, however, the more vulnerable he became to Bainbridge Colby's interpretation of events. Meanwhile, General Alvaro Obregón, Carranza's expected successor, was doing everything he could to rid himself of an image he had once projected as an extreme socialist who left the First Chief's cabinet in 1917 because Carranza was too moderate. Hints were being dropped that the Constitution would be modified to correspond with a new attitude in Chapultepec Castle.[20]

Cunard Cummins, for example, had a most satisfactory interview with Obregón. "Regarding British properties, the anti-foreign clauses of [the] Constitution, and our other grievances," the diplomat reported to Lord Curzon, "he promises all Your Lordship would desire." Sir Auckland Geddes reported from Washington in May 1920 that American officials had taken a decided interest in Obregón's political education, entertaining him with a full tour of "the naval, military and aviation Departments. . . ." If nothing untoward happened, and Obregón was elected in July, the United States would immediately recognize his government.[21]

Nothing so smooth happened, of course. Carranza refused to leave office, and was killed while attempting to march to Veracruz to rally his old supporters. Obregón had to settle for being the power behind President Adolfo de la Huerta. Bainbridge Colby lost no time in warning Geddes that the British should stand clear until Washington gave a signal it was ready to recognize, a signal that would be turned to green only when whatever government finally emerged acknowledged that Mexico could not establish and maintain order without outside assistance. There were certain provisions in the Constitution which America could not agree to, Geddes was told, and Obregón was sending a special representative to Washington to take "soundings as to the opinion of [the] United States Government." The president considered it "most undesirable" that revolutionary governments should pass out concessions covering thousands of square miles, Colby admonished Geddes finally, in the hope of gaining foreign support. Greater stability in South America could be achieved only if it were clearly understood all around that such concessions could not be considered valid.[22]

Whatever Wilson told Colby to say to the British, Under Secretary of State Norman Davis was fully confident that Obregón knew better than to try Huerta's tactics. He felt sure, moreover, that Obregón wanted to lead Mexico badly enough to accept "almost any conditions we were disposed to ask for recognition and the resumption of friendly relations." Would the general agree to "clean out from south America completely" the propaganda bureaus Carranza had established? Davis asked Iglesias Calderón, Obregón's special agent. That would be done, came the reply. Discussion shifted to Mexican willingness "to recognize as valid all of the concessions and contracts granted by or made with previous Governments." Again the answer was yes. But certain reservations had to be made, said Calderón. Under Díaz there had been "unreasonable, onerous and illegal" concessions granted. Davis assured him that the United States would never support unreasonable claims—but the terms "onerous" and "unreasonable" were vague. What concessions did Calderón have in mind? The special agent cited the immense tracts of land awarded to Lord Cowdray. Sensing a trap, the under secretary remarked that if a concession was thought to be illegal, the fact could be established by an orderly court procedure. If justice had indeed been denied, the next step was through diplomatic channels. "To this he assented."[23]

If Calderón meant what Davis heard, then the new authorities in Mexico City were at last ready to abandon the quest to force foreign investors to become Mexican citizens and give up the right to invoke diplomatic support. Any regime willing to do that, it could be argued, would find itself with less independence than Mexico enjoyed under Porfirio Díaz. Little wonder that the oil men wanted Calderón's promises engraved in a gilt-edged treaty that would take precedence over the 1917 Constitution.[24] As for the State Department, it wanted the proposal for such a pact to emanate from Mexico City. That would alleviate problems in convincing Wilson, just as it would lessen chances that some future Carranza would repudiate the agreement as imposed by "Yankee imperialism."

In September 1920 another agent, Roberto Pesquiera, a Mexican finance expert, came to New York to talk with the International Bankers' Committee. It was an unproductive session. The bankers only wanted to berate Mexico for the past, complained Pesquiera, and to issue threats. No diplomatic recognition, they warned, until their desires were met. Norman Davis tried to assure him that no "interests or groups" could deliver the United States government. Pesquiera should not be misled: a settlement of the oil question, important as that was, would not mean

automatic recognition either. The strategy appeared to be to keep the
Mexicans guessing—but to provide well-placed hints until they themselves
came up with a treaty formula or its equivalent.[24]

At this point Wilson heard from two old friends, neither of whom was
very happy about the State Department's game. One was Henry Morgenthau, the man Wilson had selected to succeed Fletcher, an appointment
the Senate had never confirmed. He wrote that Mexican authorities were
making every effort to bring the country under control. This effort could
not succeed without American support, but Mexico's need for economic
aid as well as diplomatic recognition provided the best insurance of Mexican good behavior. The new regime was prepared to accept certain condition, but not ones dictated by the oil companies. The moment was propi-
tious, moreover, because the those now in charge feared a Republican
victory in November. Finally, recognition would put Wilson in a position
to "prevent the success of the mischief-makers and jingoes in our midst
who want war."[25]

Like Morgenthau, George Creel, former head of the Committee for
Public Information, was sure that Obregón would do whatever was
needed "instantly." Wilson's Mexican policy stood out as one of his finest
achievements. "I *know* that we can bring this policy to complete success."[26]
Interested to hear more, the president instructed Colby to send for Morgenthau to have a talk about Mexico. The ambassador-designate had no
new facts, Colby reported, but of course he was glad to get his views. All
that had been received from Mexico lately were some rather "skittish"
overtures. The Mexicans always assented to American wishes at these
meetings, he went on, but things never got beyond the talking stage.[27]

Colby did as Lansing had done but Colby was more successful. He
drew Wilson's attention elsewhere by hinting at "a good deal of veiled
strategy in the situation—propagandists, press agents, informal emissaries, oil men, attorneys and various like developments. I hope we can have
a talk with you soon about the whole situation."[28] Wilson saw Creel himself, but stuck to Colby's line. Mexico had to prove it was willing to live up
to its obligations under international law, said the president, and agree
not to make Article 27 of the Constitution retroactive. Recognition could
not be given unless all the things promised by Calderón and Pesquiera
had been acted upon favorably.[29]

Relying upon Colby's word, Wilson shifted his attention back to an
ancient foe, the Republicans. If Warren Harding were elected, he told a
friend, "and gives the country the kind of government that we have every
reason to expect we shall come very close to having a revolution in this
country and the prospects that we shall have war with Mexico is [*sic*] very
great."[30] When the Republican victory took place, Wilson convinced him-

self that the oil men were now in a position to dictate policy. Preventing them from using anything the administration did to their advantage became a reason for not doing anything. That suited Colby fine.

The State Department should not act upon suggestions "from anybody connected with the oil interests down there," cautioned Wilson:

> Pardon me if this warning is superfluous. Now that an administration is about to come in that will try to upset everything that we have done in Mexico, I feel particularly solicitous lest we should prepare the way for their mischief in any way.[31]

This letter gave the secretary of state another opportunity to repudiate any outside efforts to bring about a settlement, as somehow tied in with the lurking oil interests. "Their purpose seems to be to dangle recognition and financial support in one hand," he answered the president on November 6, 1920, "and with the other to threaten intervention." By keeping Mexican needs and fears in tandem, the oil men obviously hoped to bring about "a condition whereby they can escape adequate taxation, appropriate the wealth of Mexico for themselves, fortify their monopolies, and exercise a controlling influence in the distribution of oil throughout the world."[32]

George Creel was furious about what he saw as Colby's attempt to deceive the president. The oil interests were hard at work, yes, but not as Mr. Colby suggested. He had seen a memorandum submitted to the State Department that demanded much more than a promise that Article 27 not be made retroactive, "virtually an absolute and unconditional surrender of sovereignty to the foreign oil interests . . . [by] Mexico." Colby denied the existence of such a memorandum, Creel wrote Wilson, but the secretary would not say what department policy was; if it was not what was proposed in the alleged memorandum. Instead, rumors had been put about that he, Creel, was in the employ of the Mexican government or the oil companies, or both simultaneously. Those who wanted to "guarantee their dividends with American bayonets" were calling the tune. He feared for the future.[33]

It was a tough letter, not easily dismissed. Colby steadfastly denied these accusation. But another observer, Sir Auckland Geddes, reported to London that an oil company representative had informed the embassy that State Department officials were drawing up their own memorandum—in conjunction with the oil companies—that stipulated conditions for recognition. The general feeling, however, was that the issue would carry over for the Republicans to resolve.[34]

Creel's persistence led Wilson to summons a White House conference consisting of Colby, Norman Davis, Creel, and himself. Once again the State Department prevailed, but the president now suspected that the oil companies had penetrated the secretary's office. In response to a letter from Norman Davis recommending lifting the arms embargo so that Obregón's forces might be able to carry out pacification and demobilization, Wilson issued this valedictory warning: "Men like [Edward] Doheny and others who are deeply involved in the oil intrigues have shown more and more recently their somewhat desperate anxiety to have this embargo lifted. This fills me with suspicion and I would like very much to have a memorandum from you on that aspect of the subject. We cannot be too careful not to serve these predatory interests, because they intend the demoralization of our own politics and the control of Mexican politics."[35]

If the oil men wanted to turn back the clock to 1911, Wilson still lived in the world of 1913. He knew better, of course; he knew that that era had come to an end in 1917. Soon after the Republicans came to power determined to restore "normalcy" to American life, British chargé H. G. Chilton talked with Henry Fletcher, now installed as under secretary of state. Obregón's negative response to a new draft treaty proposal had convinced him that further negotiations were not worthwhile. "He felt that it would be an extremely bad precedent to acknowledge the head of a regime which based its reply to the American proposals on a Constitution which was Bolshevistic and confiscatory in character. To do so could but encourage other South American Republics to adopt similar measures prejudicial to the very foundation of international relations."[36]

Chilton was shown the treaty proposal. The operative clause protected property rights of "whatever nature, heretofore or hereafter acquired" against "confiscation, under constitutional provisions, legislation or executive decrees or otherwise." The draft also spelled out in detail rights claimed by American property holders prior to the promulgation of the Constitution—to avoid any "misunderstanding."[37] Accepting these terms, said Mexican foreign minister Alberto Pani, would cause a new revolution. A sovereign state could not make such a contract simply in order to obtain recognition of its right to exist. Mexico could not again become a dependency.[38]

The stalemate continued. But in 1923 the Harding administration, prodded by exporters and businessmen who felt the oil companies' fears were overdrawn, edged closer to recognition. A strangely tormented voice protested in private. "I dare say you think as I do that the present administration is finding it too easy to rely on promises of the present Mexican government," Woodrow Wilson wrote to George Creel in August 1923. "It seems to me they are still upon the quicksands."[39]

As it happens, he was right. None of the special arrangements made during the 1920s resolved the fundamental issue. In 1938 Mexico nationalized the oil industry, triggering a final confrontation with the revolution that had begun a generation earlier. World War II requirements forced an adjustment with Mexican nationalization, and another generation passed before revolution in Cuba opened an era of multiplying difficulties for Wilson's successors.

The line between the "special interests" and the national interest, Wilson's crucial criterion, had already been blurred in 1919, when the State Department under both Lansing and Colby sought a remedy for revolutionary nationalism. An interdepartmental committee studying the situation reported:

> When the development of United States petroleum interests abroad is imperilled by injurious government action, or when conditions arise in any country which endanger the lives and property of United States citizens engaged in the oil industry, the policy of the United States, while necessarily controlled by its general policy as to the protection of United States interests abroad should also be guided by the realization that the confiscation or destruction of petroleum properties controlled by United States interests or the existence of conditions which make impossible their operation, is an injury to the national interests and an injury which cannot be remedied by apologies or pecuniary compensation after the damage has occurred.[40]

Events in China also foretold a confrontation, but a conflict masked by Japanese-American competition to qualify as the successor dynasty to British hegemony.

> *There was a lot of combustible material in China and if the flames were put to it the fire could not be quenched for China had a population of four hundred million people. It was symptoms of that which filled him with anxiety.*
>
> Woodrow Wilson, April 1919

Japan gave Wilson a Hobson's choice at Paris. As American policymakers had anticipated, the Japanese effort to represent Asia at the peace conference by placing on the agenda a demand for a racial equality clause in the treaty was closely linked to a narrower quest, an implied option for the Western powers: the demand that the Shantung question be settled between Japan and China alone. It was true, of course, that to grant the latter meant equality in a certain sense, albeit a backhanded sort of equality so far as the Chinese were concerned.

China depended on American support at Paris, if that situation was to be improved. American reluctance to force a League solution of the Shantung question, and to use that as the basis for expanding Chinese sovereignty, was conditioned by many factors. Granting Japan's demand for racial equality would not only have alienated the white Dominions of the British Empire, and stirred congressional ire in the United States; it would also have undermined the entire notion of Western supervision of nonwhite areas.

The longer the debate went on, moreover, the deeper became Wilson's predicament. Japan let it be known that if the West tried to interfere in Shantung, it would not join the League of Nations. Wilson yielded. Having received promises that Japan would return the peninsula to Chinese sovereignty once its right to the German possessions had been confirmed, the president sought to assure the dissatisfied Chinese delegates that their country would still enjoy greater protection than ever before. "He, himself, was prepared to advocate at the Council of the League . . . that the special positions occupied by the various nations in China should be abandoned. Japan declared that she was ready to support this."[41]

Wellington Koo, head of the Chinese delegation, dismissed Wilson's arguments with a blunt statement that China stood at a crossroads. It wanted to travel with Europe and the United States, but if justice was denied, his country might be driven to go with the Japanese. "There was a small section in China which believed in Asia for the Asiatics and wanted the closest cooperation with Japan." Wilson bridled at this, responding in a lecturing tone he often adopted when cornered. Koo must not think that an injustice was being done, he said. The sacredness of treaties had been the starting point for the recent war. The League could not be based on a foundation of broken treaties, a reference either to Anglo-Japanese arrangements for the disposition of German possessions or to Sino-Japanese understandings—neither of which any Wilson supporter had previously put in the category of treaties to be defended by the League. But the president had more to say. China should remember that it was not only Japan that had transgressed. The solution for China now was to cooperate with the other powers in undoing the trouble (a reference, apparently, to Robert Lansing's search for a lever to pry out spheres of influence, or to Wilson's promise to make China a good example of what the League could accomplish).[42]

News of the Shantung decision sent Chinese students into the streets, the beginning of a revolution that would not come to an end for thirty years. American promises meant nothing, the Chinese prime minister told Sir John Jordan. What the Paris Peace Conference had done was to convince the Chinese that might made right, hardly the sort of atmosphere for serious negotiations to end the civil war. And hardly an inducement for China to sign the peace treaty, join the League, and wait patiently for Woodrow Wilson to launch his assault on spheres of influence.[43]

When the Shantung decision became an issue in the American debate over the treaty, Wilson met it squarely; in fact his response to critics on this question was the most forthright and candid part of the final crusade. He reminded audiences of President William McKinley's outright acquiescence in the German takeover twenty years earlier. "In the message of Mr. McKinley about this transaction, he says—I am quoting his language—that inasmuch as the powers that had taken these territories had agreed to keep the door open for our commerce, there was no reason why we should object. Just so we could trade with these stolen territories we were willing to let them be stolen." Which of the gentlemen now so aroused at China's plight, he asked, would have protested then?[44]

At another stop he went after John Hay's Open Door policy, a policy he himself had once put among the great examples of American altruism. "You have heard of Mr. Hay's policy of the open door," he began. "That was his policy of the open door—not the open door to the rights of China, but the open door to the goods of America." Until the League of Nations, there had been but one avenue into China, into the affairs of all weak nations: the imperial way, whether one called it that or the "open door."[45]

Such candor—almost unheard of then or later—availed not. The Senate would not accept Wilson's treaty and League without reservations he could not abide; and in China neither side in the civil war could accept responsibility for failure to gain absolute equality.[46] Political remedies being out of the question, the burden would have to fall on the consortium negotiations. In mid-February 1919 chargé J. V. A. MacMurray reported from Tokyo that the Japanese government had agreed to American bankers' demands that both political and industrial loans be put under the consortium. This was a major concession. British bankers had also been resisting American pressure, but the Foreign Office understood that the "only remedy" for a system of uncontrolled borrowing was to establish an international authority "enjoying a practical monopoly of loan and concession business in China."[47] Political loans were those that came under the heading of currency reform, for example, while industrial loans most often meant railroads. The distinction was difficult to maintain because they were both government loans, and would both be secured by government revenue sources. Since the days of Sir Edward Grey, suspicion had existed in British business circles that the consortium would mean less for them, a fourth share across the board, or a fifth, or even a sixth, whereas in most of the areas covered by industrial loans they had established the business, and still dominated it. The breakthrough came with J. P. Morgan's assurances that consolidation of industrial and political loans would not mean an automatic division of certain contracts in order to give each participant an equal share of the required supplies. Industrial contacts would still be put up to public tender as in the past. Theoretically, at least, the British would not lose out to newcomers because of the consortium.[48]

"I find there is great interest evidenced by every one here in the new Consortium and its operations," Thomas Lamont wrote Breckinridge Long from Paris:

> It seems to be the consensus of opinion that it is the one practical thing left which is going to prevent Japan from having a free hand in China. The Shantung decision came as a pretty hard blow and was received with the keenest disappointment on all sides. I have had any number of people say to me that unless the Consortium actually functioned as outlined, our hope for any kind of square deal in the Far East was gone.[49]

Lamont's early optimism faded when it was learned that the Japanese were now insisting that both Manchuria and Mongolia be excluded from the consortium arrangement. What good was the concession if that were the case? Lansing was ready to tell Tokyo that the other three would go ahead without Japan. Lamont indicated agreement, but asked if a three-power group really made sense. Bankers at home raised a more practical issue. Without Japan, the entire economic burden would fall upon the United States, at least until Great Britain and France were able to get on their feet. "I think we want to know beyond any doubt," one of the leading bankers wrote Breckenridge Long, "that we are ready to see things through and be able to write the last chapter as well as the first one."[50]

Things would be different after World War II, with the advent of the Marshall Plan and federal lending agencies (although not really different for China). But to reconstruct the world in the 1920s, the State Department had to rely on the bankers. American policymakers were pleasantly surprised, however, by the reappearance of one British voice on the Asian scene offering the prospect of an ally against Japan in a final showdown over the consortium. "I would not yield for one moment," declared Lord Curzon. In a series of meetings held to review the China question in the summer of 1919, the foreign secretary had delivered his own lectures to the Japanese ambassador. With these latest claims, coming on top of the Shantung demand at Paris, Japan had bitten off more than anyone could allow her to chew, Curzon declared. The days when China could be cut up or divided into spheres of influence had gone by. Twenty-five years ago the European powers, and yes, Britain too, had shown no great scruple. But the ideals and principles that now moved mankind ruled out imperial pretensions, "except insofar as . . . the natural advantages of character, propinquity, and resources" allowed. Developments inside China since the signing of the peace treaty "had produced a state of affairs . . . fraught with real danger to the peace of the East." He was not finished. The secret treaties signed during the war, said Curzon, were "equally stupid and shortsighted."[51]

Did this reflect a serious turn in British policy? asked the United States ambassador. No British objections to Sino-Japanese arrangements had been lodged earlier. All along, of course, the British had felt that once the war was over a time of reckoning would come. Concessions to Japan had always been considered necessary expedients, though a different strand of thought had often become visible when Foreign Office experts looked closely at the situation. Without a connection to Japan, the British would have to face the Americans alone; and it was by no means sure that Anglo-American interests were parallel, let alone identical.

In any event, Curzon ordered the records of his conversations with the Japanese ambassador to be made available to Washington. In the American capital at that moment a determined effort was being made to force Tokyo to concede that the Versailles Treaty superseded the Sino-Japanese treaties of 1915 and 1918, under which Japan claimed the right to deal with Shantung bilaterally. Hopefully such a statement would ease criticism of the Paris decision, but Japan had thus far shown no eagerness to comply. So Curzon's messages and exchanges were indeed welcome.[52]

Finally, after what amounted to a threat that the president would reveal everything Japan had promised at Paris, the Japanese Foreign Office stated that according to a promise "which she gave to China in 1915," Japan would restore Shantung, retaining only the economic privileges originally conceded to Germany. However benign this sounded outside Japan, it reaffirmed the validity of the 1915 and 1918 treaties. And it certainly did nothing to quiet Chinese protests, or restore confidence in the West as China's protector.[53]

Nevertheless, said Lansing (taking a leaf from John Hay's notebook), no matter how ambiguous the Japanese reply was, Wilson could now put forward exactly what Tokyo had pledged to do, and judge its performance by that standard. This the president did on August 6, 1919, producing an immediate outcry in Japan that Versailles could not supersede other treaties made in good faith, nor permit third parties to interfere in such a manner.[54]

Once again Lord Curzon rose to speak for the West, this time zeroing in on the proposal Tokyo had made for joint Sino-Japanese operation of the Shantung railway. Japanese assurances of nondiscrimination were not enough, he began. Given Tokyo's control of other railways leading to

Peking and the Yangtze Valley, he must assume that "Japan was . . . establishing a stranglehold upon the Province [Shantung] which would place it eventually and for all time under control." For that reason, he concluded abruptly, he must ask Japan to consider favorably a proposal for the internationalization "of the whole of the Chinese railways."[55]

Curzon had made a remarkable turnabout, not merely from the effacement position in 1914, but also from a decade of British resistance to suggestions from any quarter for internationalizing China's railways. The turn was stimulated in part by reports from the British Chambers of Commerce in North China, which had gone on record as saying that the Shantung decision boded ill for British and American commercial interests. The effect was not limited, moreover, to Japan's control of key railways, but was bound up with a strong possibility that China would henceforth look to Japan for leadership. The only way to forestall these dangers would be to demand abrogation of the Sino-Japanese treaties, and the internationalization of all railways.[56]

For the first time, it seemed, London was ready to back a strong American policy. But was Washington? Conflicting signals were being sent out from the American capital. Lord Curzon told Ambassador John W. Davis that a reasonable compromise would be to meet Japan's desire to exclude south Manchuria from the consortium's field of operations, but stand fast against similar demands regarding Inner Mongolia.[57]

Lansing's reply to this suggestion was negative, almost belligerent in tone. If the powers displayed their resolve, it said, Tokyo would abandon all its demands. Japan knew that it could accomplish nothing without the others. But to Viscount Earl Grey, on special mission in Washington, the secretary offered a very different definition of his policy. Anglo-American cooperation was essential, he began, if Japan was to be restrained; yet he was prepared to "concede [a] special position in Manchuria and inner Mongolia to Japan but no possession of Eastern Siberia."[58]

On the domestic front, the secretary was trying an equally complicated series of maneuvers. Lansing was now urging the consortium bankers to permit the Chicago Continental and Commercial Trust Company to go ahead with negotiations for the often-stalled loan option for $30 million, promising them that if the international bankers' negotiations did result, at last, in a new consortium, the Chicago firm would surrender the contract. This idea, like the confusing response to British diplomatic initiatives, offered both flexibility and firmness. And it gave the American consortium bankers both something to think about and something to offer in return. Hopefully, it would convince everyone involved, at home and abroad, that if the negotiations failed America would go ahead with its own policy and plans.[59]

Not trusting to bank negotiations to convey his message, Lansing then told the Japanese chargé that should Tokyo accede "immediately" to Washington's insistence that no Chinese area be formally excluded, "with the understanding that all the Japanese interests now in possession of Japan, and upon which substantial progress had been made should remain to Japan . . . , I would cause to be cancelled the thirty million dollar loan and would throw it into the Consortium."[60]

British doubts about this tactic were answered by Thomas Lamont, who advised his counterpart in the British banking group, Sir Charles Addis, that the Japanese might well buckle if they believed American financial institutions were at last prepared to "furnish industrial loans to China." The stage was set, therefore, for the British and French to give an effective push as well, by telling Japan that if after a reasonable time Tokyo's reservations had not been withdrawn, they would entertain serious proposals for a three-power consortium.[61]

The explosive charge that Lansing had been getting ready for so long never went off. It fizzled yet again. The Chicago bank discovered that the Chinese could not guarantee the salt tax would be available to insure repayment; nor had the firm's inquiries turned up evidence of investor interest. Assistant Secretary Long wanted to bluff it out, but Lansing decided at once to accept a pending British proposal for an interim four-power loan, a kind of good faith statement about the prospects of success in consortium negotiations.[62]

What an anticlimax it was to all the grand hopes for the new China policy. Painful as it was to lose out because of one bank's timidity, though, at least the State Department now knew that neither conditions in China nor interest in America justified continuing the search for a way to dismantle the Far Eastern spheres of influence, which seemed now to be more permanent than the Great Wall itself.

> *I believe that if we can get the question of the Consortium settled, it will be a long step in getting Japan in line and maintaining the peace out there, including especially friendly relations between the nations of our country and of Japan.*
>
> Thomas Lamont to Colonel House,
> February 13, 1920

Lamont's words to Colonel House upon his departure for a grand tour of the Orient as chief negotiator for the consortium accurately summarized his mission. New York had not overcome Washington, but Lansing, and even more his Republican successors, had become neutral about the Chinese revolution. While we wait to see what happens, the dominant attitude was, let's hold the line on independent action; otherwise the Orient could become the scene of the opening battles in the next war.

Although Lansing had ruled out a bluff in the Chicago loan instance, the State Department's instructions to Ambassador Morris still warned that Lamont's visit meant it was now or never for the consortium. If no agreement came out of the talks, Washington would give "our support to every proper financial concern in the United States which should wish to do business on an independent basis in China."[63]

The Japanese Foreign Office had already prepared a counterproposal, a compromise wherein Tokyo would give up claims to exclude specific areas if it could pass on proposed loans under certain categories. Such a formula would only further unsettle conditions in China, Bainbridge Colby commented; Japan should be willing to trust its partners not to make loans inimical to its interests.[64] This exchange was a further indication, however, that instead of courting Chinese nationalism, American policy had become a search for ways to avoid unsettling conditions in China. To that end, a Japanese-American understanding was essential.

Lamont proved to be an exceptionally skilled negotiator. The department's original instructions were absolutely correct and would yield results, he advised from Tokyo. His discussions with Japanese bankers had left him absolutely convinced that Japan's business interests favored cooperation with the United States. American refusal to negotiate a government-to-government formula might be coupled, therefore, with private exchanges between the bankers themselves. The details of what interests would or would not come under the scope of the consortium in certain provinces could thus be resolved without resort to a government exchange, "which might be defined as recognition of spheres of influence."[65]

In a cable that passed through the State Department, Lamont then advised J. P. Morgan that there was nothing in south Manchuria or eastern Mongolia that would lead American bankers to put money in those areas unless Japan desired to go along. Lamont may have praised the State Department's adamant position, but as this message (and the words he was preparing for the Japanese) demonstrated, the purpose of the consortium was now to cement relations among the industrial powers, not to set China free. The Wilsonians may have deluded themselves in this regard, but Lamont put the record straight. The note the banker handed the Foreign Office went farther than anything that had ever passed between Washington and Tokyo toward recognizing Japan's special position on the Asian continent. It stated that the other three groups acknowledged Japan's likely need for foodstuffs from Manchuria and wool from Mongolia, as well as the requirement for "other raw materials necessary for manufacturing. . . ." Japan's role in the community of industrial nations was to be confirmed by consortium approval for its expansion onto the Asian mainland. "Recognizing as we do these facts pertaining to your economic life," it also said, "we may say that we shall view with satisfaction Japan's economic efforts to increase the output of such commodities as we describe, for we believe that by such increased output not only will Japan's population and industries be supplied but that there should result a real and favorable economic development in certain portions of the Provinces of Manchuria and Mongolia."[66]

Whether thought of as an evil necessity or welcomed as an opening of new vistas, Lamont's achievement in finding the right method and language earned him plaudits. Doubts were met by his warning, based on the Tokyo talks, that if some serious regard was not paid to Japanese interests, the current Japanese ministry might fall and be replaced by one dedicated to a purely nationalist approach. The British Foreign Office was impressed by how well Lamont had played his cards; he had given up nothing of real importance and had gained abandonment of general claims by the Japanese. He had told Japanese bankers, "who had literally beseiged him for American loans," that "unless they accept present terms they need expect no financial assistance from America."[67]

An equally difficult assignment awaited Lamont in China. In Japan discussions had taken place on the advisability of a large administrative loan to China. According to the Japanese the money could be doled out so as to insure real progress in the disbanding of troops and negotiations for reuniting the country. "Japanese Group believe," explained Lamont, "that by following this course we can avoid another upset in Government, even peaceful revolutions being always exceedingly expensive. . . ." The only alternative, Lamont agreed, was to impose a complete financial boycott on China until it set its house in order.[68]

The banker's travels in China—he visited both Peking and Canton—convinced him that the real achievement, at least for the foreseeable future, was a Japanese-American understanding on these points. True, the Japanese were not yet a first-class power, and true also, they "ought to be down on their knees in gratitude" for being invited into partnership. But Lamont and his principals had a healthy respect for Japanese potential as a sound conservative power, one that had a vital role to play in containing revolution and turmoil. The suggestion, for example, that had emananated from the Japanese bankers about the way to dole out funds to the Chinese conditioned on progress toward stability was exactly the right sort of attitude. It demonstrated, hopefully, that Japan had turned its back on the "German" methods that had brought on war and revolution in Europe.

The German example held another lesson. The problem there had been that the German military group had dominated all political questions. If that same situation was to be avoided in Asia, if the Japanese military was to be brought under control, it was necessary not to increase its influence at a crucial time in the development of Japanese capitalism. Lamont's compromise would allow time for the civilian leaders to gain the same stature and permanence in exercising political power as their counterparts in other industrial nations. Without saying so explicitly, the American bankers were trying to provide for Japan a safe transition from feudalism to industrial liberal democracy.

Before dismissing this approach too lightly as doomed to fail, the original Wilsonians had to reconsider their own ill-fated efforts to work with revolution in Mexico and China. It could be argued in this regard that Lamont, and political leaders like Herbert Hoover and Charles Evans Hughes, saw clearly enough that the major assignment ahead was to work with threatened industrial powers, seeking to bring them into the fold of liberalism, to which end the methods of the old diplomacy could be justified.

If China proper was not the place for the consortium to begin its new tasks, there was still something to be done in northern Asia. Here also was the place to start taming the Japanese military: Siberia. If the Japanese general staff was permitted to retain its stronghold there, Lamont contended in his final report on the negotiations he had so successfully brought to a conclusion, "we shall see that great region west of the Ural mountains in [the] economic grasp of Japan and [the] most valuable market in the world closed to American manufacture and export." Still, there was no reason for pessimism. 'Gradually . . . Japan will, unless the Powers continue to give her [a] free hand in China and Siberia, swing into line and learn table manners from Western Groups."[69]

The initial project for the consortium, Lamont had been advised (and believed), should be to take over management of the former Russian-owned Chinese Eastern Railway, still under inter-Allied control as a result of the anti-Bolshevik intervention. "E. H. Harriman," John F. Stevens had told Lamont, "described the Chinese Eastern as one of the greatest possibilities of any railroad property in the world. It is true. It taps a wonderful region. It is, say, thirteen or fourteen hundred miles long. It ought to have in branch lines, or feeders, like teeth in a rake as J. J. Hill used to call them, a thousand miles more."[70]

The Chinese Eastern Railway was duly placed on the agenda for the first formal meeting of the consortium bankers, along with a list of other projects for the long range that would have effectively put China under their general trusteeship. In November 1920, then, Sir Charles Addis spoke for the hopes of the consortium founders in remarks to the British China Association:

> However much we may differ as to the value of *the* League of Nations, I suppose there is no one who would question the urgent need of *a* League of Nations. Here is one [the consortium] which has already proved its usefulness in clearing up some of the misunderstandings which keep nations apart and which, administered with prudence, may yet serve to knot closer together those who have joined it.[71]

With the consortium at last settled, both at home and internationally, Lamont and State Department officials were united in a conviction that the next step had to be the unknotting of the Anglo-Japanese alliance. If China's trust was ever to be regained (still a hope, if not a policy), that had to be done. Besides, Americans did not want an inner group functioning within the consortium. It was not big enough for that. And finally, if the Japanese military group could find refuge in the alliance, Lamont's efforts would have been for nought.[72]

Hence, after an intense period of focusing on Japan, American diplomatic efforts swung around again to British responsibility for the continued unnatural state of affairs. On August 20, 1920, Norman Davis lectured Sir Auckland Geddes on the British government's various sins. Davis contended that London had given the Japanese unqualified support in Siberia. His Majesty's Government was now going to have to decide: us or them. Geddes was equally frank in responding. Of course the alliance was an embarrassment, but Britain could not very well abandon it without some solid assurances of American support for common objectives. Davis then replied that a formal Anglo-American alliance was out of the question, but perhaps something might be arranged on the pattern of the Root-Takahira Agreement.[73]

It was hard to believe Davis was serious. Surely not. Much of the difficulty in Japanese-American relations had arisen out of misunderstandings about what the Root-Takahira and subsequent agreements, most notably the Lansing-Ishii Agreement, actually meant. But leaving that aside, why had the United States suddenly started applying pressure in this fashion so soon after Lamont's less than Wilsonian arrangement with Japan? In part the answer was that policymakers believed that leniency toward Tokyo—which made them uneasy anyway—had to be counterbalanced by a firm stance on the alliance question, or Japan would become quite unmanageable. What had been given away by the house at one table in the casino must be recouped at another. And more.

But there was an additional factor. A Bolshevik negotiator had arrived in Peking to discuss the fate of the Chinese Eastern Railway. This was a bad omen. But if a contest was looming for China's future, and if the scene of the first skirmish was to be the Chinese Eastern Railway, then time was needed to construct a liberal alternative before it was too late. Davis spent much of his time these days preaching the liberal gospel not only to British diplomats, but also to Mexican recalcitrants; now he delivered another warning. By striking at the political rights of the "true Russians" in China, he told the Chinese chargé, Peking was lending color to the belief that it was "acting as a tool of Bolshevik leaders in Moscow." Davis did not believe the accusation, of course, but China's actions were liable to be construed "as part of an attempt to strike at [the] whole structure of extra-territorial rights in China."[74]

It was an odd way to appeal to the Chinese to renounce any connections with the Bolsheviks, and it amounted, however backhandedly, to a recognition that the Russian Revolution had given the Chinese, even those reactionaries who ran things in Peking, greater leverage than ever before with the Western powers. American policymakers were soon involved in an initiative that became the Washington treaty system, a model of capitalist cooperation to complete the work of making the world safe for democracy. David Lloyd George tried a very different approach at the Genoa Conference in 1922, his final attempt to reintegrate Soviet Russia into the European system.

CHAPTER THIRTEEN

The Washington Contract

*Through the forest of black coats and white collars. I could
see in profile, motionless and sober, the distinguished head
of Mr. Balfour. As the last sentences sounded and the Anglo-Japanese Alliance publicly perished, his head fell forward on his chest exactly as if the spinal chord had been
severed. It was an amazing revelation of what the Japanese
Treaty had meant to the men of a vanished age.*

An observer at the Washington Naval Conference[1]

The Washington Naval Conference, which met between November 1921
and February 1922, was often understood (at the time and later) as the
triumph of a less exalted diplomacy than Wilson practiced at Paris. Using
the "bargaining chip" of the powerful postwar fleet under construction,
Secretary of State Charles Evans Hughes successfully negotiated the most
far-reaching disarmament agreement of the century. To achieve this goal,
however, Hughes provided assurances to the European powers and Japan
that he would deal with them about China, and not the other way around.
In other words, where the Wilsonians had sought, in a variety of ways, to
pursue an independent China policy, the Republicans fulfilled Harding's
promise to return to "normalcy" in diplomacy as well as domestic policy.

From a longer perspective, nevertheless, the Washington conference
appears to have something in common also with Wilson's efforts at the
peace conference, particularly his pledge at the time of the Shantung
decision to bring China's case before an early session of the Council of the
League of Nations. The initiative for the invitations to a disarmament
conference came from the Senate, as proposed in a resolution introduced

by Republican Progressive William E. Borah, who had opposed American entry into the League. Inside the Harding administration another concern held equal or even superior priority: the Anglo-Japanese alliance. With the Soviets bidding for China's favor, the tasks confronting American policymakers became even more complicated.

> *It is impossible for China to act through the consortium until the question of the renewal of the Anglo-Japanese Alliance is determined.*
>
> Minister Charles R. Crane, March 1921

Crane's warnings awaited the Republicans when they took over the White House and the State Department. Even though its people were starving and its government was desperate for funds, he had said in an earlier message, China would not accept the stringent terms demanded by the bankers. Altogether, the situation created by the consortium agreement had not advanced cooperation and peaceful change in China; rather it had given the Peking clique more justification for a military dictatorship, in preference to foreign overlordship.[2]

The Chinese believed that American influence in the consortium would never be great enough to control the rapacious appetites of the others. So long as the Anglo-Japanese alliance remained intact, Crane insisted, Japan would have the advantage of proximity if it came to a contest between imperial rivals. Up for renewal in 1921, the Anglo-Japanese alliance had been under study in the British Foreign Office since the end of the war, when Far Eastern expert Beilby Alston first recommended replacing it with "a union, embracing the United States, Japan, and Great Britain, pledged to rehabilitate China. . . ." Further consideration had produced a competing view that held the alliance was still needed—most likely as a protection *against* Japan, or possibly as leverage against the United States, which was in the process of building a tremendous fleet.[3]

Sir Charles Eliot put the position well. He quite agreed, he said, with Viscount Kato, who had explained to him that while it might be unnecessary to make such an alliance today if it were being proposed for the first time, if it was not renewed "the position will not be the same as if it had never been made." The really great danger in the future, thought the British diplomat, was the possibility of Japan drifting away into a pact with Germany, or even with Germany and Russia together.[4]

Alston was supported by the Board of Trade, which resented Japan's use of its "special relationship" to improve its economic position in China, although it was by no means clear how disbanding the alliance would make things much different. The anti-alliance group centered their arguments on the need to create an Anglo-American fleet in the Pacific whose mere existence would "alter the whole complexion of the Far Eastern problem." Should Japan decide either to intervene in China, or, possibly, to lead a pan-Asian movement, an Anglo-Saxon fleet would provide an essential counterweight.[5]

Such were the conclusions, also, of a Foreign Office committee that reported on January 21, 1921. Renewal of the alliance would make close relations with the United States impossible. Upon those relations depended China's rehabilitation, control of Japan's aggressive tendencies, and Britain's ability to defend its own imperial interests. This last had a special significance because of the intensifying Dominion opposition to renewal, which had grown substantially since it first appeared at the time of the last renewal ten years earlier.[6]

If Curzon had any doubts that Anglo-American relations were indeed "trembling in the balance," a recent report from Sir Auckland Geddes removed them. The ambassador had called on Secretary Hughes to discuss a minor matter relating to international rights on the Japanese-mandated island of Yap. Hughes had asked for an early answer to his note requesting British support in forcing Japan to yield to Washington's desires. Geddes said the wrong thing. The British reply, he remarked casually, would no doubt contain a reference to His Majesty's obligations to Japan. According to Sir Auckland, Hughes rose from his chair as if stabbed, his face the color of "the light rings in boiled beet-root." Veins bulging, teeth bared, voice thick, the secretary delivered a forty-five minuted tirade that commenced:

> You would not be here to speak for Britain! You would not be speaking anywhere! England would not be able to speak at all it is the Kaiser (all this in a grand crescendo moving to a shouted climax)—the Kaiser who would be heard, if America seeking nothing for herself, but to save England, had not plunged into the war and (screamed) won it!! And you speak of obligations to Japan.

The Versailles Treaty had wiped out all previous obligations, insisted Hughes; and according to Geddes, the secretary "hissed" like a stage villain that Wilson had not known of your "Secret Treaty."[7]

There matters stood on the eve of a conference with Dominion leaders in the spring of 1921. They had to be told that "we had no intention of dropping the Alliance," Lloyd George said at first in cabinet discussion.

But the real position was that the only hope rested in enticing President Harding to summon a Pacific Conference where Britain, the United States, and Japan could seek to sort out all the debris left from the prewar era and find the basis for a new political arrangement, if not a formal written treaty. Isolating Japan would be a most dangerous error, he said, very likely producing instead a Russo-German-Japanese combine. "Frankly," he also admitted, "I like the Japanese."[8]

Efforts to entice Hughes and Harding on that basis failed. On the day after Lloyd George outlined his strategy, a Foreign Office representative spoke to Under Secretary Henry Fletcher. "[O]ften when they had a bad elephant in India," explained Arthur Willert, "they put him between two good elephants to make him behave, and that might be tried in the case of Japan." Fletcher made it clear that tales from the British raj held no interest for Americans.[9]

In every discussion, American officials put abrogation of the Anglo-Japanese alliance first, after which many things were possible, including naval disarmament and even a tripartite declaration of policy. In Lloyd George's mind these topics were elevated into a formal agenda for a Pacific Conference. One of the chief reasons he desired such a meeting, the prime minister told the new American ambassador, George Harvey, "was to wipe out the alliance without offending Japan." The king had sought him out also, reported Harvey, to say that while Japan had done all that had been asked of her—and while there was a certain embarrassment involved in liquidating the pact—"I want to say to you plainly that we are not going to have that treaty. Just how or when we can rid ourselves of it, I do not pretend to know but we are going to do it."[10]

The prime minister's intention, whatever motivated the king, was to secure a two-level conference. The first, a political conference, would meet in London, to be followed by a naval disarmament meeting in Washington. That way, presumably, a substitute for the Anglo-Japanese alliance could be worked out that would make it unnecessary to lose any of the advantages of the old diplomacy while the new was still too young to stand on its own feet. Delighted with Harding's decision to summon a naval conference, the prime minister was soon disabused of the notion that the United States would take part in a preliminary tête-à-tête in London. Worse still, London learned the facts of life secondhand, from Paris. The French had been invited to Washington, Lord Curzon was informed, to discuss both political and disarmament questions—and had accepted. Italy had been invited, and had likewise accepted. Holland had been left out, and was unhappy. China had been asked to attend and wanted to know if the alliance would be taken up. Japan had accepted, but with the reservation that it would only talk about disarmament. Curzon, the strongest pro-alliance member of the war cabinet, apparently thought London-Washington consultations were still in progress about the nature of the meeting to be held. This is what one would expect, he seethed, from people "who have no experience in diplomacy."[11]

Winston Churchill advised the prime minister not to send a British delegation. To be put on the same level with France and Italy in regard to Asian affairs was intolerable. Lloyd George thought the same thing. A meeting attended by such a "mob of delegates" with only a remote concern in the big issues and quite ready to give away British interests "not merely in the Pacific but in the command of the sea, that would be fatal to our interests. . . . [T]he British Empire must not be given away."[12]

The more they learned about the proposed agenda, the more British policymakers came to suspect that the "misunderstanding" about the status of the conference was intentional. It had been expanded to include internal Chinese questions. Prospects for success were dim. "It will not be easy to rebuild China in sections or compartments," read a skeptical Foreign Office memorandum, "or to leave her partially free and partially in chains. At any rate all the chains will be violently rattled before they are either left on her atrophied limbs or struck off."[13]

Even Beilby Alston thought he detected an ominous change in Washington's aspirations. It was not simply that the Americans were trying to do too much. Britain had become the enemy. He saw evidence everywhere, including in reports of American missionary attitudes in China. The missionaries were going out of their way to belittle everything British. "The only wholly virtuous and disinterested country is America, which waged no opium wars, grabbed no Chinese territory nor ever attempted to oppress the helpless downtrodden black and yellow man throughout the world, as do the British. Owing to the large sums of money—Rockefeller's millions, for instance—on which American schools and missions can draw, it seems hopeless for us to attempt to compete, but, if we care not to be relegated entirely to the background, much greater efforts than have been made heretofore will have to be put forth in order to maintain a hold on the Chinese mind, and our proper share of recognition as a Power to be reckoned with."[14]

But before Auckland Geddes could deliver an "ultimatum" barring discussion of the Anglo-Japanese treaty in front of a "mob of delegates," Secretary Hughes surprised him by saying that there would have to be private tripartite conversations apart from all the other discussions. Geddes was surprised, but not optimistic. The Americans were determined to put Japan in its place, and would listen to none of his warnings against blunt confrontation, or to his argument that Tokyo might be behaving the way it did because it feared the United States. Japan had ample opportunity economically, insisted Hughes, and would not think about pretexts for aggressive action unless it "found support in the attitude of Great Britain."[15]

The Americans, always a puzzling lot, seemed to be outdoing themselves. Having just negotiated a very much less than perfect consortium agreement with Japan, and having welcomed the Japanese to the table filled with Chinese goodies, they were now taking their displeasure out on London. How was this to be explained, except in terms of a long-range plan in the works. Japan had been coddled, in preparation for the real confrontation with Great Britain.

More so even than Lansing had been before, Hughes seemed to be rigidly set upon his course. Certainly he pursued it without ambiguity. From the British point of view, then, the Washington Naval Conference shaped up as a very dangerous affair. Lord Curzon told his colleagues that the strategy must be to limit discussion to disarmament and a tripartite declaration. Encouraged by the Americans, however, the Chinese had decided to bring Shantung to Washington. When that topic was introduced, all chance of private diplomacy among the powers would disappear. Hence the foreign secretary worked on the Chinese minister in London:

> China would do well to recognize the fact that at her very doors lay a powerful, highly organized ambitious State, whose population must inevitably overflow the territories which they at present occupy, and which would be driven to impinge upon its neighbors. Would it not be sound statesmanship to steer Japan away from the great industrial areas of China proper, and push her—so to speak—to the north . . . ?[16]

That was what his inclination would be, concluded Curzon, if he were a "Chinaman." Very different was this advice, with its insistence that China's welfare would be served by the unity of the great powers, than what he had been offering in the summer of 1919. Reality had set in. It was now apparent that the temporary effacement policy of Sir Edward Grey might be the only permanent way not simply of limiting Japan, but of preventing the Americans from doing some very foolish things. According to reports from Beilby Alston, moreover, Japanese diplomats in China were saying that if China brought up spheres of influence, their government would call upon Great Britain to surrender its privileged position in the Yangtze, France its privileges in Yunnan, and both powers plus the United States their control of Chinese customs, tax revenues, and other special rights.[17]

Clearly, someone had to save the Americans from themselves. On board ship Arthur Balfour, who led the British delegation, drafted two proposals calling for a tripartite agreement and a more general international protectorate for China. British notes of the single preliminary discussion Hughes granted indicated a favorable reception for these ideas, and a willingness to grant the existence of certain "existing facts, e.g., in Manchuria."[18]

Hughes's own notes reveal a very different emphasis. Listing the Anglo-Japanese alliance, the Root-Takahira agreement, and the Lansing-Ishii agreement, the secretary said that at the conclusion of the conference he wanted to be able to say to the United States Senate that the past had been swept away—not only the Anglo-Japanese alliance, but all the imperfections in America's record as well.[19]

> *We are taking perhaps the greatest forward step in history to establish the reign of peace.*
>
> Charles Evans Hughes
> on the Washington Naval Conference

Skeptics and critics alike were stunned by Hughes's opening speech to the conference. Calling for a ten-year naval holiday and a drastic limitation on numbers of capital ships, the secretary promised America would lead the way. Aside from everything else, the speech established him as the conference's real leader, one who just might pull off everything he had promised. In private, however, he continued to assure delegations from the West and Japan that he did not intend to play up to Chinese nationalism. America's ultimate goals for China might be very different from those of the others—who could ever say for sure?—but the secretary wanted it known that he was not naive about the prospects of stability in China in the immediate future.

China's internal discord actually helped Hughes establish a mediatory role. Thus when China's delegates presented a list of demands at the public sessions, America responded through Elihu Root at the subcommittee level with a strong affirmation of broad principles. But private assurances were also given to the Japanese that these did not apply to certain of their holdings in Manchuria.[20]

Diplomacy moved quickly, with Hughes setting the pace at all levels and inside each conference room. On November 28, 1921, for example, he told Arthur Balfour that he had approved a Japanese draft of a tripartite arrangement to replace the Anglo-Japanese alliance. He had added two modifications, however, the more significant being his insistence that France be included. This was necessary, Hughes explained, to obtain Senate approval, which an enlarged Anglo-Japanese alliance could otherwise never do. The proposed pact would not contain specific obligations, merely require the signers to consult in case of a threat to the peace. However it would function, on the other hand, there was a world of difference between three powers and four. With four it would be possible to mobilize a majority, something not thinkable in a two-party or even a three-party arrangement.[21]

Both Japan and Great Britain had been outflanked. The invitation to France, which Paris could hardly refuse, put terrific pressure on the others to go along. Signed on December 13, 1921, the Four-Power Treaty was then used by Hughes to persuade the Japanese that they were really equal, even though he wanted them to accept an inferior position in the disarmament treaty negotiations. The Five-Power Treaty that resulted from these negotiations set the ratio in capital ships at 5:5:3 for the United States, Great Britain, and Japan and 1.75 each for France and Italy. By separating political and military issues in this fashion, Hughes had further weakened the possibility of a revived "special relationship" between Britain and Japan. The third pact, the Nine-Power Treaty, also served a dual purpose. It pledged all the attending powers to support of John Hay's Open Door policy and, in doing so, set them up as stockholders with watchdog powers over management. It was like the League of Nations in miniature.[22]

Equally impressive was Hughes's management of the vexatious Shantung question. Although several State Department aides believed he gave away too much, the secretary persuaded the Chinese that there would never be a better time to settle. Any agreement reached under the auspices of this conference, he suggested, was bound to last. It would have the highest sanction and the firmest foundation. Japan had agreed to accept Chinese Treasury notes, and a fifteen-year repayment period, to bring to an end the impasse over the Shantung railway. How could China gain control of the line any sooner?

> If we were dealing with business men and great corporate interests, and not with nations, I should say that any lawyer who permitted his client under similar circumstances to lose such a chance, would be worthy of the sharpest condemnation and would receive it.[23]

Not having been exposed to Secretary Hughes's spellbinding performance, Lord Curzon remained skeptical about the practical application of the Washington treaties. They could be construed, said a Foreign Office minute, as prohibiting any power from taking action to protect its rights.[24] Well, of course, that was the problem. What would Hughes do when it came time to end the juggling act? No one could predict what would happen inside China. The treaties stood in some respects to China as the Platt Amendment did to Cuba. But in each instance, American policymakers thought they were devising a postimperialist blueprint flexible enough to permit nationalist shoots to grow safely, protected against the storms of revolution and war, espaliered along the wall of capitalist liberalism.

Even before the conference ended there were unhappy signs that all was not well. Hughes had pressed the Chinese to accept an American-sponsored plan for international control of the Chinese Eastern Railway. But in Peking the representative of the Soviet Union had warned American minister Jacob Gould Schurman that the question was one to be settled between Moscow and Peking. The Soviet government, he said, would not recognize "any infraction of the rights of the Russian working-man which may be adopted [at Washington] without the knowledge of the government which represents his will. . . ." Cumbersome, perhaps, but this assertion of class diplomacy over dollar diplomacy pointed up the need for a united front among the capitalist powers, a key factor in the origins of the Washington conference. It was essential to match terms, not an easy assignment, and to stand together behind any offer. In this case, the Russians had offered an outright return of the railroad to China, free of any charge, stipulating only that China must not surrender it in whole or in part to any third power.[25]

If he was frank with himself, Hughes knew that his offer had much less to recommend it. He could caution the Chinese about the "questionable validity" of any agreement with the Soviets, and predict the wrathful response of the "Powers to any attempt to nullify" their rights. But he could not go too far in that direction without provoking an already aroused Chinese nationalism—another reason for holding the Washington conference. Schurman tried a more subtle approach, reminding the Chinese foreign minister that China would need money to finance the running of the railroad—only to receive the unsubtle reply that China could find what it needed outside the consortium. Instructed to try again, the minister told Chinese officials that "the Powers would deplore using pressure against China and . . . hoped that China would voluntarily request cooperation." He also remarked that Washington should have shown China the advantages of meeting the powers around the council table, a reference to the terms of the Shantung settlement. But still there was no response.[26]

In May 1922 the consortium council met in London, and resolved to abstain from political interference in China. It would concentrate first on

railways. "Provided adequate security can be obtained there seems to be
no reason why the further development of railway communication in
China, in itself a potent means of unification should wait upon the solution of her administrative problem.[27] But what if there were no administration at all? The same month that the council resolved to remain aloof
from Chinese politics, there were as many as twenty factions vying for
control in Peking, and separate regimes in Mukden and Canton. The
scene resembled nothing so much as the croquet game in *Alice in Wonder-
land,* when the mallets curled up and the balls unrolled.

The threatened anarchy in China only increased fears in London,
however, of a headlong rush of Chinese nationalism against the war-
weakened barriers protecting foreigners. Now that the Chinese had seen
how easy it was to extract concessions from Washington, complained British Foreign Office advisers to Curzon, concessions far beyond what they
might expect from normal channels, the Chinese might next question
"the authority and prestige of the Diplomatic Corps at Peking, which the
Chinese Government should be taught to respect as the chief advisers of
the Powers from whom there is no higher court of Appeal." The place to
begin correcting this error, however, was not Peking, but Washington.
"While for the moment economically all the advantages lie with the
Americans," observed "old China hand" Victor Wellesley, "their ignorance and lack of experience in dealing with orientals both politically and
economically unfit them for taking the leading part at any rate for a long
time to come, in the destinies of the Far East, and it ought not to be
difficult for us in spite of the manifest disadvantages resulting from the
war to retain our leadership if the problem is tactfully and discreetly
handled."[28]

He would soon have his opportunity to find out.

> *I have always assumed [that the consortium] quite
> consciously recognized that banking transactions are
> not mere adventitious opportunities to sell the use of
> money.*
>
> Charles Evans Hughes to Thomas Lamont,
> April 1922

When the Washington conference broke up there was also pending a
Chinese loan request for $100 million, to be secured by the salt tax and
customs revenues to guarantee that they would be paid. In this instance,
however, the American group saw an opportunity not only to be assured

of repayment on new loans, but also to recoup losses from the prewar era. J. P. Morgan & Company, the spokesman for both the first and second consortium groups, advised the State Department that it opposed consideration of the Chinese proposal because it lacked a provision to pay American bondholders for losses suffered in previous China ventures. "It must be clear that we cannot consider operation under which we should be guilty of completely neglecting [the] interests of investors holding bonds in default."[29]

Hughes's assistants in the State Department were appalled at the narrow focus of the bankers, and convinced the secretary to send a fifteen-page letter to New York. It was time to impress upon the financiers, said J. V. A. MacMurray, that they had responsibilities to the American business community in general. Surely part of their duty was to see to it that Americans were able to avail themselves "of the opportunity for commercial expansion in the remaining undeveloped markets of the world." The bankers had known about China's unsettled condition, and that there was a long climb ahead. But American trade and industry demanded new outlets, and "our financial interests must cooperate with them if they are to preserve healthy conditions for their own growth." Nor did their duty end there. "The existence of a Consortium has . . . become an integral part of the international political situation which we are congratulating ourselves upon having established in the Far East."[30]

MacMurray was joined by Stanley K. Hornbeck, who complained that the bankers simply lacked "an adequate conception of the present as a moment of special opportunity for themselves, with their money, and with the public's money, to build a great financial port of entry for American influence and commerce in the new 'far West' of Eastern Asia." New York's timidity (or cupidity) was incomprehensible in Peking, agreed Minister Schurman. Unless the American bankers seized the reins in the consortium, not only would American business suffer, but the old "competitive system" would storm back, to trample out what progress had been made. It was not good enough to say that China must first unify itself. The fact was that Peking could not order the tuchuns and warlords to put down their arms. "To realize the situation by analogy let us suppose that in the days of Boss Tweed the city government he gave New York had been moved by some foreign influence to protest against the Boss system, to demand the Boss's withdrawal, and the dispersal of the army of heelers he maintained to corrupt the electorate and stuff the ballot boxes." But all that mattered very little, Schurman continued. The customs would still be collected by foreigners, who would, in turn, continue to pay China's obligations even if Peking disappeared from the face of the earth. "The obvious comment in Peking is that when bonds of the Chinese Govern-

ment are gilt-edged, the Consortium will not need to float them." State
Department officials carefully marked all the critical passages in Schurman's letter, and forwarded it, under Hughes' signature, to Thomas Lamont's special attention.[31]

At about the same time a new loan proposal arrived from China. In
two parts, it asked first for a $2 to $4 million monthly advance over a
period of six months, and second for a $100 million loan to finance all the
unsecured debt. British officials, who had been wary of the earlier proposal because any loan secured by customs was a form of tax on trade,
now did an abrupt about-face.[32] In the first place, the new proposal called
for putting the unsecured debt on the salt tax rather than on a customs
increase. But there was a more important difference. "The Bolshevik
Government is now represented at Peking by an agent of particularly
dangerous type in the shape of Mr. [Adolph] Joffe." If China was not
helped along the path of righteousness by getting aid in meeting its pressing financial needs, there was a good chance that its unpaid troops and
civil servants would fall prey to Bolshevik propaganda. "But for this profound change of circumstances," said Victor Wellesley, "I would have
preferred to await the result of the next struggle. . . ."[33] It was decided
that someone must go to Washington to get things moving. Wellesley got
the job. It would have to be handled very delicately, he wrote, for "any
suspicion on the part of the Americans that we were trying to knobble
them would be fatal."[34]

But the American bankers had dug in against Washington's pressure,
even though the new Chinese proposal had seemed to carry the promise
of repayment on old loans. Lamont tried not to have a confrontation,
however, with the secretary of state. As for the assertion he had heard in
the State Department that the Japanese were leading the bankers by the
nose, Lamont told Hughes, he could only repeat what he had recently
told the head of the Yokohama Specie Bank about the American view. No
loan was likely at the present time, but the consortium should not break
off negotiations. Things might take a sudden turn for the better, who
could tell? Thus far, he ended, the Japanese had shown a good disposition "to play the game."[35]

By whose rules was the game being played? wondered China experts
in the department. The consortium's attitude no doubt influenced the
administration's rejection of a proposal submitted by the National City
Bank for loaning $20 million to a Japanese organization, the Oriental
Development Company. Proceeds of this loan were to be used in projects
in the South Seas, Singapore, Manchuria, and Mongolia. The Far Eastern
Division of the State Department collaborated on a memorandum to
Hughes that asserted the money would be spent to the detriment of

American enterprise in third countries. Tokyo had played this game before; it had improvised its own rules and sought to turn the Anglo-Japanese alliance into a "foreign capital and Japanese brains" team for exploiting China. Now Japanese leaders wanted the Americans to play.

Had the consortium been active, it seems less likely that the Far Eastern Division would have been so agitated. As it was, the National City Bank project highlighted for policy planners "a line of conflict, clearly drawn, between American ideals and policy and Japanese intentions and practices. . . ." What MacMurray, Hornbeck, and Schurman had been arguing was a political question, though it was put in economic terms. If the bankers could not combine service to capitalism and to "nationalist" revolution, the field would be left to the forces alien to American-style liberalism: Bolshevism or Japanese-led pan-Asianism. "Japan is steadily entrenching herself," predicted the Far Eastern Division's memorandum, "against the day when she may bid defiance to those governments, especially the American, which advocate respect for the territorial integrity and sovereignty of China and for the open door. . . ."[36]

When Victor Wellesley arrived, the New York–Washington dispute was near its height. He found himself preaching to the convinced in the State Department. Traveling north, he found New York apathetic. The bankers could not even be roused, Sir Victor reported to Curzon, "by the remark that, after all, it was an American policy that we were trying to support." Looking for the answer, the British expert thought he perceived it in friction within the American banking group. Mr. Lamont, he understood, no longer called the shots. "In fact," Wellesley remarked, "he has lost his grip."[37]

Lamont's grip was firm enough. During all the years he had been watching events in China, began his reply to the barrage of State Department letters, he had looked in vain for the appearance of a strong man, or men, who could by wisdom, force, and patriotism begin to lift that huge country out of its morass. "I almost despair that he or they will ever come." Perhaps China's future was destined otherwise. Perhaps it would be determined by the autonomous provinces, whose interest in a central government would be minimal. And perhaps, also, that would not be so bad for all concerned. But it was impossible for American banks to lock up their capital waiting for China to work out its salvation. Neither could they commend Chinese promises to American investors to pay unless these were backed up by "definite liens upon free and assured revenues, or liens upon constructive enterprises. . . ."[38]

These assertions of the primacy of banking considerations marked a significant turning point in the 1920s. Much as they had hoped (as had Lamont) for a Chinese renaissance, the State Department now fell back before what seemed to be reality. At the Washington conference, American policymakers, even Hughes, had assumed they were integrating the consortium into a streamlined Wilsonian policy. They had also hoped, in a somewhat less self-conscious fashion, to complete the integration of political ideology and economic thought among the capitalist powers, and between those powers and undeveloped areas. They were prodded along, as noted, by the appearance of Soviet representatives and influence in China. But now events unforeseen by either Lamont or Hughes set American policy in a different direction.

> *It is our wish to make every American feel perfectly safe in coming into the Yangtze valley to live or to transact business, until such time as the Chinese themselves are able to afford these guarantees—guarantees which every Chinese citizen freely enjoys in America.*
>
> Rear Admiral W. W. Phelps,
> Commander of the American Yangtze Patrol Force,
> September 1, 1923

On May 6, 1923, bandits held up an express train near Lin-ch'eng in Shantung, took nineteen foreign passengers hostage, and held them for ransom. Consortium representatives in Peking called it the "gravest act of barbarism since [the] Boxer siege." Upon further consideration, however, it was decided that the affair offered an opportunity to demand effective control of China's modernization. "It appears to us that the powers have a great opportunity now of putting an end to military misgovernment in this country, which is a rapidly increasing danger to life and property, and is a fundamental obstacle to any attempt at reform."[39]

Thus far consortium representatives and their home offices had never agreed on prospects for China loans. The kidnapping incident did suggest to some that it was time to redefine the results of the Washington Naval Conference: concessions to Chinese nationalism had produced nothing but woe (though so far these had barely touched Western rights in China), and had shown the need to abandon the "new diplomacy" in favor of a frankly "trustee" policy. Schurman reported that sentiment was running in favor of drastic action: "Even the sweeping away of the Chinese Government and the setting up of an international agency is seriously discussed." What would Washington think, he asked, about creating a foreign force to prevent future outrages of this sort?[40]

Gunboat patrols had been in existence since the days of the Boxer

Rebellion, but the thought of an international police force to keep order on Chinese railroads was a quantum leap for the consortium. "The present seems a favorable time," group representatives in Peking were advised, "for an attempt to overcome the Chinese objection to an amalgamated railway system under effective foreign managers and technical experts. We think this may be done by proposing the increase of foreign supervision over each individual line with a view to a composite railway loan secured on the revenues of all Government railways."[41]

If New York had reversed itself, and now wanted to do something big, so had Washington. After consulting with President Harding, Hughes instructed Schurman that American participation in such a fanciful scheme would be unwise. It was bound to fail. And when it did, all that would be left was Chinese bitterness against all foreign interests; or, if that did not happen, the scheme would require such compromises that American national interests would suffer. The secretary did not elaborate on this last point, but went ahead to suggest that the administration did not oppose using force for a specific object, if that would enhance foreign prestige in China. Possibly certain railways could be occupied for a time. What did the minister think of this alternative?

Very little, it appeared. A general plan was the only way to solve the problem of warlordism. An international board of audit might, as a first step, be imposed on the Chinese railways, said Schurman's reply. "This would strike at [the] tap root of militarism and, therefore, militarists who set up and pull down cabinets and even presidents who opposed the plan. Students and champions of unabridged sovereignty of China will also oppose it."[42]

Whether stated in Hughes's objections or in Jacob Gould Schurman's affirmations of this latest "internationalization" plan, American policy toward the Chinese revolution had come full circle since the days of Wilson. Lin-ch'eng was a blessing in disguise, insisted Victor Wellesley, who was not at all troubled that high policy could be altered by such an incident, in a manner reminiscent of the interventions of the imperial era. "At last," he exulted, "we have got the Consortium to work & can give it our blessing." He even pressed Sir Charles Addis, head of the British group, to take a look at the entire China landscape to see if there were not "new and hitherto untried sources of revenue" that might be "particularly suitable for foreign control." The outlook for intergroup cooperation had never seemed brighter, and refocusing the China question in this direction would also lessen pressure on the tariff issue.[43]

Support for strong action was also voiced by the British Federation of Industries. Despite years of disorder, its director, R. T. Nugent, wrote Curzon, the China trade had held up well. But the kidnapping outrage

endangered the British commercial position. The federation would, consequently, favor creating a special gendarmerie, trained and commanded
by competent foreign officers, to keep the main trade routes open.[44]

"Nothing can be more fatal than a display of weakness," concurred
Wellesley. "The prestige of the European races has been steadily declining in the Far East ever since the Russo-Japanese War and it has suffered
a severe blow as the result of the Great War. It has never been at a lower
ebb than at present. We of all nations, with our enormous political and
economic interests in Asia can least afford to risk a rebuff at the hands of
the Chinese and expose our impotency to the whole world." An international police force, he reminded colleagues, would also put a check on the
ever-present danger that Japan might jump the traces in hopes of leading
Asia against the world. For that reason, of course, it would be difficult to
line up Tokyo. And the Americans were, as usual, standoffish, though
relying as much as the rest upon special privileges from the past. But the
attempt had to be made to find a unified policy. "All that is necessary is to
grasp the nettle firmly."[45]

Willingness to grasp the nettle was not enough. Neither Washington
nor Tokyo was prepared to support a British initiative. British prestige
was bound to suffer the most when it became known that its plan had
been rejected by the others. "[W]hereas in the days gone by we could
make things uncomfortable for China," lamented Foreign Office official
J. F. Brenan, "or the Chinese thought we could, they now know that we
are not really prepared to do anything, and have called the bluff."[46]

In the aftermath of the Lin-ch'eng affair, Wellesley pondered a very
different approach to China, possibly a conference of warlords. That
might be the only way to avoid future trouble. Indeed, Sun Yat-sen was
already threatening action against the customs houses in the areas he
controlled. British investments in China were of the magnitude of more
than £120 million, broken down in Sir Victor's calculations into £11 million in railways, £16 million in other loans, and nearly £100 million annually in trade. "Were it not for the danger to these interests, the internal
troubles of China might leave us unconcerned." As he saw it, the only
alternative was to summon a conference of the warlords, to see "what
common ground exists between them." At first sight the chances for anything significant emerging seemed remote. Yet the tuchuns were motivated by personal ambition and the desire to accumulate wealth. If the
capitalist powers were stymied, so were they. The costs of maintaining
their armies and the fear of defeat were mounting, making it less and less
possible for them to go on. "To use a Chinese expression, they are 'riding
a tiger' and are at a loss to know how to approach the problem."

The capitalist powers had two things to offer. They could promise financial assistance, by a distribution of the customs and salt revenues among the provinces, and security from attack. Put the warlords on salary, in other words. It had been tried successfully in India—still worked, in fact. The more he turned these thoughts over, the better Wellesley liked the idea. It was a corrective to recent overmeddling in Chinese affairs—prompted by an unnamed power. "The more one examines the problem the more one becomes impressed with the view that there is substantial justice in the demands of the Provinces for a share of the revenues, a principle which was always recognized and acted upon until the disappearance of the Manchu Dynasty, and that it will be impossible for the Powers in the long run to continue to bolster up an unrecognized Central Government at the expense of the Provinces."[47]

The idea that modern nationalism could be contained within a conclave of warlords was a novel solution, perhaps, but not entirely remote from Lloyd George's proposal that emerged at the Paris Peace Conference for summoning the Russian "tuchuns" to Prinkipo. And it was at least distantly related to aspects of Wilson's handling of the Mexican Revolution. In order to give the warlords their annual stipends it would be necessary to meddle in Chinese affairs, however, so that the revenues could be collected according to ways set down in the Boxer protocols that granted the foreign powers control of Chinese customs and certain taxes.

Relegating Sun Yat-sen to tuchun status was psychologically satisfying as well. Let him hold his principality and do with it what he liked, so long as the general order remained unchanged. The transformation of China's image in Washington from a modernizing power into several practically autonomous "Indian states" thus had appeal, not only because of the obvious difficulty all the foreign powers had experienced since the end of the war, but because it promised to head off future trouble with a Chinese leader whose ambitions might exceed the proper grasp of a native prince.

Sun Yat-sen was not oblivious to all the signs. Sometime previous to the Lin-ch'eng incident Jacob Gould Schurman had traveled to Canton and heard a startling proposal from Sun. The Kuomintang leader urged the United States to take the lead in calling for a joint military intervention that would extend to all the provincial capitals. Schurman did not need to refer the idea to Washington; the answer was no. The kidnapping "outrage" gave Sun an opportunity to recast his proposal as a general manifesto to the great powers. That "deplorable bandit" attack had occurred, said his declaration, because the great powers had thrown in their lot with the militarists. "Unconsciously, perhaps, they have thus done something which they have professed they would not do, that is, intervened in China's internal affairs by practically imposing on the country a government repudiated by it." The only way to rectify this situation was for them to withdraw recognition from Peking, and continue to withold it until a government was established that was truly representative.[48]

Schurman acknowledged it was an adroit maneuver. A later Kuomintang leader, Chiang Kai-shek, would propose something similar to Americans during World War II: a major campaign in China that would not only defeat the Japanese, but eradicate Communist opposition to his government. But, as in that later era, Washington declined the offer.[49]

The manifesto having failed, as Sun no doubt knew it would, Canton sent a note to the diplomatic corps on September 5, 1923, protesting the customs administration and outlining what it could do with its share of the proceeds if the monies were fairly distributed—roads, currency reform, river conservancy projects, suppression of piracy, and purchases of armored launches.

Another adroit maneuver—and equally unacceptable. As far as any great threat to close down the customs houses and levy special taxes in their place on foreign trade, Hughes had one position. "[T]his Government would of course regard such action as subversion of the treaty basis of foreign trade with China." The Washington conference, it now appeared beyond a shadow of doubt, had not repealed the Boxer Rebellion treaty system.[50] On December 1, 1923, the American chargé in China reported that the signers of the Five-Power Treaty—all but Japan—had agreed that if Sun attempted to make good his threat, a naval demonstration would have to take place. J. V. A. MacMurray, once the leading champion of Paul Reinsch's legacy of working with Chinese nationalism, fully agreed. With their vast interests in China, he advised Secretary Hughes, the British could not permit the customs to be disrupted. "Our interests are similar in principle; and it is believed that it would be unwise to admit tacitly a lesser interest in the question through taking a course of action substantially different or decidedly weaker than the British will unquestionably pursue." Sun's charade would collapse, he predicted, if the foreign powers stood together.[51]

Holding aloof at this time would create the impression that the United States was content to play a lesser role in Chinese affairs than Italy. Hughes explained all this to President Calvin Coolidge, who replied, "I think the naval units should be sent."[52] One question had been settled, at least for the time being: America was one of the great powers, not their tutor. More than that, however, it now saw China through the eyes of a great power. Schurman traveled again to Canton to see if Sun was willing to listen to reason. He impressed the American as bent on martyrdom. All the more reason, the minister reported home, to prevent even a single day's disruption of the customs. Actually, Sun made a counterproposal that Schurman chose to withhold for a time. He did not again ask for an

American-led military expedition against the provinces, but he did want Hughes to summon a conference—this time inside China—of Chinese leaders. The minister had replied only that the American people and government were opposed to intervention in the domestic affairs of other nations.[53]

Sun's threat to halt the customs collection faded before the counter-threat of a naval demonstration. A decade had passed since Woodrow Wilson had brought to an end American participation in the first China consortium, explaining that its conditions for loans touched very closely the administrative independence of China itself. "The awakening of the people of China to a consciousness of their responsibilities under free government," he said then, "is the most significant, if not the most momentuous, event of our generation. With this movement and aspiration the American people are in profound sympathy."[54]

CHAPTER FOURTEEN

Hard Road to a Stalemate

We must show Labour that the Government mean to be masters, I need hardly say this Government, but government of the land; but we must carry with us every phrase of rational sane well-ordered opinion. . . . There must be no suspicion that we are utilizing conditions in order to carry out or to return to a reactionary regime.

David Lloyd George, private letter,
September 1920

Peace with Soviet Russia had become the prime minister's dominant theme, the key to maintaining peace at home and himself in power. Every setback he took not as evidence of the impossibility of his task, but of the stupid shortsightedness of critics. He even began to see himself as both arbiter between factions within the Soviet government and peacemaker among the former Allies, on top of his role as master of domestic political affairs.

When Russian delegates returned to London in early August to continue the suspended trade talks, anti-Soviet feelings ran high. The Red Army was pressing forward toward Warsaw. At the second Comintern congress in Moscow, Lenin was predicting that Polish workers would greet the army's arrival as a sign for a general uprising. With the prospect of the Russian Revolution once again becoming the European revolution—if not indeed the world revolution—the Anglo-Russian negotiations took on sinister overtones of deceit and betrayal.

General Sir Henry Wilson, chief of the imperial general staff, told his minister, War secretary Winston Churchill, that "we soldiers might have to take action." Churchill agreed that the prime minister's attitude gave cause for concern. "[I]t will take some explaining to ease my mind of the suspicion that LG is a traitor," Wilson confided to his diary.[1] Few would go that far, but even the prime minister's closest friends were concerned about his risk-taking.

> *There has been too much concerning all this as conferring a boon on Bolshevik Russia.*
>
> David Lloyd George to the cabinet, November 1920

At the time a message came in from Moscow agreeing to British conditions for resuming the trade talks, British industrial production had fallen by over 18 percent and unemployment had risen to 22 percent of those insured. Even those who encouraged anti-Soviet hysteria could never quite forget that before the war Russia had provided Britain with a £27 million market. That was Lloyd George's ace in the hole. But it was the only one he held.[2]

"This is a great occasion," the prime minister said of the about-to-be-resumed negotiations. A friend, Lord Riddell, asked if it was all so simple. Had the Russians agreed to cease propaganda? Lloyd George brushed that aside as no longer worthy of comment: "I don't think that arises now." Riddell was not to be hushed up. Lenin was out to destroy civilization, he said. "No doubt Lenin is thinking of the day when he will string you up to a lamp-post in Whitehall!" Perhaps he was, mused the prime minister, but the Bolsheviks were bound to quarrel and fall out. Krasin, the leader of the delegation, was not a Bolshevik at all.[3]

Nevertheless, when the talks began on August 4, 1920, Lloyd George led off with an ultimatum. If Moscow did not accept an armistice in three days' time in the Russo-Polish war, the fleet would sail to the Baltic. There was growing suspicion, he said, that the Soviets were using the trade talks as a cover for a campaign to defeat the Poles. To take off some of the political heat, Lloyd George also appealed to President Wilson. While "we are by no means out of the wood," he wrote, the threat to break off the trade talks had proven more effective against the Red Army than anything Pilsudski had thrown against it. If the Russians came to their senses and agreed to an armistice, it could lead to real peace in Europe from end to end. Should such a peace conference take place, he would very much like to have an American present—not merely an observer, but someone with formal authority to take part. "It would make a great difference . . ."[4]

Lloyd George had been successful in 1917, when he had sought out
Wilson to defeat the Germans, promising America a lead position in the
peace conference. Now his appeal for help in making peace with Russia
met a chilly response. Wilson did not answer for three months, but the
prime minister learned much sooner what Americans thought. As it happened, the Italian ambassador had called at the State Department to
inquire if the United States would agree to meet with the Soviets. Secretary of State Colby did not equivocate. The United States desired a free
and independent Poland, and would not object to an armistice, he explained. But it could not approve of a general European conference that
would lead to recognition of the Soviet government and settlement of
questions having to do with the "former Russian Empire" on the basis of
dismemberment. "We are unwilling that while it is in the grip of a non-
representative government, whose only sanction is brutal force, Russia
shall be weakened still further by policy of dismemberment, conceived in
other than Russian interests." Without desiring to interfere in any way,
Colby's reply continued, the United States hoped that the Russian people
would soon find a "way to set up a government representing their free
will and purpose." When that time arrived, America would consider what
practical assistance it could offer the Russian people, provided only that
in the meantime they had not placed themselves beyond the pale by
oppression of the Poles. Let it not be thought that American unwillingness to recognize the Soviets, concluded the note, was based upon a refusal to countenance any particular "political or social structure which the
Russian people may see fit to embrace." Still unable to square the right of
self-determination with Bolshevism, American policymakers continued to
chase the democratic spirit through the unhospitable corridors of revolution, hoping it would emerge at the other end, where a peaceful resolution of social questions along liberal lines would become the business of
national leaders and international conferences.[5]

How could one conduct relations with the Soviet regime, the note
went on, an "antigovernment" that made no bones about its belief that
"the very existence of Bolshevism in Russia, the maintenance of their own
rule, depends, and must continue to depend, upon the occurrence of
revolutions in all other great civilized nations, including the United
States . . . ?" Driven by their grim creed, the Bosheviks must go on promoting revolution to the end of time. Only if their rule prevailed outside
Russia, and spread country by country, could the Bolsheviks ever feel
secure that they were anything more than a political faction exercising a
brutal tyranny—and therefore always in danger of the righteous wrath of
the Russian people.

When he finally answered Lloyd George's letter, Wilson added only that if it had been left alone, Bolshevism would have burned itself out. If the Allies had not intervened in the first place, and if they would now let well enough alone, the Russian question would settle itself. Looked at from Lloyd George's perspective, what Colby and Wilson appeared to be calling for was a new revolution. At least, those were the words and phrases—"no practicable and permanent settlement involving Russian territory and rights can be arrived at until the great Russian people can express themselves through a recognized Government of their own choice"—that had been used with Germany in demanding the kaiser's overthrow. "Wilson, not Lenin," suggests one historian, "may have been Europe's most dangerous revolutionary."[6] He was also a prosperous one, Lloyd George complained, who was perfectly willing to see European buyers dependent upon high-priced American grain.

For reasons not yet entirely clear, the Red Army suffered a serious defeat before the gates of Warsaw, easing somewhat Lloyd George's problems at home with his Russian policy.[7] Inside the cabinet, however, Churchill and Curzon were forming an alliance against him, using as their latest ammunition a powerful indictment against the Russian delegates constructed out of intelligence intercepts. They pressed for publication of the intercepts to expose the scope and insidious nature of Bolshevik activities; their position parodied Trotsky's original conviction that publicizing the secret treaties would produce irresistible demands for an immediate peace.[8]

Lloyd George urged them to consider what would happen if their demand was met. Workingmen, he wrote to disgruntled cabinet members on September 2, 1920, would suspect that expulsion of the trade delegation—for that is what Churchill and Curzon wanted—had nothing to do with such misdeeds, but was a desperate act of the ruling class. Bolshevik propaganda was, in reality, so crude that the more of it that became available to workers, the better. Restarting the Russian trade, on the other hand, would be of great value. "We are in for a period of unemployment and increase in unemployment is a far more formidable peril than all the lunacies of Lenin." Germany had already recovered enough to put in a successful bid to supply Russia with an order of thousands of locomotives. The United States, whatever Wilson had to say, would not stay out of the competition. "America will issue sanctimonious proclamations denouncing Bolshevism whilst at the same time encouraging Bolshevist representatives to come to the states and negotiate contracts."[9]

Cabinet dissidents feared using the press to try to go over the prime minister's head. And with good reason. Should the working classes unite in opposition to the Constitution, Lloyd George reminded Andrew Bonar Law, the outlook would be grave, especially if they were joined by "what I call intellectual liberalism. . . ." The more anxious the critics became, the more telling was such a rebuttal. The intercepts were not published, nor were the Russians sent packing.[10]

Within the cabinet, moreover, the Churchill-Curzon group had suffered an important defection. Sir Robert Horne, president of the Board of Trade, switched sides. A gloomy economic forecast by the Manufacturer's Association was the ostensible reason. Winter promised worse unemployment, said Horne. "Traders say they have never known the textile trade so bad. . . . The effects of the McKinley Tariff [an American measure enacted in the 1890s] were not nearly so bad as now." That was a pointed reference, certainly, and it provided what the prime minister had been saying. If Britain did not act, others certainly would—the Germans and yes, even the Americans, who were flocking to Baltic cities with their order books. The Russians were ready to place large orders, concluded Horne, backed by £10 million in gold security deposits. The business community wanted the trade, although former concessionaires and creditors would raise objections.[11]

Then it was Andrew Bonar Law's turn. He was the Conservative party spokesman in the coalition, so what he said carried great weight. "We have been playing with the Russian situation too long. . . . We are in for bad employment. There is some business to be got in this way. If we make no agreement the effect on the public mind of the imaginary value of trade which would never take place, but which they *think* would take place if there were an agreement, would be very bad."[12]

With Law's imprimatur, Lloyd George was free to go ahead with the negotiations. Up to now, he told the cabinet, he had deferred a good deal "to the feelings of some of my colleagues, and now I must make up my mind. . . ." There was no use allowing hatred for the Bolsheviks to harm the nation. He had talked with many businessmen who shared his fears about the next eighteen months. "We may have the worst period of unemployment any of us have known." What would happen, then, if it leaked out that His Majesty's Government had turned down orders for £10 million at a time when the nation was spending nearly half that sum to succor the unemployed?

As for propaganda, was there really any way to stop it? Should a single pamphlet be published in India, "our officials who are violently anti-Bolshevik, will hold that the conditions have not been fulfilled." It was no use saying that an agreement could be signed in six months if Soviet behavior merited it. By that time England would be in serious economic difficulty. Businessmen wanted the trade. Naturally financiers wanted their money back—who could blame them? "But the pressure from the Midlands is all the other way."[13]

Unusual support for Lloyd George's position that the heart of the matter was European reconstruction, even more than British trade prospects, came in an article by H. G. Wells, who had traveled to Russia. Wells's point was that if the Bolsheviks were thwarted in Europe, they would "asiatize" their movement. As this was exactly the opposite of what Lord Curzon had been saying, it caused some notice (mostly unfavorable) in the Foreign Office. But at least one foreign policy adviser, R. H. Hoare, agreed. "In one way or another we must presumably pick up the Marxian glove, but why not do it in Europe, rather than on the comparatively unknown ground of Asia?" Hoare argued that the trade talks should be pursued to the end. That way if trade failed to materialize, the domestic aspect of the Red Menace would evaporate, yet the Russians would not be able to claim that they had been driven eastwards.[14]

In Russia, Wells's piece began, he had seen a film of a great "festival" at Baku, where Zinoviev of the Comintern, Hungary's Bela Kun, and "our Mr. Jack Quelch" had gone on a pilgrimage to raise the Asiatic proletariat. "They went to beat up the class-conscious wage slaves of Persia and Turkestan. They sought out factory workers and slum dwellers in the tents of the Steppes." At the assembly all swore undying hatred of capitalism and especially of British imperialism.

A gentleman from the Baku neighborhood, wrote Wells, dressed in fur-trimmed jacket and high boots, did a dance with knives clenched in his teeth and balanced on top of his forehead. "He is now rolled up in my keeping, ready to dance again when opportunity offers. I tried to find out whether he was a specimen Asiatic proletarian, or just what he symbolized, but I could get no light on him. But there are yards and yards of film of him. I wish I could have resuscitated Karl Marx, just to watch that solemn stare over the beard, regarding him."

Talks with fellow writer Maxim Gorky put the film in perspective. Gorky was frankly obsessed with a vision of Russia abandoning Europe and going East. The "ideal figure" of the new Soviet republic was a huge worker holding a hammer or sickle. "A time may come, if we maintain the European blockade . . . when that ideal may give place altogether to a nomadic-looking gentleman from Turkestan. We may drive what will remain of Bolshevik Russia to the steppes and the knife. . . . Asia will resume. The simple ancient rhythm of the horseman plundering the peasant and the peasant waylaying the horseman, will creep back across the plains to the Niemen and the Dniester. The cities will become clusters of ruins in the waste; the roads and railroads will rot and rust; the river traffic will decay." If the West isolated Russia, the days of Genghis Khan would return, when the conqueror from the East sat astride his stallion outside the gates of Western Europe.[15]

> *There is every prospect that Russia may sink into complete*
> *anarchy. Unless the Russians can improve their transport,*
> *and re-create a portion of their trade, the country is*
> *doomed. This is one of those cases in which one feels that*
> *one cannot stand aside. One must do something to endeavor*
> *to avert such a catastrophe.*
>
> David Lloyd George, December 1920

Here were images far different from his original description of bulging grain bins. Lloyd George could pick the argument he thought would do the most good. To meet Foreign Office objections, the prime minister had prepared a list of specified areas and countries where the Soviets must accept a ban on propaganda. The Russians should submit a similar list, he suggested to Krasin: "[T]here is no objection to your naming every country in the world." What better way to expose the foolishness of any list of proscribed areas? Foreign Affairs Commissar Chicherin took him up on it and sent Krasin a list. Lloyd George was no doubt delighted. Now he could rid himself of the whole business with a playacting display of indignation at Russian effrontery and sweep the table clean. If others did not see Lloyd George's clever trap, Sir Eyre Crowe in the Foreign Office certainly did. This was tantamount to equalizing the two sides, he warned Curzon. And that should be the last thing any responsible minister should wish to do. To avoid it, at least a selection of the intercepts should be published. That would silence those "virtuous persons" who were declaring that there was nothing to choose between the Bolshevik government and His Majesty's Government.[16]

But it was too late. The final version of the trade agreement, signed on March 16, 1921, merely required the Russian government to refrain from encouraging the "peoples of Asia" to take actions contrary to British interests, "especially in India and in the Independent State of Afghanistan." British signers gave similar undertakings in regard to countries that had once formed part of the Russian empire. No matter how it might be explained, this exchange of vows sealed the question of recognition, for the agreement presumed that the Soviets could speak for the Russian people on such issues, and that the British could if necessary call the Soviets to account about things besides trade questions. In a very real sense, as Foreign Office officials understood, the Conservatives had tripped themselves up. The restrictions they wanted to impose on propaganda, the promises they wished to extract on the prerevolutionary debt, and anything else of this nature, all worked to enlarge British relations with the Soviets. The Bolsheviks were now a successor government that could assert a legitimate claim to full standing among the nations of the world.[17]

Despite the efforts of various labor organizations to make the case for Russian trade in the United States, the Wilson administration had largely succeeded in blunting arguments that trade deals with Russia could provide significant relief from problems connected with America's transition to a peacetime economy.[18] Things were somewhat different under Harding, however. On the day that the Anglo-Russian agreement was announced, Commerce Secretary Herbert Hoover in the new Republican administration suggested to Charles Evans Hughes that it would be unfair to American traders not to accept Russian gold in payment for exports. If the British accepted it, the gold would no doubt filter out into the world anyway. The British had made a mistake, but Americans should not lose out as a result. Until the Soviets abandoned their lunatic policies, Hoover said, they would have nothing to trade except gold, platinum, and jewelry. Yet it could not be denied that the British trade agreement would postpone indefinitely Lenin's political demise, and stimulate partial economic recovery in Soviet Russia. Looked at from America, Hoover told a member of the British embassy, the agreement appeared to be the first of several planned steps to enable British capitalists to regain lost properties in Russia. He expected the Germans to follow suit.[19]

Hoover's policy was shaped by conflicting needs. He was determined to meet British and German competition, but not just for the sake of immediate trade advantages. These were secondary to his long-range concern: to have a foothold inside Russia when the inevitable change came. For domestic political purposes, as well as consistency, however, he had to assert that there had been no change. "Hoover Opposes Trade Deal with Soviet Russia" read a headline based on press statements from his office. But what he actually said was that the new administration would not negotiate a formal agreement. The British pact was political, not economic, the commerce secretary insisted, because under the Soviet system production would never return to anything near normal. "The real blockade has been the failure of the Russians to produce anything except gold and platinum to trade with."[20]

Secretary of State Hughes responded to overtures for talks with Maxim Litvinov with a brief lecture insisting that the only hope for the Russian people rested in abandonment of communism, a system that made a resumption of productivity so obviously impossible. "Production is conditioned upon the safety of life, the recognition by firm guarantees of private property, the sanctity of contract, and the rights of free labor."[21]

It suited American policymakers perfectly well that Britain should not reap any great harvest in the Russian trade. But the summer of 1921 brought news of a Russian famine, the result of so many years of turmoil capped by what was to become a persistent problem of peasant resistance to delivering foodstuffs to the cities except in exchange for goods. On August 5, 1921, the Russian trade delegation appealed to Lloyd George for help in obtaining clothing, boots, and agricultural implements. The request triggered a new round of debate over the issues of credit and Soviet willingness to recognize the tsarist debts. Behind that debate, of course, was the larger dispute over whether Lloyd George's policy had ever been the right one. Must His Majesty's Government compound the original error, argued critics, by extending itself to save the fanatical Bolsheviks from their own folly?[22]

Supporters of the prime minister pointed out that all the Western nations were in a bind. To send aid would further legitimize Bolshevik authority, but to deny it would not only be criticized as cruel, it might strengthen the grip of the Lenin regime by making it appear Russia had no friends. "All neighboring states as well as Germany," advised Sir Robert Hodgson from the newly opened trade office in Moscow, "are making preparations to send assistance. Great Britain having concluded an agreement with a view to commercial advantage would be placed in an invidious position by standing aloof."[23]

Lord Curzon, meanwhile, was working on a way of disengaging from this Russian tangle. He and his aides were busy culling the best tidbits from what intelligence sources had provided recently for a formal protest note. The intercepts had dried up, but instead of reducing the role of the intelligence professionals this added to their aura of being men who had access to secret doings and documents.[24] The finished product was dispatched to Moscow on September 7, 1921. Citing secret transactions—interspersed with public statements available to anyone—it pictured an active conspiracy operating day and night to destroy the British empire. The better relations foreseen at the time of the signing of the trade agreement could not be realized, Lord Curzon wrote at the end of the note, if these activities did not come to a halt.[25]

The protest note boosted morale in the Foreign Office. J. D. Gregory minuted, for example, that it had been thought (obviously by the prime minister) that the Soviets were moving to the right, but that that theory was false. What was true was that the Lenin regime was about to disintegrate into anarchy. "Its disappearance would therefore alter little from that point of view, whilst from every other it would relieve Europe of a nightmare. It is understood to be also the view of the Govt of India that complete anarchy in Russia would be preferable to the existing regime."[26]

Congratulations were a bit premature. If Curzon had hoped to make it possible to start all over, he soon discovered that the trade agreement was not so easily dispensed with. If he hoped to isolate the Soviets from outside support without making it appear that Britain had acted invidiously after lusting for trade, he would be disappointed for a very surprising reason. Curzon was undone by Herbert Hoover's offer to organize a private relief effort in the United States.

The first indication of trouble came in the failed mission of Leslie Urquhart, who had gone to Moscow to explore the possibility of resuming management of his nationalized mining properties. When negotiations stalled, Urquhart blamed the Hoover offer, and Maxim Litvinov made no secret of Russian plans to play off the capitalist nations against one another. Such practices were hardly unique in international relations, but it did confirm that the famine negotiations had much political content, on both sides.[27]

Worse was to come. The protest note boomeranged. Instead of the abject apology that the Foreign Office had expected, the Soviet reply was a point-by-point refutation. In one instance, a man who the protest note claimed had delivered a subversive speech against British imperial interests had in fact been locked up in jail at the time. In *Pravda*, Karl Radek taunted Lord Curzon for having been duped by crude forgeries that had already appeared in the "RUSSIAN WHITE PRESS, MAKING EVERYONE LAUGH." Not only were the British wrong, they had been taken in like gullible innocents. Curzon vented his disappointment in a minute to his subordinates: "I can only regard this as a humiliating conclusion to an episode upon which . . . I ought never to have been allowed to embark."[28]

The next important communication from Moscow was an expected denunciation of Western insistence upon recognition of Russia's prerevolutionary debt in exchange for famine aid. What was interesting about Chicherin's letter, however, was the way it wove together ritual Soviet assaults on capitalist misdeeds with Lenin's decision to undertake a New Economic Policy that, if it was to work, depended upon expanding economic relations with the outside world.[29] From the beginning, Chicherin's letter read, the Soviets had wished to work with foreign capitalists. To that end, it had always intended to recognize the old debts; but Western leaders had to recognize as well that world recovery without Russia was impossible. Actually it was fortunate that a workers' and peasants' government existed in Russia, because only such a government could really work with foreign capitalists. "The selfish interests of separate groups of capitalists do not prevent them [workers and peasants] from working for the restoration of the national prosperity. The Workers and Peasants Government is guided by the interest of the masses, which is in the last analysis that of all society." It would be hard to fault the Bolsheviks for a lack of ingenuity, whatever else one thought about them. After declaring that no people could be obliged "to pay those debts which are as chains riveted on it through long centuries," Chicherin said that the Soviets were ready to make concessions, especially to the small bondholders in France for whom the tsarist debt was a vital matter of personal concern. The first step was to call an international conference. How much more sensible that would be than to continue the futile interventionist schemes still being hatched in the West. Doomed to fail anyway, they would only make matters worse for everyone by delaying Russia's recovery.[30]

The Russian note was also an example of Wilsonian public diplomacy carried to its logical end; it was published almost simultaneously with its delivery to Whitehall. The British reply suggested an international commission to investigate the famine and relief problems. The Foreign Office pressed this idea because it would forestall the inevitable "movement from many quarters to rush H.M.G. into a general peace conference [with Russia alone]."[31] Moscow's rejoinder was simple. Russia could not possibly give rational answers to debt claims except at an international conference—where all questions could be considered. The day had passed when the Soviet government could be excluded from international gatherings and when decisions reached in its absence could be imposed upon Russia.[32]

Pravda, meanwhile, continued to pick apart what was left of the British protest note in an effort to expose the futility of such methods. Lord Curzon had pictured to the world propaganda trains rushing eastwards filled with leaflets printed in all languages. "Our trains are neither in Afghanistan nor in Persia," *Pravda* declared, "and could not be seen there by any witness for the single reason that neither of these countries possess railways."[33]

> The Bolsheviks must face the tribunal of civilized nations in full conference, and they must bring with them something quite definite, viz., recognition of their responsibility for old debts and claims of every description. This really means that the Soviets are called upon to put again into full force the right to private property, with all the consequences ensuing from this principle.
>
> London *Daily Telegraph*,
> December 18, 1921

Satisfying as these exchanges might be psychologically, the impasse was intolerable on all other grounds. Both Lloyd George and his opponents now realized that the final issue would depend upon an international conference. In mid-December 1921, the prime minister told the cabinet he thought that the Germans would have to be brought into any plan for Russia's rehabilitation. They were the experts on Eastern Europe. Despite the short lapse of time since the argument had been that Germany must be denied any advantages in Russia, the cabinet approved opening discussions with the French on "a scheme for the formation of a syndicate of Western Powers (and possibly the United States) for the economic reconstruction of Russia, subject to possible conditions, e.g. recognition of Russian debts, the control of Russian Railways and Customs and diplomatic recognition of the Soviet Government."[34]

The parallel with the Washington Naval Conference and the second consortium for China was striking, and was made even stronger when in early January 1922 the Supreme Allied Council meeting in Cannes accepted the British prime minister's idea for a general European economic conference to which both outcast powers, Germany and Soviet Russia, would be invited as equals.[35] Every bit as skilled, indeed more so, than Charles Evans Hughes, Lloyd George did not have the same backing as the American secretary. Whether he could make up for that shortage was the question.

Had the United States participated in the Genoa conference in the spring of 1922 things might have had a different ending. But probably not. Curzon had hoped to enlist the Americans in support of the Foreign Office's plan for an international relief commission, but Hughes made it plain that the United States would shun all Allied entanglements: "It desires to avoid direct dealings with [the] Soviet regime and also to keep a free hand without becoming unnecessarily involved in the plans of other governments."[36]

How much less likely it was, then, that the Americans would agree to be part of Lloyd George's very different plan for European rehabilitation. Warned by the American ambassador on another occasion that his government would not shake hands with the Russians, Lloyd George had tried to make light of Anglo-American divisions. "I'll tell you what you do," he had said. "If you don't want to shake hands with the Bolsheviks, you let us do it, and then you shake hands with us."[37]

Russia's appeal for international aid to combat famine struck Commerce Secretary Herbert Hoover as an ideal way for America to take up an active role in Russia without giving its regime moral or political support, and without being criticized as part of another Allied interventionist plan. Hoover's demands of the Russians were only two in number. They would have to release Americans held since the civil war, and allow his agents to supervise the distribution of foodstuffs and supplies inside Russia. Agreement was reached easily and the Hoover volunteers went to work.[38]

Although Hoover admitted later that American relief helped the Soviets to consolidate their power, at the time he imagined he was laying the groundwork for a large American role in some future non-Bolshevik Russia. For the same reason he opposed a State Department proposal to use Germany as a middleman in regaining entry into Russia. This indirect trade that the State Department now apparently wanted to see restarted was nothing more than a malignant offshoot of the old German imperialism. Besides, at the end of the prewar era American industry had begun to best the Germans in direct trade competition in Russia. Russians liked Americans better than Germans. And they respected the American government more than those that had thus far extended diplomatic recognition. These factors would give the United States "certain undoubted commercial advantages" when the proper moment arrived. "The hope of our commerce lies in the establishment of American firms abroad, distributing American goods under American direction; in the building of direct American financing and, above all, in the installation of American technology in Russian industries."[39]

Lloyd George's idea of Germany as middleman struck the Foreign Office as morally "deplorable" as well. But the prime minister saw it only as a means to an end. On February 10, 1922, he stressed the same pragmatic approach to Krasin in explaining to him the stipulations of the Cannes resolutions which required the Soviets to acknowledge the debts and either restore or indemnify owners of property confiscated or nationalized during or since the revolution. Even an extremist Labour government in Britain, he told Krasin, "would never repudiate the debts incurred by its predecessors." Table your own claims, he repeated, that was the way to play the game. If Moscow wished to "niggle," he warned, "we should never have the Conference this side of the Day of Judgment."[40]

Krasin, not averse to practicing some of Lloyd George's preaching for his own purposes, told the United States consul general in London that the prime minister had promised that diplomatic recognition would follow the Genoa conference. The Russian was probably trying to nudge the Americans into some gesture of their own, and interpreting Lloyd George's remarks to suit that end. When a cabinet committee appointed by Lloyd George reported that the Cannes resolutions did commit the great powers to recognition if the Soviets met the stipulated conditions, however, charges were raised that the prime minister had gone too far on his own.[41]

With trouble welling up behind him, the prime minister tried to relieve the pressure by gaining French support. He hoped that Eduard Beneš of Czechoslovakia would act as his advocate in Paris. But while Beneš imagined himself to be a mediator in East-West disputes, he took a more cautious attitude about formal recognition, explaining that he thought Genoa was to be a station along the road. Final action would depend on Moscow's willingness to cease propaganda and grant liberty to its people. Well, replied Lloyd George, France had had a treaty with Russia before the war. Had this contained a clause requiring the tsar to prove his commitment to liberty? Could one ask more of the Bolsheviks than the French had demanded of the Romanovs?

Outmaneuvered by a grand master, Beneš backed off to allow the prime minister to present his positive arguments. "We were an industrial nation dependent to a great extent on markets for our industry," Lloyd George told him. "Only a one-seventh part of our population was agricultural. . . . International trade was essential to us. We had two millions unemployed which constituted our devastated area. We had to spend £100,000,000 to keep the unemployed alive. Hence, we intended to make peace. We wished to go forward with France, and it would be very foolish for France to drive us to go forward with Russia and Germany for economic reasons."[42]

Beneš now understood what was expected of him. The real place for mediation was between England and France. "It must be remembered," the prime minister told the Czech at their next encounter, "that Great Britain had never fought Germany before the war, and that the population was largely Teutonic in its remoter origins." The Germans were a great trading people; so were the British. The French were not. "Trade was life to us, and if it we were attacked in our trade, and France stood in the way we should drift towards other friends." If something solid emerged from Genoa, the United States might also participate.

At a third meeting Lloyd George stressed that it was really the Russians and Lenin who were at a disadvantage. The Bolsheviks knew that Russia had to return to Europe. "If Lenin came back from Genoa with nothing in his hands, he would be overthrown." If the great powers should say to his representative, Here is a syndicate with £25,000,000 to put Russia's railways in order, Lenin would willingly "pay the price." Italy had seen the light; if Czechoslovakia came along, too, how could the conference fail?

How could France hold out, he meant.[43] At a stormy meeting with Raymond Poincaré on February 25, 1922, Lloyd George warned the French leader that his obstinacy threatened to drive Great Britain into "a new grouping on political questions." After an exchange of mutual recriminations that reached all the way back to prewar questions, the prime minister insisted that Poincaré's proposal to postpone recognition would destroy the conference. Russia would make no concessions unless recognition came first, and Allied financiers would not put up the money until relations had been established. Recognition meant, furthermore, that Russia would have to obey the rules. As matters stood, the Soviets had everything to gain by not doing so. But try as he might, even threatening not to put the much-desired Anglo-French treaty of guarantee before Parliament until other questions were settled, the only concession he could wring from Poincaré was an agreement that the Genoa meeting should begin in early April 1922. To a defector at home, Lloyd George pleaded the case that Cannes committed the honor of the government. Recognition must be granted if the Bolsheviks accepted the conditions of the invitation. "We must act straightforwardly even with the Revolutionaries."[44]

On March 15, 1922, Chicherin sent a telegram to the Entente governments. Although like its predecessor it was cast as an indignant warning against trying to impose a trusteeship on Russia, also like the previous message it offered assurances that the Soviets wanted to work with Western capitalism. Indeed, it went beyond previous assurances, due to the announcement of the New Economic Policy. "The interests and rights of foreigners holding property in Russia," it said, "are effectively guaranteed by the present Soviet legislation."[45]

Clever, said one Foreign Office official; the Soviets now seemed to be appealing to capitalists in an effort to bring pressure on Western nations, perhaps in the hope that the general design of bringing Russia along step by step would be abandoned in a free-for-all to get the best lots in Russia. The workers had failed to force recognition; now the owners would be tried.[46] Chancellor of the Exchequer Austen Chamberlain also hoped that the prime minister would not get carried away by Chicherin's effusions. Churchill was threatening to resign, he advised him. The coalition could not stand his defection, because "he was more Tory than the Tory Ministers." Britain, moreover, could not go it alone without France.[47]

Britain could not go to Genoa tied to French chariot wheels, Lloyd George responded. If the "Communist Party" came out on top inside Russia, it was true nothing could be done. "If, on the other hand, the party that is prepared to surrender its Bolshevism and to make terms with the Western capitalists has captured the Soviet authority, then it would be folly not to help Russia to return to the community of civilized nations." And if Churchill wanted to push matters to an extreme, then the cabinet would have to choose. If there was a failure "through our fault" in the project of European reconstruction, "there will be such a revolt amongst the working classes of this country that no Government could withstand it, and our great industrial leaders will sympathize with that revolt."[48]

As it happened, another Conservative minister in the cabinet, Stanley Baldwin, had just completed a report on trade prospects that confirmed every dire prophecy Lloyd George had uttered. Export trade was essential to Britain, said the report, because of all the powers it was the one that was overindustrialized. War had thrown the automatic machinery of trade and credit out of gear. "For three years we have been trying to start this machine: with difficulty the cog wheels are being fitted and some are revolving, but in Europe the damage is almost irreparable and the whole refuses to function because a part will not work." Baldwin's focus was on the reparations mess. "My fear is that we may find even after an expansion of trade that we shall have with us a pool of unemployed who will quickly degenerate into unemployable and hence a perpetual danger to the social and political life of the country."[49]

Lloyd George sent a copy of the report to Chamberlain, remarking that French policy on reparations would drive Germany to Bolshevism or imperialism. Nor could anyone govern in Britain under conditions that would make it impossible for him to do his duty to the trader and the workingman. Chamberlain agreed, but that did not solve the Churchill problem. He had learned the prime minister had planted a story in the press that he would part with his dearest political friend rather than abandon his plans. How could Churchill see this as anything but a direct challenge? The coalition's survival depended upon compromise. "Your policy of appeasement is clearly right," Chamberlain told Lloyd George. But was it so certain that Genoa would be a success? The French desire for a probationary period before de jure recognition did not seem so unreasonable. "I am most anxious to remove difficulties from the path, but I cannot affront the opinion of practically the whole of my party on a matter of this kind in which I think their attitude is entirely reasonable." After all, he closed, both Frenchmen and Americans were trading with Russia without recognizing the Soviets. His experience in the City did not reveal any great anxiety among the financiers, nor were the manufacturers demanding recognition.[50]

The showdown came on March 26, 1922, when Lloyd George used the Baldwin report as backing for his position that the unsettled political state of Europe damaged trade prospects, no matter what the bankers or manufacturers said. Theirs was a narrow angle of vision. At least half of Europe was under the shadow of war, a situation that had to be corrected before the wheels of trade and industry could turn with anything approaching normal speed. The degree of recognition might be debated. And he conceded that Britain should not act alone (which left open the possibility, however, of its acting with Italy and the rest and leaving France to do as it wished). Under no circumstances should Paris be given a veto over British policy, for France was the nation least interested in Russian trade. Lenin's New Economic Policy, he concluded, was a decision to abandon communism. If the Russians came prepared to negotiate, "we should give every support to anti-Communist elements in Russia."

Suppose the prime minister was correct, retorted Churchill, and a power struggle was going on in Moscow. The Bolshevik representative to Genoa would be out to get concessions that would permit his government to triumph, to rivet its shackles on the ignorant peasants. Meanwhile, three million "intelligent" Russians living in exile would be struck with despair if Great Britain recognized the Soviet Union. He was bitterly sorry that at a time of strong conservative majorities in a country devoted to monarchy it was proposed to accord such supreme favor and patronage to the Bolsheviks.

Austen Chamberlain engineered a compromise that limited the prime minister's freedom of action at Genoa. If a general consensus appeared, but only if that were to happen, the prime minister could agree to a limited form of recognition. To satisfy home opinion, furthermore, Lloyd George agreed to tell the House of Commons that the Russians would have to meet various conditions before full and ceremonial recognition could be accorded. The Soviets would have to demonstrate, for example, that they exercised full control over the Third International and could command it to carry out Russia's engagements.[51]

In that case, of course, back-bench Conservatives could go on living in the coalition, and also in the fictional world of Victorian grandeur and native uprisings.

Genoa is an armed city. There are cavalry patrols along the roads; the railways are guarded for miles out; the pavements are permanently lined with carabinieri and there are infantry pickets every fifty yards.

John Duncan Gregory to Miles Lampson,
April 14, 1922

While the cabinet concerned itself with a compromise formula that would hold the coalition together, the Foreign Office, together with experts from the other Allied countries, effectively cut the ground from under the prime minister by preparing a list of twenty-eight articles that would have required the Soviets to turn over control of their domestic affairs to a more powerful consortium than was planned for China. Included here was a pledge that foreigners might request that laws of their homeland apply to all contracts; another stipulated that all multilateral conventions and agreements predating the revolution should still apply; yet another demanded that free collective bargaining between employer and employee should determine wages and so on. All these were to be in addition to earlier demands that the Soviets recognize the prerevolutionary debts—and assent to a specific mechanism for their payment.[52]

Even should the Russians jump through the hoop, H. F. Maxse told his Foreign Office colleagues, France had no intention of recognizing the Soviet government. "If this attitude is persisted in, it can only mean the withdrawal of either the French or the Russian delegates from Genoa." Was that so bad? queried Ronald Lindsay. "It appears then that at Genoa we shall be confronted with the choice of having the Bolsheviks as our friends for the immediate future, or the French. I prefer the latter; and if somewhere in the future we may have to part company with France, I hope we shall not then insult her by saying that we prefer Moscow."[53]

Lloyd George could propose whatever his heart desired, but the prime minister was not at the Paris Peace Conference any more. The days of the Big Four were over. Yet he could not complain about Louis Barthou's opening statement at Genoa: "Europe is covered with ruins. It would be madness to suppose that a magic wand could rebuild on these shattered ruins the enchanted castles of our dreams. It would be still worse, more disastrous and more destructive, to sit with our arms folded by the way-side and do nothing, because there is much to do."[54]

When Chicherin then concluded his opening statement on the need for economic cooperation and tabled a disarmament proposal, however, he was cut short by a less conciliatory Barthou. Russia had not been invited to offer proposals, he said, only to receive Allied conditions. As he had at home during the Anglo-Soviet trade talks, Lloyd George sought to use private conversations to get the conference restarted on a more positive note. But Chicherin was determined to take the opportunity to denounce the twenty-eight articles. How would the leaders of the French Revolution have responded to a demand from Pitt that they restore British property? "Everyone in Russia had formed the impression that the old world was done with, and that everything belonging to it had disappeared," Chicherin declared. Anyway, whatever justice there was in the Allied claims had vanished with the invasion and the intervention; yet the experts even wanted Russia to pay interest at a rate equal to the annual value of prewar exports.[55]

There were diehards in all governments, Lloyd George told the Russian. After the French Revolution it had taken twenty-years to realize the folly of such efforts. This time it had only taken three. But the right to self-determination could not be confused with the willingness of others to trade. British businessmen wanted more trade, but there was still ample room in India and South America. If the Soviets could not agree to a debt settlement and give assurances of reasonable treatment, traders would "wipe Russia off the map. . . ."

"It was now proposed," replied Maxim Litvinov wryly, that the Russian delegation "should go back to their people and say, 'Congratulate us! We have come back to you with another 20 billions of debts. Perhaps some capital will be found for us—perhaps not. Perhaps someone will give us a loan—perhaps not.' But, anyhow, the position would be worse than before." Nevertheless, the Russians agreed to submit to Moscow Lloyd George's formula for scaling down the debt and the interest. The prime minister's proposal said nothing about compensation for the intervention, only that the debts were being scaled down because of Russia's "serious economic condition." The draft agreement also exempted private debts, stipulating that foreign nationals "could not be deprived of rights to the return of their property."[56]

"Mr. Lloyd George's sleeves were empty," quipped John Maynard Keynes, so that "there was no basis for a bargain." Britain simply demanded that the Soviets "unsay their doctrine," without offering anything in return. Keynes also faulted the prime minister for the one thing Lloyd George thought most important: the creation of an atmosphere. He should also have consulted his experts more, instead of exhausting them in the "drafting of endless subterfuges. . . ." The criticism was far wide of the mark, for the creation of an atmosphere was the only hope the prime minister had for defeating the experts' subterfuges.[57]

Excluded from these private sessions was the Foreign Office's chief expert, J. D. Gregory, who much preferred it that way. He saw all he wanted to see of the Russians at the plenary sessions. Chicherin looked "the degenerate he is," wrote Gregory, and except for him and Krasin, the rest, he imagined, were all Jews. The two who came to the plenary session looked to him as if they had stepped out of a Drury Lane pantomime, "real melodramatic cut-throats from the 'Babes in the Wood'—!" "It is very unpleasant to reflect that the main interest here is centered on the future relations between them and ourselves." Distrust of Lloyd George did not blind Gregory, however, to what had been offered to the Russians. It was no compromise, he reported. The atmosphere suggested that "we are here to do something big" to recreate Europe, but everything else contradicted that impression.[58]

Two days later, on Easter Sunday, April 16, 1922, something big was done. The German and Russian delegations had reached a momentous agreement across the lake at Rapallo. "It was at once realized," Gregory cabled London, "that [the] whole situation was transformed." The French wanted to denounce the perfidious behavior of the two probationers and withdraw. That would only make matters worse, observed a discouraged Lloyd George. He had felt this coming for more than a year. To continue to isolate Germany and Russia would solve nothing. The populations of those countries would leap into one another's arms. It was all coming true just as he had feared.[59]

The Russo-German agreement, the prime minister argued at the next plenary session, made it all the more necessary to reach an understanding with Russia. "Our policy should be to do our best to detach the Russian people from the German combination. The Germans had stolen a march on us, but we must not accept diplomatic defeat. We must make the Russian people look to us, and not to Germany for their help. If we did not, he would hesitate to shoulder the responsibility for what might happen."[60]

Genoa ended in disarray. The French press even hinted that Rapallo was a clever part of British strategy. And Lloyd George, in the wake of this massive failure, placed his signature on a peevish final memorandum dated May 2, 1922, which, in even harsher terms than before, demanded Russian acquiescence in capitalist rules of the game. The only enticement he offered to the Russians was a promise of direct government assistance through credits for the export of British goods under the Trade Facilities Act. He would ask Parliament, Lloyd George said, for an additional £25 million for this purpose.[61]

Whether the Soviets would have agreed to any terms Lloyd George suggested remains moot, but their reply of May 10 correctly stated that the Allies had made "no precise proposals" for assistance to Russia and, more generally, that "the problems of the future, which interest everyone, have been subordinated to the interests of the past, which affect only certan groups of foreigners." It must be, continued the response, that the capitalist powers felt economic recovery took second place to the need to "defeat" Russia by a more subtle form of intervention. And to disguise this obsession, the Allied memorandum had tried to render plausible the absurd idea that economic isolation would injure only Russia. If Russia must pay for collaboration, others would suffer more for their doctrinaire intransigence.[62]

Ideological fervor permeated Genoa, disrupting the atmosphere for Lloyd George's efforts. But surely, just as important in determining the French attitude was that, lacking capital to invest in Russia, they were, along with the Belgians, more interested in collecting past debts. For his part, Lloyd George was ready to split with the Allies, even before he saw the Soviet response, and permit each creditor nation to negotiate its own arrangements. British property holders were more reasonable, he thought, and would make out better than those who "insisted on standing out for the last penny."[63]

Lloyd George's domestic critics found themselves, perhaps for the first time, doubting the wisdom of the hard line and what it had brought in the wake of Genoa. Churchill never doubted, of course, but inside the Foreign Office Owen O'Malley drew out the consequences of the Lloyd George memorandum. It asked everything, said O'Malley, and offered nothing in return. The Russians could not accept it without endangering the position of the present government in the eyes of its supporters. It would please no one with strong views on Russia, neither anti-Bolshevik nor pro-Bolshevik.

> Neither will it be of use as propaganda or as a rallying point for neutral or moderate opinion. For those purposes a perfectly candid document would be required; and this memo is not perfectly candid. The implied promises of benefits to Russia thro' Trade Facilities Act, Exports Credits, International Corporation are pure eyewash & will be recognized as such by everyone familiar with those Acts and projects.
>
> The French policy of ostracism of Russia and the ultra-Radical policy of recognition plus loans were both possible policies. They may both have been mistaken policies or they may not, but they were defensible with candid arguments. But the policy presented in this memorandum and the negotiations which produced it is neither flesh, fowl nor good red herring and it will render relations between ourselves & Russia more difficult than before.[64]

Everyone was worse off because of Genoa, ended O'Malley. The best thing to do now was to put the subject of Russia to sleep for six months. Lord Curzon agreed: "There is a great deal in Mr. O'Malley's argument." What had to be done, right away, said Austen Chamberlain, was to get out a white paper describing all the violations and hostile acts perpetrated by the Soviets so as "to get a clear idea of the strength of our case."[65]

The years subsequent to the collapse at Genoa saw a series of desperate individual initiatives, beginning with Rapallo. France's decision to go it alone on reparations and the occupation of the Ruhr followed. Then Italy moved toward ultimate disaster behind Mussolini. After Lenin's death, Josef Stalin set out to prove that socialism could exist in one country, whatever the cost. The decade ended with the Great Depression. And Hitler.

> *The sum of the whole matter is that . . . our civilization cannot survive materially unless it can be redeemed spiritually. . . . Only thus can discontent be driven out and all the shadows lifted from the road ahead.*
>
>   Woodrow Wilson,
>   "The Road Away from Revolution," 1923

Former president William Howard Taft offered Lloyd George some consolation in the summer of 1922. Russia must wait, he said. "Russia . . . was an unorganized country and could therefore collapse without the terrible results which must follow in Germany. The Russian people were moreover impractical and rather indeterminate in character. Revolution and Bolshevism would be much more serious in Germany."[66]

With the return of European prosperity, Lloyd George's dark prophecies were forgotten. Indeed, when the Ramsay MacDonald government sought to extend credits to the Soviet Union, the former prime minister was among the first to denounce the plan. Still later, he imagined an alliance against Bolshevism between Hitler's Germany and Great Britain, calling Hitler upon his return from a visit "a born leader. A magnetic, dynamic personality with a single-minded purpose."[67]

As the revolutionary tide receded, leaving behind but a few pools of discontent, the fear that had reached its height from 1917 to 1921 also went away. The Conservatives in Great Britain followed Chamberlain's advice to make as strong a case as possible against Bolshevism, and otherwise leave Russia alone. As foreign secretary in the mid-1920s, Chamberlain did just that, completing his work with the Locarno Pact that brought together future NATO allies Germany, Italy, France, and Great Britain. Much of the success of containment in the 1920s (and in the 1940s) was based upon the availability of American money. At Paris, frustrated Wilsonians had recoiled at the Keynes plan, calling it an ingenious scheme for subordinating American concerns to Allied reparations policy, and calculated to promote state interference in the world economy. From one perspective it was too radical, from another too conservative.

Nevertheless, American money, in the form of private loans, came to Europe in a tidal wave during the 1920s, and appeared to have a greater force behind it than the revolutionary thrust that came from Russia out of the war. Republican "banker diplomacy" also worked reasonably well for a decade in controlling the revolution in Mexico and striking a bargain with Japanese interests in Asia. As Taft had said of Russia, China could wait. Wilson had given his approval to the initial efforts to reform and reformulate "Dollar Diplomacy" when he still believed that the war against Germany would mobilize world opinion to such an extent that imperialism would give way to trusteeship, the "special interests" to a capitalist commitment to the general welfare. Once the gamble was lost, he had no other plan to offer. The painful process of trying to devise an economic intervention plan in Russia, which he finally gave up, left him desolate of any idea that would not somehow conflict with his liberal beliefs, or his faith that he could use the power of the state to correct what had gone wrong both inside and outside America.

"I don't know exactly what I am", Lloyd George had said in 1913. He was true to his word. He had practically no stake, as Wilson did, in ideology. Not any more. His program for reengaging both America in 1917 and Russia in 1922 had as its primary concern victory and the restoration of British trade. Without that, nothing else was possible. But that did not mean he lacked subtlety, a subtlety that went beyond cleverness in besting opponents in debate. Had he thought it possible to crush the Bolsheviks within a reasonable time, and with a reasonable expenditure, he would have been inclined to give it a try, along with his old political comrade Winston Churchill.

As it turned out, Wilson was paralyzed by ideological difficulties, Lloyd George by political ones. They both foresaw the future with terrible accuracy. When Genoa collapsed, and with it his last hope of preserving the balance at home, Lloyd George despaired of what would happen if the West forced Russia into Germany's arms. With diminishing resources, Great Britain was left to manage Wilson's League; with seemingly limitless resources, the United States was left with no political responsibility. The division was a fateful one.

At the end, Wilson pronounced a judgment on his era:

> The world has been made safe for democracy. There need now be no fear that any such mad design as that entertained by the insolent and ignorant Hohenzollerns and their counselors may prevail against it. But democracy has not yet made the world safe against irrational revolution. That supreme task, which is nothing less than the salvation of civilization, now faces democracy, insistent, imperative. There is no escaping it, unless everything we have built up is presently to fall in ruin about us; and the United States, as the greatest of democracies, must undertake it.

Lloyd George, as befitted his reputation, regretted missed opportunities. "I'll tell you what to do. If you don't want to shake hands with the Bolsheviks, you let us do it, and then you shake hands with us."[68]

Notes

PROLOGUE

1. Charles Seymour, ed., *The Intimate Papers of Colonel House*, 4 vols. (Boston, 1926–28), 4:282; "Conference on *George Washington* with Wilson," Dec. 10, 1918, notes by Charles Seymour, copy in Wilson Papers, Princeton University (hereafter Wilson Collection, P).

2. Ray Stannard Baker and William E. Dodd, eds., *The Public Papers of Woodrow Wilson: War and Peace*, 2 vols. (New York, 1927), 1:326.

3. Ibid., pp. 342–44.

4. Lloyd George, *Memoirs of the Peace Conference* (New Haven, 1939), p. 111.

5. Quoted in Seth Tillman, *Anglo-American Relations at the Paris Peace Conference of 1919* (Princeton, 1961), p. 68.

6. Harold Nicolson, *Peacemaking, 1919* (New York, 1965 ed.), pp. 40–42.

7. William Maxwell Aitken, Lord Beaverbrook, *Men and Power, 1917–1918* (New York, 1956), p. xvii.

8. A. J. P. Taylor, "Lloyd George: Rise and Fall," in *Essays in English History* (New York, 1976), 261; Peter Rowland, *David Lloyd George* (New York, 1975), pp. 469–70.

9. Lloyd George, *Memoirs of the Peace Conference*, pp. 112–17; United States, Department of State, *Papers Relating to the Foreign Relations of the United States* (Washington, various dates), (hereafter *FR*), *Russia, 1919*, pp. 1–2.

10. Rowland, *Lloyd George*, pp. 473–74.

11. Tillman, *Anglo-American Relations at Paris*, p. 135; John Silverlight, *The Victors' Dilemma: Allied Intervention in the Russian Civil War* (London, 1970). p. 10.

12. Lloyd George, *Memoirs of the Peace Conference*, pp. 112–17.

13. Quoted in Betty Miller Unterberger, "Woodrow Wilson and the Russian Revolution," in Arthur S. Link, ed., *Woodrow Wilson and a Revolutionary World, 1913–1921* (Chapel Hill, N.C., 1982), p. 81.

14. Winston S. Churchill, *Great Contemporaries* (Chicago, 1973, ed.), p. 132.

15. See Arno J. Mayer, *Politics and Diplomacy of Peacemaking: Containment and Counterrevolution at Versailles, 1918–1919* (New York, 1970).

16. Derby to Balfour, Dec. 22, 1918, *Balfour Papers*, British Museum, London (hereafter, BM).

17. Derby to Balfour, Dec. 24, 1918, ibid.

18. Baker and Dodd, *Public Papers: War and Peace* 1:353.

CHAPTER ONE. WHAT COMES OF EMPIRE

1. Thomas Packenham, *The Boer War* (New York, 1979), pp. 492–94.

2. Ibid.

3. See the discussion of American attitudes in Howard K. Beale, *Theodore Roosevelt and the Rise of America to World Power* (Baltimore, 1956), pp. 95–101.

4. Quoted in Keith Hutchison, *The Decline and Fall of British Capitalism* (New York, 1950), p. 28.

5. D. C. M. Platt, "Economic Factors in British Policy during the 'New Imperialism,' " *Past and Present*, no. 39 (April 1968): 120–38. For the larger context, see idem, *Finance, Trade, and Politics in British Foreign Policy, 1815–1914* (Oxford, 1968), pp. 362–65.

6. John A. Hobson, *Imperialism* (London, 1938 ed.), p. 360.

7. Bernard Porter, *The Lion's Share: A Short History of British Imperialism, 1850–1970* (New York, 1975), pp. 120–48.

8. Hobson, *Imperialism*, p. 360.

9. Ibid., p. 92.

10. J. L. Garvin, *The Life of Joseph Chamberlain*, 3 vols. (London, 1934), 3:20.

11. Memorandum, Nov. 9, 1901, Lansdowne Papers, FO 800/115, Public Record Office, London (hereafter PRO).

12. Quoted from Winston Churchill's biography of his father by Robert Rhodes James, *Churchill: A Study in Failure, 1900–1939* (London, Penguin ed., 1973), p. 21.

13. Winston S. Churchill, *The World Crisis, 1911–1918*, 2 vols. (London, 1964 ed.), 1:22.

14. Bernard Semmel, *Imperialism and Social Reform: English Social-Imperial Thought, 1895–1914* (New York, 1968 ed.), pp. 84–85.

15. Richard Shannon, *The Crisis of Imperialism, 1865–1915* (London, 1976 ed.), pp. 351–52; Alfred Gollin, *Balfour's Burden: Arthur Balfour and Imperial Preference* (London, 1965), pp. 44–46.

16. Harry Browne, *Joseph Chamberlain, Radical and Imperialist* (London, 1974), p. 65.

17. G. R. Searle, *The Quest for National Efficiency: A Study in British Politics and Political Thought, 1899–1914* (Berkeley, 1971), pp. 146–47; Michael Barratt Brown, *After Imperialism* (London, 1963), pp. 104–5.

18. Blanche Dugdale, *Arthur James Balfour*, 2 vols. (New York, 1937), 1:328.

19. John Grigg, *Lloyd George: The People's Champion, 1902–1911* (Berkeley, 1978), p. 63.

20. Ibid., p. 77.

21. See George Dangerfield, *The Strange Death of Liberal England, 1910–1914* (New York, 1935), pp. 214–330; James, *Churchill*, p. 49; Searle, *The Quest*, pp. 177–92.

22. Grigg, *Lloyd George*, p. 307.

23. Kenneth Young, *Arthur James Balfour* (London, 1963), pp. 277–84.

24. London *Times*, June 1, 1910, clipping in Grey Papers, FO 800/93, PRO.

25. Searle, *The Quest*, pp. 177–82; Grigg, *Lloyd George*, pp. 362–68; Robert J. Scally, *The Origins of the Lloyd George Coalition: The Politics of Social Imperialism, 1900–1918* (Princeton, 1975), pp. 172–96.

26. *War Memoirs* 1:21.

27. Grigg, *Lloyd George*, pp. 308–9.

28. Shannon, *Crisis*, p. 428.

29. *Essays in English History*, pp. 268–69.

30. Churchill, *World Crisis* 1:114–15.

31. Ibid., p. 123.

32. James, *Churchill*, pp. 66–67; Shannon, *Crisis*, pp. 459–65.

33. Shannon, *Crisis*, p. 465.

CHAPTER TWO. THE AMERICAN ANSWER

1. Arthur S. Link, David W. Hirst, John E. Little et al., eds., *The Papers of Woodrow Wilson*, 40 vols. to date (Princeton, 1966–) (hereafter *PWW*), 12:362.

2. Ibid., p. 213.

3. Ibid., p. 216.

4. Quoted in Beale, *Roosevelt and the Rise of America*, p. 101; see also pp. 102–15.

5. "The American Commercial Invasion of the World," *Harper's Weekly* 45 (Feb. 16, 1901): 174–75.

6. Link, *PWW* 12:222.

7. For an excellent description of this apprehension, see David Healy, *U.S. Expansionism: The Imperialist Urge in the 1890s* (Madison, Wis., 1970), chap. 1.

8. Ibid., p. 23.

9. Carroll D. Wright, "Industrial Necessities," *The Forum* 2 (November 1886): 308–15.

10. Quoted in Edward Crapol, *America for the Americans* (Westport, Conn., 1973), p. 147.

11. The debate is in *North American Review* 150 (January 1890): 1–54.

12. *The New Empire: An Interpretation of American Expansion, 1860–1898* (Ithaca, N.Y., 1963), p. 267.

13. Lloyd to John C. Pirie, Dec. 30., 1895, Henry Demarest Lloyd Papers, Minnesota Historical Society, St. Paul, Minnesota. Also see William Appleman Williams, *The Roots of the Modern American Empire* (New York, 1969), esp. chap. 14.

14. James D. Richardson, *A Supplement to a Compilation of the Messages and Papers of the Presidents* (Washington, 1902), pp. 292–96.

15. Kasson to George B. Cortelyou, Oct. 19, 1901, Theodore Roosevelt Papers, Library of Congress, Washington, D.C.

16. Roosevelt to Sen. William E. Chandler, Nov. 2, 1901, ibid.

17. Roosevelt to Butler, May 27, 1902, ibid.

18. Roosevelt to Butler, Aug. 22 and 29, 1902, ibid.

19. Quoted in Beale, *Roosevelt and the Rise of America*, p. 149.

20. Richardson, *Supplement to Messages of the Presidents*, p. 338. Roosevelt's first annual message, written in the immediate aftermath of McKinley's assasination, stressed that anarchy was an international problem calling for a special agreement among nations: "Anarchy is a crime against the whole human race; and all mankind should band against the anarchist. His crime should be made an offense against the law of nations, like piracy and that form of mansteailing known as the slave trade; for it is of far blacker infamy than either. It should be so declared by treaties among all civilized powers" (ibid., p. 318). Thus did questions of social unrest intersect with foreign policy even in TR's day, and preview attitudes among Woodrow Wilson's advisers concerning relations among nations to stabilize and develop the "waste places" of the earth. (See below, nn. 44 and 45.)

21. Ibid., p. 336.

22. Roosevelt to George Otto Trevelyan, Aug. 18, 1906, in Elting E. Morison, et al., eds., *The Letters of Theodore Roosevelt*, 8 vols. (Cambridge, 1951–54), 5:365–66.

23. Speech, March 13, 1907, in Link, *PWW* 17:82–83.

24. Ibid., p. 324.

25. Ibid., p. 337.

26. Ibid. 20:366–67.

27. See Arthur S. Link, *Woodrow Wilson and the Progressive Era* (New York, 1954).

28. Speech, May 23, 1912, Link, *PWW* 24:413–28.

29. Link, *Wilson and Progressive Era*, p. 21; Link, *PWW* 20:14.

30. Link, *PWW* 20:17.

31. Ibid., pp. 38–40.

32. Ibid., pp. 400–413.

33. John Wells Davidson, ed., *The Crossroads of Freedom* (New Haven, 1956), pp. 416–17.

34. Wilson to McAdoo, Nov. 19, 1911, William Gibbs McAdoo Papers, Library of Congress, Washington, D.C.

35. Ray Stannard Baker, *Woodrow Wilson: Life and Letters*, 8 vols. (Garden City, N.Y., 1927–39), 4:128–29.

36. Link, *PWW* 17:135.

37. See Lloyd C. Gardner, "Commercial Preparedness," in William Appleman Williams, *The Shaping of American Diplomacy*, 2 vols. (Chicago, 1970), 2:54–58.

38. *The New Industrial Day* (New York, 1912), pp. 46–47.

39. Bryan to Wilson, rec'd Apr. 30, 1913, encl. copy of *St. Louis Post-Dispatch*, Apr. 20, 1913, Woodrow Wilson Papers, Library of Congress, Washington, D.C. (hereafter Wilson Papers, LC).

40. Ibid.

41. Link, *PWW* 25:24–25.

42. Cary Grayson Diary, Dec. 11, 1918, copy in the possession of Arthur S. Link.

43. *Philip Dru: Administrator* (privately printed, 1912), p. 272.

44. House Diary, May 9, 1913, in Seymour, *Intimate Papers* 1:239.

45. House to Wilson, June 26, 1914, Link, *PWW* 30:256–57.

46. House to Wilson, Aug. 22, 1914, ibid., pp. 432–33.

CHAPTER THREE. INTERVENTION IN MEXICO

1. Spring-Rice to Grey, July 21, 1913, FO 371 1674/35096, PRO, and Spring-Rice to Grey, July 21, 1913, Grey Papers, FO 800/83, PRO.

2. Quoted in John Milton Cooper, Jr., *Walter Hines Page: The Southerner as American, 1855–1918* (Chapel Hill, N.C., 1977), p. 267.

3. Ibid., p. 266.

4. Hale to Bryan, June 18, 1913, Department of State Records, Decimal File (hereafter SD) 812.00/7798½, National Archives of the United States, Washington, D.C. (hereafter NA).

5. Ambassador Henry Lane Wilson was convinced that would be the outcome. For his views see United States Senate, Committee on Foreign Relations, *Investigation of Mexican Affairs: Preliminary Report and Hearings*, 66th cong., 2d sess., 2 vols. (Washington, 1920), 2:2258. For background on European radicalism and the revolution see James D. Cockcroft, *Intellectual Precursors of the Mexican Revolution, 1910–1913* (Austin, Tex., 1968); and on agrarian factors, Eric Wolf, "Mexico," in *Peasant Wars of the Twentieth Century* (New York, 1969), pp. 3–50.

6. Wilfley to Taft, May 7, 1911, William Howard Taft Papers, Library of Congress, Washington, D.C. See also H. Percival Dodge to Philander C. Knox, May 25, 1911, SD 710.11/60, NA.

7. Knox to Speyer & Co., May 1912, SD 812.51/46a, NA, and Montgomery Schuyler to Knox, Nov. 12, 1912, SD 812.51/48, NA, and Dec. 28, 1912, SD 812.51/52, NA. See also Edgar Turlington, *Mexico and Her Foreign Creditors* (New York, 1930), pp. 246–47.

8. H. L. Wilson to Knox, Feb. 18, 1913, United States, Department of State, *FR, 1913*, pp. 720–21. Sir Francis Stronge to Grey, Feb. 21, 1913, FO 371 1671/8498, PRO.

9. Strong to Grey, Feb. 25, 1913, FO 371 1671/9099, PRO.

10. Wilson to Knox, Feb. 26, 1913, *FR, 1913*, pp. 741–42.

11. See Robert F. Smith, *The United States and Revolutionary Nationalism in Mexico, 1916–1932* (Chicago, 1972), pp. 16–17; and Howard F. Cline, *The United States and Mexico*, rev. ed. (New York, 1963), pp. 133–39.

12. Estimates are in Smith, *U.S. and Revolutionary Nationalism*, pp. 5–10; Peter Calvert, *The Mexican Revolution, 1910–1914: The Diplomacy of Anglo-American Conflict* (Cambridge, 1968), pp. 20–21; and Charles C. Cumberland, *The Mexican Revolution: The Constitutionalist Years* (Austin, Tex., 1972), pp. 89–91.

13. *FR, 1913*, p. 760.

14. Bryce to Grey, Feb. 25 and 28, 1913, FO 371 1671/8976, PRO.

15. Grey minute on Stronge to Grey, Feb. 28, 1913, FO 371 1671/9678, PRO.

16. E. David Cronin, ed., *The Cabinet Diaries of Josephus Daniels, 1913–1921* (Lincoln, Neb., 1963), pp. 6–7.

17. Ibid., pp. 42–43; Baker, *Wilson: Life and Letters* 4:243; Arthur S. Link, *Wilson: The New Freedom* (Princeton, 1956), p. 354.

18. Josephus Daniels, *The Wilson Era, Years of Peace—1910–1917* (Chapel Hill, N.C., 1944), p. 182; H. L. Wilson to Bryan, May 15, 1913, SD 812.00/7652, NA.

19. Stronge to Grey, May 14, 1913, FO 371 1673/24920, PRO.

20. House Diary, Mar. 26 and 27, April 1, and May 2, 1913, Edward M. House Papers, Yale University, New Haven.

21. Friedrich Katz, *The Secret War in Mexico: Europe, The United States and the Mexican Revolution* (Chicago, 1981), p. 165. Professor Katz's book is perhaps the most useful study of the diplomacy of the Mexican Revolution available. Many conclusions presented here parallel his findings.

22. Link, *The New Freedom*, p. 349; House Diary, May 2, 1913, House Papers.

23. Spring-Rice to Grey, May 19, 1913, FO 371 1673/24127, PRO.

24. Ibid., and Calvert, *Mexican Revolution*, pp. 191–92.

25. Bryan to Wilson, July 19, 1913, William Jennings Bryan Papers, Library of Congress, Washington, D.C.; Link, *The New Freedom*, pp. 356–57.

26. Stronge to Grey, Aug. 20, 1913, FO 371 1675/38609, PRO.

27. William S. Dodd and Ray Stannard Baker, eds., *The Public Papers of Woodrow Wilson*, 8 vols. (New York, 1925), 3:45–46.

28. Spring-Rice to Grey, Oct. 6, 1913, FO 371 1677/45563, PRO.

29. Edith O'Shaughnessy, *A Diplomat's Wife in Mexico* (New York 1916), pp. 9–15.

30. Carden to Grey, Sept. 12, 1913, FO 371 1676/43839; see also Calvert, *Mexican Revolution*, pp. 221–23.

31. Calvert, *Mexican Revolution*, pp. 226–29.

32. O'Shaughnessy to Bryan, Oct. 11, 1913, *FR, 1913*, p. 837; Calvert, *Mexican Revolution*, pp. 231–34; O'Shaughnessy, *Diplomat's Wife*, pp. 9–10.

33. Link, *The New Freedom*, p. 367; Kendrick A. Clements, "Woodrow Wilson's Mexican Policy, 1913–15," *Diplomatic History* 4 (Spring 1980): 113–36.

34. See the excellent treatment of the Mobile address in Calvert, *Mexican Revolution*, pp. 250–51; Lloyd C. Gardner, "Woodrow Wilson and the Mexican Revolution," in Link, *Wilson and a Revolutionary World*, pp. 3–49.

35. House Diary, Oct. 30, 1913, House Papers.

36. *Philip Dru*, pp. 279–81.

37. Tyrrell to Grey, Nov. 14, 1913, FO 371 1678/52367, PRO; and Link, *The New Freedom*, p. 375.

38. Grey to Spring-Rice, Nov. 11, 1913, FO 371 1678/51806, PRO.

39. Link, *The New Freedom*, pp. 382–83.

40. Ibid., 385–86.

41. House Diary, Dec. 23, 1913, House Papers.

42. Grey to Spring-Rice, Feb. 4, 1914, FO 371 2025/5647, PRO; Spring-Rice to Grey, Feb. 3, 1914, FO 371 2025/6621; on Wilson and Villa, see Clarence C. Clendenen, *The United States and Pancho Villa: A Study in Unconventional Diplomacy* (Ithaca, N.Y., 1961), chap. 5, esp. pp. 60–61; and Katz, *The Secret War*, chap. 8.

43. Spring-Rice to Grey, Feb. 7, 1914, FO 371 2025/7144, PRO.

44. Katz, *The Secret War*, p. 150.

45. Memorandum by Thomas Hohler, Feb. 11, 1914, FO 371 2025, PRO.

46. Spring-Rice to Grey, Mar. 2, 1914, Grey Papers, FO 800/84.

47. Ibid.

48. Lind to Bryan, Mar. 27, 1914, Wilson Papers, LC.

49. P. Edward Haley, *Revolution and Intervention: The Diplomacy of Taft and Wilson with Mexico, 1910–1917* (Cambridge, Mass., 1970), pp. 130–31.

50. Grey to Spring-Rice, April 8, 1914; Spring-Rice to Grey, April 8, 1914, FO 371 2026/15749, PRO.

51. Department of State to the British Embassy, April 10, 1914, FO 371 2027/16436, PRO.

52. Link, *The New Freedom*, p. 395.

53. Daniels, *The Wilson Era, 1910–1917*, pp. 193–95.

54. Carranza to Wilson, April 22, 1914; Bryan to Letcher, April 24, 1914, both in *FR, 1914*, pp. 483–86.

55. Wilson to Garrison, Aug. 8, 1914, in Link, *PWW* 30:360–61.

56. See Gardner, "Wilson and the Mexican Revolution," where this point is elaborated upon at greater length.

57. *Address of President Wilson at Independence Hall, July 4, 1914* (Washington, D.C., 1917).

58. Wilson to Page, June 1, 1914, Ray Stannard Baker Papers, Library of Congress, Washington, D.C.; Wilson to Page, June 4, 1914, Walter Hines Page Papers, Library of Congress, Washington, D.C.

59. Grey to Colville Barclay, July 2, 1914, FO 371 2030/30568, PRO.

60. Lansing to Wilson, Aug. 9, 1915, Wilson Papers, LC.

61. Ibid.

62 Barclay to Grey, Aug. 13, 1915, FO 371 2402/117782, PRO.

63. Wilson to Lansing, Aug. 8, 1915, SD 812.00/15752½, NA.

64. See Friedrich Katz, "Pancho Villa and the Attack on Columbus, New Mexico," *American Historical Review* 83 (February 1978): 101–30; and Katz, *The Secret War*, pp. 298–305.

65. Katz, *The Secret War*, pp. 298–305.

66. Ibid.

67. House to Wilson, April 7, 1916, Wilson Papers, LC; Wilson to House, June 22, 1916, Baker Papers; House to Wilson, June 25, 1916, Wilson Papers, LC.

68. Hohler to Grey, May 25, 1916, FO 371 2700/100832, PRO, and Grey's minute on same.

69. Claude Dawson to Lansing, Aug. 11, 1916, SD 812.6363/245, NA.

70. *FR, 1917*, pp. 1062–63; Spring-Rice to Balfour, Mar. 1, 1917, FO 371 2959/45836, PRO.

71. On Carranza's maneuvers see Ramón Eduardo Ruíz, *The Great Rebellion: Mexico, 1905–1924* (New York, 1980), chap. 20.

72. For a longer discussion of this ambiguous situation, see Lloyd Gardner, *A Covenant with Power: America and World Order from Wilson to Reagan* (New York, 1984), chap. 1.

73. Grey to Spring-Rice, Nov. 12, 1916, FO 371 2706/235235, PRO; Grey to Thurston, Nov. 22, 1916, FO 371 2705/22882, PRO; Anderson Diary, Nov. 13 and 15, 1916, Chandler P. Anderson Papers, Library of Congress, Washington, D.C.

74. For background see Marvin D. Bernstein, *The Mexican Mining Industry, 1890–1950* (Albany, N.Y., 1964), pp. 78–80. On July 21, 1908, Consul General Benjamin Ridgely advised the State Department about pending mining legislation, "It is certain that this plan, if promulgated, will operate to the serious disadvantage of American enterprises already existing in Mexico and it is equally certain that it will prevent American capital in the future from seeking investments here." Pressure was put on Díaz to oppose any such legislation. State Department Numerical File, 4021/ 16, NA. See also David Thompson to Secretary of State, July 28, 1908, SD 4021/18, NA.

75. *FR, 1917*, pp. 947–57.

76. Memorandum by Polk, Nov. 23, 1916, SD 812.6363/270, NA; undated memorandum by Hohler, FO 371 2706/230070, PRO.

77. Undated Hohler memorandum, FO 371 2706/230070, PRO.

78. Smith, *U.S. and Revolutionary Nationalism*, pp. 96–97; Lansing to Ed Smith, Mar. 3, 1917, Robert Lansing Papers, Library of Congress, Washington, D.C.

79. Spring-Rice to Balfour, Mar. 16, 1917, FO 371 2959/57292, PRO.

80. Gardner, "Wilson and the Mexican Revolution."

81. Wilson to Mrs. Galt, Aug. 18, 1915, Link, *PWW* 34:240–44.

CHAPTER FOUR. UPHEAVAL IN CHINA

1. Draft of an article, enclosed in Reed to Joseph P. Tumulty, June 30, 1914, Link, *PWW* 30:231–38.

2. Grey to Jordan, Oct. 31, 1912, Grey Papers, FO 800/44, PRO.

3. Books on the China consortium include Charles Vevier, *The United States and China, 1906–1913: A Study of Finance and Diplomacy* (New Brunswick, N.J., 1955), and, in a broader context, Jerry Israel, *Progressivism and the Open Door: America and China, 1905–1921* (Pittsburgh, Pa., 1971). A study which puts emphasis on China's role in involving the United States is Michael Hunt, *Frontier Defense and the Open Door Policy* (New Haven, 1973). Finally, one should not forget Herbert Croly, *Willard Straight* (New York, 1924), a still useful insight into the Progressive worldview and China's place in it.

4. Huntington Wilson to H. P. Fletcher, Oct. 20, 1909, SD 5767/101; Wilson to Whitelaw Reid, Oct. 17, 1909, SD 5315/551A; Reid to Knox, Oct. 18, 1909, SD 5315/552, all in NA; *FR, 1910*, pp. 234–35.

5. Jan. 6, 1910, *FR, 1910*, pp. 243–45. See also Walter V. Scholes and Marie V. Scholes, *The Foreign Policies of the Taft Administration* (Columbia, Mo., 1970), pp. 172–73.

6. Grey to James Bryce, Jan. 7, 1911, Grey Papers, FO 800/83, PRO.

7. O. Edmund Clubb, *Twentieth-Century China* (New York, 1964), pp. 38–40.

8. Ibid., pp. 41–42.

9. Scholes and Scholes, *Taft Administration*, pp. 232–33; Morgan & Co. to Knox, Feb. 26, 1912, SD 893.51/777, NA.

10. Reid to Knox, June 27, 1912, SD 893.51/969; Knox to Mitchell Innes, July 2, 1912, SD 893.51/977; Calhoun to Knox, July 9, 1912, SD 893.51/989; Knox to American Embassy, July 18, 1912, SD 893.51/1012A, all in NA.

11. Quoted in Scholes and Scholes, *Taft Administration*, p. 172.

12. Ibid., 156.

13. On British policy and its background, see C. J. Lowe and M. L. Dockrill, *The Mirage of Power: British Foreign Policy, 1914–1922*, 3 vols. (Boston, 1972), 2:274; Ian Nish, *Alliance in Decline* (London, 1972), pp. 68–69; and Robert J. Gowen, "Great Britain and the Twenty-One Demands of 1915: Cooperation versus Effacement," *Journal of Modern History* 43 (March 1971): 76–101.

14. *FR, 1913*, p. 170.

15. Minute, Mar. 19, 1913, FO 371 1593/13033, PRO.

16. Bryce to Grey, Mar. 21, 1913, FO 371 1593/15570, PRO.

17. Ibid., and Bryce to Grey, April 1, 1913, FO 371 1593/17041, PRO.

18. The Wilson statement is put into a context of the president's developing attitudes

toward both Mexico and China in Lloyd C. Gardner, *Wilson and Revolutions: 1913–1921* (Philadelphia, 1976), pp. 64–65.

19. Williams to Bryan, July 11, 1913, *FR, 1913,,* pp. 183–86; Bryan to Williams, Sept. 11, 1913, ibid., pp. 186–87.

20. See Paul S. Reinsch, *An American Diplomat in China* (New York, 1922), pp. 62–69.

21. "Interview," Nov. 27, 1913, Paul S. Reinsch Papers, State Historical Society, Madison, Wisconsin.

22. Ibid.

23. Reinsch to Bryan, Dec. 2, 1913, ibid. On Reinsch's various projects, see Israel, *Progressivism and the Open Door,* pp. 132–37.

24. Grey to Sir Conyngham Greene, Feb. 2, 1914, FO 371 1941/5325, PRO; Peter Lowe, *Great Britain and Japan, 1911–1915* (New York, 1969), pp. 149–59.

25. "Memorandum Communicated to the French Embassy," Mar. 17, 1914, FO 371 1941/9937, PRO.

26. Ibid.

27. Quoted in Lowe, *Britain and Japan,* p. 165.

28. Minute on Jordan to Grey, Feb. 27, 1914, dated Mar. 18, 1914, FO 371 1938/11587, PRO.

29. Jordan to Grey, Mar. 15, 1914, FO 371 1941/11461, PRO; and see Grey to Jordan, Mar. 20, 1914, FO 371 1941/12350, PRO.

30. London *Times,* Mar. 23, 1914, clipping in FO 371 1938, PRO.

31. Charles R. Crane to Wilson, Aug. 2 or 3, 1914, Wilson Papers, LC.

32. See Madeline Chi, *China Diplomacy, 1914–1918* (Cambridge, Mass., 1970), pp. 1–17; Lowe, *Britain and Japan,* pp. 181–91, 218.

33. Jordan to Grey, Aug. 19, 1914, and minutes thereon, FO 371 2017/40873, PRO; and Chi, *China Diplomacy,* pp. 7–8.

34. Grey to Greene, "Very Confidential," Aug. 22, 1914, FO 371 2017/43718, PRO. Emphasis added. See also Colville Barclay to Grey, Aug. 17, 1914, FO 371 2017/403550, PRO.

35. Spring-Rice to Grey, Aug. 25, 1914, Grey Papers, FO 800/84, PRO.

36. Lowe, *Great Britain and Japan,* p. 194.

37. Bryan to Wilson, Oct. 2, 1914, Bryan Papers.

38. Chi, *China Diplomacy,* pp. 26–27, 31.

39. Reinsch, *American Diplomat in China,* pp. 129–30.

40. Wilson to Bryan, Jan. 25, 1915, Bryan Papers; Reinsch to Bryan, Feb. 1, 1915, forwarded to Wilson, Wilson Papers, LC.

41. E. T. Williams to Bryan, Feb. 2, 1915, Wilson Papers, LC.

42. Ibid.

43. Wilson to Reinsch, Feb. 8, 1915, ibid.

44. Spring-Rice to Grey, April 2, 1915, FO 371 2323/38669, PRO; "Papers Communicated by the Japanese Ambassador," April 28, 1915, FO 371 2323/51932, PRO; Gowen, "Great Britain and the Twenty-One Demands"; Lowe, *Great Britain and Japan,* p. 246.

45. Wilson to Bryan, May 10, 1915, Bryan Papers; Arthur S. Link, *Wilson: The Struggle for Neutrality* (Princeton, N.J., 1960), pp. 307–8; Lowe, *Britain and Japan,* p. 251.

46. Lowe, *Britain and Japan,* pp. 232–34; Grey to Spring-Rice, Feb. 12, 1915, FO 371 2322/18530, PRO.

47. Feb. 19, 1915, FO 371 2322/19478, PRO.

48. Gowen, "Great Britain and the Twenty-One Demands."

49. Spring-Rice to Grey, April 2, 1915, FO 371 2323/38669, PRO.

50. Reinsch to Wilson, Mar. 5, 1915, with enclosures, Wilson Papers, LC; Wilson to B. Howell Griswold, Jr., June 8, 1915, ibid.; Burton F. Beers, *Vain Endeavor: Robert Lansing's Attempts to End the Japanese-American Rivalry* (Durham, N.C., 1962), pp. 74–75; Reinsch to Lansing, Dec. 15, 1915, SD 893.77/1498, NA; Willard Straight to Lansing, Dec. 21, 1915, ibid., 1502.

51. Reinsch to Lansing, April 3, 1916, Wilson Papers, LC.

52. Wilson to Lansing, April 7, 1916, SD 793.94/516½, NA.

53. Andrew Nathan, *Peking Politics, 1918–1923* (Berkeley, 1976), p. 25.

54. Lansing to Wilson, June 15, 1916, SD 893.51/1652, NA; Wilson to Lansing, June 21, 1916, ibid., 3009.

55. Spring-Rice to Grey, June 20, 1916, FO 371 2651/120021, PRO; Lansing to Reinsch,

June 20 and 27, 1916, SD 893.51/1652, NA; E. T. Williams to Lansing, June 21, 1916, ibid., William Phillips to Polk, July 12, 1916, Frank L. Polk Papers, Yale University; Phillips to Polk, July 13, 1916, ibid.

56. Schiff to Polk, Oct. 10, 1916, and Williams to Polk, Oct. 11, 1916, Polk Papers.

57. Polk to Schiff, Oct. 18, 1916, ibid.; Guthrie to Lansing, Aug. 1, 1916, SD 793.94/538½, NA.

58. Paolo E. Colletta, ed., "Bryan Briefs Lansing," *Pacific Historical Review* 27 (Nov. 1958): 383–96; House Diary, July 24, 1915, House Papers.

59. Guthrie to Lansing, Sept. 25, 1916, SD 793.94/540½, NA.

60. Israel, *Progressivism and the Open Door*, pp. 140–42; Beers, *Vain Endeavor*, pp. 104–5.

61. *New York Times*, Nov. 17, 1916, clipping in FO 371 2652, PRO; see also Beers, *Vain Endeavor*, pp. 86–87.

62. Undated minute on Barclay to Grey, Nov. 17, 1916, FO 371 2652/232539, PRO.

63. Grey to Spring-Rice, Mar. 23, 1916, FO 371 2653/57229, PRO; Grey to Spring-Rice, April 8, 1916, FO 371 2645/66319, PRO.

64. Jordan to Grey, April 14, 1916, FO 371 2656/88887, PRO; Minutes by Lyon and Gregory, undated and April 28, 1916, on Willard Straight to Foreign Office, April 26, 1916, FO 371 2656/79845, PRO.

65. Grey to British Ambassadors in Paris, St. Petersburg, and Tokyo, June 12, 1916, FO 371 2651/110613, PRO.

66. Undated minute on Greene to Grey, June 25, 1916, FO 371 2651/122439, PRO; Grey to Greene, June 27, 1916, ibid., 124742.

67. Greene to Grey, July 10, 1916, FO 371 2651/163748, PRO; Grey to Jordan, July 31, 1916, ibid., 146765; Grey to Greene, July 31, 1916, FO 371 2652/150708, PRO.

68. Reinsch to Lansing, Nov. 15, 1916, SD 893.811/235, NA.

69. *FR, 1917*, pp. 161–63, 170–71; Beers, *Vain Endeavor*, pp. 94–95; memorandum by Lansing, Jan. 25, 1917, *FR, 1917*, pp. 117–18.

70. Ibid.

71. Guthrie to Lansing, Jan. 27, 1917, *FR, 1917*, p. 118; Nish, *Alliance in Decline*, pp. 198–207.

72. Spring-Rice to Balfour, Jan. 18, 1917, FO 371 2907/23664, PRO.

73. Minute, Jan. 31, 1917, on ibid.; Nish, *Alliance in Decline*, pp. 203–5; Greene to Balfour, Jan. 27, 1917, FO 371 2950/22099, PRO.

74. Quotation from Nish, *Alliance in Decline*, p. 208; see also War Cabinet Meeting (hereafter WC) 51, Feb. 1, 1917, WC 54, Feb. 5, 1917, and WC 63, Feb. 12, 1917, all in Cabinet Office Papers (hereafter CAB) 23/1, PRO.

75. Reinsch to Lansing, Jan. 19, 1917, Wilson Papers, LC.

76. Reinsch, *American Diplomat in China*, pp. 246–47, 251–52; Reinsch to Lansing, Feb. 6, 1917, *FR, 1917, Supplement I*, pp. 401–2.

77. Lansing to Reinsch, Feb. 10, 1917, 1 p.m. and 4 p.m., *FR, 1917, Supplement I*, p. 408.

78. Reinsch to Lansing, Feb. 12, 1917, Breckinridge Long Papers, Library of Congress, Washington, D.C.; Reinsch to Wilson, Feb. 4, 1917, Wilson Papers, LC.

79. Memorandum by E. T. Williams, Feb. 17, 1917, Long Papers; Lansing to Reinsch, Feb. 17 and 26, 1917, *FR, 1917, Supplement I*, pp. 410–11; Beers, *Vain Endeavor*, pp. 98–100.

80. Lansing to Reinsch, Mar. 12, 1917, *FR, 1917, Supplement I;* p. 419.

81. Minute on Alston to Foreign Office, April 6, 1917, FO 371 2911/62811, PRO.

82. Balfour to Alston, Mar. 8, 1917, FO 371 2916/47792, PRO; Minutes of Second Meeting of IWC, Mar. 22, 1917, Austen Chamberlain Papers, Birmingham University, Birmingham, England, AC 20/8/3.

83. Balfour to Lloyd George, April 27, 1917, FO 371 3119/86512, PRO.

84. Minute, April 26, 1917, FO 371 2911/87032, PRO.

CHAPTER FIVE. EXPLODING GERMANY

1. For a general survey of the development of British war aims, see V. H. Rothwell, *British War Aims and Peace Diplomacy, 1914–1918* (Oxford, 1971).

2. Quoted in Michael Fry, *Lloyd George and Foreign Policy*, vol. 1, *The Education of a Statesman: 1890–1916* (Montreal, 1977), p. 247.

3. Page to Wilson, Aug. 3, 1914, Wilson Papers, LC.

4. See Zara S. Steiner, *Britain and the Origins of the First World War* (London, 1977), pp. 116–17.

5. Memorandum, by Sir Francis Bertie, July 4, 1914, Francis Bertie Papers, FO 800/177, PRO.

6. Steiner, *Britian and the First World War*, p. 150.

7. Arno Mayer, "Domestic Causes of the First World War," in Leonard Kreiger and Fritz Stern, eds., *The Responsibility of Power* (New York, 1967), p. 290; Grey of Fallodon, *Twenty-Five Years, 1892–1916*, 2 vols. (London, 1925), 2:55.

8. Steiner, *Britain and the First World War*, p. 234.

9. Grey, *Twenty-Five Years* 2:163.

10. Ibid., pp. 317–18.

11. Alexander P. Noyes, *The War Period of American Finance* (New York, 1926), pp. 52, 62–63, 66–67; Link, *Struggle for Neutrality*, p. 81.

12. Link, *Struggle for Neutrality*, pp. 82–83.

13. Ibid., p. 87; see also McAdoo, *Crowded Years*, pp. 304–5. J. P. Morgan to Wilson, Sept. 4, 1914, and Seth Low to Wilson, Aug. 29, 1914, Wilson Papers, LC.

14. Henry Lee Higginson to Wilson, July 30, 1914, July 31, and Aug. 4, Wilson Papers, LC.

15. Seth Low to Wilson, Aug. 29, 1914, ibid.

16. Quoted in Baker, *Wilson: Life and Letters* 4:372–73.

17. House to Wilson, Aug. 22, 1914, Wilson Papers, LC; Link, *Struggle for Neutrality*, p. 50.

18. House Diary, Sept. 28, 1914, House Papers.

19. Link, *Struggle for Neutrality*, p. 205.

20. Ibid., pp. 210–11; House Diary, Dec. 20, 1914, House Papers; Seymour, *Intimate Papers* 1:341–42; Ernest May, *The World War and American Isolation, 1914–1917* (Cambridge, Mass., 1959), pp. 81–83; and see Patrick Devlin, *Too Proud to Fight: Woodrow Wilson's Neutrality* (New York, 1975), pp. 245–46.

21. Seymour, *Intimate Papers*, 1:340–42; Rothwell, *British War Aims*, p. 22.

22. Anderson Diary, Jan. 9, 1915, Anderson Papers.

23. Rothwell, *British War Aims*, pp. 22–26.

24. House Diary, Feb. 10 and 11, 1915, House Papers; Seymour, *Intimate Papers* 1:350–51.

25. House to Wilson, Feb. 15, 1915, Wilson Papers, LC.

26. Ibid.

27. Seymour, *Intimate Papers* 1:372–73; Link, *Struggle for Neutrality*, pp. 221–22; Wilson to House, Feb. 20, 1915, and House to Wilson, Feb. 23, 1915, Wilson Papers, LC.

28. May, *American Isolation*, pp. 100–109.

29. House to Wilson, May 14, 1915, Wilson Papers, LC; see also House to Wilson, May 9, 1915, House Papers.

30. Grey to House, June 6, 1915, Seymour, *Intimate Papers* 2:54; House to Wilson, June 3, 1915, House Papers.

31. Wilson to House, May 18, 1915, Baker Papers; Sen. Morris Shepard to Bryan, May 29, 1915, SD 763.72112/365, NA.

32. Spring-Rice to Grey, July 15, 1915, Grey Papers, FO 800/95, PRO.

33. Wilson to House, Aug. 5, 1915, Baker Papers; McAdoo to Wilson, Aug. 21, 1915, United States Senate, Special Committee, *Hearings before the Special Committee Investigating the Munitions Industry*, 74th Cong., 2d sess., 40 pts. (Washington, 1937), pt. 27, pp. 8398–99; German Embassy to Secretary of State, Aug. 22, 1915, SD 763.72112/1504, NA; Wilson to House, Aug. 31, 1915, Wilson Papers, LC.

34. Wilson to House, Aug. 21, 1915, Baker Papers; McAdoo to Wilson, Aug. 21, 1915, Senate Committee, *Munitions Industry*, pt. 26, pp. 8123–25; Lansing to Wilson, Sept. 6, 1915, FR, Lansing Papers 1:144–47.

35. Wilson to Lansing, Aug. 26, 1915, FR, Lansing Papers 1:144; May, *American Isolation*, p. 41.

36. Wilson to House, Sept. 7, 1915, Baker Papers.

37. Fry, *Lloyd George and Foreign Policy* 1:220–23; and see George W. Egerton, *Great Britain and the Creation of the League of Nations* (Chapel Hill, N.C., 1978), pp. 25–31.

38. Wilson to House, Dec. 24, 1915, Baker Papers; House Diary, Jan. 6, 1916, House Papers.

39. House Diary, Jan. 6, 1916, House Papers.

40. House to Wilson, Jan. 11, 1916, Wilson Papers, LC.

41. House to Wilson, Feb. 10 and 11, 1916, ibid.; House Diary, Feb. 10–14, House Papers; Seymour, *Intimate Papers* 2:171–72, 174–76.

42. Seymour, *Intimate Papers* 2:180–82; House to Wilson, Feb. 16, 1916, Wilson Papers, LC.

43. Seymour, *Intimate Papers* 2:225–27.

44. House to Wilson, April 3, 1916, Wilson Papers, LC; House to Grey, April 6 and 7, 1916, House Papers.

45. Grey to House, April 7, 1916, House Papers.

46. House to Wilson, April 22, 1916, Wilson Papers, LC; May, *American Isolation*, p. 252; House Diary, May 3, 1916, House Papers.

47. House Diary, May 9, 1916, House Papers; House to Grey, May 10 and 11, 1916, Wilson Papers, LC; Seymour, *Intimate Papers* 2:278–80.

48. Seymour, *Intimate Papers* 2:278–80.

49. House Diary, May 13, 1916, House Papers; House to Wilson, May 14, 1916, Wilson Papers, LC.

50. Wilson to House, May 16, 1916, Baker Papers.

51. Wilson to House, May 18, 1916, ibid.

52. Grey to House, May 29, 1916, House Papers.

53. Grey to Spring-Rice, July 29, 1916, Grey Papers, FO 800/86, PRO.

54. See the discussion in Egerton, *Great Britain and the Creation of the League*, pp. 31–33.

55. H. W. V. Temperley, ed., *A History of the Peace Conference of Paris*, 6 vols. (London, 1921), 5:366–69.

56. Lansing to Wilson, June 23, 1916, *FR, Lansing Papers,* 1:311–12; and see Carl Parrini, *Heir to Empire: United States Economic Diplomacy, 1916–1923* (Pittsburgh, Pa., 1969).

57. George Creel, "The Next Four Years: An Interview with the President," *Everybody's Magazine* 36 (Feb. 1917): 129–39; "Annual Message," Dec. 5, 1916, *FR, 1916*, p. xii.

58. "The Blunder of the Allied Economic Conference in Paris in June, 1916," Aug. 25, 1917, Robert Lansing Papers, Library of Congress, Washington, D.C.

59. Ibid.; "The President's Attitude Toward Great Britain and its Dangers," Sept. (n.d.) 1916, ibid.

60. Seymour, *Intimate Papers* 2:316–17.

61. Gerard to Lansing, Sept. 25, 1916, *FR, 1916, Supplement*, p. 55.

62. May, *American Isolation*, p. 394; and see Fritz Fischer, *Germany's Aims in the First World War* (New York, 1967), pp. 292–93.

63. Senate Committee, *Munitions Industry*, pt. 28, 8734–35.

64. House Diary, Oct. 27, 1916, House Papers; Wilson to W. P. G. Harding, Nov. 26, 1916, ibid.

65. House Diary, Nov. 17, 1916, House Papers: Wilson to House, Nov. 24, 1916, Baker Papers.

66. May, *American Isolation*, p. 365; Lansing to Grew, Nov. 29, 1916, *FR, 1916, Supplement*, pp. 70–71; Grew to Lansing, Dec. 1, 1916, SD 763.72119/190, NA; "What Will the President Do?," Dec. 3, 1916, Lansing Papers; Lansing to Wilson, Dec. 10, 1916, Wilson Papers, LC.

67. "Minutes of a Meeting at 10 Downing St.," Dec. 26, 1916, CAB 28/2, IC-13a, PRO.

68. Harold I. Nelson, *Land and Power: British and Allied Policy on Germany's Frontiers, 1916–1919* (London, 1963), pp. 11–13.

69. Ibid., p. 16; Arthur Marwick, *Britain in the Century of Total War* (London, 1968), pp. 90–91.

70. Robert J. Scally, *The Origins of the Lloyd George Coalition: The Politics of Social-Imperialism, 1900–1918* (Princeton, 1975), pp. 344–48.

71. Ibid., p. 350.

72. Ibid., p. 354.

73. See note 67 above.

74. Rothwell, *British War Aims*, p. 65.

75. House to Wilson, Jan. 20, 1917, Wilson Papers, LC; see Arno J. Mayer, *Wilson vs. Lenin: Political Origins of the New Diplomacy* (Cleveland, 1964), p. 158; Seymour, *Intimate Papers* 2:417–18.

76. Mayer, *Wilson vs. Lenin*, pp. 160–62.

77. See, for example, Fischer, *Germany's Aims in the First World War.*
78. Quoted in May, *American Isolation,* pp. 367–68.
79. "Memorandum on the Severance of Diplomatic Relations with Germany," Feb. 4, 1917, Lansing Papers.
80. Lansing to Page, Feb. 8, 1917, SD 763.72119/483A, NA.
81. Page to Lansing, Feb. 10, 1917, SD 763.72119/488, NA.
82. Spring-Rice to Balfour, Feb. 23, 1917, Balfour Papers, BM.
83. Page to Lansing, Mar. 5, 1917, Senate Committee, *Munitions Industry,* pt. 28, pp. 8504–5.
84. Lansing to House, Mar. 19, 1917, House Papers.
85. "Proces-verbal of the First Meeting of the Imperial War Cabinet," Mar. 20, 1917, Chamberlain Papers, AC 20/8/2.

CHAPTER SIX. THE RUSSIAN GLACIER

1. Balfour to Lloyd George, April 27, 1917, FO 371 3119/86512, PRO.
2. Francis to Wilson, Feb. 22, 1917, Wilson Papers, LC.
3. On this point see Mark Ferro, *The Russian Revolution of February, 1917,* trans. J. G. Richards (Englewood, N.J., 1972), chap. 1; Norman Stone, *The Eastern Front, 1914–1917* (London, 1975), pp. 18–30.
4. Quoted in A. J. P. Taylor, *The Struggle for Mastery in Europe, 1848–1918* (Oxford, 1954), pp. 509–10.
5. Michael G. Ekstein and Zara Steiner, "The Sarajevo Crisis," in F. H. Hinsley, *British Foreign Policy under Sir Edward Grey* (London, 1977), p. 408.
6. Taylor, *Struggle for Mastery,* p. 540.
7. Buchanan to Grey, Mar. 13, 1915, Bertie Papers, FO 800/177, PRO; also Memorandum, Mar. 16, 1915, ibid.
8. "The War and Russian Social Democracy," in *Selected Works,* 12 vols. (New York, 1934), 5:126.
9. See Stone, *Eastern Front,* chaps. 7–8; Grey, *Twenty-Five Years* 2:217–18.
10. Buchanan to Grey, Nov. 5, 1915, Grey Papers, FO 800/25, PRO.
11. Link, *Struggle for Neutrality,* p. 205.
12. Marye to Bryan, Dec. 28, 1914, SD 661.1112/14, NA; Lansing to Marye, June 19, 1915, SD 711.612/240A, NA; Charles Gwynne to Lansing, Jan. 6, 1916, SD 611.0031/80, NA; Willard Straight to Lansing, Jan. 14, 1916, Lansing Papers.
13. George Frost Kennan, *Russia Leaves the War* (Princeton, 1956), pp. 35–38; Lansing to Straight, Jan. 20, 1916, Lansing Papers; Straight to Henry P. Fletcher, Feb. 24, 1917, The Willard Straight Papers, Cornell University, Ithaca, New York.
14. Francis to Wilson, April 8, 1916, SD 711.612/247½, NA; Francis to Lansing, April 10, 1916, ibid.; Francis to House, April 13, 1916, House Papers.
15. Francis to Lansing, May 1 and 2, 1916, *FR, Lansing Papers* 2:309–13; see also David Francis, *Russia from the American Embassy* (New York, 1921), pp. 8–9.
16. Francis to Lansing, May 20, 1916, *FR, Lansing Papers* 1:148–50; Samuel McRoberts to Frank Vanderlip, May 24, 1916, SD 861.51/110, NA; Lansing to Francis, June 8, 1916, ibid.; Francis to Lansing, June 19, 1916, SD 861.51/117, NA; Francis to Lansing, May 29, 1916, Wilson Papers, LC; Francis to Lansing, Oct. 24, 1916, Lansing Papers.
17. Lloyd George, *The War Memoirs of David Lloyd George,* 2 vol. ed. (London, 1936), 1:552–53, 562–63.
18. Ibid., p. 930.
19. Edward Crankshaw, *The Shadow of the Winter Palace: The Drift to Revolution, 1825–1917* (London, 1976), p. 310; Sir George Buchanan, *My Mission to Russia and Other Diplomatic Memories,* 2 vols. (London, 1923), 2:44–50.
20. Lloyd George, *War Memoirs* 1:950.
21. Buchanan to Balfour, Mar. 15, 1917, FO 371 2995/56428, PRO.
22. Ibid.
23. Charles Hardinage to Buchanan, Mar. 16, 1917, ibid.
24. Balfour to Buchanan, Mar. 16, 1917, FO 371 2998/57216, PRO.
25. Balfour to Buchanan, Mar. 17, 1917, Balfour Papers, FO 800/205, PRO.

26. Balfour to Buchanan, Mar. 17, 1917, FO 371 2995/57143, PRO; Buchanan to Balfour, Mar. 18, 1917, FO 371 2998/58189, PRO.

27. Ibid.

28. 91 *H.C. Debates,* 5th ser., cols. 1472–73, 1538.

29. Ibid., cols. 2090–92.

30. For texts see Anthony Summers and Tom Mongold, *The File on the Tsar* (New York, 1976), pp. 244, 246; see also Harold Nicolson, *King George the Fifth* (New York, 1953), p. 299.

31. Lloyd George, *War Memoirs* 1:971–72.

32. WC 100, Mar. 21, 1917, CAB 23/2, PRO; Balfour to Buchanan, Mar. 21, 1917, FO 371 2998/59540, PRO.

33. Lloyd George, *War Memoirs* 1:972–73; Balfour to Buchanan, Mar. 23, 1917, FO 371 2998/62911, PRO.

34. Lloyd George, *War Memoirs* 1:973–75.

35. Summers and Mongold, *File on the Tsar,* p. 249; see also WC 118, April 13, 1917, CAB 23/2, PRO.

36. Ibid., and Balfour to Buchanan, April 13, 1917, Balfour Papers, FO 800/205, PRO.

37. Compare Lloyd George, *War Memoirs,* 1:975–76, and Buchanan to Balfour, April 15, 1917, Balfour Papers, FO 800/205, PRO; Summers and Mongold, *File on the Tsar,* p. 252; see also Bernard Pares, *The Fall of the Russian Monarchy* (New York, 1939), pp. 478–79; Keith Middlemas, ed., *Thomas Jones: Whitehall Diary,* vol. 1, *1916–1925* (London, 1969), pp. 25–26; Paul B. Johnson, *Land Fit for Heroes: The Planning of British Reconstruction, 1916–1919* (Chicago, 1968), p. 38.

38. Francis to Lansing, Mar. 18, 1917, *FR, Russia, 1918* 1:5–6; N. Gordon Levin, *Woodrow Wilson and World Politics* (New York, 1968), chap. 1.

39. House to Wilson, Mar. 17, 1917, Wilson Papers, LC.

40. Francis to Lansing, Mar. 19, 1917, *FR, 1918, Russia* 1:7.

41. Francis to Lansing, April 6, 1917, ibid. 3:2–3, 4–10.

42. Ibid.

43. Francis to Lansing, Mar. 23, 1917, ibid. 1:15–16.

44. Rex A. Wade, *The Russian Search for Peace, February–October, 1917* (Stanford, Calif., 1969), pp. 28–29.

45. Buchanan, *My Mission to Russia* 2:111–12; Buchanan to Balfour, April 8, 1917, FO 371 2996/73018, PRO.

46. House to Wilson, April 10, 1917, Wilson Papers, LC.

47. Spring-Rice to Balfour, April 10, 1917, FO 371 2996/73701, PRO.

48. Lansing to Wilson, April 12, 1917, SD 763.72/3800½, NA.

49. Lansing to Wilson, April 12, 1917; Wilson to Lansing, April 12, 1917, *FR, Lansing Papers* 2:326–27.

50. Wilson to Lansing, April 19, 1917, SD 763.72/4031½, NA; House to Wilson, April 20, 1917, Wilson Collection, P.

51. Wise to Wilson, April 27, 1917; Wilson to Wise, April 28, 1917, Wilson Collection, P; House to Wilson, April 13, 1917, ibid.; Lansing to Wilson, April 30, 1917, SD 763.72/4386½, NA; William Appleman Williams, *American-Russian Relations, 1781–1947* (New York, 1952), pp. 86–87.

52. Walling letter forwarded to Lansing, May 3, 1917, SD 763.72/4390½, NA.

53. Lansing to Wilson, April 30, 1917, Wilson Collection, P.

54. Lansing to Wilson, May 17, 1917, ibid.; Balfour to Cecil, May 23, 1917, FO 115/2317, PRO.

55. Wilson to George Creel, May 18, 1917, Wilson Collection, P; *FR, 1917, Supplement 2* 1:71–73; House to Wilson, June 5, 1917, Wilson Collection, P.

56. Page to Wilson, June 8, 1917, Wilson Collection, P.

57. Howard to Balfour, April 14, 1917, FO 371 3005/77528, PRO.

58. Wade, *Russian Search for Peace, chap. 4;* J. M. Winter, "Arthur Henderson, the Russian Revolution, and the Reconstruction of the Labour Party," *Historical Journal* 15 (Dec. 1972): 753–73; WC 144, May 23, 1917, CAB 23/2, PRO; Buchanan to Balfour, May 17, 1917, FO 371 2998/100809, PRO.

59. Buchanan to Balfour, May 17, 1917, FO 371 2998/100809, PRO.

60. Cecil to Bertie, May 8, 1917, FO 371 3005/94018, PRO.

61. George Curzon, "Policy in View of Russian Developments," May 12, 1917, G.T. 703, copy in Chamberlain Papers, AC 20/9/24; Wade, *Russian Search for Peace,* pp. 57–58; Howard to Balfour, May 20, 1917, FO 371 3005/101686, PRO.

62. Lloyd George to Buchanan, May 21, 1917, FO 371 3005/102621, PRO.

63. David Marquand, *Ramsay MacDonald* (London, 1977), pp. 207–9, 213–14; Lloyd George, *War Memoirs* 2:1124–25; William H. Buckler to House, May 31, June 8, June 14, 1917, Wilson Collection, P.

64. Winter, "Arthur Henderson," pp. 753–73.

65. Stephen Roskill, *Hankey: Man of Secrets*, vol. 1 (London, 1970), pp. 418–19.

66. Wade, *Russian Search for Peace*, pp. 106–7; Lloyd George, *War Memoirs* 2:1131–32.

67. Trevor Wilson, ed., *The Political Diaries of C. P. Scott, 1911–1928* (London, 1970), p. 299; Wade, *Russian Search for Peace*, pp. 108–9.

68. Mark Ferro, *The Great War, 1914–1918*, trans. Nicole Stone (London, 1973), pp. 197–8; Winter, "Arthur Henderson," pp. 753–73.

69. Lloyd George, *War Memoirs*, 2:1133–35; Wade, *Russian Search for Peace*, pp. 108–11.

70. Steven R. Graubard, *British Labour and the Russian Revolution* (Cambridge, Mass., 1956), pp. 27–28.

71. Ibid., pp. 3–5; 97 *H.C. Debates* 5th ser., Aug. 13, 1917, cols. 928–32.

72. Lloyd George, *War Memoirs* 2:1130, 1134–35.

73. See W. B. Fest, "British War Aims and German Peace Feelers During the First World War," *Historical Journal* 15 (June 1972): 285–308; Wade, *Russian Search for Peace*, pp. 110–12, 114–17, 160; 97 *H.C. Debates*, 5th ser., Aug. 16, 1917, cols. 1498, 1505, 1523, 1525.

74. Wade, *Russian Search for Peace*, pp. 110–12, 114–17.

75. Root to Lansing, June 17, 1917, *FR, 1918, Russia* 1:120–27.

76. Spring-Rice to Balfour, Aug. 16, 1917, quoted in Sterling J. Kernek, "Distractions of Peace During War: The Lloyd George Government's Reaction to Woodrow Wilson, December 1916–November, 1918," in *Transactions of the American Philosophical Society*, n.s., 65, no. 2 (1975): 54.

77. Transcription of shorthand notes, Aug. 3, 1917, Wilson Collection, P. Question mark in original.

78. Wilson to House, Aug. 16, 1917; House to Wilson, Aug. 19, 1917, Wilson Collection, P.

79. House to Wilson, Aug. 19, 1917, Wilson Collection, P.

80. Lansing to Wilson, Aug. 19, 1917, SD 763.72119/792½, NA.

81. Kernek, "Distractions of Peace," pp. 52–53.

82. House to Wilson, Aug. 15, 1917, Wilson Collection, P.

83. Ibid.

84. Memorandum, Aug. 9, 1917, reprinted in Robert Lansing, *The War Memoirs of Robert Lansing* (Indianapolis, 1935), pp. 337–38.

85. *FR, 1917, Supplement* 2 1:177–79.

86. Eastman to Wilson, Sept. 8, 1917, Wilson Collection, P.

87. Memorandum, Sept. 19, 1917 by Henry Morgenthau, ibid.

88. WC 223, Aug. 24, 1917, CAB 23/3, PRO.

89. WC 229, Sept. 7, 1917, CAB 23/4, PRO; WC 230, 231, Sept. 10 and 12, 1917, CAB 23/4, PRO; Richard Ullman, *Anglo-Soviet Relations, 1917–1921*, 3 vols. (Princeton, 1961–72), 1:11–12.

90. Rothwell, *British War Aims*, pp. 106–10.

91. Ullman, *Anglo-Soviet Relations* 1:15; Buchanan to Balfour, Oct. 20, 1017, FO 371 3011/203530, PRO.

92. Balfour to Buchanan, Oct. 24, 1917, FO 371 3011/205303, PRO.

93. Quoted in Williams, *American-Russian Relations*, pp. 102–3.

94. Francis to Lansing, Nov. 2, 1917, *FR, Russia, 1918* 2:26–27.

95. Jane Degras, ed., *Soviet Documents on Foreign Policy*, (New York, 1951), 1:1–3; E. H. Carr, *The Bolshevik Revolution, 1917–1923*, 3 vols. (London, 1953), 3:6–10.

96. Buchanan to Balfour, Nov. 18, 1917, FO 371 3124/220186, PRO.

97. Reprinted in Gardner, *Wilson and Revolutions*, pp. 90–91.

CHAPTER SEVEN. IDEOLOGICAL FRONT LINES

1. Minutes of War Cabinet 295, Dec. 10, 1917, quoted in C. J. Lowe and M. L. Dockrill, *The Mirage of Power: British Foreign Policy, 1914–1922*, 3 vols. (Boston, 1972) 3:664–69.

2. Edgar Sisson, *One Hundred Red Days* (New Haven, Conn., 1931), p. 29; see also Buchanan to Balfour, Nov. 19, 1917, FO 371 2999/221684, PRO.

3. Summers to Lansing, Nov. 17, 1917, *FR, 1918, Russia* 3:234–35.

4. Newton D. Baker to Wilson, Nov. 23, 1917, with encl., Wilson Papers, P.

5. "Memorandum . . . for the War Cabinet," Dec. 22, 1917, FO 371 3018/241447, PRO.

6. Ibid., and WC 280, Nov. 22, 1917, CAB 23/4, PRO.

7. House to Lansing, Nov. 24, 1917, SD 861.51/277, NA; House Diary, Nov. 16, 1917, quoted in Ullmann, *Anglo-Soviet Relations* 1:26.

8. "Notes of a Conversation Held at the Ministry of Foreign Affairs," Paris, Nov. 30, 1917, FO 371 2955, PRO; House to Wilson, Dec. 2, 1917, *FR, 1918, Russia* 1:255.

9. WC 280, Nov. 22, 1917, CAB 23/4, PRO.

10. Ullman, *Anglo-Soviet Relations* 1:43–44; "Memorandum . . . for the War Cabinet," Dec. 22, 1917, FO 371 3018/241447, PRO; Buchanan to Balfour, Nov. 27, 1917, FO 371 3017, PRO.

11. Buchanan to Balfour, Nov. 29, 1917, FO 371 3018/228823, PRO; WC 286, Nov. 29, 1917, CAB 23/4, PRO; "Memo" to CIGS, Nov. 20, 1917, FO 371 3018/226952, PRO.

12. WC 289, Dec. 3, 1917, CAB 23/4, PRO; Cecil to Buchanan, Dec. 3, 1917, FO 371 3018/229192, PRO; Cecil to Barclay, Dec. 3, 1917, FO 371 3018/226952, PRO.

13. Wilson to House, Dec. 1, 1917, Wilson Collection, P.

14. House to Lansing, Dec. 2, 1917, *FR, 1918, Russia* 2:583–84.

15. Quoted in N. Gordon Levin, *Woodrow Wilson and World Politics* (New York, 1968), p. 59.

16. Creel to Sisson, Dec. 3, 1917, Wilson Collection, P.

17. Lansing to Francis, Dec. 6, 1917, *FR, 1918, Russia* 1:289; Lansing to Smith, Nov. 26, 1917, ibid. 2:582.

18. "Memorandum on the Russian Situation," Dec. 2, 1917, quoted by Lansing in *War Memoirs*, pp. 339–43.

19. See George F. Kennan, *Soviet-American Relations, 1917–1920*, 2 vols. (Princeton, 1956–58), 1:158–59.

20. Spring-Rice to Balfour, Dec. 8, 1917, FO 115/2245, PRO.

21. Spring-Rice to Balfour, Dec. 7, 1917, Balfour Papers, FO 800/209, PRO.

22. Spring-Rice to Balfour, Dec. 13, 1917, FO 115/2245, PRO.

23. Lansing to Wilson, Dec. 12, 1917, and Wilson to Lansing, Dec. 12, 1917, Wilson Papers, P; Spring-Rice to Balfour, Dec. 13, 1917, FO 115/2318, PRO; Lansing to Wilson, and Wilson's note, Dec. 10, 1917, *FR, Lansing Papers* 2:343–46.

24. Spring-Rice to Balfour, Dec. 8, 1917, FO 371 3000/233343, PRO; Lansing to Wilson, Dec. 12, 1917, with encl., *FR, Lansing Papers* 2:345–46.

25. Lansing to Wilson, Dec. 12, 1917, with encl, *FR, Lansing Papers* 2:345–46; and Cronin, *Daniels Diaries*, p. 252; Page to Lansing, Dec. 18, 1917, *FR, 1918, Russia* 2:591–92; Page to Lansing, Dec. 21, 1917, ibid., pp. 595–99; Crosby to Lansing, Dec. 27, 1917, ibid., 697–700.

26. Roland Morris to Lansing, Dec. 24, 1917, *FR, 1918, Russia* 2:11–13; "Memorandum of an Interview," ibid.; John F. Stevens to Daniel Willard, ibid. 3:213–14; Page to Lansing, Dec. 29, 1917, ibid. 1:330–31; Sharp to Lansing, Dec. 23, 1917, ibid. 2:596–97.

27. Quoted in Williams, *American-Russian Relations*, p. 118.

28. "Memorandum of Conversation with Colonel Thompson of the American Red Cross," Dec. 14, 1917, FO 371 3018/238606, PRO.

29. Ibid., Minutes by Sir George Clerk, Dec. 14, 1917, and Hardinage, Dec. 15, 1917.

30. WC 302, Dec. 19, 1917, CAB 23/4, PRO.

31. Eric Drummond to R. Cecil, Dec. 21, 1917, FO 371 3283/741, PRO.

32. Cronin, *Daniels Diaries*, pp. 262–63; Kennan, *Soviet-American Relations* 1:245–46; Creel to Wilson, Dec. 31, 1917, Baker Papers; Diary Entry, Jan. 2, 1918, House Papers.

33. Francis to Lansing, Dec. 24, 1917, *FR, 1918, Russia* 1:324–26; Francis to Lansing, Jan. 2, 1918, ibid., pp. 421–22.

34. Francis to Lansing, Jan. 2, Jan. 1, 1918, ibid., pp. 421–22, 418.

35. Francis to Lansing, Dec. 31, 1917, ibid., pp. 405–6.

36. Lansing to Wilson, Jan. 2, 1918, *FR, Lansing Papers* 2:346–48.

37. Spring-Rice to Balfour, Jan. 4, 1918, in Stephen Gwynn, ed., *The Letters and Friendships of Sir Cecil Spring-Rice*, 2 vols. (Boston, 1929), 2:422–25.

38. Diary entry, Jan. 9, 1918, House Papers; Sisson, *One Hundred Red Days*, pp. 208–9; Francis to Lansing, Jan. 12, 1918, *FR, 1918, Russia* 1:426.

39. Sisson, *One Hundred Red Days*, pp. 208–9.

40. Mayer, *Wilson vs. Lenin*, pp. 322–27, 322–27; Rothwell, *British War Aims*, pp. 151–53.

41. R. H. Bruce Lockhart, *Memoirs of a British Agent* (New York, 1932), pp. 228–29; E. H. Carr, *The Bolshevik Revolution*, 3 vols. (London, 1950–53) 3:45–46. WC 294, Dec. 7, 1917, CAB 23/4, PRO; Memorandum, Dec. 11, 1917, FO 371 3018/234843, PRO; Cecil to Spring-Rice, Jan. 5, 1918, FO 371 3298/4299, PRO.

42. Sir C. Greene to Balfour, Jan. 5, 1918, FO 371 3288/3384, PRO; Greene to Balfour, Jan. 11, 1918, FO 371 3289/7698, PRO.

43. Balfour to Greene, Jan. 16, 1918, FO 371 3289/9343, PRO.

44. Cited in David R. Woodward, "The British Government and Japanese Intervention in Russia During World War I," *Journal of Modern History*, 46(Dec. 1974): 663–85.

45. WC 327, Jan. 21, 1918, CAB 23/5, PRO. The historical battle over the motives for intervention in Russia will rage on until the end of time. For some it is merely a matter of emphasis; for others the ideological questions are as alive today as they were when the participants attempted to sort out the factors for themselves. The latest entry on the side of seeing the intervention as purely military in nature (although he is not shy about presenting evidence that can be interpreted differently) is Michael Kettle, *The Allies and the Russian Collapse, 1917–1918* (Minneapolis, 1981), pp. 218–19.

46. WC 327, Jan. 21, 1918, CAB 23/5, PRO.

47. WC 330A, Jan. 24, 1918, CAB 23/13, PRO.

48. Eric Drummond to Wiseman, Jan. 30, 1918, Balfour Papers, FO 800/223, PRO; Wiseman to House, Jan. 30, 1918, House to Wilson, Jan. 31, 1918, Wilson Papers, LC.; Wilson to Lansing, Jan. 20, 1918, *FR, Lansing Papers* 2:351; Cronin, *Daniels Diaries*, pp. 269–70; House to Wilson, Feb. 2, 1918, Wilson Papers, LC; Wiseman to Drummond, Jan. 30, 1918, Balfour Papers, BM; Colville Barclay to Balfour, Jan. 31, 1918, FO 371 3289/20280, PRO; Balfour to Wiseman, Feb. 8, 1918, Balfour Papers, BM; Wiseman to Drummond, Feb. 3, 1918, CAB 21/45, PRO.

49. Wilson to Lansing, Feb. 4, 1918, SD 861.00/1097, NA.

50. Wilson to Lansing, Feb. 4, 1918, SD 861.01/14½, and Wilson to Lansing, Feb. 4, 1918, with encl., Wilson Collection, P.

51. Memorandum, Feb. 5, 1918, SD 861.01/14½, NA.

52. Lansing to Wilson, Feb. 9, 1918, SD 861.00/4212, NA.

53. Leon Trotsky, *My Life: An Attempt at an Autobiography* (Harmondsworth, Eng., 1975), pp. 393–400.

54. John H. Wheeler-Bennett, *Brest-Litovsk, the Forgotten Peace: March 1918* (London, 1963), pp. 224–27, 237.

55. Trotsky, *My Life*, pp. 397–99.

56. WCs 340 and 341, Feb. 7 and 8, 1918, CAB 23/5, PRO.

57. Middlemas, ed., *Whitehall Diary* 1:48–51; Roskill, *Hankey: Man of Secrets* 1:493–94; Carr, *Bolshevik Revolution* 3:43; Kettle, *Allies and Russian Collapse*, pp. 222–28.

58. Balfour to Lockhart, Feb. 9, 1918, FO 371 3198/21928, PRO.

59. Wiseman to Reading, Feb. 12, 1918, Reading Papers, FO 800/223, PRO; Wilton B. Fowler, *British-American Relations, 1917–1918: The Role of Sir William Wiseman* (Princeton, 1969), pp. 170–71; Balfour to Frederick Lindley, Feb. 13, 1918, FO 371 3298/15369, PRO.

60. Balfour to Lindley, Feb. 13, 1918, FO 371 3298/15369, PRO.

61. Lockhart to Balfour, Feb. 13, 1918, FO 371 3284/29096, PRO; Lockhart to Balfour, Feb. 13, 1918, FO 371 3298/29431, PRO.

62. Lockhart to Balfour, Feb. 16, 1918, FO 371 3299/31645, PRO; Lockhart to Balfour, Feb. 16, 1918, FO 371 3299/32015, PRO; Minutes, Feb. 19, 1918, on FO 371 3299/32150, PRO.

63. Balfour to Lockhart, Feb. 21, 1918, FO 371 3299/31645, PRO; Balfour to Bagge, Feb. 22, 1918, FO 371 3283, PRO; Kettle, *Allies and Russians Collapse*, pp. 230–36.

64. Lockhart, *British Agent*, pp. 228–29; Carr, *Bolshevik Revolution*, 3:45–46.

65. Lockhart, *British Agent*, pp. 228–29.

66. Lindley to Balfour, Feb. 24, 1918, FO 371 3284/37365, PRO.

67. Lockhart to Balfour, Feb. 25, 1918, FO 371 3284/37676, PRO.

68. Ullmann, *Anglo-Soviet Relations* 1:104–5.

69. Lansing to Wilson, Feb. 15, 1918, *FR, Lansing Papers* 2:352–53; Lansing to Francis, Feb. 18, 1918, *FR, 1918, Russia* 1:383.

70. Lansing to Wilson, Feb. 16, 1918, SD 763.72Su/32½, NA; Wilson to Lansing, Feb. 16, 1918, ibid.

71. William Phillips to Lansing, Feb. 16, 1918, *FR, 1918, Russia* 1:383.
72. Levin, *Wilson and World Politics*, p. 72.
73. Lansing to Francis, Feb. 19, 1918, SD 861.77/297b, NA.
74. Lansing to Paul Reinsch, Feb. 13, 1918, *FR, 1918, Russia* 2:44–45; Moser to Lansing, Feb. 3, 1918, ibid. 3:219–20; Stevens to Lansing, Feb. 10, 1918, ibid., p. 220; Morris to Lansing, Feb. 17, 1918, ibid., pp. 220–21.
75. Francis to Lansing, Feb. 24, 1918, ibid. 1:387.
76. See the discussion in Kennan, *Soviet-American Relations* 1:434–40.
77. Summers to Lansing, Feb. 23, 1918, *FR, 1918, Russia* 2:53–54.
78. House to Wilson, Mar. 3, 1918, Wilson Papers, LC; Diary entry, Mar. 2 and 3, 1918, House Papers.
79. *FR, 1918, Russia* 2:67–68.
80. Lockhart, *British Agent*, pp.236–37.
82. Lockhart to Balfour, Mar. 2, 1918, FO 371 3285/40028, PRO.
82. Balfour to Lockhart, Mar. 4, 1918, FO 371 3285/40028, PRO.
83. Lockhart to Balfour, Mar. 8, 1918, FO 371 3285/43859, PRO; Balfour to House, Mar. 6, 1918, Lloyd George Papers, F/60/2/46, The House of Lords, London.
84. Kennan, *Soviet-American Relations* 1:510–11.
85. Kettle, *Allies and Russian Collapse*, p. 259.
86. Francis to Lansing, *FR, 1918, Russia* 1:394–95.
87. Ibid., pp. 395–96; Kennan, *Soviet-American Relations* 1:510–11.
88. *FR, 1918, Russia*, 1:399–400; Kennan, *Soviet-American Relations* 1:515–17; Degras, *Soviet Documents on Foreign Policy* 1:59–61.
89. Carr, *Bolshevik Revolution* 3:69.

CHAPTER EIGHT. VISIONS IN A CLOUDED PRISM

1. D. C. Watt, *A History of the World in the Twentieth Century, Part 1, 1899–1918* (London, 1967), pp. 322–23.
2. Wiseman to Drummond, Mar. 27, 1918, Reading Papers, FO 800/23, PRO.
3. Lockhart to Balfour, Mar. 18, 1918, FO 371 3285/50480, PRO.
4. Ullman, *Anglo-Soviet Relations*, 1:132–33.
5. *FR, 1918, Russia* 1:485–86.
6. Ibid., pp. 486–88; Wilson to Lansing, Mar. 28, 1918, with encl., SD 763.72119/1530½, NA; Wilson to House, Mar. 22, 1918, Baker Papers; Wiseman, "Notes on an Interview," April 1, 1918, Balfour Papers, BM.
7. Draft to Lockhart, April 3, 1918, FO 371 3285, PRO; Balfour to Lockhart, April 10, 1918, FO 371 3285/62282, PRO.
8. Balfour to Lockhart, April 13, 1918, FO 371 3285, PRO; Balfour to Lockhart, April 10, 1918, FO 371 3285/62282, PRO.
9. Middlemas, *Whitehall Diary* 1:59.
10. WC 395, April 19, 1918, CAB 23/6, PRO.
11. Minute, April 24, 1918, on Lockhart to Balfour, April 21, 1918, FO 371 3285/72443, PRO.
12. Reading to Balfour, April 25, 1918, FO 371 3285/75420, PRO.
13. Francis to Lansing, May 2, 1918, *FR, 1918, Russia* 1:519–21.
14. Reinsch to Lansing, April 10, 1918, ibid. 2:117–18.
15. Wilson to Lansing, April 18, 1918, *FR, Lansing Papers* 2:360.
16. Wilson to Lansing, May 20, 1918, and Lansing to Wilson, May 21, 1918, with encl., Wilson Papers, LC.
17. Levin, *Wilson and World Politics*, p. 96.
18. Lansing to Wilson, May 16, 1918, SD 861.00/1894½, NA; Lansing to Wilson, with encl., May 28, 1918, SD 861.00/1907½, NA; *FR, 1918, Russia*, 2:484–85.
19. Lansing to Wilson, June 13, 1918, Wilson Papers, LC.
20. Wiseman to Drummond, June 14, 1918, Balfour Papers, BM.
21. Kennan, *Soviet-American Relations* 2:387.
22. Levin, *Wilson and World Politics*, p. 99.
23. Wilson to Lansing, June 17, 1918, *FR, Lansing Papers* 2:360.

24. Kennan, *Soviet-American Relations* 2:217–24.

25. Ibid., pp. 144–45.

26. WC 409 A, May 11, 1918, CAB 23/14, PRO.

27. See David R. Woodward, "The British Government and Japanese Intervention in Russia During World War I," *Journal of Modern History* 46 (Dec. 1974): 663–85.

28. Lockhart to Balfour, May 9, 1918, FO 371 3285/84749, PRO; Lockhart to Balfour, May 16, 1918, FO 371 3285/89389, PRO.

29. Greene to Balfour, May 15, 1918, FO 371 3183/87990, PRO.

30. WC X-3, May 17, 1918, CAB 23/17, PRO; WC 413, May 17, 1918, CAB 23/6, PRO.

31. Memorandum, May 18, 1918, FO 371 3443/89880, PRO.

32. Lockhart to Balfour, May 26, 1918, FO 371 3286/95628, PRO.

33. WC 427, June 6, 1918, CAB 23/6, PRO; Cecil to Lloyd George, June 7, 1918, The Robert Cecil Papers, BM.

34. WC X-15, June 19, 1918, CAB 23/17, PRO; Balfour to Milner, June 18, 1918, Balfour Papers, FO 800/205, PRO; Reading to Balfour, June 16, 1918, ibid.

35. Balfour to Milner, June 18, 1918, Balfour Papers, FO 800/205, PRO.

36. Balfour to Reading, June 20, 1918, Reading Papers, FO 800/223, PRO.

37. House to Wilson, June 21, 1918, Wilson Papers, LC.

38. Balfour to Reading, June 21, 1918, FO 371 3324/110145, PRO.

39. Bullitt to House, June 24, 1918, House Papers.

40. Lansing to Wilson, June 28, 1918, with encl., Wilson Papers, LC.

41. Kennan, *Soviet-American Relations* 2:392–93; Reading to Balfour, June 28, 1918, FO 371 3324/114697, PRO.

42. "Memorandum on the Siberian Situation," July 4, 1918, Lansing Papers; Kennan, *Soviet-American Relations* 2:394–96.

43. "Memorandum of a Conference in the White House," July 6, 1918, *FR, 1918, Russia* 2:262–63; Cronin, *Daniels Diaries*, pp. 317–18.

44. Cronin, *Daniels Diaries*, pp. 317–18.

45. House to Wilson, July 6, 1918, Wilson Papers, LC.

46. Wilson to House, July 8, 1918, House Papers.

47. Reading to Balfour, July 9, 1918, Reading Papers, FO 800/223, PRO; Lansing to Wilson, July 9, 1918, *FR, 1918, Russia* 2:267–68.

48. Reading to Balfour, June 25, 1918, FO 371 3286/114321, PRO; WC 435A, June 24, 1918, CAB 23/14, PRO; Ullman, *Anglo-Soviet Relations* 1:208–10; WC X-17, June 26, 1918, CAB 23/17, PRO.

49. Lloyd George to Reading, July 10, 1918, Reading Papers, FO 800/224, PRO; Ullman, *Anglo-Soviet Relations* 1:219–20; Balfour to Reading, July 11, 1918, FO 371 3324/118072, PRO; WC 444, July 11, 1918, CAB 23/7, PRO; Reading to Balfour, July 16, 1918, FO 371 3324/124239, PRO.

50. Lockhart to Balfour, July 6, 1918, FO 371 3287/123371, PRO; see also, FO 371 3287/134850, PRO.

51. WC 446, July 16, 1918, CAB 23/7, PRO; *FR, 1918, Russia* 3:134–36; ibid. 2:287–90.

52. Ibid. 3:134–36.

53. Ibid., p. 136.

54. Minutes and Memoranda, July 22–26, 1918, filed in FO 371 3287/120025, PRO.

55. Cecil to Balfour, July 29, 1918, Balfour Papers, FO 800/205, PRO.

56. Polk to Wilson, Aug. 2, 1918, and Wilson to Polk, Aug. 8, 1918, Wilson Papers, LC; Ullman, *Anglo-Soviet Relations* 1:258–59; Barclay to Reading, Aug. 11, 1918, FO 371 3224/138830, PRO; Balfour to Barclay, Aug. 12, 1918, FO 371 3224/138572, PRO; Barclay to Balfour, Aug. 14, 1918, FO 371 3224/141371; *FR, 1918, Russia* 2:344–50; Wilson to Lansing, Aug. 23, 1918, *FR, Lansing Papers* 2:378–79.

57. Wilson to Polk, Aug. 8, 1918, Wilson Papers, LC; Kennan, *Soviet-American Relations* 2:403–4.

58. Wilson to Lewis, July 24, 1918, Wilson Papers, LC.

59. Richard Goldhurst, *The Midnight War: The American Intervention in Russia, 1918–1920* (New York, 1978), pp. 90–93; Cole to Lansing, Sept. 10. 1918, *FR, 1918, Russia* 2:527–30.

60. Cole to Lansing, Sept. 10, 1918, *FR, 1918, Russia* 2:527–30; see also pp. 499–500.

61. Ullman, *Anglo-Soviet Relations* 1:238–40.

62. Francis to Lansing, Aug. 2, 1918, *FR, 1918, Russia* 2:505–6.

63. Wilson to Lansing, Sept. 5, 1918, SD 861.00/7381, NA.

64. Ibid.
65. *FR, 1918, Russia* 3:77–78.
66. Francis to Lansing, Oct. 24, 1918, ibid., p. 79; Poole to Lansing, Nov. 13, 1918, ibid. 2:567–68.
67. Morris to Lansing, Sept. 8, 1918, ibid. 3:245–46.
68. N. D. Baker to Wilson, Nov. 27, 1918, Baker Papers; Baker to Wilson, Nov. 6, 1918, Wilson Papers, LC.
69. Graves to Baker, Nov. 22, 1918, Wilson Papers, LC.
70. Lansing to Wilson, Sept. 9, 1918, encl. Admiral Knight to Daniels, Sept. 6, 1918, Wilson Papers, LC.
71. House Diary, Sept. 24, 1918, House Papers.
72. Ibid., Sept. 19, 1918.
73. Acting Secretary of State to Diplomatic Representatives of the Allies and China, Oct. 10, 1918, *FR, 1918, Russia* 3:147–50; Francis to Lansing, Oct. 17, 1918, ibid., pp. 155–57.
74. Whitehouse to Lansing, Oct. 12, 1918, ibid., pp. 154–55; Lansing to Whitehouse, Oct. 22, 1918, ibid., p. 158.
75. Whitehouse to Lansing, Oct. 29, 1918, ibid., p. 160; Long to Whitehouse, Oct. 31, 1918, ibid.
76. Levin, *Wilson and World Politics*, p. 126; Fowler, *British-American Relations*, pp. 288–89.
77. Martin Gilbert, *Winston S. Churchill*, vol. 4, *1917–1922* (London, 1975), pp. 227–28.
78. Levin, *Wilson and World Politics*, p. 126; Fowler, *British-American Relations*, pp. 227–28.
79. Mayer, *Wilson vs. Lenin*, pp. 62–63.
80. Inga Flota, *Colonel House in Paris: A Study of American Policy at the Paris Peace Conference, 1919* (Copenhagen, 1973), pp. 35–37.
81. Lansing to Ed Smith, Oct. 12, 1918, Lansing Papers.
82. Phillips to Lansing, Oct. 14, 1918, SD 860C.00/10, NA.
83. Roskill, *Hankey* 1:614; Middlemas, *Whitehall Diary* 1:67–70.
84. SWC, IC 88, Nov. 1 & 2, 1918, CAB 28/5, PRO; Lionel Kochan, *The Struggle for Germany, 1914–1945* (New York, 1967), pp. 9–11.
85. Kochan, *Struggle for Germany*, pp. 11–12; Mayer, *Wilson vs. Lenin*, pp. 100–103.
86. Mayer, *Wilson vs. Lenin*, pp. 148–49.
87. WC 502, Nov. 14, 1918, CAB 23/8, PRO.
88. Churchill, *The Aftermath* (London, 1929), p. 20.
89. Lansing to Wilson, Nov. 9, 1918, with encl., Wilson Collection, P.
90. Wilson to Lansing, Nov. 20, 1918, *FR, Paris Peace Conference* 2:268–71; Lansing to Wilson, Nov. 26, 1918, ibid.
91. Seymour, *Intimate Papers* 4:282; "Conference on *George Washington* with Wilson," Dec. 10, 1918, notes by Charles Seymour, copy in Wilson Collection, P.

CHAPTER NINE. THE OUTSKIRTS OF PARIS: MEXICO AND CHINA

1. Spring-Rice to Balfour, Mar. 16, 1917, FO 371 2959/57292, PRO.
2. Anderson Diary, Dec. 29, 1916, and Jan. 3, 1917, Anderson Papers; Memorandum, Mar. 12, 1917, FO 371 2959/65315, PRO.
3. Memorandum, Mar. 12, 1917, FO 371 2959/65315, PRO.
4. Anderson Diary, Mar. 8, 10, 29, April 6 and 10, 1917, Anderson Papers.
5. Fletcher to Lansing, April 10, 1917; Lansing to Wilson, April 11, 1917; Wilson to Lansing, April 11, 1917, all in Baker Papers.
6. Spring-Rice to Foreign Office, April 19, 1917, FO 371 2690/81713, PRO.
7. Lansing to Fletcher, April 28, 1917, Wilson Collection, P.
8. Anderson Diary, May 7, 1917, Anderson Papers.
9. Fletcher to Lansing, June 25, 1917, SD 812.51/293, NA; Anderson Diary, May 7, 1917, Anderson Papers; Minute by R. Sperling, June 4, 1917, FO 371 2961/110559, PRO; H. A. Cummins to Balfour, June 22, 1917, FO 371 2961/148197; Memorandum by Thurston, June 23, 1917, FO 371 2961/148197, PRO.
10. Spring-Rice to Balfour, July 11, 1917, FO 371 2961/137700, PRO; Minute by Sperling, Dec. 10, 1917, FO 371 2964/230821, PRO; *FR, 1917*, pp. 296–98; Spring-Rice to Balfour, July 9, 1917, FO 371 2961/136311, PRO; Anderson Diary, July 17, 1917, Anderson Papers.

11. Anderson Diary, July 17, 1917, Anderson Papers.

12. Spring-Rice to Balfour, July 23, 1917, FO 371 2962/146167, PRO; Long Diary, July 20, 1917, Long Papers.

13. Spring-Rice to Balfour, July 21, 1917, FO 371 2962/146167, PRO; Fletcher to Lansing, Aug. 2, 1917, SD 812.51/312, NA; Lansing to Fletcher, Aug. 8, 1917, ibid.; *FR, 1917*, pp. 1013–14, 1072; Spring-Rice to Balfour, Nov. 20, 1917, FO 371 2964/222080, PRO.

14. Canova to Lansing, Oct. 25, 1918, SD 812.51/382, NA; Memorandum, Dec. 10, 1917, FO 371 2964/230821, PRO.

15. Anderson Diary, Oct. 3, 1917, Anderson Papers.

16. Cummins to Balfour, Mar. 10, 1918, FO 371 3242/44928, PRO.

17. Reading to Balfour, encl. Cummins to Reading, Mar. 9, 1918, FO 371 3242/47237, PRO.

18. Reading to Balfour, Mar. 12, 1918, FO 371 3242/46840, PRO; Balfour to Reading, Mar. 16, 1918, FO 371 3242/46840, PRO; Wiseman to Drummond, Mar. 14, 1918, Balfour Papers, BM; Director of Military Intelligence to Balfour, Mar. 18, 1918, FO 371 3242/49735, PRO.

19. Director of Military Intelligence to Balfour, Mar. 18, 1918, FO 371 3243/49735, PRO; and "Mexican Situation," Mar. 16, 1918, FO 371 3242/49375, PRO; Memorandum, Mar. 25, 1918, FO 371 3242/56916, PRO; Reading to Balfour, Mar. 20, 1918, with minutes, FO 371 3243/52362, PRO.

20. Lansing to Fletcher, Mar. 19, 1918; Fletcher to Lansing, April 3, 1918, *FR, 1918*, pp. 705–7, 712–14; Extract from a letter from Percy S. Bullen to Sir John M. Le Sage, June 18, 1918, FO 800/209, PRO; Copy of transcript, undated, in Wilson Collection, P.

21. Copy of transcript, undated, Wilson Collection, P.

22. Ibid.

23. Fletcher to Lansing, July 1, 1918; Lansing to Fletcher, July 6, 1918, *FR, 1918*, pp. 594–97, 627–29; Undated Memorandum, [July 1918], FO 371 3245/136685, PRO.

24. Polk to Wilson, July 31 and Aug. 1, 1918, Wilson Papers, LC; Wilson to Polk, Aug. 2, 1918, ibid.; Bruere to Wilson, Aug. 15, 1918, ibid.

25. Wiseman to Drummond, Aug. 20, 1918, FO 800/225, PRO; Thurston to Balfour, Aug. 24, 1918; Balfour to Thurston, Aug. 27, 1918, FO 371 4245/146522; see also Fowler, *British-American Relations*, pp. 211–12.

26. Lamont to Auchinloss, with encl., Oct. 10, 1918, SD 812.51/544, NA; J. P. Morgan & Co. to Morgan, Grenfell, Oct. 10, 1918, Fletcher Papers.

27. Minutes on copy of cable from J. P. Morgan & Co. to Morgan, Grenfell, Oct. 10, 1918, FO 371 3246/172195, PRO.

28. "Brief Review of Carranza's Efforts to Confiscate American-owned Oil Properties in Mexico," Dec. 4, 1919, Fletcher Papers.

29. "Conference between Mr. Garfield . . . and Officials of the Department," Nov. 12, 1918, SD 812.6363/415, NA; Lamont to Polk, Nov. 18, 1918, *FR, 1919* 2:644–45; Fletcher to Lamont, Dec. 4, 1918, Fletcher Papers; Lamont to Fletcher, Dec. 6, 1918, ibid.; Lamont to Acting Secretary of State, Dec. 13, 1918, *FR, 1919* 2:546–47.

30. Fletcher to Lamont, Dec. 18, 1918, Fletcher Papers; Fletcher to Lansing, Dec. 23, 1918, SD 812.51/480, NA.

31. "Memorandum Re: Mexico," Jan. 17, 1919, Balfour Papers, BM; Minute by R. S. Seymour, Jan. 28, 1919, FO 371 3826/19579, PRO.

32. *New York World*, Feb. 6, 1919.

33. *New York Times*, Jan. 23, 1919.

34. Ibid.; Reading to Balfour, Mar. 8, 1919, FO 371 3827/42036, PRO; Chargé in Mexico to Acting Secretary of State, Mar. 4, 1919, *FR, 1919* 2:593; Reading to Balfour with minutes, Mar. 6, 1919, FO 371 3827/36015, PRO.

35. Reading to Balfour, Mar. 19, 1919, FO 371 3827/43604, PRO; Polk to Wilson, Mar. 1, 1919, with encl., SD 812.00/23111a, NA.

36. Lowe and Dockrill, *Mirage of Power* 2:297.

37. Lansing to Reinsch, April 16, 1917, *FR, 1917*, p. 187; see also Lansing to Wilson, April 12, 1917, and Wilson to Lansing, April 13, 1917, Baker Papers.

38. Lansing to French Ambassador, May 1, 1917, *FR, 1917*, p. 188.

39. *FR, 1917*, pp. 48–49; undated minute by Robert Cecil on Page to Balfour, June 4, 1917, FO 371 2911/111948, PRO.

40. Japanese Ambassador to Lansing, June 15, 1917, *FR, 1917*, pp. 71–72; Lansing to

Japanese Ambassador, July 6, 1917, SD 793.94/570, NA; *FR, 1917*, pp. 260–62; Memorandum of Conversation, July 10, 1917, Breckinridge Long Papers, Library of Congress, Washington, D.C.

41. Lansing to Jusserand, Aug. 24, 1917, SD 893.77/1608, NA; Lansing to Spring-Rice, Aug. 24, 1917, encl. in Colville Barclay to Foreign Office, Aug. 27, 1917, FO 371 2914/185234, PRO.

42. Minutes on Spring-Rice to Foreign Office, Sept. 25, 1917, FO 371 2914/186943, PRO.

43. Jeffrey J. Safford, *Wilsonian Maritime Diplomacy, 1913–1921* (New Brunswick, N.J., 1978), pp. 129–33.

44. Lansing, *War Memoirs*, pp. 291–92.

45. "Memorandum of a Conference with Japanese Special Ambassador," Sept. 6, 1917, SD 793.94/583A, NA.

46. Spring-Rice to Foreign Office, Sept. 8, 1917, FO 371 2914/175980, PRO.

47. Spring-Rice to Lansing, Sept. 8, 1917, *FR, 1917*, pp. 195–96.

48. Lansing to British Embassy, Sept. 20, 1917, ibid., pp. 197–98.

49. Minute by T. H. Lyons, undated, on Spring-Rice to Balfour, Oct. 5, 1917, FO 371 2914/207211, PRO.

50. "Memorandum of a Conversation with Viscount Ishii at My Residence," Sept. 22, 1917, *FR, Lansing Papers* 2:435–36; Lansing, *War Memoirs*, pp. 294–96.

51. Memorandum, Sept. 26, 1917, Long Papers; Memorandum by Long, Oct. 25, 1917, and by J. V. A. MacMurray, July 9, 1921, both in SD 793.94/609, NA; Lansing, *War Memoirs*, pp. 301–4.

52. Lansing, *War Memoirs*, pp. 303–4; *FR, Lansing Papers* 2:451–52; see also "Memorandum of a Conversation with Chinese Minister," Dec. 3, 1917, Long Papers.

53. Minute on Barclay to Foreign Office, Nov. 6, 1917, FO 371 2954/213295, PRO; Nish, *Alliance in Decline*, pp. 222–23.

54. Committee for Public Information, press release, May 26, 1918, Lansing Papers; Page to Balfour, Nov. 7, 1917, FO 371 2954/213773, PRO; C. Clive Bayley to Spring-Rice, Nov. 28, 1917, FO 371 2920/244145, PRO.

55. Spring-Rice to Foreign Office, Nov. 27, 1917, FO 371 2954/226515, PRO; Morgan, Grenfell to J. P. Morgan & Co., Mar. 2, 1917; American Group to Lansing, Mar. 8, 1917, *FR, 1917*, pp. 126–28.

56. Long to E. T. Williams, Mar. 13, 1917, SD 893.51/1755, NA; *FR, 1917*, pp. 129–30.

57. Lansing to Wilson, June 25, 1917, Wilson Papers, LC.

58. Memorandum, July 30, 1917, Long Papers.

59. Balfour to Spring-Rice, Aug. 18, 1917, FO 371 2908/160020, PRO.

60. Memorandum, Oct. 18, 1917 and Long to Wilson, Oct. 20, 1917, Long Papers; British Embassy to Secretary of State, Oct. 3, 1917, *FR, 1917*, pp. 144–45.

61. Diary entry, Nov. 9, 1917, Long Papers.

62. Reinsch to Lansing, Dec. 20, 1917; Lansing to Reinsch, Jan. 24, 1918, Reinsch Papers.

63. Wilson to Lansing, Nov. 20, 1918; Lansing to Wilson, Nov. 25, 1918, Wilson Papers, LC.

64. Wilson to Lansing, Mar. 10, 1918, Wilson Papers, P.

65. Reinsch to Lansing, April 13, 1918, SD 893.51/1890, NA; Reinsch to Lansing, April 27, 1918, SD 893.51/1893, NA.

66. Lansing to Wilson, June 20, 1918, *FR, 1918*, pp. 169–71; Redfield to Lansing, June 4, 1918, with encl., SD 893.51/1903, NA; "Memorandum of a Conversation with American Bankers," June 29, 1918, Long Papers; Certain bankers to Lansing, July 8, 1918; Lansing to Certain bankers, July 9, 1918, *FR, 1918*, pp. 172–75.

67. Diary entry, July 12, 1918, Long Papers.

68. Jordan to Balfour, Oct. 23, 1918, FO 371 3191/205337, PRO.

69. Jordan to Balfour, Nov. 10, 1918, FO 371 3191/186939, PRO.

70. Minute, Dec. 2, 1918, on ibid.; Jordan to Macleay, Dec. 4, 1918, Macleay's minute, Dec. 12, 1918, FO 371 3191/203506, PRO.

71. Balfour minute on Jordan to Macleay, Dec. 4, 1918, FO 371 3191/203506, PRO.

72. Crane to Wilson, Dec. 12, 1918, Wilson Papers, LC; Reinsch to Lansing, Dec. 20, 1918, SD 893.77/1723, NA; Memorandum, Nov. 27, 1918, *FR, Paris Peace Conference* (hereafter *PPC*), 2:509–11; Polk to Commissioners to Negotiate Peace, Dec. 21, 1918, ibid., pp. 517–18.

73. Morris to Lansing, Nov. 15 and Nov. 27, 1918, *FR, PPC* 1:489–90, 490–92.
74. Polk to Commission to Negotiate Peace, Jan. 5, 1919, ibid. 2:519.

CHAPTER TEN. WILSON AND LLOYD GEORGE IN PARIS

1. Martin Gilbert, *Churchill* 4:229.
2. Ibid., pp. 229–31.
3. Churchill, *The Aftermath*, p. 169.
4. WC 515, Jan. 10, 1919, CAB 23/9, PRO.
5. Wilson to Lansing, Jan. 10, 1919, quoted in Mayer, *Politics and Diplomacy of Peacemaking*, p. 424; Wilson to McAdoo, Jan. 9, 1919, SD 871.51/141, NA; Vopicka to Lansing, Dec. 24, 1918, SD 871.00/57, NA.
6. Meeting of the Supreme War Council, Jan. 12, 1919, *FR, PPC* 3:469–77.
7. Ullman, *Anglo-Soviet Relations* 2:99–100; Notes of a Conversation, Jan. 12, 1919, *FR, PPC* 3:482–94.
8. Notes of a Conversation, Jan. 16, 1919, *FR, PPC,* 3:578–93.
9. Balfour to Lloyd George, Jan. 1919, Lloyd George Papers, F/2/4/7; Ullman, *Anglo-Soviet Relations* 2:105–7; *FR, PPC* 3:647–54, 663–68.
10. *FR, PPC,* 3:647–54, 663–68.
11. Ibid.
12. Churchill, *The Aftermath*, p. 170.
13. Ullman, *Anglo-Soviet Relations* 2:114–15; Polk to Lansing, Feb. 1, 1919, *FR, Russia, 1919*, pp. 38–39.
14. Ibid.
15. *FR, PPC* 3:649.
16. Mayer, *Politics and Diplomacy of Peacemaking*, p. 444.
17. Lloyd George to Kerr, Feb. 12, 1919, Lloyd George Papers, F/89/2/8.
18. Ullman, *Anglo-Soviet Relations* 2:118–21; Silverlight, *The Victors' Dilemma*, pp. 150–51; Lord Riddell, *Intimate Diary*, pp. 21–24.
19. Melville Stone to Wilson, encl. transcript, Feb. 10, 1919, Wilson Papers, P.
20. *New York Herald*, Feb. 14, 1919, ibid.
21. "Minutes of the 14th Session of the Supreme War Council," Feb. 14, 1919, *FR, PPC* 3:1039–44.
22. Churchill to Lloyd George, Feb. 15, 1919, Lloyd George Papers, F/8/3/16.
23. "Notes of a Conversation," Feb. 15, 1919, *FR, PPC* 4:1–21.
24. Gilbert, *Churchill* 4:248, 249–56.
25. Lloyd George to Churchill, Feb. 16, 1919, Lloyd George Papers, F/8/3/18.
26. Lansing to Polk, Feb. 17, 1919, *FR, Russia, 1919*, pp. 68–69; Wilson to the Council, Feb. 19, 1919, ibid., pp. 71–72.
27. "Notes of a Conversation," Feb. 25, 1919, *FR, PPC* 4:117–37; Wilson to House, Feb. 20, 1919, Wilson Papers, LC; "The Russian Situation," Feb. 26, 1919, Balfour Papers, BM.
28. Mayer, *Politics and Diplomacy of Peacemaking*, pp. 464–65; Lansing to Polk, Feb. 24, 1919, *FR, Russia, 1919*, p. 74.
29. Kerr to Lloyd George, Feb. 18, 1919, Lloyd George Papers, F/89/2/23; Lloyd George, *Memoirs of the Peace Conference*, p. 244.
30. Carr, *Bolshevik Revolution* 3:117, 123–24.
31. Lincoln Steffens, *The Autobiography of Lincoln Steffens* (New York, 1931), pp. 792–93; *FR, Russia, 1919*, pp. 74–82. Lenin was quite candid with Steffens about what reciprocal relations with the Soviet government would mean for both sides. Steffens had asked the Russian leader if in signing the Bullitt agreement he was giving assurances that a flock of Russian propagandists would not flood Central and Western Europe. "No," came his reply. "A propagandist, you know, is a propagandist," he said. "He must propagand." Propaganda went on inside Russia. If the borders were opened, of course propagandists would move back and forth. "We can agree not to send them to you, and we can agree that if they do go, they shall be subject to your laws, but we—nobody can make a propagandist stop propaganding" (Steffens, *Autobiography*, pp. 796–97).
32. Flota, *Colonel House in Paris*, pp. 152, 158.
33. Cary Grayson Diary, March 10, 1919, copy in possession of Arthur S. Link.

34. Minutes of the Meeting of the Supreme War Council, Mar. 17, 1919, *FR, PPC* 4:356–85.

35. Grayson Diary, Mar. 24, 1919.

36. Riddell, *Intimate Diary,* pp. 38–39; Mayer, *Politics and Diplomacy of Peacemaking,* p. 585; John M. Thompson, *Russia, Bolshevism, and the Versailles Peace* (Princeton, 1966), pp. 234–36.

37. Thompson, *Russia, Bolshevism, and Versailles,* pp. 242–43; Paul Mantoux, *Paris Peace Conference, 1919: Proceedings of the Council of Four* (Geneva, 1964), p. 1.

38. "Some Considerations for the Peace Conference before They Finally Draft Their Terms," Mar. 25, 1919, Wilson Papers, LC; Mayer, *Politics and Diplomacy of Peacemaking,* pp. 580–84.

39. Mantoux, *Paris Peace Conference,* pp. 27, 32–34, 35–63.

40. Hoover to Wilson, April 3, 1919, Wilson Papers, LC.

41. Cited in Herbert Hoover, *The Ordeal of Woodrow Wilson* (New York, 1958), pp. 135–36.

42. Ibid., pp. 140–41.

43. Hoover to House, April 19, 1919, House Papers.

44. Lansing to Polk, April 21, 1919, SD 600.1115/85, NA; American Mission to Polk, April 23, 1919, SD 864.00/73, NA; Lansing to Wilson, April 25, 1919, Wilson Papers, LC. The record of American anger at Allied manipulation against American commerce in Central Europe, as they termed it, can be followed in these documents: Lansing to Polk, April 16, 1919, SD 871.51/158, NA; Davis to Rathbone, April 18, 1919, SD 871.51/160, NA; Polk to Lansing, May 1, 1919, Wilson Papers, LC; Lansing to Wilson, May 3, 1919, ibid.; Wilson to Davis, May 17, 1919, ibid.; Bratianu to Davis, May 17, 1919, SD 871.51/179, NA.

45. Hoover to Wilson, April 11, 1919, Wilson Papers, LC.

46. Wilson to Hoover, April 15, 1919, in Hoover, *Ordeal of Wilson,* p. 148.

47. Lloyd George to Wilson, April 23, 1919, Wilson Papers, LC; Ray Stannard Baker, *Woodrow Wilson and World Settlement: A History of the Peace Conference* 3 vols. (New York, 1923), 2:288–90.

48. Davis to Rathbone, April 25, 1919, Wilson Papers, LC; Baker, *Wilson and World Settlement* 2:288–90; Leffingwell to Davis, April 28, 1919, SD 102.1/1979, NA; Rathbone to Davis, April 28, 1919, The Norman Davis Papers, Library of Congress, Washington, D.C.

49. Diary entry, May 19, 1919, The Thomas Lamont Papers, Harvard University Business School, copy in Wilson Collection, P.

50. Copy of Speech, May 9, 1919, Wilson Collection, P.

51. Big Four to Nansen, April 17, 1919, *FR, Russia, 1919,* pp. 108–9.

52. Ibid., p. 111; Churchill to Lloyd George, April 20, 1919, Lloyd George Papers.

53. *FR, Russia, 1919,* pp. 111–15.

54. Thompson, *Russia, Bolshevism and Versailles,* pp. 258–67; *FR, Russia, 1919,* pp. 246–48; American Mission to Polk, Jan. 31, 1919, ibid.; Diary entry, Jan. 30, 1919, Vance McCormick Diary, Wilson Papers, LC.

55. Polk to Lansing, Feb. 4, 1919, *FR, Russia, 1919,* pp. 248–49.

56. Polk to Lansing, Mar. 13, 1919, Wilson Papers, LC.

57. Bliss to Wilson, May 9, 1919, Wilson Papers, P; *FR, PPC* 5:528–29.

58. Lansing to Wilson, Mar. 22, 1919, Wilson Papers, LC; Phillips to American Mission, Mar. 28, 1919, ibid.

59. Knox to War Office, Mar. 10, 1919, FO 371 4094/42833, PRO.

60. Eliot to Balfour, April 5, 1919, FO 371 4095/53753, PRO.

61. Minutes on ibid.; and "The Case for Recognition of Admiral Kolchak's Government in Siberia," April 11, 1919, FO 371 4095/60524, PRO.

62. Churchill to Borden, May 1, 1919, copy in Wilson Collection, P.

63. WC 563, May 6, 1919, CAB 23/10, PRO.

64. Memorandum, May 9, 1919, Wilson Papers, P.

65. *FR, PPC* 5:560.

66. Ullman, *Anglo-Soviet Relations* 2:166–69.

67. A. H. Frazier to Wilson, with encl., May 17, 1919, Wilson Papers, LC; "Notes of a Meeting Held at President Wilson's Residence, May 19, 1919, *FR, PPC* 5:705–11.

68. Gregory to Hoover, June 4, 1919, Wilson Papers, LC; Taylor to Hoover, June 6, 1919, ibid.

69. Hoover to Wilson, June 9, 1919, Wilson Papers, LC; Bliss to Wilson, June 10, 1919,

ibid.; Diary entry, June 11, House Papers; Wilson to House, June 10, 1919, Wilson Papers, LC; Wilson to Bliss, June 16, 1919, ibid.

70. Thompson, *Russia, Bolshevism and Versailles*, pp. 210–11; Mayer, *Politics and Diplomacy of Peacemaking*, pp. 830–46.

71. Halstead to American mission, Aug. 5, 1919, SD 864.00/104, NA.

72. American mission to Lansing, Aug. 7, 1919, SD 864.00/107, NA; Wilson to Lansing, Aug. 8, 1919, SD 864.00/111½, NA; Polk to Lansing, Aug. 9, 1919, SD 871.51/187, NA.

73. Mayer, *Politics and Diplomacy of Peacemaking*, pp. 845–51; David Burner, *Herbert Hoover: A Public Life* (New York, 1979), pp. 123–25.

74. Kerr to Lloyd George, Aug. 21, 1919, Lloyd George Papers, F/89/4/160.

75. *FR, Russia, 1919*, pp. 375–78; Gilbert, *Churchill* 4:297–99; WC 578 and 578A, June 11, 1919, CAB 23/15, PRO.

76. Gilbert, *Churchill* 4:299–300; WC 580A, June 18, 1919, CAB 23/15, PRO.

77. Diary entry, June 23, 1919, Vance McCormick Diary, Wilson Papers, LC.

78. Polk to Morris, July 11, *FR, Russia, 1919*, p. 390; for remainder of correspondence, ibid., pp. 396–422.

CHAPTER ELEVEN. AT ARM'S LENGTH AND BEYOND

1. Riddell, *Intimate Diary*, p. 118.

2. Tumulty to Wilson, June 4, 1919, Wilson Collection, P.

3. Thomas Lamont to Wilson, June 23, 1919, and Wilson to Lamont, June 24, 1919, ibid.

4. Wiseman to Balfour, July 18, 1919, ibid.

5. Lansing to Gary M. Jones, Aug. 4, 1919, Lansing Papers.

6. "The Spread of Bolshevism in the United States," July 26, 1919, ibid.

7. "Memorandum by Mr. Tumulty," Aug. 7, 1919, and Tumulty to Wilson, Aug. 28, 1919, Wilson Collection, P; Lansing to Wilson, Aug. 7, 1919, and D. C. Poole, "Memorandum Concerning the Purposes of the Bolsheviki Especially with Regard to World Revolution," undated [Aug. 7, 1919], both ibid.

8. Wilson to Lansing, Aug. 14, 1919, Wilson Papers, LC.

9. Palmer to Wilson, July 30, 1919, Wilson Collection, P.

10. Wilson to Palmer, Aug. 1, 1919, ibid.

11. These excerpts, and others, were sent on to American representatives in the anti-Bolshevik areas of Russia; Sept. 9, 1919, *FR, Russia, 1919*, pp. 119–20.

12. Tumulty to Lansing, Oct. 28, 1919, SD 861.00/5655, NA.

13. Lansing to Tumulty, Oct. 29, 1919, SD 861.00/5655, NA; Lansing to Polk, Nov. 17, 1919, Polk Papers; Lansing, "One Point of View of the Murders at Centralia, Washington," Lansing Papers.

14. Churchill, *The Aftermath*, p. 276.

15. Maurice Cowling, *The Impact of Labour, 1920–1924* (Cambridge, 1971), p. 421.

16. Ibid., pp. 43–44; James, *Churchill: Study in Failure*, p. 155; Kenneth O. Morgan, *Consensus and Disunity: The Lloyd George Coalition Government, 1918–1922* (Oxford, 1979), pp. 48–49; WC 606A, Aug. 5, 1919, CAB 23/15, PRO.

17. Churchill, *The Aftermath*, pp. 253–55.

18. WC 598, July 23, 1919, WC 599, July 25, 1919, WC 601, July 29, 1919, WC 612, Aug. 12, 1919, all in CAB 23/11, PRO.

19. Davis to Lansing, Nov. 15, 1919, *FR, Russia, 1919*, p. 122.

20. 121 *H.C. Debates*, Nov. 17, 1919, cols. 688–96.

21. Ibid., pp. 715–26.

22. Ullman, *Anglo-Soviet Relations* 2:308–10.

23. Davis to Lansing, Dec. 3, 1919, *FR, Russia, 1919*, pp. 126, 128–29; Lansing to Davis, Dec. 4, 1919, ibid., pp. 129–30.

24. Lansing to Wilson, Dec. 4, 1919, Wilson Papers, LC.

25. Transcript of Interview in Walter Weyl Papers, June 27, 1919, copy in Wilson Collection, P.

26. For business interest in the new Russia see SD 611.119/436, 439, 442, 448, 450, NA; Phillips to Lamont, Sept. 13, 1919, *FR, Russia, 1919*, p. 158.

27. J.H. Fulton, National City Bank, to B. Long, July 22, 1919, and Lansing to National City Bank, Aug. 18, 1919, SD 861.51/637, NA; J. J. Hertmanowicz to Lansing, July 25, 1919, Long to Hertmanowicz, Aug. 1, 1919, SD 661.1115/6, NA; Polk to Lansing, Oct. 8, 1919, SD 860c.00/31, NA; Jerome Landfield to B. Long, Sept. 23, 1919, SD 125.0061/167, NA; Phillips to Shipping Board, Oct. 22, 1919, SD 661.119/469A, NA; Bristol to Lansing, Nov. 11, 1919, SD 661.1112/18, NA.

28. Lenroot to Lansing, Nov. 3, 1919, and Lansing to Lenroot, Nov. 18, 1919, SD 661.119/469, NA; Phillips to Wadsworth, Nov. 1, 1919, FR, Russia, 1919, pp. 161–62; A. Mitchell Palmer to Tumulty, with enc. Jennings to Wilson, Nov. 5, 1919, SD 661.119/478, NA.

29. Lansing to Wilson, Aug. 30, 1919, with encl., Wilson Collection, P; Lansing to Ira Harris, Sept. 3, 1919, and Harris to Lansing, Sept. 8, 1919, SD 861.51/658 and 664, NA; Phillips to American embassy, Tokyo, Sept. 27, 1919, FR, Russia, 1919, pp. 582–83; Lansing to Ernest Harris, Sept. 30, 1919, SD 861.51/675, NA.

30. Morris to Lansing, Oct. 31 and Nov. 1, 1919, FR, Russia, 1919, pp. 588–94.

31. Lansing to Morris, Nov. 19, 1919, ibid., pp. 597–99.

32. Lansing to Polk, Oct. 14, 1919, SD 860c.00/31, NA.

33. It first appeared in December 1919, and is reprinted in The Collected Works of John Maynard Keynes, vol. 2 (London, 1971).

34. Ibid., pp. 183, 185–87.

35. Geddes to Foreign Office, July 11, 1920, FO 371 4100/208345, PRO.

36. Secretary's Note of a Conference, Dec. 11, 1919, CAB 23/35, and CAB 23/18, Dec. 12, 1919, PRO.

37. Ullman, Anglo-Soviet Relations 3:317–18, 326–27.

38. "Notes of a Meeting of the Heads of Delegations . . . ," Jan. 14, 1920, FO 371 4032/179077, PRO.

39. Ullman, Anglo-Soviet Relations 3:329–30.

40. "Notes of a Cabinet Conference," Jan. 18, 1920, S-11, CAB 23/35, PRO.

41. Ullman, Anglo-Soviet Relations 3:342–44; H. A. Grant-Watson to Curzon, Jan. 27, 1920, FO 371 4032/175068, PRO; Poole to Adee, Jan. 17, 1920, SD 861.51/731, NA; Lindsay to Curzon, Jan. 21, 1920, FO 371 4032/174469, PRO.

42. J. G. Lay to Adee, Feb. 6, 1920, SD 661.119/494, NA; Adolf Berle to Colby, Feb. 7, 1920, SD 661.1115/29, NA.

43 Stevens to Colby, Feb. 11, 1920, SD 861.77/1363, NA; Lamont, Memorandum, undated, May 1920, handed to Colby by Roland Morris, June 8, 1920, SD 861.77/1574, NA.

44. Schoenfeld to Colby, Feb. 12, 1920, and same to same, same date, SD 661.1112/20 and 21, NA.

45. Carr, The Bolshevik Revolution, 3:314–17; Dresel to Colby, Feb. 12, 1920, with encl., SD 661.001/13, NA.

46. Polk to Wilson, Mar. 3, 1920, SD 661.1115/339, NA.

47. Polk to Wilson, Mar. 10, 1920, with Wilson's notations, Wilson Papers, P.

48. Anderson, "Russian Developments as Seen through Copenhagen and as Affecting American Trade," undated, Mar. 1920, SD 661.001/27, NA.

49. Davis to Colby, Mar. 14, 1920, Polk Papers.

50. Wilson to Polk, Mar. 18, 1920, Wilson Papers, LC.

51. Ullman, Anglo-Russian Relations 3:89–91; Colby to American Embassy, London, Mar. 24, 1920, SD 661.1115/33, NA.

52. Balfour to Lloyd George, Feb. 6, 1920 and Lloyd George to Balfour, Feb. 18, 1920, Lloyd George Papers, F/3/5/1 and F/3/5/3.

53. Grant Watson to Curzon, April 7, 1920, FO 371 4033/190737, PRO.

54. Carr, Bolshevik Revolution 3:154–61.

55. Colonel Tallents to Curzon, April 22, 1920, British Documents on Foreign Policy (hereafter BDFP), (London, v.d.) 1st. ser., 11:298–302; Curzon to Tallents, June 16, 1920, ibid., pp. 356–57.

56. Chicherin to Curzon, April 29, 1920, with minutes by Howe, May 1, Gregory, May 1, and Curzon, May 2, 1920, FO 371 3981/195172, PRO.

57. O'Malley to Gregory, April 21, 1920, FO 371 4033/193988, PRO.

58. Note by Curzon for the cabinet, May 27, 1920, BDFP, 1st. ser., 12:723–26.

59. Curzon to Lloyd George, May 28, 1920, ibid., pp. 726–28; Conclusions of a Conference of Ministers, May 28, 1920, CAB 23/21, PRO; Conclusions of a Conference of Ministers, June 3, 1920, CAB 23/21, PRO.

60. Wilson, *Diaries of C. P. Scott*, pp. 326–27.

61. Intercept, dated June 12, 1920, Lloyd George Papers, F/12/3/50.

62. Ullman, *Anglo-Soviet Relations* 3:105.

63. "Note by Mr. Krasin," June 29, 1920, FO 371 4036/207569, PRO; see also *BDFP*, 1st. ser., 8:380–88; and Ullman, *Anglo-Soviet Relations* 3:123–24.

64. *BDFP*, 1st. ser., 8:380–88; Ullman, *Anglo-Soviet Relations* 3:123–24.

65. Chicherin to Curzon, July 8, 1920, FO 371 4036/207633, PRO; Ullman, *Anglo-Soviet Relations*, 3:144–45; "Notes of a Conversation . . .," July 8, 1920, *BDFP*, 1st. ser., 8:490–91.

66. Geddes to Curzon, June 6, 1920, FO 371 4035/202138, PRO.

67. Geddes to Lloyd George, June 8, 1920, Lloyd George Papers, F/60/4/2.

68. Cummings Diary, May 31, 1920, copy in Wilson Collection, P.

69. Gompers to Colby, June 8, 1920; Colby to Wilson, June 11, 1920; Colby to Gompers, June 12, 1920, all in Bainbridge Colby Papers, Library of Congress, Washington, D.C.

70. Geddes to Curzon, June 20, 1920, *BDFP*, 1st ser., 12:739–40.

CHAPTER TWELVE. THE SHAPE OF THINGS TO COME

1. Lamont to J. P. Morgan, Mar. 18, 1920, SD 893.51/2718, NA.

2. Geddes to Curzon, July 12, 1920, FO 371 4494/4773, PRO.

3. Bruere to Cabrera, May 2, 1919; Cabrera to Bruere, May 14, 1919, Fletcher Papers.

4. Bruere to Cabrera, May 29, 1919; Bruere to Fletcher, with encl., May 29, 1919, ibid.

5. "Brief Review of Carranza's Efforts to Confiscate American-owned Oil Properties in Mexico," Dec. 4, 1919, ibid.

6. Walker to Fletcher, Aug. 12, 1919, ibid.

7. Polk to American Legation, Mar. 15, 1919, SD 821.51/97, NA; Hoffman Philip to Lansing, Mar. 27, 1919, SD 821.51/100, NA; Philip to Lansing, Mar. 27, 1919, SD 821.51/99, NA; Lansing to Philip, Aug. 9, 1919, *FR, 1919* 1:737–38; A. Mitchell Palmer to Lansing, Aug. 13, 1919, SD 821.6363/60, NA; Lansing to Palmer, Aug. 23, 1919, ibid.; Lansing to Philip, Aug. 13, 1919, SD 821.6363/58, NA.

8. Lansing to Philip, Aug. 21 and 28, 1919, *FR, 1919* 1:743–44, 772–74.

9. Phillips to Summerlin, July 21, 1919, *FR, 1919* 2:572.

10. Summerlin to Lansing, July 30, 1919, ibid., pp. 573–74.

11. Lansing to Wilson, Aug. 18, 1919, SD 812.00/23111b, NA; Lansing to Wilson, Aug. 21, 1919, SD 812.00/23111c, NA; Wilson to Lansing, Aug. 22, 1919, Wilson Papers, P.

12. Summerlin to Lansing, Sept. 3, 1919, *FR, 1919* 2:531–34.

13. Summerlin to Lansing, Sept. 2, 1919, ibid., pp. 607–10.

14. Smith, *U.S. and Revolutionary Nationalism*, pp. 157–60; "Method of Determining a Course of Action When an International Dispute Becomes Acute," Nov. 17, 1919, Lansing Papers; Cronin, *Daniels Diaries*, p. 461.

15. "Interview with the Mexican Ambassador Regarding Jenkins Case, Nov. 28, 1919, Lansing Papers; Diary entry, Nov. 28, 1919, Long Papers; Smith, *U.S. and Revolutionary Nationalism*, pp. 165–66.

16. Lansing to Wilson, Dec. 5, 1919, Wilson Papers, LC.

17. Lansing to Wilson, Dec. 19, 1919, Wilson Papers, LC.

18. Fletcher to Lansing, Dec. 11, 1919, Fletcher Papers; Fletcher to Lansing, Dec. 22, 1919, ibid.; Lansing to Wilson, Jan. 3, 1920, Wilson Papers, LC.

19. Lansing to Wilson, Jan. 3, 1920, Wilson Papers, LC.

20. Cummins to Curzon, Mar. 24, 1920, with minutes, FO 371 4491/1686, PRO; Ruíz, *The Great Rebellion*, pp. 174–78.

21. Cummins to Curzon, April 13, 1920, FO 371 4492/2283, PRO; Geddes to Curzon, May 6, 1920, two cables, FO 371 4492/2875 and 2897, PRO.

22. Geddes to Curzon, June 20, 1920, with minutes, FO 371 4494/4136, PRO.

23. Davis to Wilson, June 25, 1920, Wilson Papers, LC; Wilson to Davis, June 26, 1920, ibid.; Davis to Wilson, July 21, 1920, Davis Papers; Smith, *U.S. and Revolutionary Nationalism*, pp. 178–79.

24. Geddes to Curzon, July 12, 1920 , FO 371 4494/4773, PRO; Smith, *U.S. and Revolutionary Nationalism*, p. 179; Cowdray to Cecil Harmsworth, July 23, 1920, FO 371 4495/5046, PRO; Memorandum of Conversation with Mexican Ambassador, Aug. 30, 1920, Davis Papers; "Memorandum of a Conversation with Mr. Pesquiera," Sept. 23, 1920, ibid.

25. Morgenthau to Wilson, Sept. 23, 1920, Colby Papers.

26. Creel to Mrs. Wilson, Sept. 17, 1920, Wilson Papers, LC.

27. Wilson to Colby, Sept. 24, 1920; Colby to Wilson, Sept. 25, 1920, Colby Papers.

28. Colby to Wilson, Sept. 25, 1920. ibid.

29. Smith, *U.S. and Revolutionary Nationalism*, p. 181; Wilson to Colby, Sept. 27, 1920, Colby Papers.

30. Diary Entry, Oct. 5, 1920, Homer S. Cummings Papers, copy in Wilson Collection, P.

31. Wilson to Colby, Nov. 5, 1920, SD 812.00/26464, NA.

32. Colby to Wilson, Nov. 6, 1920, Wilson Papers. LC.

33. Creel to Colby, Nov. 12, 1920, copy to Mrs. Wilson, Nov. 15, 1920, Wilson Papers, LC.

34. Geddes to Curzon, Nov. 16, 1920, FO 371 4497/8091, PRO.

35. Colby to Wilson, Nov. 20, Wilson to Colby, Nov. 20, 1920 and Nov. 22, 1920, Wilson Papers, LC; Smith, *U.S. and Revolutionary Nationalism*, pp. 182–83; Wilson to Davis, Nov. 23, 1920, Wilson Papers, LC.

36. Chilton to Curzon, June 8, 1921, FO 371 5584/4496, PRO.

37. Ibid.

38. Ibid.

39. Smith, *U.S. and Revolutionary Nationalism*, p. 189.

40. Economic Liaison Committee, "Petroleum Policy of the United States," undated (1919), Polk Papers.

41. "Notes of a Meeting . . . ," April 22, 1919: 11:30 a.m. and 4:30 p.m., *FR, PPC*, 5:123–33, 138–48.

42. Ibid.

43. Andrew J. Nathan, *Peking Politics,* pp. 158–60; Jordan to Curzon, May 14, 1919, FO 371 3683/75614, PRO.

44. Address at Palace Hotel, San Francisco, Sept. 17, 1919, Wilson Papers, LC.

45. Quoted in Joseph Tumulty, *Woodrow Wilson As I Know Him* (New York, 1921), pp. 380–2.

46. Nathan, *Peking Politics,* p. 162; Jordan to Curzon, May 17, 1919, FO 371 3683/77728, PRO.

47. W. G. Max Müller, "China Loans and Concessions," Feb. 21, 1919, FO 371 3690/37459, PRO.

48. Ibid.

49. See H. D. Marshall to Long, May 20, 1919, Long Papers.

50. Nish, *Alliance in Decline,* pp. 274–75; William Roger Louis, *British Strategy in the Far East, 1919–1939* (Oxford, 1971), pp. 28–29; Hugh Wallace to Acting Secretary of State, June 21, 1919, FR, 1919, 1:453–55; H. D. Marshall to Long, June 21, 1919, Long Papers.

51. Minute July 16, 1919, FO 371 3691/102801, PRO; Curzon to Alston, July 18 and 11, 1919, *BDFP,* 1st. ser., 6:613–18, 634–39.

52. Diary entry, July 18, 1919, Long Papers; Polk to Long, July 18, 1919, Wilson Papers, LC; Memorandum of Conversation by Breckinridge Long, July 19, 1919, ibid.

53. Memorandum of a Conversation with the Japanese Chargé, Aug. 1, 1919, Long Papers; Text of press statement, Aug. 2, 1919, Wilson Papers, LC.

54. Lansing to Wilson, Aug. 4, 1919; Wilson to Lansing, Aug. 6, 1919, Wilson Papers, LC.

55. Curzon to Alston, Aug. 11, 1919, *BDFP,* 1st. ser., 6:666–68.

56. British Chambers of Commerce at Tientsin, Cheefo, and Shanghai to Foreign Office, Aug. 15, 20, and 29, 1919, FO 371 3695/117200, 119371, 123132, PRO; Press clippings in Lansing Papers; Lindsay to Balfour, Aug. 13, 1919, FO 371 3695/115608, PRO; Lindsay to Balfour, Aug. 15, 1919, *BDFP,* 1st. ser., 6:680.

57. Curzon to Alston, Sept. 25, 1919, *BDFP,* 1st. ser., 6:734–36; Minutes on Jordan to Curzon, Sept. 29 and Oct. 1, 1919, FO 371 3691/134376, PRO; Curzon to Alston, Oct. 7, 1919, *BDFP,* 1st. ser., 6:758–59.

58. Grey to Curzon, Oct. 10, 1919, *BDFP,* 1st. ser., 6:776; Lansing to John W. Davis, Oct. 11, 1919, *FR, 1919,* 1:493–96; Memorandum by Tilley, Oct. 16, 1919, FO 371 3691/139674, PRO.

59. "Memorandum of a Telephone Conversation with Mr. Thomas Lamont," Oct. 14, 1919, Long Papers; Long to Lamont, Oct. 16, 1919, ibid.; Lansing to Davis, Oct. 22, 1919, *FR, 1919* 1:527–28.

60. Memorandum of a Conversation, Oct. 27, 1919, SD 893.51/2504, NA.

61. Addis to Curzon, Oct. 30, 1919, with encl., FO 371 3691/147676, PRO; Lansing to Lamont, Oct. 30, 1919, Long Papers.

62. Vice President of Chicago Continental and Commercial Bank to J. V. A. MacMurray, Oct. 30, 1919, *FR, 1919* 1:530–52; Diary entry, Oct. 31, 1919, Long Papers; William Phillips to J. J. Abbott, Oct. 31, 1919, *FR, 1919* 1:532–33.

63. Secretary of State to Morris, Feb. 7, 1920, *FR, 1920* 1:627–28; Japanese embassy to State Department, Mar. 2, 1920, ibid., pp. 500–503.

64. Colby to Davis, Mar. 6, 1920, ibid., pp. 503–5.

65. Morris to Secretary of State, Mar. 8, 1920, ibid., pp. 506–7; Morris to Secretary of State, Mar. 11, 1920, SD 893.51/2707, NA.

66. Addis to R. H. Clive, with encl., Mar. 25, 1920, FO 371 5298/276, PRO.

67. Louis, *British Strategy*, p. 32; Alston to Curzon, Mar. 28, 1920, *BDFP*, 1st. ser., 6:1059.

68. Lamont to Norman Davis, June 14, 1920, Davis Papers; Morris to Colby, April 8, 1920, SD 893.51/2765, NA; Lamont, "Report on Negotiations," undated [May 1920], Davis Papers.

69. Lamont, "Report on Negotiations," Davis Papers.

70. Lamont to Davis, June 14, 1920, ibid.; Memorandum to Colby, June 8, 1920, SD 861.77/1574, NA.

71. London *Times*, Nov. 23, 1920, clippings in FO 371 5302/2899, PRO.

72. Lamont to Davis, June 14, 1920, Davis Papers.

73. Memorandum of a Conversation, Aug. 20, 1920, Davis Papers.

74. Geddes to Curzon, Oct. 5, 1920, *BDFP*, 1st. ser. 14:150.

CHAPTER THIRTEEN. THE WASHINGTON CONTRACT

1. Quoted in Louis, *British Strategy*, pp. 107–8.

2. Crane to Colby, Oct. 25, 1920, *FR, 1920* 1:665; Crane to Hughes, Mar. 23, 1921, SD 793.94/1170, NA.

3. Alston to Sir John Tilley, Oct. 7, 1919, FO 371 5340/177312, PRO; "Memorandum on the Effect of the Anglo-Japanese Alliance upon Foreign Relationships," Feb. 28, 1920, FO 371 5340/150925, PRO.

4. Eliot to Curzon, June 17, 1920, *BDFP*, 1st. ser., 14:42–48.

5. Fountain to Committee of Imperial Defence, June 28, 1920, FO 371 5359/1455, PRO; Memorandum, Aug. 1, 1920, *BDFP*, 1st ser., 14:81–86.

6. Report of the Anglo-Japanese Alliance Committee, Jan. 21, 1921, *BDFP*, 1st ser., 14:221–27.

7. Geddes to Curzon, April 15, 1921, encl. in Curzon to Lloyd George, April 20, 1921, Lloyd George Papers, F/13/2/19.

8. CAB 43 (21), May 30, 1921, CAB 23/25, PRO.

9. Memorandum of a Conversation, May 31, 1921, SD 741.9411/96, NA.

10. Geddes to Curzon, July 7, 1921, *BDFP*, 1st. ser., 14:328–29; George Harvey to Hughes, July 8, 1921, SD 500.A4/1, NA.

11. From a copy in FO 371 6676/2563, PRO; Memorandum by Miles Lampson, July 19, 1921, with minute by Curzon, FO 371 6659/2635, PRO.

12. Churchill to Lloyd George, July 18, 1921; Lloyd George to Churchill, July 18, 1921, both in Lloyd George Papers, F/9/3/68 and F/9/3/69.

13. Memorandum, July 24, 1921, *BDFP*, 1st. ser., 14:345–51.

14. Alston to Curzon, Aug. 13, 1921, with encl., FO 371 6668/3821, PRO; Alston to Curzon, Aug. 18, 1921, FO 371 6659/3511, PRO.

15. Curzon to Geddes, Sept. 18, 1921, *BDFP*, 1st. ser., 14:398; "Memorandum of an Interview with the British Ambassador," Sept. 20, 1921, *FR, 1921*, 1:71–74. All the important portions of this conversation were not included in the printed volume cited. See SD 500.A4/190½, NA.

16. Curzon to Alston, Oct. 24, 1921, *BDFP*, 1st. ser., 14:451–52.

17. Alston to Curzon, Oct. 25, 1921, FO 371 6660/3971, PRO.

18. Memorandum, Nov. 11, 1921, *BDFP*, 1st. ser., 14:470–71.

19. "Memorandum in Outline Form," Nov. 11, 1921, *FR, 1922* 1:1–3.

20. See Warren I. Cohen, *America's Response to China* (New York, 1971), pp. 104–6.

21. Balfour to Lloyd George, Nov. 29, 1921, Lloyd George Papers, F/61/1/7; and the less detailed Balfour to Lloyd George telegram of that date in *BDFP*, 1st. ser., 14:522–23. See also, *FR, 1922* 1:5–6, 84–86.

22. China's input into the three treaties was of no consequence.

23. Hughes to Jacob Gould Schurman, Jan. 22, 1922, *FR, 1922* 1:941. See also E. T. Williams to Hughes, Jan. 24, 1922, SD 793.94/1306, NA; Hughes to J. V. A. MacMurray, Jan. 26, 1922, SD 793.94/1265, NA.

24. Balfour to Lloyd George, Feb. 6, 1922, Lloyd George Papers, F/61/3/7. On what Hughes was trying to do see Akira Iriye, *After Imperialism: The Search for a New Order in the Far East, 1921–1931* (New York, 1973).

25. Hughes to American Legation, Dec. 24, 1921, SD 861.77/2364a, NA; Hughes to Schurman, Dec. 24, 1921, *FR, 1922*, 1:874–75; Soviet delegate to Schurman, Dec. 21, 1921, ibid., p. 876; Schurman to Hughes, Dec. 27, 1921, ibid., p. 877.

26. Hughes to Schurman, Dec. 31, 1921, *FR, 1922* 1:877; Hughes to Schurman, Feb. 3, 1922; Schurman to Hughes, Feb. 22, 1922, ibid., pp. 882–83, 886–88.

27. *FR 1922*, 1:774–79. See also Roberta Dayer, *Bankers and Diplomats in China, 1917–1925* (London, 1981), pp. 123–27.

28. Wellesley Minute in FO 371 7984, PRO; Dayer, *Bankers and Diplomats*, pp. 123–32.

29. Morgan & Co. to Hughes, Jan. 6, 1922, SD 893.51/3678, NA.

30. MacMurray to Hughes, April 3, 1922, SD 893.51/3777, and Hughes to Lamont, April 13, 1922, *FR, 1922* 1:764–65.

31. Hornbeck quoted in Dayer, *Bankers and Diplomats*, p. 132. Schurman to Hughes, Oct. 3, 1922, SD 893.51/4049, NA.

32. Addis to Morgan, Jan, 3, 1922, SD 893.51/3678, NA; see also Sir N. Stabb to Victor Wellesley, Jan. 4, 1922, FO 371 7984/63, PRO.

33. Sir N. Stabb to Curzon, Oct. 5, 1922, FO 371 7985/3128, PRO; Minutes by Carr, Oct. 5, and Wellesley, Oct. 12, 1922, ibid.

34. Minute by Wellesley, Nov. 13, 1922, on Auckland Geddes to Curzon, Oct. 24, 1922, FO 371 7985/3403, PRO.

35. Lamont to Hughes, Dec. 15, 1922, SD 893.51/4118, NA.

36. See Joan Hoff Wilson, *American Business and Foreign Policy, 1920–1933* (Boston, 1973), pp. 205–18; and the memorandum, "South Manchurian Railway Co: Proposed Loan to," April 30, 1922, SD 893.51/4364, NA.

37. Wellesley to B. C. Newton, Jan. 12, 1923, FO 371 9200/147, PRO; Wellesley to Curzon, Jan. 15, 1923; ibid.; Hughes to Warren, Jan. 12, 1923, *FR, 1923*, 1:526–27; Wellesley to Curzon, Feb. 26, 1923, FO 371 9200/523, PRO.

38. Lamont to Hughes, Jan. 26, 1923, SD 893.51/4165, NA.

39. Morgan, Grenfell to J. P. Morgan & Co., rec'd May 10, 1923, *FR, 1923* 1:542–43.

40. Ibid., pp. 639–40; Schurman to Hughes, May 26, 1923, ibid., p. 648.

41. Minute, June 1, 1923, on Macleay to Curzon, May 19, 1923, FO 371 9189/1538, PRO; "Minutes of a Meeting of the Consortium Council," May 28, 1923, FO 371 9202/1667, PRO.

42. Schurman to Hughes, June 6, 1923, *FR, 1923* 1:653–54; Schurman to Hughes, June 8, 1923, SD 893.51/4324, NA.

43. Dayer, *Bankers and Diplomats*, p. 156.

44. Nugent to Curzon, June 14, 1923, FO 371 9190/1841, PRO.

45. Macleay to Curzon, June 19, 1923, with minute by Wellesely, June 22, 1923, FO 371 9190/1897, PRO.

46. British Embassy to Department of State, June 19, 1923, *FR, 1923* 1:661; Hughes to Schurman, June 23, 1923, ibid., pp. 666–68; Macleay to Curzon, Aug. 2, 1923, with minutes, FO 371 9192/2320, PRO; minute by Brenan, Dec. 8, 1923, FO 371 9193/3522, PRO.

47. "Memorandum on the China Situation," Oct. 3, 1923, FO 371 9193/3120, PRO.

48. Manifesto dated June 29, 1923, *FR, 1923* 1:511–23.

49. Schurman to Hughes, Sept. 22, 1923, SD 893.51/4419, NA.

50. Hughes to Schurman, Oct. 20, 1923, SD 893.51/4419, NA.

51. Memorandum, Dec. 4, 1923 SD 893.51/4432, NA.

52. Bell to Hughes, Dec. 5, 1923, *FR, 1923* 1:561; Hughes to Peking, Dec. 6, 1923, SD 893.51/4432, NA.

53. Bell to Hughes, Jan. 8, 1924, encl. Schurman to Hughes Jan. 6, 1924, SD 893.51/4519, NA.

54. *FR, 1913*, pp. 170–71.

CHAPTER FOURTEEN. HARD ROAD TO A STALEMATE

1. Gilbert, *Churchill*, 4:424–5; Ullman, *Anglo-Soviet Relations* 3:274–82.

2. Riddell, *Intimate Diary*, pp. 220–21; Dan P. Silverman, *Reconstructing Europe after the Great War* (Cambridge, Mass., 1982), pp. 242–43.

3. Riddell, *Intimate Diary*, pp. 226–27.

4. "Draft Notes of a Conference Held at 10, Downing Street . . . ," Aug. 4, 1920, *BDFP*, 1st. ser., 8:670–80; Lloyd George to Wilson, Aug. 5, 1920, Wilson Papers, P.

5. From a draft dated Aug. 9, 1920, Wilson Papers, P.

6. "Memorandum of a Conversation with the British Ambassador," Aug. 20, 1920, Davis Papers; Silverman, *Reconstructing Europe*, p. 250; Wilson to Lloyd George, Nov. 3, 1920, Wilson Papers, P.

7. See Thomas Fiddick, "The 'Miracle of the Vistula': Soviet Policy versus Red Army Strategy," *Journal of Modern History* 45 (Dec. 1973): 626–43.

8. See Gilbert, *Churchill* 4:424–25.

9. "Memorandum on the Proposal to Expel Messrs. Kameneff and Krassin [*sic*]," Sept. 2, 1920, CAB 21/173, PRO.

10. Lloyd George to Bonar Law, Sept. 4, 1920, quoted in Ullman, *Anglo-Soviet Relations* 3:299.

11. CAB 61 (20), Nov. 17, 1920, CAB 23/23, PRO.

12. Ibid.

13. Ibid.

14. Clipping from *Sunday Express* in FO 371 5422/2435, with minute by Hoare, Nov. 15, 1920, PRO.

15. Ibid.

16. Notes of a Conference, Dec. 21, 1920, *BDFP*, 1st ser., 8:879–92; Minute by Crowe, Feb. 10, 1921, on Chicherin to Curzon, Feb. 4, 1921, FO 371 6853/1665, PRO.

17. See Robert Horne to Krasin, Mar. 16, 1921, FO 371 6854/3438, PRO.

18. See, for example, Chicago Federation of Labor to Colby, Jan. 4, 1921, SD 661.119/585, NA; Alexander to Wilson, Jan. 22, 1921; Wilson to Alexander, Jan. 24, 1921, Wilson Papers, LC.

19. Hoover to Charles Evans Hughes, Mar. 16, 1921, *FR, 1921* 2:762–63; Geddes to Curzon, Mar. 22, 1921, FO 371 6854/4088, PRO.

20. *New York Times*, Mar. 22, 1921.

21. Hughes to Litvinov, Mar. 25, 1921, SD 661.1115/275A, NA.

22. "Notes of Interview with Members of the Russian Trade Delegation," Aug. 5, 1921, *BDFP*, 1st. ser., 20:704–5.

23. Hodgson to Curzon, Aug. 11, 1921, ibid., pp. 741–49.

24. See Christopher Andrew, "The British Secret Service and Anglo-Soviet Relations in the 1920s, Part I: From the Trade Negotiations to the Zinoviev Letter," *Historical Journal* 20 (1977): 673–706.

25. Curzon to Hodgson, Sept. 7, 1921, *BDFP*, 1st. ser., 20: 741–49.

26. Sept. 12, 1921, FO 371 6851/10364, PRO.

27. Hodgson to Curzon, Sept. 22, 1921, with minutes, FO 371 6855/10713, PRO; Hodgson to Curzon, Sept. 22, 1921, *BDFP*, 1st. ser., 20:768–70.

28. Translation of article in FO 371 6855, dated Sept. 24, 1921, PRO; Curzon's handwritten minute in FO 371 6855, PRO.

29. See minute by Gregory, Nov. 2, 1921, FO 371 6856/12389, PRO.

30. Chicherin to Lloyd George, Oct. 28, 1921, Lloyd George Papers, F/58/2/26.

31. "Recognition of Debts by Soviet Government," Oct. 27, 1921, FO 371 6932/12227, PRO; Gregory to Krasin, Nov. 1, 1921, *BDFP*, 1st. ser., 20:798–801.

32. "Memorandum by Mr. Klishko," Nov. 16, 1921, FO 371 6933/12733, PRO.

33. *Pravda*, Nov. 18, 1921, translation in FO 371 6856, PRO.

34. Minutes, Dec. 16, 1921, CAB 93 (21), CAB 23/27, PRO.

35. Carr, *The Bolshevik Revolution* 3:356–58; Silverman, *Reconstructing Europe*, p. 259.

36. Harvey to Hughes, Aug. 23, 1921; Hughes to Harvey, Aug. 25, 1921, *FR, 1921* 2:818–19.

37. Lord Beaverbrook, *The Decline and Fall of Lloyd George* (New York, 1963), p. 292.

38. See *FR, 1921* 2:804–17.

39. Carr, *Bolshevik Revolution* 3:342–43; Joan Hoff Wilson, *Ideology and Economics, U.S. Relations with the Soviet Union, 1918–1933* (Columbia, Mo., 1974), pp. 21–25; Hughes to Hoover, Dec. 1, 1921, with encl., *FR, 1921* 2:785–86.

40. Minute, Feb. 1, 1922, FO 371 8190/4327, PRO; Memorandum of a Conversation, Feb. 10, 1922, CAB 23/35, PRO.

41. Silverman, *Reconstructing Europe*, pp. 260–61.

42. "Memoranda of Conversations with Beneš," Feb. 16, 17, 20, 1922, S-42, S-43, S-46, CAB 23/36, PRO; Silverman, *Reconstructing Europe*, pp. 259–60.

43. See *BDFP*, 1st. ser., 20:156–59.

44. British notes, Feb. 25, 1922, *BDFP*, 1st. ser., 19:170–92; Beaverbrook, *Decline of Lloyd George*, p. 293.

45. Telegram, Mar. 15, 1922, FO 371 8186/2548, PRO.

46. Minute, ibid., Mar. 20, 1922.

47. Chamberlain to Lloyd George, Mar. 21, 1921, Chamberlain Papers, AC 23/6/18.

48. Lloyd George to Chamberlain, Mar. 22, 1922, ibid., AC 23/6/19; Riddell, *Intimate Diary*, pp. 368–70.

49. "Memorandum to the Prime Minister on Trade," Mar. 23, 1922, Chamberlain Papers, AC 23/6/28.

50. Chamberlain to Lloyd George, Mar. 23 and 25, 1922, ibid., AC 23/6/20, AC 23/6/22.

51. CAB 21 (22), Mar. 26, 1922, CAB 22 (22), Mar. 27, 1922, CAB 23/29, PRO; Conclusions of Conference of Ministers, April 2, 1922, CAB 23/29, PRO.

52. "Report of the British Committee . . . ," Mar. 28, 1922, *BDFP*, 1st. ser., 19:257–58.

53. Ibid., pp. 276–78.

54. Minutes of the First Plenary Session, April 10, 1922, ibid., pp. 334–57.

55. Ibid.; Minutes of an Informal Meeting, April 14, 1922, ibid., pp. 380–409.

56. Ibid., and Minutes of a Meeting, April 15, 1922, ibid., pp. 409–21 and appendix.

57. Silverman, *Reconstructing Europe*, p. 265.

58. Gregory to Miles Lampson, April 14, 1922, FO 371 8187/3704, PRO.

59. Gregory to Curzon, April 17, 1922, FO 371 8187/3583, PRO.

60. Minutes of a Meeting, April 18, 1922, *BDFP*, 1st. ser., 19:446–52.

61. Silverman, *Reconstructing Europe*, p. 266.

62. Ibid., and "Reply of the Russian Delegation to the Memorandum of May 2, 1922," FO 371 8190/4657, PRO.

63. Silverman, *Reconstructing Europe*, p. 267.

64. Minutes, May 8 and 19, 1922, FO 371 8189/4322, PRO.

65. Curzon to Chamberlain, May 13, 1922; Chamberlain to Curzon, May 15, 1922, Chamberlain Papers, AC 23/6/33, and /40.

66. Notes of a Conversation, July 5, 1922, CAB 23/36, PRO.

67. See Martin Gilbert and Richard Gott, *The Appeasers* (London, 1967), pp. 35–36.

68. "The Road Away from Revolution," in Dodd and Baker, *Public Papers of Woodrow Wilson* 6:536–39; Beaverbrook, *Decline of Lloyd George*, p. 292.

Index